RECONSTRUCTING RAWLS

RECONSTRUCTING RAWLS

THE KANTIAN FOUNDATIONS OF JUSTICE AS FAIRNESS

ROBERT S. TAYLOR

THE PENNSYLVANIA STATE UNIVERSITY PRESS
UNIVERSITY PARK, PENNSYLVANIA

Library of Congress Cataloging-in-Publication Data

Taylor, Robert S., 1968–
Reconstructing Rawls : the Kantian foundations of justice as fairness / Robert S. Taylor.
p. cm.
Summary: "Compares the theories of John Rawls and Emmanuel Kant, and offers an internal critique and reconstruction of justice as fairness, reconceiving it as a comprehensive, universalistic Kantian liberalism"—Provided by publisher.
Includes bibliographical references (p.   ) and index.
ISBN 978-0-271-03772-1 (pbk. : alk. paper) 978-0-271-03771-4 (cloth : alk. paper)
1. Justice.
2. Rawls, John, 1921–2002.
3. Kant, Immanuel, 1724–1804—Political and social views.
I. Title.

JC578.T39 2011
320.01'1—dc22
2010031598

Copyright © 2011 The Pennsylvania State University
All rights reserved
Printed in the United States of America
Published by The Pennsylvania State University Press,
University Park, PA 16802-1003

The Pennsylvania State University Press is a member of the
Association of American University Presses.

It is the policy of The Pennsylvania State University Press to use
acid-free paper. Publications on uncoated stock satisfy the minimum
requirements of American National Standard for Information Sciences—
Permanence of Paper for Printed Library Material, ANSI Z39.48–1992.

Contents

List of Illustrations   vii
Preface and Acknowledgments   ix
List of Abbreviations   xiii
List of Acronyms   xv
Introduction   xvii

Part 1: Kantian Affinities

1
Rawls's Kantianism   3

Part 2: Reconstructing Rawls

2
The Kantian Conception of the Person   59

3
The Priorities of Right and Political Liberty   115

4
The Priority of Civil Liberty   152

5
The Priority of Fair Equality of Opportunity   173

6
The Difference Principle   192

Part 3: Kantian Foundations

7
Justifying the Kantian Conception of the Person   231

8
The Poverty of Political Liberalism   249

Conclusion:
Justice as Fairness as a Universalistic
Kantian Liberalism   301

References   318
Index   326

Illustrations

Figures

1. Parallel autonomy and priority hierarchies xxi
2. Finite rational agency 14
3. Justice as fairness as Kantian constructivism 23
4. Partial taxonomy of duties in Kant's late moral philosophy 77
5. Model of agency 106
6. Hierarchy of communities 113
7. The self-respect argument 157
8. Decision rules under uncertainty 195
9. Depicting Conditions 2 and 3 196
10. Depicting Conditions 1–4 216
11. Model overlapping consensus 247
12. Utilitarian civil libertarianism 282

Tables

1. A lexical ordering 151
2. Payoff matrix 195

Preface and Acknowledgments

This book has one overarching goal: to reclaim Rawls for the Enlightenment—more specifically, the Prussian Enlightenment. His so-called political turn in the 1980s, motivated by a newfound interest in pluralism and the accommodation of difference, has been unhealthy for autonomy-based liberalism and has led liberalism more broadly towards cultural relativism, be it in the guise of liberal multiculturalism or critiques of cosmopolitan distributive-justice theories. I believe it is time to redeem *Theory*'s implicit promise of a universalistic, comprehensive Kantian liberalism, a promise that went unredeemed in Rawls's lifetime but on which this book attempts to deliver. Reconstructing Rawls on Kantian foundations leads to some unorthodox conclusions about justice as fairness, to be sure: for example, it yields a more civic-humanist reading of the priority of political liberty, a more Marxist reading of the priority of fair equality of opportunity, and a more ascetic or antimaterialist reading of the difference principle. It nonetheless leaves us with a theory that is still recognizably Rawlsian and reveals a previously untraveled road out of *Theory*—a road very different from the one Rawls himself ultimately followed.

Traveling this road has, without exaggeration, taken me nearly two decades. While I was an undergraduate at the University of Tennessee at Knoxville in the early 1990s, I completed a senior thesis on Michael Sandel's communitarian critique of Rawls, thus initiating a long, almost continuous engagement with contemporary analytic political philosophy. My myriad discussions there with Tom Ungs, Alex Smith, Larry Hall, and Bob Gorman—who showed near-superhuman patience with me as an annoyingly earnest and rigidly libertarian undergrad—further sparked my interest in liberal egalitarianism, classical liberalism, and political theory more broadly. A fateful decision to pursue a doctorate in economics at Duke University led to a profitable seven-year detour, during which I continued to examine Rawls and even taught an interdisciplinary class on contemporary analytic political philosophy.

After four years of teaching economics, I decided in 1998 to return to graduate school at the University of California at Berkeley to pursue my first intellectual love on a full-time basis. I recall and appreciate the warm—if slightly puzzled—support of Tom Ungs, Alex Smith, and Kip Viscusi (my former dissertation advisor), who agreed to write letters of reference for what must have looked like a quixotic venture. I am also grateful to David Collier at Berkeley for his role in securing my admission to the political science program; by taking a chance on a weird applicant, he made it possible for me to shift my intellectual and professional trajectory. While at Berkeley, I had the good fortune of having several excellent teachers whose classes reintroduced me to the contemporary analytic and/or Enlightenment traditions of moral and political thought, especially Chris Kutz, Samuel Freeman, Sam Scheffler, and Shannon Stimson (my dissertation advisor). I also benefited from interaction with an unusually active and organized cohort of political theory Ph.D. students, including Robert Adcock, Yvonne Chiu, James Harney, Alison Kaufman, Jimmy Klausen, Robyn Marasco, Mike Signer, Sharon Stanley, Simon Stow, and Carla Yumatle. I am especially grateful for the close and enduring friendships I developed both with Yvonne and with Robert and Alison (now happily married), whose support and feedback as well as companionship on hikes around the Bay Area I greatly valued.

After graduation from Berkeley, short teaching stints at Duke and Stanford allowed me to meet some wonderful scholars whose encouragement during a sometimes rough transition period I appreciated: at Duke, Craig Borowiak, Charles-Philippe David, Peter Euben, Jason Frank, Ruth Grant, and Elisabeth Vallet; at Stanford, Rob Reich, Debra Satz, Tamar Schapiro, Mary Sprague, Peter Stone, Jonathan Wand, and Allen Wood. Landing my current job at UC Davis was nothing short of a godsend: the research support has been matchless, and my colleagues (especially Yuch Kono and my fellow theorist John Scott) are a delight, making my job more entertaining than I could have possibly imagined.

The list of people I must thank for comments, criticisms, recommendations, and support regarding this book is long and includes most of those mentioned above:

Robert Adcock	Eamonn Callan	Peter Euben
Facundo Alonso	Yvonne Chiu	Jim Fishkin
Dick Arneson	John Christman	Samuel Freeman
Nigel Ashford	Neal D'Amato	Bill Galston
Chuck Beitz	Meir Dan-Cohen	Amy Gutmann
Corey Brettschneider	Jerry Dworkin	Vicki Hsueh
Thom Brooks	Lisa Ellis	Brad Inwood
Barbara Buckinx	Dave Estlund	Alex Kaufman

Alison Kaufman	Josh Parsons	Shannon Stimson
Steven Kelts	Rodney Peffer	Peter Stone
Loren King	Larry Peterman	Simon Stow
Jimmy Klausen	Eric Rakowski	Tracy Strong
George Klosko	Rob Reich	Patrick Suppes
Niko Kolodny	David Reidy	Nick Tampio
Sharon Krause	Patrick Riley	John Tomasi
Chris Kutz	Connie Rosati	Chad Van Schoelandt
Chris Laursen	Debra Satz	Manuel Vargas
Mika LaVaque-Manty	Tamar Schapiro	Geoffrey Vaughan
Jacob Levy	Sam Scheffler	Pekka Väyrynen
David Lieberman	John Scott	Gerry Vildostegui
Steve Macedo	Brian Shaw	Drew Volmert
Robyn Marasco	Susan Shell	Jay Wallace
Dean Mathiowetz	Seana Shiffrin	Lael Weis
Simon May	Paul Sniderman	Howard Williams
Jamie Mayerfeld	Sarah Song	Ed Wingenbach
Donald Moon	Sharon Stanley	Allen Wood
Miko Nincic	Peter Steinberger	Carla Yumatle

I offer special thanks to Sandy Thatcher, former director at Penn State University Press, for shepherding my book through the publication process, as well as Jon Mandle and Tony Laden for their thoughtful, challenging reviews—the book is much improved because of them.

Chapters 2, 4, and 5 contain materials originally published in, respectively, "Kantian Personal Autonomy," *Political Theory* 33, no. 5 (October 2005): 602–28; "Rawls's Defense of the Priority of Liberty: A Kantian Reconstruction," *Philosophy and Public Affairs* 31, no. 3 (Summer 2003): 246–71; and "Self-Realization and the Priority of Fair Equality of Opportunity," *Journal of Moral Philosophy* 1, no. 3 (November 2004): 333–47. I thank the publishers for their permission to include them here.

Finally, I am grateful to Mom and Yvonne for their love, encouragement, and patience, and I hereby dedicate figure 11 to Yvonne.

Abbreviations

I will use the two- to four-letter abbreviations listed below for the primary texts of Rawls and Kant. All of my references to Kant will contain such an abbreviation in addition to the standard *volume:page* references to the Prussian Academy edition of Kant's collected works (Kant 1900)—except for references to the *Critique of Pure Reason,* which will be to pages in the first (1781 or "A") and second (1787 or "B") editions of that work. I also note below the particular English translations of Kant that I use.

Rawls's Primary Texts

CP	*Collected Papers* (Rawls 1999a)
DJ	"Distributive Justice" (CP 130–53)
DJSA	"Distributive Justice: Some Addenda" (CP 154–75)
IMT	"The Independence of Moral Theory" (CP 286–302)
IOC	"The Idea of an Overlapping Consensus" (CP 421–48)
IPRR	"The Idea of Public Reason Revisited" (Rawls 1999b, 129–80; CP 573–615)
JF	*Justice as Fairness: A Restatement* (Rawls 2001)
JFPM	"Justice as Fairness: Political Not Metaphysical" (CP 388–414)
KCE	"A Kantian Conception of Equality" (CP 254–66)
KCMT	"Kantian Constructivism in Moral Theory" (CP 303–58)
LHMP	*Lectures on the History of Moral Philosophy* (Rawls 2000)
LHPP	*Lectures on the History of Political Philosophy* (Rawls 2007)
LP	*The Law of Peoples* / "The Law of Peoples" (Rawls 1999b, 1–128 / CP 529–64)
ODPE	"Outline for a Decision Procedure in Ethics" (CP 1–19)
PL	*Political Liberalism* (Rawls 1993)
SJ	"The Sense of Justice" (CP 96–116)
SRMC	"Some Reasons for the Maximin Criterion" (CP 225–31)
SUPG	"Social Unity and Primary Goods" (CP 359–87)
TJ	*A Theory of Justice* (Rawls 1971, 1999c; revised edition used unless noted)

Kant's Primary Texts

CJ   *Critique of the Power of Judgment* (Kant 2000)
CPrR   *Critique of Practical Reason* (Kant 1996, 133–272)
CPuR   *Critique of Pure Reason* (Kant 1998a)
GMM   *Groundwork of the Metaphysics of Morals* (Kant 1996, 37–108)
MM   *The Metaphysics of Morals* (Kant 1996, 353–604)
PP   "Toward Perpetual Peace: A Philosophical Project" (Kant 1996, 311–52)
Rel   *Religion Within the Boundaries of Mere Reason* (Kant 1998b, 31–192)
T&P   "On the Common Saying: That May Be Correct in Theory, But It Is of No Use in Practice" (Kant 1996, 273–310)
WIE   "An Answer to the Question: What Is Enlightenment?" (Kant 1996, 11–22)
WOT   "What Does It Mean to Orient Oneself in Thinking?" (Kant 1998b, 1–14)

Acronyms

This book uses a large number of terms of art, most of which are drawn from Rawls's or Kant's own texts. In order to save space, I employ a host of acronyms to stand in for them. I define them all when they are first used, but on the (reasonable) supposition that readers will have a hard time keeping up with them, I offer a comprehensive list below.

CC	constitutional consensus
CD	comprehensive doctrine
CI	categorical imperative
DP	difference principle
EL	equal-liberty principle
FA	formula of autonomy
FEO	fair-equality-of-opportunity principle
FH	formula of humanity
FKE	formula of the kingdom of ends
FLN	formula of the law of nature
FUL	formula of universal law
$MA_{(K)}$	moral autonomy (Kantian)
OC	overlapping consensus
OP	original position
$PA_{(K)}$	personal autonomy (Kantian)
PCD	partially comprehensive doctrine
PCJ	political conception of justice
RCD	reasonable comprehensive doctrine
$SR_{(K)}$	self-realization (Kantian)
UCD	unreasonable comprehensive doctrine
UPR	universal principle of right
UPV	universal principle of virtue
VI	veil of ignorance
$Will_A$	practical reason or *Wille*
$Will_B$	free choice or *Willkür*
WOS	well-ordered society

Introduction

In his essay "Two Concepts of Liberalism," William Galston distinguishes between two varieties of liberal theory.[1] The first—Enlightenment liberalism—stresses the development and exercise of our capacity for *autonomy*, understood as "individual self-direction" and entailing a "sustained rational examination of self, others, and social practices"; this is the liberalism of not only Kant and Mill but also a number of contemporary thinkers, including Don Herzog, Stephen Macedo, Jeremy Waldron, and the preeminent Kantians (Barbara Herman, Christine Korsgaard, Onora O'Neill, Allen Wood, etc.).[2] The second—Reformation liberalism—emphasizes *diversity* and the toleration that encourages it, where diversity is understood simply as "differences among individuals and groups over such matters as the nature of a good life, sources of moral authority, reason versus faith, and the like"; this is the liberalism of not only Madison and Isaiah Berlin but also contemporary thinkers such as Galston himself, Charles Larmore, and Donald Moon.[3] These two varieties of liberal theory are often mutually supporting—as Galston puts it, "the exercise of autonomy yields diversity, while the fact of diversity protects and nourishes autonomy"—but in a surprising number of cases they conflict, whether over the accommodation of group difference, the design of civic education, or the promotion of liberal values internationally.[4] In fact, much of the so-called liberalism/multiculturalism debate is an intramural affair, pitting Enlightenment and Reformation liberals against one another.[5]

---

1. Galston (1995). His distinction between "Enlightenment" and "Reformation" liberalisms was anticipated by Charles Larmore's distinction between "Kantian" and "modus vivendi" liberalisms and Donald Moon's distinction between "traditional" and "political" liberalisms, respectively; see Larmore (1987) and Moon (1993).
2. Galston (1995, 521, 523, 525). He identifies Herzog, Macedo, and Waldron as Enlightenment liberals.
3. Ibid., 521, 525–27. He identifies himself, Madison, and Berlin as Reformation liberals, at least implicitly. Locke is harder to categorize. The *Letter Concerning Toleration* has both Enlightenment and Reformation components: some of its arguments focus on the idea that only a "free faith" can have any worth in the eyes of God, while others place emphasis on the peace and security that will follow from toleration of diverse sects—see Locke (1990, 19, 65, 71).
4. Galston (1995, 521). Regarding the third case, see Mehta (1999) on Mill, Burke, and British colonialism.
5. See, e.g., Laden and Owen (2007), as well as the discussion in Kymlicka (2002, chap. 8).

One might reasonably ask where John Rawls, arguably the greatest political philosopher of the twentieth century, would fall in this debate. He certainly had many Enlightenment-liberal credentials: he taught several famous Kantians (e.g., Herman, Korsgaard, and O'Neill), lectured on Kant extensively, and characterized his magnum opus, *A Theory of Justice* (1971), as "highly Kantian in nature."[6] By the same token, though, Rawls's later work *Political Liberalism* (1993) "applies the principle of toleration to philosophy itself," thus taking a diversity-based approach that has been a major influence on such Reformation liberals as Galston, Larmore, and Moon.[7] We might therefore understand Rawls's intellectual trajectory as the opposite of the historical one: it begins with the Enlightenment and ends by circling back to the Reformation.

This depiction of his trajectory is far too crude, however. *Political Liberalism* may be a Reformation-liberal text, but is *Theory* really an Enlightenment-liberal one—or, more precisely, is it a Kantian-liberal one? Many scholars have called Rawls's Kantian credentials into question, including Kerstin Budde, Otfried Höffe, Oliver Johnson, Larry Krasnoff, and Andrew Levine (see Budde 2007, Höffe 1984, Johnson 1974, Krasnoff 1999, and Levine 1974). Other scholars (e.g., Larmore) have discerned certain justificatory ambiguities in *Theory*, such as the commingling of Enlightenment-liberal and Reformation-liberal elements.[8] Most importantly, Rawls himself saw a strong continuity between the arguments of *Theory* and *Political Liberalism*, suggesting that the Kantianism of the former work may have been oversold, not only by himself but by others as well.[9]

I will therefore begin in chapter 1 by showing just how Kantian Rawls was during his most Kantian period—roughly, from *Theory of Justice* to his "Kantian Constructivism in Moral Theory" (1980) and "Social Unity and Primary

---

6. TJ xviii. The Kant lectures take up approximately half of LHMP. A number of Rawls's students, including those listed above, contributed to an edited volume that took its inspiration from Rawls's approach to teaching the history of moral and political philosophy—see Reath, Herman, and Korsgaard (1997).

7. PL 10. Galston, however, denies that the later Rawls is a Reformation liberal, arguing that he "attempts to give due weight to our deepest differences [but] ultimately fails to take those differences seriously enough" (1995, 518–21).

8. Larmore (1987, 125): "*Theory of Justice* harbors, side by side, the Kantian and modus vivendi approaches. Rawls's later writings, and particularly his Dewey Lectures [i.e., KCMT], have put the second approach in the center where it belongs."

9. JFPM 388–89. Rawls explicitly "put aside the question whether the text of *A Theory of Justice* supports different readings from the one I sketch here" (388). One of the most important tasks of my book will be to provide just such an alternative reading. Among those who seconded Rawls's self-described Kantianism were Darwall (1976, 1980), Davidson (1985), and Guyer (2000, 262–86).

Goods" (1982).[10] I demonstrate here that Rawls's theory is even more Kantian in this period than has generally been recognized: from his Kantian conceptions of person and society to his construction procedure (including the formal constraints of the concept of right, the veil of ignorance, and the thin theory of the good) and on through the principles, institutions, and psychology of justice that this procedure generates, his insights track those of Kant nearly one for one. Alternative readings of *Theory* and other works of this period are possible—as Rawls himself argues and as I will show in chapter 7—but their essentials are profoundly and almost unremittingly Kantian.

The interpretive work of chapter 1 provides the essential backdrop for the reconstructive task of part 2 (chapters 2-6), which shows just how dependent Rawls's arguments for the most distinctive features of justice as fairness—namely the lexical priorities of right, political liberty, civil liberty, and fair equality of opportunity plus the difference principle—are upon his extreme and controversial Kantian conception of the person. Its very extremity and controversiality will only become clear, however, in the process of (re)constructing his arguments for these features: through a procedure of "backwards engineering," I will show that any conception of the person that is capable of grounding the arguments for these features must be one that is itself grounded in Kant's model of finite rational agency, properly elaborated. These reconstructions of Rawls's arguments are required because either (1) they are incomplete (as with the priority of liberty and the difference principle) or (2) they are basically missing (as with the priority of fair equality of opportunity). Moreover, the principles of justice that these arguments sustain play such a central, consistent role in the various incarnations of Rawls's theory—from *Theory* (1971) and *Political Liberalism* (1993) to *Justice as Fairness: A Restatement* (2001)—that flaws in their justification imperil his evolving political project.[11] This reconstructive task occupies the heart of my book, supported by the prior interpretive work of chapter 1, which not only offers materials for this task but also assures us that a Kantian reconstruction does no violence to Rawls's texts.

---

10. Samuel Freeman identifies Kantian constructivism as a "transition stage" in Rawls's thought (CP xi). Stephen Darwall (1980) is the only other scholar to have carried out a *comprehensive* examination of Rawls's Kantianism, but he did not have access to KCMT when he wrote his essay. My chapter 1 is therefore the first comprehensive examination of Rawls's Kantianism in light of his Kantian-constructivist writings, which do much to elucidate the nature (and limits) of his Kantianism.

11. For example, Rawls devotes a huge amount of text to defending the priority of liberty and the difference principle in *Political Liberalism* and *Justice as Fairness: A Restatement*, respectively; see PL 289-371 and JF pts. II and III.

I begin this task in chapter 2 by presenting a more detailed and comprehensive Kantian conception of the person than Rawls uses in his own works, but one that is required to justify his theory's most distinctive features. This conception of the person, based upon Kant's own model of finite rational agency, is a hierarchy of Kantian conceptions of autonomy: in descending order, they are Kantian moral autonomy, Kantian personal autonomy, and Kantian self-realization. The constituent conceptions of this hierarchy offer the most compelling interpretations of their parent concepts and can be reached along both deductive and inductive routes. The first route utilizes a procedure analogous to Rawls's four-stage sequence to derive the lower conceptions from higher ones along with their associated plans and rules, while the second constructs an ideal cognitive-developmental psychology, an epicyclic system using an iterative model of agency to explain the emergence of higher conceptions from lower ones.[12] This hierarchy of Kantian conceptions will be used in later chapters to ground a parallel hierarchy of lexical priorities, with the priorities of right and political liberty at the top, the priority of civil liberty in the middle, and the priority of fair equality of opportunity (or FEO) at the bottom. This rich system of relationships is depicted graphically in figure 1. Notice that all priorities as well as their grounding conceptions of autonomy can be traced back to a Kantian conception of moral autonomy—a result anticipated by Kant in his *Groundwork*, as I shall argue (see GMM 4:415–17).

Chapters 3 through 6 then review the various arguments Rawls makes for the distinctive features of his theory and show that only those arguments securely grounded on the hierarchical conception of persons presented in chapter 2 offer genuine promise. Chapter 3 does this for the priorities of right and political liberty, arguing that they are founded on a Kantian conception of moral autonomy and also that (contrary to Rawls's assertion in his famous "Reply to Habermas") political liberty takes priority over civil liberty in his theory, giving it a somewhat civic-humanist character (PL 206, 413). Chapter 4 reveals the grave inadequacy of two of his three arguments for the priority of (civil) liberty and shows how the third and most promising one, which grounds this priority on a Kantian conception of personal autonomy, can be bolstered. Chapter 5 offers for the first time a defense of the priority of fair equality of opportunity—which is entirely (and peculiarly) missing from the

---

12. Rawls's four-stage sequence is described at TJ §31. This ideal cognitive-developmental psychology loosely tracks Rawls's own discussion of psychological "stage theories," such as those of Piaget and Kohlberg, in TJ chap. 8.

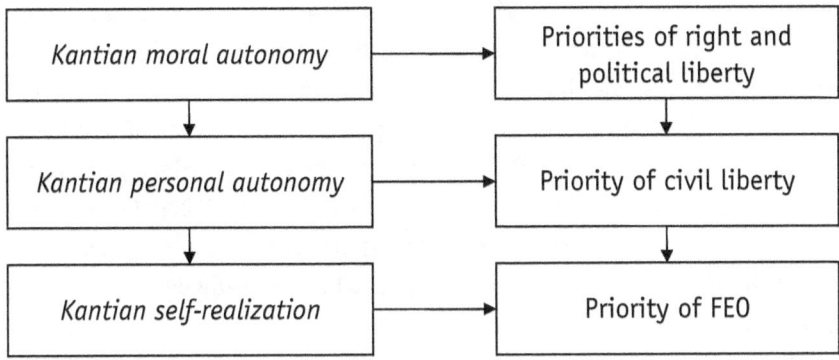

Fig. 1 Parallel autonomy and priority hierarchies

corpus of Rawls's texts—a defense that is constructed with existing resources in *Theory* (including the Aristotelian Principle and the concept of Humboldtian social union) and grounded on a Kantian conception of self-realization through work, which has Marxist undertones. Finally, chapter 6 explicates and gives additional support for his notorious difference principle. I contend here that his latter-day defenses of the difference principle (especially those present in *Justice as Fairness: A Restatement*) are inadequate and that the most compelling case for it can be made by means of a reconstructed version of an earlier defense—namely, the formal one elaborated in *Theory* §26 (see esp. TJ 132–35). This reconstructed defense relies, though, on a whole series of Kantian assumptions about asceticism, the unavoidable ends of duty and finitude, and the essential nature of persons. As one moves through these five reconstructive chapters, the extent to which justice as fairness depends upon specifically Kantian presuppositions becomes increasingly apparent, strongly reinforcing the conclusions of chapter 1.[13]

In part 3 of the book, I turn to "reflective equilibrium," Rawls's innovative technique of moral justification, and to its role in vindicating his Kantian conception of the person. In chapter 7, I describe this technique, developed in both *Theory* and "The Independence of Moral Theory" (1975), and point to its ambiguous treatment of moral objectivity. This ambiguity is reflected in Rawls's evasive answer to a central question: how can we bring about a coincidence of

---

13. Cf. S. Freeman (2007a, 183), where he maintains that "this deep Kantian argument plays no central role in solving the problems, dealt with in parts I and II of *A Theory of Justice*, of (1) eliciting the reasonable principles of a just constitution, and (2) deciding the institutions that satisfy them."

reflective judgments among moral agents, which he maintains is "a necessary condition for objective moral truths" (IMT 290)? One answer suggested by Rawls—namely, a reliance on "self-evident first principles," like Kant's practical postulate of freedom—is rejected during the 1980s in favor of another: by way of preexisting (near) consensus on considered convictions of justice found in "a democratic society under modern conditions" (IMT 289; KCMT 305-6). I enumerate Rawls's powerful reasons for rejecting the first answer and then describe in great detail the mature theory that he eventually developed from the second answer in *Political Liberalism*.

In chapter 8, I contend that the Reformation-liberal answer given in *Political Liberalism* to the above question—roughly, that justice as fairness can serve as the focus of an overlapping consensus of the reasonable comprehensive doctrines present in modern liberal democracies—is impoverished in at least two senses. First and more narrowly, no comprehensive doctrine but the Kantian one is capable of endorsing the strong Kantian conception of the person that underwrites justice as fairness. Thus, no overlapping consensus on justice as fairness is possible; the best that can be hoped for is an overlapping consensus on a *class* of liberal political conceptions of justice, with justice as fairness as just one competitor conception among others, its centrality determined through political competition and the strength of the supporting socioeconomic interests. Second and more broadly, even if we assumed justice as fairness could act as the focus of an overlapping consensus, the system of justification involved would offer us little moral guidance, whether in a domestic or an international context, regarding the appropriate width and content of overlapping consensus: because political liberalism has no *independent* criterion of reasonableness, it cannot refuse extension of the scope of toleration to include illiberal, even indecent groups and nations. Moreover, its agnosticism regarding the width and content of overlapping consensus, which is a form of cultural relativism, would lead to a dramatically diminished role for political philosophy, effectively turning it into a handmaid of the social sciences. These are sharply revisionist claims, of course, but I believe they are borne out by the chapter's arguments, which as a whole suggest the profound poverty of political liberalism and Reformation liberalism more generally.

Finally, the conclusion offers an alternative way to answer the question of justification, showing that a Kantian conception of the person must, unsurprisingly, be grounded in a Kantian way: on a practical postulate of freedom as a necessary presupposition of finite rational agency. I argue here, however, that this defense need not rely upon Kant's transcendental idealism, that is, we can dispense with metaphysics in grounding Kantian liberalism—even the "thin" metaphysics of Kant—rendering the postulate potentially ratifiable by a wide variety of persons as well as belief systems.[14] This justificatory approach is Rawls's "road not taken," and by following it ourselves, we can turn justice as fairness into an authentically comprehensive and universalistic liberalism, thereby fulfilling the implicit promise of *Theory* and helping secure its place within the canon (Frost 1969, 105).

Even if this reconstruction of Rawls's Kantian liberalism is found uncompelling by some persons, it can still be seen by them as a worthy companion to other cosmopolitan Enlightenment liberalisms—for example, Millian plural-perfectionism, Benthamite or Sidgwickian liberal utilitarianism, and Lockean religious liberalism—in the fight against illiberal principles and institutions around the globe, including theocratic, secular authoritarian, and totalitarian regimes and their sustaining ideologies. While Reformation liberalism is virtually impotent in such contexts, too unsure of its own relevance in illiberal societies, universalistic Enlightenment liberalisms are not hobbled by such doubts. Their very diversity is a source of strength, in fact, because different Enlightenment liberalisms are likely to appeal to different individuals, groups, and societies. As I contend in the conclusion, these liberalisms offer us the vision of a liberal world order ("a republicanism of all states, together and separately," as Kant put it) and a mode of justification addressed to all men and women as human beings, not as members of various religious, racial, and national groups (MM 6:354). Their optimistic cosmopolitanism makes them worthy of our allegiance and—if the arguments of this book are sound—makes the Kantian liberalism of a reconstructed Rawls the most worthy of them all.

---

14. Rawls himself claims to offer a detranscendentalized Kant, one contained "within the framework of an empirical theory" (TJ 226–27). While I share Rawls's aspirations, I believe that he dispenses with too much of Kant's practical philosophy in the process: a genuinely *Kantian* liberalism must be based upon a practical postulate of freedom, as I will argue in the conclusion; without this presupposition of finite rational agency, justice as fairness will simply be one more variety of heteronomous liberalism, retaining the form but not the substance of an autonomous theory.

PART 1

Kantian Affinities

1

Rawls's Kantianism

I. Introduction

Numerous scholars have questioned the depth of Rawls's Kantianism. For example, in their early responses to *Theory*, Andrew Levine and Oliver Johnson cast aspersions on Rawls's Kantian credentials, and they were not alone.[1] More recently, it has become common for people (especially political liberals) to point out that §40 of *Theory* is entitled "A Kantian *Interpretation* of Justice as Fairness," suggesting that justice as fairness, *though not itself Kantian*, can be given such an interpretation.[2] In the original preface to *Theory*, however, Rawls himself asserts that his theory of justice is "highly Kantian in nature," an assertion that is echoed in papers including "A Kantian Conception of Equality" (1975) and "Kantian Constructivism in Moral Theory" (1980) (KCE 264–66; KCMT 303–5). Even as late as 1997, Rawls refers to *Theory*'s version of justice as fairness as a "comprehensive liberal doctrine," one inspired in large part by Kant and with aspirations beyond mere justice.[3] Samuel Freeman has remarked upon the extent of this inspiration:

---

1. Levine (1974), Johnson (1974). Others have criticized Rawls's purported Kantianism more selectively, such as Höffe (1984), Krasnoff (1999), and Budde (2007). His Kantianism has been defended by, among others, Darwall (1976, 1980), Davidson (1985), and Guyer (2000, 262–86).

2. This point has been made to me several times in seminar settings and is perhaps turning into "folk wisdom," i.e., claims that everyone believes to be true but nobody has bothered to (dis)prove.

3. IPRR 614. Doctrines are *comprehensive*, according to Rawls, when they include "conceptions of what is of value in human life, and ideals of personal character, as well as ideals of friendship and of familial and associational relationships, and much else that is to inform our conduct, and in the limit to our life as a whole" (PL 13).

Rawls's lengthy lectures on Kant (nearly 200 pages in *LHMP*) indicate that Kant is the philosopher who most profoundly influenced him. From the idea of "the priority of the right over the good" and the Kantian interpretation of justice as fairness in *A Theory of Justice*, to Kantian (and later Political) Constructivism and the Independence of Moral Theory, then the conception of moral personality and the distinction between the Reasonable and the Rational in *Political Liberalism*, and finally the rejection of a world state and the idea of a "realistic utopia" in Rawls's *Law of Peoples*, one can discern that many of Rawls's main ideas were deeply influenced by his understanding of Kant.[4]

Kant's influence is most visible in *Theory* and in several essays leading up to Rawls's so-called political turn in the mid-1980s, which was marked by the publication of "Justice as Fairness: Political Not Metaphysical" (1985) and "The Idea of an Overlapping Consensus" (1987). I will hereafter refer to this decade-plus interlude of maximal Kantian influence as Rawls's "Kantian period."[5] Prior to this period, Rawls mentioned Kant only sporadically, and after it, he explicitly rejected many essential elements of Kant's thought, as we shall eventually see.[6]

Though several authors have written on Rawls's Kantianism, only Stephen Darwall (1980) has systematically reviewed the Kantian elements in Rawls's thought. Unfortunately, this excellent piece was written prior to the publication of Rawls's "Kantian Constructivism in Moral Theory," in which Rawls begins to reinterpret his own Kantianism. In what follows, therefore, I will offer a comprehensive Kantian reinterpretation of Rawls's *Theory* using Kantian constructivism as an organizing framework; this reinterpretation will lay the groundwork for the reconstructive work I do in part 2 of the book and provide a useful and methodical review of the components of justice as fairness. In section II of this chapter, I define constructivism and describe its variants as well as its competitors. In section III, I discuss *Kantian* constructivism, investigate

---

4. S. Freeman (2007b, 21). Freeman also claims that Kant's political writings had relatively little influence on Rawls, the main exception being his work on international justice (22; see, e.g., LP 86). As I will argue in this chapter, the influence was more substantial than this, though Rawls rarely invokes Kant's political works explicitly.

5. Samuel Freeman (CP xi) refers to this as a "transition stage" in Rawls's thought, one leading to political liberalism.

6. The only time prior to *Theory* that Rawls engages with Kant in any substantive way is in his Kantian interpretation of the difference principle in "Distributive Justice: Some Addenda" (1968), which is not long thereafter rolled into *Theory*. See DJSA 167–69 and TJ 156–58.

its function, and explore the question of how constructivist Kant's own doctrine is. In section IV, I systematically reinterpret Rawls's justice as fairness as a Kantian-constructivist doctrine and reveal its intimate relationship to Kant's own constructivism, something that Rawls spends surprisingly little time doing. Lastly, in section V, I discuss the differences between their respective theories. Some of these differences are possibly more apparent than real—or so I will suggest—but several are not, and one in particular does indeed mark a decisive break with Kant: Rawls's fateful decision in "Kantian Constructivism" to ground his conception of persons in democratic culture rather than in practical reason, a decision that points the way to his later political liberalism. This parting of ways with Kant—its nature, its justification, and its cost—will be the subject matter of part 3 of the book.

II. Constructivism: Definition, Variants, and Competitors

"Constructivism" is the name of one general approach to moral theorizing, with "moral" understood here as encompassing both matters of justice (right) and matters of ethics (virtue).[7] According to Onora O'Neill, one of its foremost practitioners, it can be characterized—and simultaneously distinguished from alternative approaches—by three interlocking claims:

1. "Ethical principles or claims may be seen as the *constructions of human agents*" (O'Neill 2003, 348). Rather than seeing moral principles as part of a "moral order that is prior to and independent of our conception of the person and the social role of morality" and that can be accessed by way of theoretical reason, constructivists view such principles as the products or artifacts of our practical reason (KCMT 344; Korsgaard 2003, 117).
2. "Ethical reasoning can be *practical*—[that is,] it can establish practical prescriptions or recommendations which can be used to **guide action**" (O'Neill 2003, 348; emphasis added in bold). Rather than simply describing the moral realm and our navigation of it, constructivists believe that any normative concept "refers schematically to the solution of a

---

7. Constructivism has other meanings outside moral philosophy: see O'Neill (2003, 347–48) and PL 90–91n, 102–3.

practical problem" and that our conception of ourselves (our "practical identity") "both embodies the problem and serves as an aid in finding the solution" (Korsgaard 1996b, 115; 2003, 99).

3. "It can *justify* those prescriptions or recommendations . . . [showing that] **objectivity** in ethics is not illusory" (O'Neill 2003, 348). Rather than characterizing moral claims as subjective, culturally determined, or otherwise arbitrary, constructivists believe these claims can be vindicated in such a way that they hold across individuals and groups who confront the same (set of) moral problems—as Christine Korsgaard puts it, "if you recognize the problem to be real, to be yours, to be one you have to solve, and the solution to be the only or the best one, then the solution is binding upon you" (2003, 16).

These claims are necessary and sufficient criteria for a moral theory to be deemed constructivist; theories failing to meet one or more of these criteria are alternatives to constructivism, several of which I will discuss shortly.

The best way to understand these criteria is to describe briefly several moral theories that meet all three and therefore qualify as constructivist doctrines. Kant's moral theory, for example, starts with the problem posed by the existence of a plurality of finite rational beings who are free but necessarily interacting. Roughly, the problem is how these beings can maintain their freedom given such interaction—and not merely their external freedom, which can be infringed by others, but their internal freedom as well, which is violated if the laws such beings inevitably follow are not a product of their own legislative wills. His solution, discussed more fully in the next section, is the categorical imperative, a product of their law-giving wills against which their actions and motives for action can be tested for universalizability (and therefore consistency with the actions and motives of others) and from which can be derived general principles of right and virtue. Kant believes that this is the problem that *we* face as human beings, and insofar as he is right about the problem and its solution, that solution is binding upon us. As we'll see in the following sections, Rawls's characterization of the problem and its solution is rather similar to Kant's, but narrower (focused primarily on justice and external freedom) and lower order (focused less on "screening devices" for testing principles of justice than on those principles themselves).[8]

8. For different characterizations of Kant's and Rawls's respective problems and solutions, see Korsgaard (1996b, 115; 2003, 112–16) and O'Neill (2003, 362). Korsgaard and O'Neill might

Though *Kantian* constructivist theories are probably the most dominant, there is nothing about constructivism that excludes non-Kantian variants. David Gauthier has described his own "morals by agreement" as constructivist, for example.[9] Gauthier's understanding of the problem is superficially like those of Kant and Rawls but with a key difference: the finite beings are seen as merely instrumentally rational in their pursuit of antecedently given ends. From a Hobbesian statement of the problem, Gauthier derives a classical-liberal solution: a limited state supervising a free market, an arrangement arrived at by means of rational bargaining. Rawls even suggested that "average utilitarianism might be presented as a kind of constructivism."[10] I will discuss and offer some criticisms of these two non-Kantian constructivisms at several points throughout the book, notably in chapters 6 and 8.[11]

Before continuing to a more detailed description of the Kantian constructivisms of Kant and Rawls, we should at least briefly consider several of their more prominent nonconstructivist competitors. The first of these competitors, *realism,* rejects the primary constructivist claim, namely, that moral principles are "constructions of reason," to use the title of O'Neill's book. Proponents of realism might have diverse substantive moral commitments—utilitarian (Sidgwick), pluralistic (Moore), or perfectionist (Leibniz)—but their views coincide on three characteristics that parallel and contrast with the three defining characteristics of constructivism: (1) moral (first) principles, rather than being

---

themselves be understood as offering variants of Kantian constructivism, but I think their approaches are better understood as *interpretations* of Kant's theory rather than *alternatives* to it—a point they themselves seem to make in their writings, and not from false modesty. O'Neill, for example, explicitly offers a "variant constructivism" as an alternative to Rawls's, but this variant turns out to rely upon her justly celebrated "alternative accounts of *Kant's* views on reason and freedom" (O'Neill 1989, 206, 212n7; emphasis added). Similarly, Korsgaard offers a constructivist theory that "derives its main inspiration from Kant, but with some modifications which I have come to think are necessary," and when it is criticized for its divergence from Kant (by G. A. Cohen and Raymond Geuss), she defends it against the charge of deviationism with a section entitled *"Apparent* Departures from Kant" (Korsgaard 1996b, 91, 234-38; emphasis added).

9. Gauthier (1989, 1997); cf. J. Buchanan (1975), who similarly derives classical-liberal conclusions from Hobbesian premises. For a discussion and critique of Gauthier's Hobbesian constructivism, see S. Freeman (2007a, 25-31, 43-44).

10. KCMT 323n1. This may be true of only some versions of utilitarianism, because as Korsgaard points out, certain utilitarians (e.g., Henry Sidgwick, John Stuart Mill on one common reading) believe that pleasure is a simple natural good, one whose normative status is not mediated through our conception of persons—but this is a variety of moral realism and violates the first criterion for a constructivist theory (Korsgaard 1996b, 40-42, 78-79; cf. KCMT 344).

11. Rawls himself criticizes Gauthier, James Buchanan, and Robert Nozick (whose views he refers to as "libertarian") for making "basic rights, liberties, and opportunities . . . depend on contingencies of history, and social circumstance and native endowment" (JF 16n16, 97). Rawls's critique of both total ("classical") and average utilitarianism is well known; see TJ §§27-28, 30.

constructions of reason, are "*self-evident truths* about good reasons," which are "fixed by a moral order that is prior to and independent of our conception of the person and the social role of morality," a moral order that is "given by the nature of things"; (2) these principles, instead of being produced by practical reason, are discerned by *theoretical* reason in our capacity as knowers, and such knowing is "not by sense, but by rational intuition"; (3) rather than being moved to act on these principles because they solve unavoidable practical problems that we face, we are *directly* motivated by them, that is, we desire to act upon them solely because we know them to be moral (first) principles.[12]

A definitive critique of realism is beyond the scope of this book, but I do want to describe two criticisms of realism that have been made by Korsgaard. First, realists tend to close off some lines of philosophical questioning by what looks like mere "fiat": when they are questioned as to *why* we must do what moral first principles require, they simply declare them to be "*intrinsically* normative" (Korsgaard 1996b, 33–34, 40–42; emphasis added). Whether they are dealing with the Platonic Form of the just city or with the natural experience of pain, realists believe the idea that we should pursue the former and avoid the latter must be self-evident, at least if these things are to have any normative force. No further argument is necessary or even possible—a stance unlikely to win over the moral skeptic or even those who are well disposed towards morality but cannot see the self-evidence of the principles in question. One potential advantage of constructivist theories is that insofar as persons share a conception of themselves and the problems they jointly face, solutions to those problems, which is what these theories claim to offer, have an obvious and unavoidable normative force.

Her second, closely related criticism involves realism's understanding of the relationship between "knowledge and action" (Korsgaard 2003, 110–12; also see Korsgaard 1996b, 16, 46, 94–97). Realists believe that once we have a knowledge of normative phenomena or facts in the world by our application of theoretical reason—we rationally intuit the intrinsic goodness of Platonic Forms or the intrinsic badness of pain—action will proceed of its own accord. Korsgaard explicitly denies this: "For even if we know what makes an action good, so long as that is just a piece of knowledge, that knowledge has to be

---

12. KCMT 343–46 (emphasis added); cf. CP 510–13. Rawls refers to realism as "rational intuitionism." I will discuss another competitor theory shortly that Rawls calls "intuitionism," so I use "realism" here both to avoid confusion and to follow more common terminological practice—see O'Neill (2003) and Korsgaard (2003).

applied in action by way of another sort of norm of action, something like an obligation to do those actions which we know to be good. And there is no way to derive such an obligation from a piece of knowledge that a certain action is good" (2003, 111). She believes that realism begs the question of how we are to bridge the worlds of knowledge and action. Why should we *do* what is good, even if by hypothesis we *know* what is good? Realism is in this case a sort of Hobbesian voluntarism: the authority of theoretical reason is imposed on our faculties of practical deliberation and action without a compelling explanation of the source of its presumed authority. As Korsgaard says, "the knowledge [of the good], being something external to the will, is just a kind of sovereign" (111). Again, constructivism provides an attractive alternative, as the authority of its pronouncements derives from practical reason itself, so that the will acts as its own sovereign: insofar as our practical faculties grapple with problems (e.g., infringements of our external and internal freedom) to which constructivist theories proffer solutions (e.g., actions and motives made consistent across persons through the categorical imperative), those faculties can genuinely adopt those solutions of their own accord and by their own authority. I will pursue this admittedly difficult thought in the following section.[13]

The second of these competitors to (Kantian) constructivism, *intuitionism*, throws out the second constructivist claim, namely, that moral theorizing can be practical, in the sense of offering us specific prescriptions and recommendations to guide action. Rawls describes intuitionist theories as follows: "first, they consist of a plurality of first principles [e.g., utilitarian, perfectionist, etc.] which may conflict to give contrary directives in particular types of cases; second, they include no explicit method, no priority rules, for weighing these principles against one another: we are simply to strike a balance by intuition, by what seems to us most nearly right."[14] These theories are pluralistic in nature and rely upon the commonsense notion that moral issues are irreducibly

---

13. Korsgaard points out that Kant has been read (by Sidgwick and Mill, for example) as a kind of realist, one who believes that "the principles of practical reason [like the Categorical Imperative] must be self-evident truths known by intuition" (2003, 106). I will defend Kant and the reconstructed Rawls from this charge in the book's conclusion. Briefly, the principles of practical reason can be derived from a postulate of freedom, but this postulate is not a self-evident truth rationally intuited but rather an unavoidable practical presupposition of agency that makes no claim to the status of knowledge.

14. TJ 30; see TJ §7 more generally. Rawls notes that theories of this sort can be found in the writings of Brian Barry, R. B. Brandt, and Nicholas Rescher. Some realist theories, which Rawls calls "rational intuitionist," are intuitionist in this second sense as well—G. E. Moore, for example, believed that pleasure and beauty are irreducible goods whose claims have to be balanced against each other through intuition (KCMT 344–45).

complex and that we cannot therefore design weighting or priority rules to adjudicate between a host of appealing fundamental values, including pleasure, beauty, perfection, etc. If intuitionism is right, then the most to which moral theories can aspire is an accurate description of the way in which individuals, interest groups, countries, etc. actually balance these competing values; given its own assumptions, intuitionism cannot prescribe or guide, that is, it cannot be practical. As Rawls points out, the only way to respond to such skepticism is to make effective arguments in favor of the very weighting or priority rules needed in order to yield a practical morality: "a refutation of intuitionism consists in presenting the sort of constructive criteria that are said not to exist."[15] I will spend the lion's share of this book making the case for Kantian versions of such rules in the domain of justice; if my case is persuasive, then intuitionism's claims will be placed in doubt.

The last of these competitors to constructivism that I will discuss, *relativism*, takes issue with the third constructivist claim, namely, that objectivity in ethics is possible. From the Sophists of ancient Greece to contemporary thinkers like Gilbert Harman and David Wong, moral relativists believe that moral principles or claims are not universal in nature but are instead contingent upon history, geography, and culture (Gowans 2008). This claim is not meant to be descriptive—it is uncontroversial that moral conventions vary spatiotemporally—but rather normative and specifically metaethical: moral practices are properly different in different cultural contexts. Moral relativism should also be distinguished from a more general moral skepticism, as moral relativists do not deny that right and wrong exist but rather deny their universality or absoluteness.

Interestingly, a moral relativist may very well deny that he rejects the third constructivist claim; indeed, he might claim constructivist credentials. If we return to the statement of the third constructivist criterion, the theory is said to hold across individuals and societies *only insofar as they confront the same problems*. Thus, a relativist might accept constructivism but deny that the problems in question are universally faced; he might instead maintain that different cultures have different problems and that moral objectivity can be vindicated solely within, or relative to, those cultures. For example, a moral relativist *cum* constructivist might say that industrialization raises certain problems (e.g., water pollution) not faced by preindustrial societies, so that

---

15. TJ 35. I offer additional criticisms of intuitionism (on grounds of generalizability and publicity) in chapter 2.

constructivist solutions to those problems apply to, and have objectivity within, industrialized societies alone.

One would be hard pressed to deny that *some* problems are culturally specific. The more pressing question, however, is whether the broader relativist claim is correct: that *all* problems are culturally specific and therefore that no universal moral theories can be constructed. As we have already seen, Kant believes that the central problems of justice and ethics are universal, so that universal principles of right and virtue are not simply possible but required; we will explore these views more systematically in the following section. Rawls's case is more complex, despite his commitment to Kantian constructivism. In his later works, at least, Rawls restricts his (ideal) theory's range of application to liberal-democratic cultures in the domestic case and to liberal as well as decent peoples in the international case, suggesting that political liberalism may itself be a constructivist-*cum*-relativist doctrine.[16] I will endorse such a reading of Rawls's late theory in part 3 of the book.

III. Kantian Constructivism: Definition and Derivation

While all of the elements of Kantian constructivism are already present in *Theory*, Rawls does not provide a systematic exposition of them before his 1980 paper "Kantian Constructivism in Moral Theory." In it, he offers the following succinct definition of Kantian constructivism: "it specifies a particular [1] *conception of the person* as an element in a reasonable [2] *procedure of construction*, the outcome of which determines the content of the first [3] *principles of justice.*"[17] Schematically, this definition can be represented as *input → process → output*. The conception of the person motivates and is mirrored by a procedure of construction, which captures its features and translates them into the language of political principles; the procedure mediates, so to speak, between an abstract ideal of personhood and more concrete principles of justice. To anticipate a bit, Rawls begins with a conception of the person as free, equal, and autonomous, with all three of these features understood in a specific (and specifically Kantian) way. He then develops a procedure of construction—the so-called original position (OP)—that reflects these features in its

16. KCMT 305-6; LP pts. I and II. Onora O'Neill (1989, 211) appears to accept this reading.
17. KCMT 304 (emphasis added). I give Kantian constructivism a quasideductive reading here; the alternative is critiqued in part 3.

constituent parts, including the formal constraints on the principles of justice, the information constraints (veil of ignorance) affecting the principle-choosing model agents in the OP, and the characteristics and motivation of such agents. These agents will, according to Rawls, choose his three principles of justice, which are lexically ordered rules for the distribution of vital social goods, including basic liberties, offices and positions, and income and wealth. So long as the OP accurately reflects a normatively guiding conception of the person, the principles that are chosen there will themselves provide political guidance.

At least two questions arise about Kantian constructivism: first, why is such a procedure of construction needed at all, and second, what makes it specifically Kantian? Regarding the first question, one might wonder why political principles cannot be *directly* derived from a normative conception of the person—why is a hypothetical procedure such as the OP needed as a mediating device? In order to answer this question, we should think about the function of mediating devices in general. The first, most obvious reason to use such devices is their heuristic function. Deriving principles of justice from a relatively abstract conception of the person is a difficult undertaking. Mediating devices can serve as bridges between them, making the intellectual task of connection easier—which probably explains why such devices (e.g., Hume's "sympathetic spectator" or the idea of a social contract) have been widely used in the history of moral and political philosophy. For example, we shall see in chapter 6 that some (including Rawls himself) have tried to derive the difference principle almost directly from the equality of moral persons. This attempt, though understandable, moves too quickly for its own good: by failing to use the OP to "unpack," so to speak, the meaning of agential equality, the argument loses its force and is in the end compelling only to those who are already committed economic egalitarians.

Another reason is that of compartmentalization. Just as sealable compartments on a ship help to protect it from catastrophic loss in case of a breach, so mediating devices act to segment arguments into stages, such that if one or more stages fail other stages can potentially be saved. For instance, a critic might take issue with Rawls's claim that his two principles of justice would be chosen in a suitably defined OP but still accept that the OP accurately reflects his conception of the person and that such a conception is normatively guiding.[18] Note that the failure of a moral argument might look quite different

---

18. Goldman (1976), for example, seems to accept Rawls's OP and the conception of the person upon which it is based but rejects the idea that the difference principle can be derived from it.

than the failure of an argument in mathematics, for example. Mathematicians should (in principle, at least) be able to concur in a judgment that an argument in their field has failed. Moral and political philosophy are patently different: philosophers (outside formal logic) may frequently have divergent judgments on whether an argument in their field has failed. But this fact makes mediating devices considerably more important in philosophy than in mathematics, *ceteris paribus*.[19] In philosophy, a multistage argument may fail at different stages for different readers, and prediction of where the argument might fail may be extremely difficult. Given this fact, the compartmentalization that mediating devices provide is an essential practice.

Regarding the second question, Rawls himself suggests that there are many varieties of constructivism, of which his is merely one example; in fact, as we saw in the last section, there could be as many varieties of constructivism as there are normatively guiding conceptions of the person.[20] What distinguishes Kantian constructivism from the other varieties is its particular and particularly rich conception of the person, which leads to a distinctive procedure of construction and set of principles.[21] What exactly does Rawls mean, though, when he describes his own constructivism as "Kantian"? He provides some guidance when he says that "the adjective 'Kantian' expresses analogy and not identity; it means roughly that a doctrine sufficiently resembles Kant's in enough fundamental respects so that it is far closer to his view than to the other traditional moral conceptions that are appropriate for use as benchmarks of comparison" (KCMT 304-5). Given this, Rawls has surprisingly little to say in "Kantian Constructivism" about Kant's own constructivism: how can we determine whether Rawls's version "sufficiently resembles" Kant's to warrant the label "Kantian" without a discussion of Kant's views?[22] Fortunately, by examining Kant's writings (especially the *Groundwork*) and by looking to Rawls's other texts, we can get a better idea of why Rawls wraps himself in the mantle of Kantianism.

19. On the use of constructivist techniques in mathematics, see PL 102-3.
20. Rawls begins KCMT by noting that there are "different kinds of constructivism" (303). Brian Barry (1989, 269-71) discusses these different kinds, which he groups into two categories: the "circumstances of justice" category, which would presumably include the theories of Hobbes and Gauthier, and the "circumstances of impartiality" category, which would include those of Rawls and Habermas.
21. Rawls contrasts the complexity of the Kantian conception of the person with that of the rational intuitionists (i.e., realists), who offer a thin "self as knower" and emphasize theoretical rather than practical reason (KCMT 346).
22. Rawls does give an account of Kant's own constructivism at LHMP 235-52; my reading is substantially different.

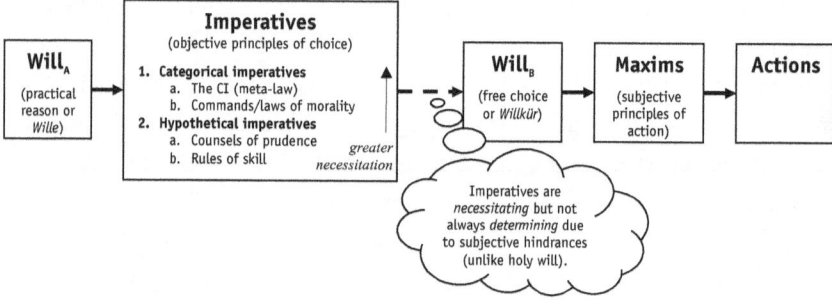

Fig. 2 Finite rational agency

In sections II and III of the *Groundwork,* Kant arguably develops a constructivist account of morality with the three components specified by Rawls: an elaborate conception of the person, a procedure of construction, and a meta-principle of morality (capturing the ethical as well as the legal/political) generated by this procedure. Let us begin with Kant's conception of the person as a finite rational being. This conception is represented diagrammatically in figure 2.[23] Kant holds that we, *qua* finite rational beings, have a twofold will: $Will_A$ (practical reason or *Wille*), which issues Imperatives, or objective principles, and $Will_B$ (free choice or *Willkür*), which should use such principles to govern its choice of Maxims (subjective principles of action) and any ensuing Actions. However, imperatives are necessitating but not therefore determining for finite rational beings like humans: although we should obey such rules, subjective hindrances (e.g., the pull of sensuality, the temptations of honor or praise, even inattention) may keep us from doing so—a situation unlike that of a "holy will" (i.e., an angelic or divine will), for which $Will_A$ and $Will_B$ are fully unified and objective principles are no longer felt as imperatives, that is, they no longer constrain or bind the agent. Our capacity to choose maxims freely according to self-authored objective principles is emblematic of our rationality; our liability to subjective hindrances in making such choices is symptomatic of our finitude.

To understand this dual nature of our will more completely, we must first understand the two conceptions of freedom associated with it: negative and positive freedom, the latter of which will play an essential role in Kant's procedure

23. Kant develops the concept of a finite rational being at both GMM 4:412–20 and MM 6:213–14, 226. Kant himself believed that the GMM description was inadequate, as it gives a unidimensional account of the will. The model of finite rational agency that I tender here therefore incorporates material from both GMM and MM. To some extent I am reconstructing the GMM model of finite rational agency in light of the later, more mature model offered in MM.

of construction. Kant says that *"will is a kind of causality of living beings . . . and freedom would be that property of such causality that it can be efficient independently of alien causes determining it."*[24] Kant refers here to negative freedom, that is, freedom from causation by "alien" (external) forces, such as nature, culture, God, etc. The kind of will described in the quotation is $Will_B$ (free choice or *Willkür*), which selects maxims that cause subsequent actions, as we have seen.[25]

However, all causality, including the causality of $Will_B$, must be governed by objective laws. This claim is a direct implication of Kant's arguments in his first *Critique*. Causation is a category of understanding, along with those under the headings of quantity, quality, modality, etc.[26] Objects must have these categorical features in order for us to have knowledge of them: Kant says that the categories apply to what we empirically intuit because it is "possible through [them] **alone** to *cognize something as an object*" (CPuR A92/B125). Only through the categories can we begin to make sense of the empirical (including the human) world, and the essential relation of "causality and dependence (cause and effect)" is one that Kant describes as universal, necessary, and law-governed (CPuR A91–92/B123–24). Categories like causality are part of the internal architecture of our theoretical or speculative reason; consequently, we necessarily seek the objectively lawful regularity of causality in our experiences—including our observations of active human wills.

An implication of this is that $Will_B$, as a kind of causality, must be governed by objective principles. If such a will is free, however, then these principles cannot be an "alien" imposition; rather, they must be self-generated and self-imposed.[27] They are generated by $Will_A$ (practical reason or *Wille*) in the form of imperatives, whereas they are imposed by $Will_B$ when it elects to follow them

---

24. GMM 4:446. The "will" here is a translation of *Wille*, not *Willkür* as I implicitly claim. As I noted earlier, I am reconstructing Kant's GMM arguments in light of his later, more mature arguments in MM.

25. As Kant says at MM 6:226, "Laws proceed from the will [*Wille*], maxims from choice [*Willkür*]. In man the latter is a free choice; the will, which is directed to nothing beyond the law itself, cannot be called either free or unfree, since it is not directed to actions but immediately to giving laws for the maxims of actions (and is, therefore, practical reason itself)."

26. See the table of the categories at CPuR A80/B106.

27. To unpack this a bit: if will is causality and all causality is law-governed, then the will must be law-governed, i.e., there is no such thing as a "lawless will." All laws governing wills can be placed into two mutually exclusive and exhaustive categories: those laws that are imposed from without (*heteronomous law*) and those that are imposed from within (*autonomous law*). If a free will is a will undetermined by alien (external) forces, then this must mean that it is undetermined by heteronomous laws, which implies (by elimination) that it must be determined—or, given our finitude, necessitated—by autonomous laws.

in its choice of maxims, which it will do when reason prevails—again, imperatives are necessitating but not therefore determining in finite rational beings due to various subjective hindrances. When we choose maxims consistent with and out of respect for self-authored moral imperatives, we are exercising the highest form of positive freedom: moral autonomy.

In order to see how Kant constructs moral imperatives—especially the meta-rule that I will call *the* categorical imperative (The CI), to distinguish it from garden-variety categorical imperatives—we must ascend the ladder of necessitation depicted in my diagram. Kant says that these three kinds of imperatives are "clearly distinguished by **dissimilarity** in the necessitation of the will. In order to make this dissimilarity evident, I think they would be most suitably named in their order by being said to be either *rules of skill, counsels of prudence, or commands (laws) of morality*."[28] I will cover them in this order, ascending the ladder of necessitation:

Hypothetical imperatives—rules of skill: These are principles of choice that instruct us how to achieve any number of possible ends. They are, in other words, principles of instrumental reason or technical imperatives. As Kant explains, they determine not "whether the end [sought] is rational and good . . . but only what one must do in order to attain it. . . . Since in early youth it is not known what ends might occur to us in the course of life, parents seek above all to have their children learn *a great many things* and to provide for *skill* in the use of means to all sorts of *discretionary* ends" (GMM 4:415). An example of a rule of skill might be "If I want to listen to the radio, then I have to plug it in and hit the power button." The most general form of such imperatives is rendered thus by Kant: "Whoever wills the end also wills (insofar as reason has decisive influence on his actions) the indispensably necessary means to it that are within his power" (GMM 4:417). Notice two things about Kant's rendering. First, rules of skill are necessitating only insofar as the end to which the rules suggest the means is actually willed by the agent; there is nothing in these rules that mandates or even so much as suggests ends themselves. For this reason, rules of skill are only weakly or conditionally necessitating. Second, even if the rules are necessitating for an agent, they are determinative of his action only insofar as "reason has decisive influence." Thus, whenever agents reject maxims inconsistent with such rules of skill (e.g., "when I want

---

28. GMM 4:416. Kant tends not to treat the "mere concept of a categorical imperative," The CI, as a separate kind of categorical imperative, but I think it clarifies the exposition to do so (GMM 4:420). Consequently, I have four kinds of imperatives where he has three.

to listen to the radio, I will pray for it to turn on"), they are exercising positive freedom, at least in a weak sense, for they are selecting maxims of action to be consistent with self-authored objective principles of practical reason.[29]

Hypothetical imperatives—counsels of prudence: These are principles of choice that instruct us how to achieve the universal subjective end of happiness. Kant offers as examples of such counsels "regimen, frugality, courtesy, reserve, and so forth, which experience teaches are most conducive to wellbeing on the average" (GMM 4:418). These counsels obviously lack the precision of many imperatives of skill due to the indeterminacy of our individual conceptions of happiness: Kant describes happiness as "a fluctuating idea" and "not an ideal of reason but of imagination, resting merely on empirical grounds"; it is a moving target, in short, making prudential counsels that aim towards it "so tenuous that everyone must be allowed countless exceptions in order to adapt his choice of a way of life to his particular inclinations and his susceptibility to satisfaction and still, in the end, to become prudent only from his own or others' misfortunes" (GMM 4:399, 418; MM 6:216). Despite the ambiguity involved, however, these counsels are more necessitating than rules of skill due to the universality of happiness as a subjective end among finite rational beings; our interest in our own welfare is not something that can be casually given up, unlike lower-order discretionary ends.[30] As with rules of skill, however, following self-authored counsels of prudence in the choice of maxims is an exercise of positive freedom that I will identify below with *personal autonomy.*

Categorical imperatives—commands/laws of morality: These are principles of choice that are not contingent on our adoption of any particular end, unlike the rules of skill or counsels of prudence. As Kant says, "the unconditional command leaves the will no discretion . . . so that it alone brings with it that necessity which we require of a law" (GMM 4:420). Additionally, unlike counsels of prudence, commands of morality are not to be "adapted" to fit individual circumstances: they are equally binding on all agents and command without

---

29. Henry Allison notes that positive freedom is a "capacity to act on the basis of imperatives (which includes, *but is not limited to,* the categorical imperative)" (Allison 1990, 85). In other words, positive freedom can be exemplified by the selection of maxims consistent with rules of skill or counsels of prudence, not just commands of morality.

30. As Allen Wood notes, "What binds me to act on a counsel of prudence is . . . the conception of myself as a single self with a conception of its own good. My commitment to an end I have set can be abandoned at my discretion, but my rational commitment to prudence cannot be abandoned as if it were an arbitrary end" (Wood 1999, 74).

favor. Examples of moral laws include "Do not lie for personal advantage" and "Do not murder." Owing to their categorical nature, they are fully necessitating imperatives, and by conscientiously following such self-authored moral laws in our choice of maxims we exercise the highest form of positive freedom: *moral autonomy.*

Categorical imperatives—The CI: This is a metaprinciple of choice, one that persons can use to "screen" all proposed practical principles. To understand its form and see how it can be derived, consider that what makes an imperative categorical is its unconditionality. Therefore, to discover the highest form of categorical imperative—what Kant calls the "mere concept" of a categorical imperative—we must imagine a perfectly unconditional objective principle of choice. This principle would have to abstract away from anything that could condition it—motives, ends, qualities of person, even subject matter (e.g., lying or murder)—leaving nothing but "universality of law as such"; the idea of screening practical principles for this characteristic gives us the first formulation of The CI, known as the formula of universal law (FUL): "Act only in accordance with that maxim through which you can at the same time will that it become a universal law" (GMM 4:421). To adopt such a principle and use it for screening maxims is to achieve the highest form of moral autonomy. In the other imperatives discussed above there remains a sort of residual heteronomy: the motives, ends, qualities of person, and subject matter that condition them are the contingent products of nature, culture, etc.[31] Only in the case of The CI, which abstracts away from all of these things, do we have an example of ideally autonomous law, one generated by pure practical reason. Consequently, an autonomous will is governed first and foremost (though not, of course, exclusively) by The CI, that is, perfectly unconditioned moral law.

If finite rational agency of the kind modeled above is Kant's conception of the person and The CI is his metaprinciple of morality, then what precisely is the procedure of construction that generates this metaprinciple? His procedure of construction is implicit in the ascent of the ladder of necessitation just described. We ascend the ladder and rise through progressively higher forms of imperatives by abstracting more and more from natural and social contingency; only when we have stripped away everything that could condition

---

31. For example, Kant says that "happiness contains all (and also not more than) that which nature provides us" (T&P 8:283), suggesting that nature is the source of all (subjective) ends, incentives, etc. Note, however, that Kant thinks of human culture as the ultimate end of nature, so the two are not really separate (CJ 5:429–34; Yovel 1980, 195).

our self-legislation of practical principles do we achieve a lawmaking position of perfect autonomy and positive freedom. Kant says as much while discussing the fifth formulation of The CI (formula of the kingdom of ends [FKE]):

> By a *kingdom* I understand a systematic union of various rational beings through common laws. Now since laws determine ends in terms of their universal validity [FUL], if we **abstract from the personal differences of rational beings as well as from all the content of their private ends** we shall be able to think of a whole of all ends in systematic connection (a whole both of rational beings as ends in themselves [FH] and of the ends of his own that each may set himself), that is, . . . a kingdom of ends, which is possible in accordance with the above principles.[32]

This "systematic union" can achieve its reconciliation of all ends of rational beings only through common laws, and just as we can imagine such reconciliation only by abstracting from all forms of conditionality, so we can generate laws capable of governing this kingdom only through a like procedure of abstraction.

We can now see that Kant's moral philosophy is properly categorized as constructivist on Rawls's own definition of the term: it contains a complex conception of the person that serves as an element in a procedure of construction that generates an objective moral principle. Moreover, as Kant indicates in his later writings, The CI has both legal/political and ethical components: the universal principle of right (UPR) and the universal principle of virtue (UPV), respectively (MM 6:230, 395). (Duties of right, such as the duty of noncoercion, are subject to external enforcement but do not require the adoption of particular moral ends, whereas duties of virtue, such as a duty of respect, are not subject to external enforcement but do require the adoption of such ends, e.g., humanity as an end in itself—in other words, they must be discharged for the right reasons in order to be considered virtuous.)[33] The UPR, which decrees that "any action is right if it can coexist with everyone's freedom in accordance with a universal law," is intended to guide the creation and enforcement of

---

32. GMM 4:433. The CI's Formula of Humanity (FH) is "so act that you use humanity, whether in your own person or in the person of any other, always at the same time as an end, never merely as a means" (GMM 4:429).

33. MM 6:379–83. Kant notes that duties of right themselves can be discharged virtuously if one makes "the right of humanity, or also the right of human beings, one's *end*" (MM 6:390–91).

law in Kant's social-contract state and consequently functions as a metaprinciple of justice (MM 6:230, 395). Thus, the objective moral principle generated by Kant's procedure of construction is both legal/political and ethical, and the former element acts as a screening device for principles of justice. Kant's own constructivism is consequently broader and higher order than Rawls's; it encompasses Kantian constructivism but also transcends it by (1) providing guidance on ethical as well as political matters and (2) constructing a screening or selection device for principles of justice rather than the principles themselves.[34]

Now that we have fully explored the relationship between, first, Kant's moral theory and constructivism and, second, Kant's constructivism and Kantian constructivism, we are finally in a position to ask in what way Rawls's own theory of justice—justice as fairness—is a variety of Kantian constructivism and then to ask how Kantian justice as fairness is.[35] Kant and Rawls may both be practitioners of Kantian constructivism, in other words, but how close are their practices of it? We will not get a full answer to this question until I explain in the next section how Rawls interprets justice as fairness as a Kantian-constructivist theory, but we can already see how close their practices are by looking at Rawls's 1975 essay "A Kantian Conception of Equality." In this essay, Rawls explicitly connects Kant's conceptions of negative and positive freedom (discussed above) to features of the OP: the veil of ignorance hides information regarding both natural and social contingencies because, as Rawls notes, "by negative freedom Kant means being able to act independently from the determination of alien causes; to act from natural necessity is to subject oneself to the heteronomy of nature"; parties behind the veil in the OP choose the principles of justice that recognize our status as free and equal beings and that will realize this freedom and equality in major social institutions, and by

---

34. I am not saying, of course, that Kant failed to reach substantive political conclusions in his Doctrine of Right. For example, implicit in the UPR (and The CI of which it is a component) is the idea of citizens (persons) as free, equal, and independent (T&P 8:290; cf. MM 6:313-14). On the basis of this idea of equality, Kant denies that any hereditary prerogatives (such as nobility by birth) can be just—at least as a matter of conclusive rather than provisional right (T&P 8:292-94; MM 6:329). What I *am* saying is that Kant never used his constructivism to derive detailed, ordered principles of justice like Rawls does. Rather, he used it only to suggest the *broad outline* of a just political order: republican government, perpetual peace through pacific federation, and cosmopolitan right (PP 8:348-60; MM 6:340-41, 350-53). As we shall see, Rawls's justice as fairness can be seen as an attempt to further flesh out the implications of treating citizens as free, equal, and independent.

35. Other Kant scholars have explored these relationships as well. Larry Krasnoff, for example, agrees that "the CI is a constructed procedure" but comes to this conclusion by way of a reconstruction of GMM I rather than an exegesis of GMM II and III, as I have offered (1999, 402-3).

doing so they reflect our capacity for autonomy or positive freedom (KCE 264–66; cf. TJ 222, 225). Rawls makes numerous similar connections in §40 of *Theory* ("A Kantian Interpretation of Justice as Fairness"), but I will review these below in the context of Rawls's own defense of his Kantian-constructivist credentials.

Before turning to this task, though, I should point out that Rawls's justice as fairness has aspirations beyond Kantian constructivism's restricted concern with political principles, towards something closer to Kant's own broader, moral constructivism. Rawls notes in *Theory* that "justice as fairness is not a complete contract theory. For it is clear that the contractarian idea can be extended to the choice of more or less an entire ethical system, that is, to a system including principles for all the virtues and not only for justice. Now for the most part I shall consider only principles of justice and others closely related to them; I make no attempt to discuss the virtues in a systematic way. Obviously if justice as fairness succeeds reasonably well, a next step would be to study the more general view suggested by the name 'rightness as fairness.'"[36] In §§18, 19, 51, and 52 of *Theory*, Rawls does offer a preliminary discussion of principles that would apply to individuals rather than institutions of the basic structure, involving obligations of fairness and fidelity, natural duties of mutual aid and respect, and supererogatory actions such as benevolence, heroic self-sacrifice, etc. However, he does not systematically develop a Rawlsian doctrine of virtue (or even a broader, nonpolitical doctrine of right) in *Theory*, and in his later works he abjures any such ambitions.[37] Nevertheless, as I will maintain below, Rawls's political theory systematically intrudes into what Kant at least would think of as the domain of ethics, not just in *Theory* but throughout his writings. When Rawls sympathetically discusses Kant's belief that "a sense of justice is a necessary condition of the worthiness to be happy," when he asks us to "think of the notion of a well-ordered society as an interpretation of the idea of a kingdom of ends," when he speaks of our first moral power "to act from (and not merely in accordance with) principles of justice," and when he says that if "human beings are largely amoral, if not incurably cynical and self-centered, one might ask, with Kant, whether it is worthwhile for human

---

36. TJ 15. In fact, Rawls calls the first two elements of his construction procedure "formal constraints of the concept of right" because "they hold for the choice of all ethical principles and not only for those of justice" (TJ 112).

37. For example, PL 99. Also see Hill (1989b), who doubts that Rawls's Kantian constructivism could be successfully extended to embrace ethical as well as political theory.

beings to live on the earth," Rawls seems to be gesturing towards broader concerns about ethical living and the highest good for man (SJ 115; KCE 264 [cf. TJ 221]; KCMT 312; LP 128). As I suggest below, it is especially at moments such as these that his brand of Kantian constructivism begins to approach Kant's own and his Kantianism becomes more than simply aspirational.

IV. Justice as Fairness as Kantian Constructivism: Diagram and Details

To what degree is Rawls's justice as fairness a Kantian-constructivist doctrine, and how close is it to Kant's own constructivism? In this section, I will review Rawls's interpretation of justice as fairness as a variety of Kantian constructivism, which according to Rawls's definition "specifies a particular [1] *conception of the person* as an element in a reasonable [2] *procedure of construction*, the outcome of which determines the content of the first [3] *principles of justice*" (KCMT 304; emphasis added). As I do so, I will compare its features to those of Kant's constructivism, pointing out similarities and discussing Rawls's own understanding of his Kantianism, especially as revealed in *Theory*. I offer a diagrammatic summary of Rawls's interpretation in figure 3, with a separate box for each of the three components of Kantian constructivism; these three components will be described in the following three subsections, respectively.

A. The Kantian Conception of the Person

Rawls begins with a conception of individuals as "free and equal moral persons."[38] The moral quality is primary, as we shall see, whereas the qualities of freedom and equality, though important, are largely derivative of it. Rawls assumes that all persons possess two moral powers, reasonableness and rationality, at least to a required minimum, and that their possession entitles them to equal justice.[39] The first moral power of *reasonableness* is "the capacity for

---

38. KCMT 309; cf. TJ 221: "free and equal rational [i.e., moral: Reasonable and Rational] beings"; cf. MM 6:314, where Kant characterizes citizens as free, equal, and independent.

39. TJ 442: "The capacity for moral personality is a *sufficient* condition for being entitled to equal justice. Nothing beyond the essential minimum is required. Whether moral personality is also a *necessary* condition I shall leave aside." On this last point, however—which is clearly relevant for the question of animal rights—Rawls later says that "while I have not maintained that the capacity for a sense of justice is necessary in order to be owed the duties of justice, it does seem that we are not required to give strict justice anyway to creatures lacking this capacity.... They are outside the scope of the theory of justice, and it does not seem possible to extend the

Kantian conception of the person
{ INPUT }

1. **Moral** (autonomous)
    a. *Reasonable* (morally autonomous)
    b. *Rational* (personally autonomous)
2. **Free**
    a. *Self-originating sources of valid claims*
    b. *Rational revisability of ends*
    c. *Responsibility for ends*
3. **Equal** (as subjects and authors of law)

reflected in

Procedure of construction: The original position (OP)
{ PROCESS }

1. **Formal constraints on the alternative principles**
    a. *Generality*
    b. *Universality*
    c. *Publicity*
    d. *Ordering*
    e. *Finality*
2. **OP information structure: Veil of ignorance (VI)**
3. **OP parties and their rationality: Thin theory of the good**
    a. *Three regulative interests*
        i. Highest-order interest in reasonableness
        ii. Highest-order interest in rationality
        iii. Higher-order interest in determinate conception of the good
    b. *Social primary goods*
    c. *Mutual disinterest*

generates

Principles, institutions, and psychology of justice
{ OUTPUT }

1. **Principles**
    a. *Priority of right*
    b. *Three principles of justice* (lexically ordered)
        i. Equal liberty (EL)
        ii. Fair equality of opportunity (FEO)
        iii. Difference principle (DP)
2. **Institutions**
    a. *Basic structure*
    b. *Well-ordered society* (WOS)
3. **Psychology**
    a. *Respect* (moral shame vs. guilt)
    b. *Good of the sense of justice*

Fig. 3 Justice as fairness as Kantian constructivism

an effective sense of justice, that is, the capacity to understand, to apply and to act from (and not merely in accordance with) the principles of justice" (KCMT 312). Rawls's theory of justice intrudes into the ethical domain here, at least as it is understood by Kant: rightful action is action merely in accordance with law, according to Kant, without regard for intention, which is why even a "nation of devils" can be capable of justice; to act from principles of right— that is, to act rightfully out of a respect for humanity and the moral law—is to act virtuously or ethically as well as justly.[40] I will return to this point below when I discuss Rawls's concept of a well-ordered society, which he compares to Kant's ideal ethical commonwealth, the kingdom of ends.

Closely related to the idea of reasonableness is Rawls's concept of full autonomy. This is the kind of autonomy achieved by citizens in a well-ordered society when they affirm, publicly recognize, and act from the principles of justice that would be chosen in a suitably characterized OP (KCMT 315). Full autonomy includes reasonableness but goes beyond it to emphasize our authorship of the principles of justice. Full autonomy is nearly identical to Kant's concept of moral autonomy, which as we have seen is the choice of maxims of action consistent with and respectful of self-authored moral imperatives. Citizens who are fully autonomous similarly act from principles of justice whose authorship they claim via the justificatory apparatus of the OP. Because this fuller capacity must implicitly be part of Rawls's conception of the person—if our authorial capacity were not part of our self-conception as moral persons, we would be incapable of imagining the development of it in a well-ordered society—I will expand the definition of reasonableness to include it; I will associate the public recognition and affirmation of principles of justice instead with the idea of a well-ordered society. With this modification, which I will defend more fully in chapter 3, reasonableness becomes nearly identical to Kant's concept of moral autonomy, which Rawls sees as the central idea of Kant's ethics.[41]

Rawls defines the second moral power of *rationality* as the "capacity to form, to revise, and rationally to pursue a conception of the good" (KCMT 312).

---

contract doctrine so as to include them in a natural way" (TJ 448); cf. MM 6:442-43, where Kant expresses very similar sentiments.

40. MM 6:380, 390-91; PP 8:366. On this point, see Höffe (1984, 121-22).

41. TJ 221. I say "nearly identical" here to emphasize as I did earlier that Kant's constructivism is broader and higher order than Rawls's Kantian constructivism—though as we have just seen, and will continue to see, there are ethical elements to Rawls's political thought that reflect a deeper Kantian sensibility.

He associates the successful execution of a plan of life, which implements our conception of the good, with happiness, and he argues that the rational pursuit of it must be consistent with principles of deliberative rationality, including "the adoption of effective means to ends; the balancing of final ends by their significance for our plan of life as a whole and by the extent to which these ends cohere and support each other; and finally, the assigning of a greater weight to the more likely consequences" (TJ 359–60, 365; KCMT 316 [cf. TJ §64]). The formation and revision of a plan of life, on the other hand, is the creative side of the moral power of rationality. Though it involves working with our current set of aims, interests, and desires, Rawls stresses that these elements of our conception of the good are subject to rational adherence, alteration, and even rejection; in other words, the moral power of rationality makes us the ultimate authors of our identity: "The aim of deliberation is to find that plan which best organizes our activities and influences the formation of our subsequent wants so that our aims and interests can be fruitfully combined into one scheme of conduct. Desires that tend to interfere with other ends, or which undermine the capacity for other activities, are weeded out; whereas those that are enjoyable in themselves and support other aims as well are encouraged" (TJ 360–61). Far from taking the elements of our plan of life as givens, Rawls's understanding of rationality requires us to harmonize them by trimming some and nurturing others. Exercising rationality is like tending our garden: we must work with the vegetation at hand according to certain rules, but over time we can change its composition and redirect its growth to achieve particular aesthetic or utilitarian objectives. Thus, Rawls's second moral power of rationality, which unites deliberative rationality with creative self-authorship, is simply a variation on the contemporary concept of personal autonomy.[42]

This moral power of rationality is closely related to Kantian prudential reasoning. First, it focuses on the achievement of happiness via the successful execution of a plan of life; Kantian prudential reasoning is similarly motivated by the universal subjective end of happiness, as we saw earlier. Second, Rawls notes that his idea of rationality "roughly parallels Kant's notion of hypothetical imperatives," which, as we noted above, includes both rules of skill and counsels of prudence (KCMT 308). Some of Rawls's principles of deliberative rationality seem more similar to rules of skill (including "the assigning of a

---

42. Among the many other scholars who have helped clarify this concept are Christman (1988), G. Dworkin (1988), Feinberg (1989), Frankfurt (1988), Mele (2001), Raz (1986, esp. 369–82), and Waldron (2005).

greater weight to the more likely consequences"), whereas others (like the "balancing of final ends") appear closer to counsels of prudence owing to their imprecision and even artistic quality. A third, closely related point is that just as Rawls's idea of rationality has a creative component, so Kant suggests that the happiness pursued via counsels of prudence is "not an ideal of reason but of imagination": we cannot achieve it through mechanical application of rules of skill but must rather exercise inventive judgment that "adapts [our] choice of a way of life to [our] particular inclinations and [our] susceptibility to satisfaction" (GMM 4:418; MM 6:216). Certain features of both Rawlsian rationality and Kantian prudence are better captured, I believe, by the kind of gardening metaphor I offered earlier than by mechanical metaphors of calculation and maximization.[43]

Rawls conceives of persons as being not just moral (i.e., reasonable and rational) but also free and equal; these last two attributes are largely derived from the first one, though, as we shall see. Freedom of the person has three closely related aspects. First, Rawls says that human beings are "self-originating sources of valid claims . . . in the sense that their claims carry weight on their own without being derived from prior duties or obligations owed to society or to other persons, or, finally, as derived from, or assigned to, their particular social role" (KCMT 330). In other words, persons are entitled to make claims on social institutions, in the name of their various interests, simply by virtue of their humanity. Why are such claims valid, however? Rawls later redescribes this aspect of freedom as "counting *moral personality* itself as a source of claims" (KCMT 331; emphasis added), meaning that one or both of our moral powers must be the source of the validity. I would suggest, on Kantian grounds, that what lies at the heart of both of the moral powers is the power of free choice or negative freedom (Will$_B$) and that this power is the source of the validity of free claims. The third formulation of The CI—the formula of humanity (FH)—says, "so act that you use humanity, whether in your own person or in the person of any other, always at the same time as an end, never merely as a means" (GMM 4:429). What most characterizes humanity for Kant, however, is the "capacity to set oneself an end—any end whatsoever," be it moral or nonmoral.[44] So the power of free choice itself is an object of respect and

---

43. For a more detailed discussion of the relationship between personal autonomy and Kantian prudence, see Taylor (2005, 606–9).
44. MM 6:392. Cf. Wood (1999, 120): "Preserving and respecting rational nature means preserving and respecting it in all its functions, not merely in its moral function of giving and

a source of valid claims on Kantian grounds, claims that need no extrinsic validation in the form of communal sanction, etc.

The second aspect of freedom, derived directly from rationality, is the free revisability of our conception of the good and our associated plan of life. As Rawls points out, persons "do not view themselves as inevitably tied to the pursuit of the particular conception of the good and its final ends which they espouse at any given time" (KCMT 331; cf. TJ 131). This ability to "stand apart" from our current aims, interests, and desires is the negative facet of moral personality, without which we could not exercise personal autonomy or reshape our plans for the sake of the moral law. Finally, the third aspect of freedom, of which free revisability is a necessary condition, is our responsibility for the ends that we choose. As long as fair conditions hold, "citizens are capable of adjusting their aims and ambitions in the light of what they can reasonably expect and of restricting their claims in matters of justice to certain kinds of things" and are required to do so (KCMT 332; PL 33–34). Making responsibility an aspect of freedom might seem peculiar—is obligation not a *restriction* of freedom?—but from a Kantian point of view it is unremarkable: negative freedom, as we saw earlier, is the foundation of positive freedom or autonomy; the highest form of autonomy, moral autonomy, makes us both authors and subjects of the moral law; hence, obligations deriving from moral personality are just aspects of our freedom. As authority figures are fond of saying (though presumably for different reasons), freedom and responsibility go together.

Equality is the third and final component of Rawls's conception of persons. Rawls says that "all [persons] view themselves as equally worthy of being represented in any procedure that is to determine the principles of justice that are to regulate the basic institutions of their society," and he grounds this equal worth on the first moral power, reasonableness (KCMT 333; cf. KCMT 309). Reasonable beings are capable of choosing maxims of action ($Will_B$) out of respect for moral laws, including the principles of justice; if we expand the idea of reasonableness to include capacity for authorship of moral laws ($Will_A$), as I suggested above, then each person can see himself as a colegislator of moral law with other persons. They can legislate together on an equal basis so long as their first moral powers are developed to the essential minimal degree; special judicial or legislative talents are optional, though these might qualify

---

obeying moral laws. Furthering rational nature requires furthering all the (morally permissible) ends it sets, not merely the ends it sets in response to duty."

one for special office in the governing structure of a well-ordered society (KCMT 333). Kant captures this idea of our colegislation of the moral law in the fourth formulation of The CI—the formula of autonomy (FA)—which is "the *principle* of every human will as *a will giving universal law through all its maxims,*" with such law serving as the basis for "a systematic union of rational beings," that is, "a kingdom of ends" (GMM 4:432–33). Like Rawls, Kant extends this idea of colegislation by finite rational beings to the political realm, not merely in the hypothetical sense that is most relevant here—that is, each citizen as "colegislator" of a "basic law" or "original contract," which is seen as *"only an idea* of reason"—but also in terms of real political practice, as Kant's defense of a representative, constitutional democracy in "Perpetual Peace" and the Doctrine of Right indicates to us.[45] As I shall show in chapter 3, Rawls's idea of reasonableness similarly grounds not just the hypothetical procedural equality of the OP but the political equality of citizens in a democratic state.[46]

B. The Procedure of Construction: The Original Position (OP)

Now that we have reviewed Rawls's Kantian conception of the person, we are ready to see how his conception is reflected in the second component of Kantian constructivism, which is a "reasonable procedure of construction." In justice as fairness, the original position (OP) plays this role. Most basically, the OP is intended to capture the Kantian idea that moral principles are "the objects of rational *choice,*" that is, they are constructed rather than discovered or intuited, and they are therefore emblematic of our positive freedom or autonomy (TJ 221; cf. KCE 265–66). In order for the principles chosen from this perspective to have moral force, its constituent parts must be designed to reflect the key features of a normatively compelling conception of the person, such as Rawls's Kantian conception. In what follows, I will review the three constituent parts of Rawls's OP in the same order they are introduced in *Theory*

---

45. T&P 8:294–95, 297; PP 8:349–53; MM 6:313–19, 325, 341, 345–46. For a systematic defense of Kant's democratic credentials, see Taylor (2006, 561–64).

46. Rawls explicitly links the hypothetical with the actual when he discusses the "principle of (equal) participation": "Justice as fairness begins with the idea that where common principles are necessary and to everyone's advantage, they are to be worked out from the viewpoint of a suitably defined initial situation of equality in which each person is fairly represented. The principle of participation transfers this notion from the original position to the constitution as the highest-order system of social rules for making rules. . . . The constitutional process should preserve the equal representation of the original position to the degree that this is practicable" (TJ 194–95).

§§23–25—the formal constraints on the alternative principles, the veil of ignorance, and the rationality of the parties—showing as I go how these parts reflect key features of Rawls's Kantian conception of the person.

1. The Formal Constraints on the Alternative Principles

Rawls imagines parties in the OP being presented with a list of alternative principles of justice (§21) from which they will choose. Principles on the list have to meet five formal criteria: generality, universality, publicity, ordering, and finality. Rawls says little about the justification of these formal constraints, remarking only that they are "not to be justified by definition or the analysis of concepts, but only by the reasonableness of the theory of which they are a part" (TJ 113). Is there anything to be said in their defense beyond this bald coherentist claim? Rawls does suggest that all principles of justice must discharge the task of "adjusting the claims that persons make on their institutions and one another"; principles failing to reconcile such claims would arguably fail to be principles of justice at all, as the entire purpose of distributive justice is that of "assigning basic rights and duties and determining the division of advantages" (TJ 113). For this reason, the last two criteria, *ordering* and *finality*, should be uncontroversial: unless principles impose an order on conflicting claims and serve as "the final court of appeal in practical reasoning," respectively, they cannot guarantee the definitive resolution of disputes that we all expect of such principles.[47]

That leaves us with the first three criteria, which are anything but uncontroversial, at least outside the bounds of liberal theory. Generality, which requires that we craft principles "without the use of what would be intuitively recognized as proper names, or rigged definite descriptions," would be inconsistent with principles that give differential treatment to named individuals, races, classes, etc. (like the Nuremberg Laws) or that effectively do so (like the

---

I think it is more than merely coincidental that Rawls, after a discussion of the meaning of freedom and equality in Lecture II of KCMT, finishes it up with a paragraph on citizens of a well-ordered society being "above reproach. Whatever their actions, all conform to the acknowledged requirements of justice for the most part" (333). Kant, in a central paragraph in the introduction to his Doctrine of Right, says that freedom is the only innate right, that equality is one implication of it, and that another is "a human being's quality . . . of being *beyond reproach (iusti)*, since before he performs any act affecting rights he has done no wrong to anyone" (MM 6:238). Rawls at times seems to channel Kant—and not just the ethical Kant but the political Kant as well.

47. TJ 113. As Rawls notes, the ordering criterion may not be uncontroversial to egoists, however, as even a general egoism (which directs each person to advance his own interests) fails to order conflicting claims (TJ 117).

so-called grandfather clauses of Jim Crow laws).[48] For example, gendered principles of justice appear to be at the root of various laws in the world today, such as Saudi Arabia's restrictions on driving by women, and such principles are clearly barred by generality.[49] Universality, which insists that principles "be universal in application . . . hold[ing] for everyone in virtue of their being moral persons," would be violated by a principle maintaining that some moral persons (e.g., foreigners or slaves) were neither protected nor bound by it. Historically, at any rate, this criterion has been controversial. Finally, publicity, which demands political transparency and assumes that "everyone will know about these principles [of justice] all that he would know if their acceptance were the result of an agreement," rules out any principle that could not serve as a "public conception of justice," from Plato's idealism (which must rely upon myths such as the Noble Lie to communicate its doctrine to nonguardians) to Sidgwick's esoteric utilitarianism (which might require most of a population to be unaware of eudaimonistic principles, as they would be likely to misapply them) (TJ 115, 398; Plato 1991, 93–94 [414b–415d]; Sidgwick 1981, 489–90).

Thus, unlike the ordering and finality constraints, the criteria of generality, universality, and publicity are in need of justification. Given the nature of Kantian constructivism, any such justification must be based upon the conception of the person underlying a proposed theory—in this case, Rawls's Kantian conception of the person. This is not to say that the criteria in question could not be justified on other grounds, including other conceptions of the person: for example, a utilitarian conception of the person would surely ground universality (with respect to all sentient beings). Rather, it is to say that the elements of any procedure of construction—be they criteria of the sort under consideration here or the information constraints and motivational assumptions for OP parties that we will soon encounter—must be tied to a specific underlying conception of the person for a theory to qualify as a variety of Kantian constructivism.

Justifying generality and universality on these grounds is simple. Although Rawls thinks "it is a mistake . . . to emphasize the place of generality and

---

48. This criterion is meant to apply to first principles of justice, not necessarily to lower-level laws like the ones just mentioned, which were simply used as examples. For instance, a principle of justice that distributes prizes to all on the basis of merit may be perfectly general in form, but even rules that directly derive from it (e.g., "give Prize X to Meritorious Person Y") may not be and in many cases *cannot* be.

49. A defender of such restrictions might reply that some suitably general principle is in fact at work here, like "give privileges only to those who can exercise them competently or responsibly," but if such a principle is being used to justify the exclusion of *all* women from driving, it must implicitly be relying on "rigged definite descriptions."

universality in Kant's ethics," there is no question of whether these qualities are present in either it or Rawls's own Kantian conception of the person (TJ 221). As we saw earlier, Rawls assumes that all persons possess the two moral powers, reasonableness and rationality, at least to a required minimum, and that their possession entitles them to equal justice and places them under its obligations (TJ 442). Hence, any principle of justice that is consistent with this conception must be universal in application. As we also saw, reasonable persons are morally autonomous, and moral autonomy in its highest form requires that persons abstract from all varieties of contingency, including "social position or natural endowments" (TJ 222). Thus, principles of justice must also be general in form to reflect Rawls's Kantian conception.

Justifying publicity is slightly more complex, in part because of the richness of Rawls's concept of publicity, which has three levels.[50] The first level of publicity requires all principles to be publicly known and understood, meaning not simply that everyone knows and understands the principles but that there is a broad awareness of this universal knowledge and understanding. The first level seems roughly equivalent to Kant's concept of publicity in "Perpetual Peace," which is simply the requirement that principles of justice be openly acknowledged.[51] The second level of publicity requires a broad and open knowledge of "the general beliefs in the light of which first principles of justice themselves can be accepted, that is, the theory of human nature and of social institutions generally" (KCMT 324; cf. TJ 398). That is, the principles of justice implicitly rely upon certain assumptions about person and society (e.g., that persons in fact have a capacity for autonomy or that a society based upon toleration and equality before the law is in fact feasible) that must be verifiable via "publicly shared methods of inquiry . . . familiar from common sense" (KCMT 324). Finally, the third and deepest level of publicity requires that the complete justification of the principles of justice "be publicly known or, better, at least publicly knowable" (KCMT 324). All citizens must have access to and be able to understand the complex of arguments that would justify the

---

50. I very roughly follow KCMT 324–25 here. Both here and elsewhere, Rawls tends to conflate publicity with other elements of a well-ordered society (e.g., the mutual acceptance of principles of right, the justice of the institutions making up the basic structure of such a society, etc.). Here I focus on the more natural, restricted sense of publicity as general exposure, openness, or transparency; the parenthetical features are *products* of a Kantian constructivism rather than elements of the procedure of construction itself.

51. PP 8:381–86. I am referring here to the first, negative "transcendental formula of public right: 'All actions relating to the rights of others are wrong if their maxim is incompatible with publicity'" (PP 8:381).

principles of justice. Whether this third level is even possible or not is surely an open question, as it would seem to demand the *capacity* at least for understanding philosophically rigorous argumentation, one that many, if not most, people might simply lack even if properly trained and socialized. We should perhaps think of the third level of publicity as an unachievable (but still guiding) ideal or standard.

These three levels of publicity, which are jointly referred to by Rawls as the *full publicity condition,* can be linked to Rawls's Kantian conception of the person by means of our first moral power as well as our equality. As we have seen, reasonableness involves moral autonomy, but in order to see *ourselves* as the authors of the principles from which we act, we must know what the principles are, what assumptions they entail, and how these principles and their assumptions can be justified. Full publicity is therefore implicit in the very idea of moral autonomy. Moreover, in order for us to see *other people* as our colegislators of moral principles (FA) and coparticipants in a possible kingdom of ends that reconciles the ends of all rational beings (FKE), we must first see that they themselves know what the moral principles are, what assumptions they entail, and how these principles and their assumptions can be justified. Full transparency is thus a necessary condition for genuinely autonomous moral community—the kind of community that Rawls uses as a model for his well-ordered society, as we shall later see (Taylor 2010).[52]

2. The OP Information Structure: The Veil of Ignorance (VI)

In addition to these formal constraints on the choice of alternative principles, parties in the OP are also subject to certain information constraints, captured by the metaphor of the veil of ignorance (VI). The VI denies parties in the OP access to "certain kinds of particular facts": "No one knows his place in society, his class position or social status; nor does he know his fortune in the distribution of natural assets and abilities, his intelligence and strength, and the like. Nor, again, does anyone know his conception of the good, the particulars of his rational plan of life, or even the special features of his psychology such as his aversion to risk or liability to optimism or pessimism. More than this, I assume that the parties do not know the particular circumstances of their own society . . . [or] to which generation they belong" (TJ 118). Nothing is revealed to parties in the OP except general facts and scientific theories about human

---

52. Rawls himself connects publicity to the idea of a kingdom of ends at TJ 115 and 221.

society as well as knowledge of their own motivation, which is given by the Thin Theory of the Good (to be discussed below). They know, for example, that human societies are under Humean circumstances of justice (including moderate scarcity and limited benevolence), and they have a full command of the social and physical sciences; as Rawls explains, "the parties are presumed to know whatever general facts affect the choice of principles of justice. There are no limitations on general information, that is, on general laws and theories" (TJ 109–12, 119). In short, Rawls is striving for the thickest feasible VI: he "starts by allowing the parties no information and then adds just enough so that they can make a rational agreement" on principles of justice (KCMT 335–36).

What justifies such a thick VI, and how is it connected to the Kantian conception of the person? Part of the justification is practical. Because the parties know nothing of their individual situations, there is no basis for bargaining, and any argument that is compelling to one OP agent should be compelling to all; we can therefore "view the agreement in the original position from the standpoint of one person selected at random" (TJ 120–21). A thick VI thus makes it more likely that the OP will generate a unique set of principles rather than a range of possibilities; it makes choice in the OP decision-theoretic rather than game-theoretic and therefore less complex, *ceteris paribus*.

Simplifying decisions in the OP, while helpful, cannot be the only or the most important reason for a thick VI, however. Kantian constructivism requires that features of the procedure of construction reflect those of the underlying conception of the person, from which it draws moral force. For this reason, Rawls also argues that the VI is "necessary to establish fairness between the parties," which it does by reflecting their negative freedom and their equality (KCMT 310). First, the VI deprives OP parties of any information that would enable them to make a heteronomous choice; they consequently choose, Rawls says, from a position of negative freedom, one independent of the "alien causes" of natural and social contingency (KCE 265; cf. TJ 222). Second, the VI situates parties in the OP "symmetrically with respect to each other," which reflects the equality of those they represent (KCMT 336). As we have seen, all persons capable of exercising the two moral powers to a sufficient degree have a legitimate claim to be equally represented in any procedure of construction, and the VI imposes equality in the OP by denying parties knowledge of their individuating characteristics: without such knowledge, parties are incapable of gaining bargaining advantages over one another, and each party will be persuaded by the same arguments that persuade the others. More broadly, the VI guarantees the reasonableness of the OP and what emerges from it; by situating OP parties symmetrically with respect to one another, it assures that the terms of social cooperation that arise will be fair ones, reflecting norms of reciprocity instead of replicating preexisting inequalities (KCMT 316).

The VI is one of the most Kantian features of Rawls's procedure of construction, and he himself contends that "the notion of the veil of ignorance is implicit, I think, in Kant's ethics" (TJ 118n, 121). This may be something of an understatement, for as we saw above, Kant says that in order for us to imagine a kingdom of ends we must "abstract from the personal differences of rational beings as well as from all the content of their private ends" (GMM 4:433). The similar process of abstraction needed to create the perfectly unconditioned objective principle of choice—The CI (FUL)—requires us to remove all residual heteronomy from the principle (in the form of motives, ends, qualities of person, and subject matter) in a manner remarkably similar to that of the VI.[53] Rawls makes use of this technique of abstraction for narrower and more concrete purposes than Kant—to construct principles of justice rather than metaprinciples of morality—but his motivation is essentially the same: to ensure the choice of principles of justice that best "express our nature as free and equal rational beings" (TJ 222). For Rawls as for Kant, all legislative authority derives from abstraction from contingency, and such abstraction lays the groundwork for political and ethical autonomy.

3. The OP Parties and Their Rationality: The Thin Theory of the Good

We have now seen the two ways in which the OP parties are constrained in their choice of principles of justice: by formal constraints on the alternative principles and by the VI. Choice must be *motivated* in some fashion, however, whether it is constrained or unconstrained, and we have yet to see why parties in the OP make the choices that they do. The usual reasons for choice are absent in the OP, thanks to the VI: OP parties are unaware of the particular interests, desires, and ends of those whom they represent, so these things cannot (heteronomously) motivate their choice of principles of justice. Rawls's

---

53. Critics of Rawls's Kantian credentials have argued that the VI stops short of the level of abstraction that would be required for true autonomy, as it fails to filter out information that is peculiar to *human* nature and society (e.g., the Thin Theory of the Good, the circumstances of justice), making principles that emerge from the OP anthropocentric rather than universally applicable to all finite rational beings, as Kant intended. (See, e.g., Johnson [1974] and Levine [1974], as well as Darwall [1976], who replies to Johnson.) I will respond to this criticism below, arguing that it attends insufficiently to the Kantian notion of *finitude* and the way it can justify the inclusion of such information in the OP.

Thin Theory of the Good is meant to fill this motivational lacuna for parties in the OP and to do so in a way that reflects our autonomy.

The Thin Theory of the Good has three distinct but tightly intertwined motivational components: the three regulative interests (principal), the social primary goods (derived), and mutual disinterest (interpersonal). The OP parties are characterized by what Rawls calls "rational autonomy," which differs from full autonomy (discussed above) in two ways: first, parties in the OP lack the first moral power of reasonableness, which is reflected in the VI instead; second, the parties have the "three regulative interests" instead of the particular interests of those whom they represent (KCMT 308, 313). The three regulative interests are derived from Rawls's Kantian conception of the person, specifically from the two moral powers of reasonableness and rationality. The OP parties have two highest-order interests in the development and exercise of these respective powers; the first two regulative interests are therefore direct reflections of our nature as moral persons, so the advancement of them is unproblematically autonomous.[54] OP parties have another, higher-order interest in "protecting and advancing their conception of the good, whatever it may be," that is, they know that the people whom they represent have a "determinate scheme of final ends, a particular conception of the good," but they do not know its exact nature due to the VI (KCMT 313). As noted earlier, our freedom is reflected in "not requiring parties to justify claims" based upon this interest (KCMT 334).

The connection between this higher-order interest and Rawls's Kantian conception of the person is not obvious; in fact, it appears straightforwardly heteronomous given its dependence on a particular conception of the good, which is necessarily tied up with specific interests, ends, and desires. True, an OP party is unaware of what these interests, ends, and desires are, due to the VI, but that merely renders the higher-order interest generally rather than specifically heteronomous. The key to seeing the autonomous aspect of this interest is to recognize that for Rawls, pursuing a particular conception of the good—whatever its content—is about executing a *rational* plan of life (TJ §63). So OP parties, when they advance their higher-order interest, are advancing some set of specific (but unknown) interests, ends, and desires that have already been subjected to rational critique via the second moral power. Because of such

---

54. As I argued above, reasonableness is a kind of *moral* autonomy, while rationality is a type of *personal* autonomy. As we shall see, the former takes priority over the latter, as the former involves full abstraction from contingency, which is impossible for the latter and therefore limits its authority.

mediation, fostering a person's good in this way is not purely heteronomous. This being said, it is still largely heteronomous due to the origin of these interests, ends, and desires in nature and culture and to the limited degree of detachment from them achieved through rationality (as compared to reasonableness). Consequently, Rawls emphasizes that the higher-order interest is subordinate to the highest-order interests, for the autonomous needs of moral personality take absolute priority over the largely (though not wholly) heteronomous needs of a determinate plan of life.[55]

Some scholars have suggested that Rawls's later account of the three regulative interests is a major departure from the way he portrays agent motivation in *Theory*.[56] Though there is a limited truth in this, the differences can easily be exaggerated. Consider, for example, Rawls's distinction in *Theory* between our "fundamental interests," such as our religious interest and our interest in integrity of our person, and our "highest-order interest" in the free revisability of our other interests—including fundamental ones—and in the social conditions necessary to support such revision (e.g., the priority of liberty) (TJ 131–32, 475–76). The fundamental interests are basically a variety of higher-order interest, as the former are central components of most conceptions of the good and make "it legitimate for [individuals] to make claims on one another concerning the design of the basic structure of society" (TJ 131). The highest-order interest, on the other hand, is just equivalent to Rawls's later second-highest-order interest in the development and exercise of the second moral power of rationality. Thus, even in *Theory* we can see the regulative interests beginning to play a central role in agent motivation.

Though the three regulative interests play the principal motivational role for parties in the OP, the parties are more immediately (if derivatively) focused on acquiring the generic means to pursue these interests: social primary goods, including "rights, liberties, and opportunities, and income and wealth" (TJ 54). Some who question Rawls's Kantian credentials have asserted that when OP parties choose principles of justice to maximize their bundle of social primary goods they are choosing heteronomously and exercising Hobbesian rather than Kantian rationality (see, e.g., Levine 1974, esp. 50–51, 55, 57; Johnson 1974).

---

55. KCMT 313, 317. Of course, a plan of life may include the pursuit of objective moral ends (such as self-perfection and the happiness of others); to the extent that it does, it becomes as much of a moral enterprise as the exercise and development of the two moral powers. I will return to this point in chapter 2.
56. Bernard Yack, for example, speaks of Rawls's "amoral conception of the primary goods all individuals seek" in *Theory* (1994, 243n34); cf. Davidson (1985, 77n35).

As Rawls argues, however, the pursuit of social primary goods is autonomous, not heteronomous: "Were the parties moved solely by lower-order impulses, say for food and drink, or by certain particular affections for this or that group of persons, association, or community, we might think of them as heteronomous and not as autonomous. But at the basis of the desire for primary goods are the highest-order interests of moral personality and the need to secure one's conception of the good (whatever it is). Thus the parties are simply trying to guarantee and to advance the requisite conditions for exercising the powers that characterize them as moral persons."[57] The autonomous quality of this pursuit becomes even more evident (as we shall later see) when parties choose lexically ordered principles of justice that elevate the status of certain goods (e.g., basic liberties) that play a special role in the development and exercise of the two moral powers.

The critics would no doubt respond by focusing attention on one's higher-order "need to secure one's conception of the good (whatever it is)" and arguing that the incorporation of such heteronomous concerns into the motivational structure of the OP is distinctly un-Kantian. Before moving on to the interpersonal component of agent motivation, I want to address this charge, as I think it reveals a fundamental misunderstanding not of Rawls's theory but of Kant's, because his moral theory incorporates these same concerns in a number of different ways. The subjects of his moral theory are, after all, *finite* rational beings, that is, needy and vulnerable beings who seek their own happiness and necessarily feel the moral law as a restraint, even if they attain perfect virtue. Human beings are neither angels nor gods, and a moral theory that ignored their finitude would be of no practical interest. Kant's moral theory is definitely not such a theory, despite caricatures that make it out to be. First, as we saw above, Kant's model of finite rational agency involves the testing of maxims of action—motivated by subjective desires, interests, and ends—against those objective principles generated by our practical reason; without these maxims, there would be no work for Kant's moral theory to do. Second, the generation of these maxims is motivated by the universal subjective end of happiness, which Kant himself builds into the idea of the complete good, the architectonic objective end of pure practical reason (CPrR 5:110–11). Third, vulnerability is assumed in Kant's writings on both ethics and politics:

---

57. KCMT 315; cf. SUPG 365–68. Rawls's account in *Theory* admittedly focuses too heavily on the third, higher-order regulative interest of securing the means for achieving a determinate conception of the good; see TJ 223 as well as Rawls's "correction" at SUPG 365n5.

Kant's perfect duty against deception, for example, would be pointless if we were not the sort of creatures who could be fooled, and Kant's defense of a social-contract state and property rights is predicated on our exposure to assault and theft.[58] These features of finite rational beings influence not just the subject matter but the structure of Kant's moral theory; without them, his doctrine would be rendered otiose.

Perhaps the most striking way that finitude enters Kant's moral theory is in his discussion of the imperfect duties of virtue, including beneficence and self-perfection (GMM 4:423; MM 6:444–61). Rawls says Kant's defense of these duties "tacitly relied upon some account of the primary goods," but he does not explicitly argue for this claim.[59] If we reconstruct Kant's FUL argument for the imperfect duty of beneficence, we can then justify Rawls's assertion. To show that a maxim of nonbeneficence cannot be universalized (which FUL requires), I will use Rawls's own method of applying FUL via FLN (formula of the law of nature), what he calls the "four-step CI-procedure."[60] The four steps of this procedure are as follows:

1. State the maxim (subjective principle of action; e.g., if C[ondition], I should A[ction]).
2. Generalize the maxim (e.g., if C, *one* should A).
3. Restate the generalized maxim as a law of nature (e.g., if C, *everyone will* A).
4. Append this law of nature to existing ones; observe the new "social equilibrium" (E).

In some cases, E will simply be inconceivable; if so, we say that the maxim in question generates a contradiction in conception. This will occur (Kant

---

58. GMM 4:422; MM 6:312. The UPR (part of The CI), by demanding that the external freedom of each person be reconciled with that of others, provides the basis not just for a social-contract state with enforcement powers but for a system of property rights that secures individual domains of freedom from encroachment by others. The motive for such encroachment and for the political/legal system that protects against it, however, is our universal vulnerability to physical need and violence. Without these vulnerabilities, a political/legal system would have no point—as both Hobbes *and* Kant were well aware.

59. KCE 265. He implicitly provides a partial defense at LHMP 233–34.

60. LHMP 167–70. The FLN reads, "act as if the maxim of your action were to become by your will a universal law of nature" (GMM 4:421). In short, if we want to know what it would be like to universalize a maxim, we can best think of the universalized maxim as being a law of nature, which is the only other kind of truly universal law with which we are familiar—laws of nature become a "type" for laws of freedom. Laws of nature would include both social science laws (e.g., the economic law of demand) and physical laws (e.g., Newton's laws of motion).

contends) when the maxim violates a perfect duty, such as noncoercion or nondeception. In other cases, E will be conceivable but unwillable; if so, we say that the maxim generates a contradiction in will. This will occur when the maxim violates an imperfect duty, such as beneficence or self-perfection.[61] A maxim of nonbeneficence should therefore generate a contradiction in will.

Suppose one thinks about adopting a maxim of nonbeneficence of the form "if I see others in need, I will never provide any help—nor will I ever ask for any myself." Putting this maxim through the CI-procedure, we generate a social world E that is certainly conceivable, if rather harsh. However, it is not willable, at least according to the following argument:

1. Finite rational beings *unavoidably* will some ends (due to duty and finitude).
2. "Whoever wills the end also wills . . . the indispensably necessary means to it."
3. No one can be certain that the help of another will *never* be a "necessary means" to the ends that they unavoidably will (again due to finitude: no omniscience).
4. Therefore, no one can will E, which would eliminate *all* mutual aid.[62]

Notice two things about this argument. First, it relies only on weak claims (of finitude, minimal uncertainty, etc.). Second, it reaches a similarly weak conclusion: only complete nonbeneficence is ruled out—as one would expect in the case of an imperfect duty, where one has "a latitude for doing more or less, and no specific limits can be assigned to what should be done" (MM 6:393).

We can now see the truth of Rawls's claim that Kant "tacitly relied upon some account of primary goods." Given a Kantian conception of the person, some ends must be willed because of either duty (e.g., the development and exercise of the two moral powers) or finitude (e.g., enough food, water, and shelter for survival, which is a condition for all other willing and must therefore be a component of any determinate conception of the good). We cannot choose maxims that, if universalized, rule out our access to the "necessary means" to achieve these ends, whether such means come in the form of generalized aid from others or more specific forms: money for food, opportunities for work, etc.

61. GMM 4:424; the FUL beneficence argument is at GMM 4:423.
62. GMM 4:417. In reconstructing Kant's argument here, I follow the lead of Herman (1993, 45–72).

Thus, just as Rawls asserted, Kant implicitly relies upon some idea of social primary goods as necessary conditions for the advancement of unavoidable ends.[63]

We have now seen the principal and derived motivational components of Rawls's Thin Theory of the Good—the three regulative interests and the social primary goods—and how they can be defended from charges of being heteronomous, un-Kantian corruptions of Rawls's theory. The final, interpersonal component of the Thin Theory—mutual disinterest—opens the Theory to the charge of egoism, however. Rawls (in)famously conceives of OP parties as "not taking an interest in one another's interests," that is, being focused exclusively on their own three regulative interests and the acquisition of social primary goods to support these interests (TJ 12). The charge of egoism is easy to rebut, however, once we examine Rawls's reasons for making this assumption. First, Rawls assumes it for parsimony, that is, for the sake of thin motivational assumptions: "The postulate of mutual disinterest in the original position is made to insure that the principles of justice do not depend upon strong assumptions. Recall that the original position is meant to incorporate widely shared and yet weak conditions. A conception of justice should not presuppose, then, extensive ties of natural sentiment. At the basis of the theory, one tries to assume as little as possible" (TJ 111–12). A second and related reason—but one more tightly tied to Rawls's Kantianism—is that assuming the parties are altruistic limits the applicability of the principles that emerge from the OP to those people who happen to have altruistic plans of life, which would violate the universality criterion. Assuming mutual disinterest, on the other hand, places no limits on the contents of plans of life: mutually disinterested parties pursuing their higher-order interest in unknown but determinate conceptions of the good make no assumptions about the egoism or altruism of the conceptions; they simply attempt to maximize social primary goods on the understanding that this will best support whatever conceptions of the good those whom they represent happen to have; thus any principles they choose will apply to all persons, regardless of the nature of their ends.[64] These minimalist assumptions are also more consistent with the freedom of moral persons: by putting no limits on the content of their final ends, the assumption of mutual

---

63. Also see Rawls's discussion of the role of "true human needs" in Kant's practical philosophy (LHMP 173–75, 232–34, 251) and Darwall's own very different attempt to implant an account of social primary goods in Kant (1980, 325–26, 332–36).

64. TJ 223–24. Social primary goods are just as important for altruists as for egoists, of course, not just because all have a duty to develop their two moral powers but also because altruistic projects require resources—and the more the better.

disinterest reflects the idea that personal identities should be self-authored, not predetermined by prior social or even moral claims, which are themselves objects of construction (TJ 223–24). Finally and perhaps most fundamentally, the reasonable desire for reciprocity and fair play, as one manifestation of concern for others, is already captured by the formal constraints on choice in the OP, especially the VI. Building such altruistic assumptions into the motives of OP parties would be "double counting," so to speak. For all these reasons, the charge of egoism is baseless, and mutual disinterest can be given a Kantian grounding just like the first two components of the Thin Theory of the Good.

C. The Principles, Institutions, and Psychology of Justice

Now that we have examined Rawls's Kantian conception of the person and the procedure of construction (the OP) that embodies it and channels its moral force, so to speak, we can go on to ask what principles of justice would be chosen in it and what implications they would have for the design of social institutions and the psychology of citizens. In a sense, social institutions and citizen psychology in a well-ordered society are as much the product of choice, through political reform and socialization, as the principles that govern that society. The normatively guiding ideal of person, mediated by procedure and resulting principle, must direct the restructuring of existing practices and attitudes; their current status and history are relevant, of course, but mostly because some peoples—thanks to good leadership or favorable historical accidents—will be closer to the ideal than others, and some practices and attitudes will be harder to alter than others.[65] All ideal theory must ultimately be supplemented by nonideal theory, which will provide assistance in the transition to a just society, but such a transition must eventually be made, and an accommodation with current injustices can only be justified as a temporary matter.[66]

---

65. Rawls introduces the concept of a four-stage sequence to describe how we should think about applying principles of justice chosen in the OP to existing societies (TJ §31). The Rawlsian ideal can justifiably vary across societies, of course, as "the traditions, institutions, and social forces of each country, and its particular historical circumstances" may affect which institutional arrangement is most just; Rawls believes this is true of the choice between property-owning democracy and liberal socialism (TJ xiv–xvi, 242). Also, the measure of deference that should be given to existing practices and attitudes, whether in the choice of principles or in their application, is partly a function of his theory's justificatory apparatus(es), which I will detail in part 3 of the book.

66. Rawls discusses nonideal theory sporadically in *Theory*, only taking it up systematically in his discussion of civil disobedience and conscientious objection (TJ 7–8, 212, 215–20, 267; TJ §§53, 55–59). It plays a more central role in *The Law of Peoples,* but the part addressing nonideal

1. The Principles of Justice

Before describing the three lexically ordered principles that Rawls says will be chosen in his OP, I should briefly discuss the metaprinciple that governs the application of these principles vis-à-vis other normative considerations: the *priority of right*. For Rawls, the three principles of justice take absolute priority over all other normative considerations, including those of welfare, efficiency, perfection (understood as "the achievement of human excellence in art, science, and culture"), piety, and glory; in short, "the concept of right is prior to that of the good," regardless of the goodness under consideration.[67] The priority of right requires that citizens subordinate the pursuit of their conceptions of the good to the demands of justice and modify those elements of their conceptions that are inconsistent with it (KCMT 317).

As Rawls notes, the priority of right is a Kantian doctrine. Kant gives a concise definition of the priority of right in "Theory and Practice": "the incentive which the human being can have *before* a goal (end) is set for him can obviously be nothing other than the law itself through the respect that it inspires (without its being determined what end one may have and may attain by complying with it)" (T&P 8:282 [emphasis added]; cited at TJ 28n16). As we saw above, counsels of prudence and rules of skill can provide us with guidance regarding how best to pursue the universal subjective end of happiness, the desire for which is implanted in us by nature, but to show respect for ourselves as autonomous beings, we must subordinate this pursuit to the highest objective principles of choice—the categorical imperatives, including The CI—that we author with our own pure practical reason. Using Kant's terms, Rawls describes this subordination in the context of his OP: "Empirical practical reason is represented by the rational deliberations of the parties; pure practical reason

---

theory deals only marginally with transitions to a just society. The guidelines for the duty of assistance discussed there are suggestive, however (LP §15).

67. TJ 21–23, 26–28, 266, 285–92. Rawls defines *teleological* theories as those (1) defining the good independently from the right and (2) defining the right as that which maximizes the good, where the good can be welfare, perfection, etc. He defines *deontological* theories simply as nonteleological ones, i.e., ones lacking features (1) and/or (2). Justice as fairness is a deontological theory lacking feature (2): it does not maximize the good. Rawls implies that it does meet condition (1): full conceptions of the good (unlike the Thin Theory of the Good) are defined independently from the right, though they must subordinate themselves to it. See TJ 21–22, 26. This being said, Rawls does eventually argue that a "disposition to take up and to be guided by the standpoint of justice accords with the individual's good"; see his so-called congruence argument, summarized in TJ §86, which addresses the worry that justice is merely an alien imposition on our independently defined conception of the good.

is represented by the constraints within which these deliberations occur."[68] This hierarchy of pure practical reason and the principles/constraints that it generates over empirical practical reason with its prudential counsels and technical rules is a direct implication of Rawls's commitment to moral autonomy, which (as Rawls himself argues) is the central feature of Kant's practical philosophy.[69]

Given the extreme quality of the priority of right, one might reasonably ask how such a strong priority over other important values could be justified. Why can't justice be sacrificed for the sake of welfare or perfection or piety, at least when the rate of exchange is highly favorable? As we have seen, this priority is built into the very framework of Rawls's Kantian constructivism and reflects his conception of the person as morally autonomous. This realization should lead us to restate the question: why should a conception of the person as morally autonomous take such priority over other, perhaps equally compelling, conceptions of the person as a sensuous being or artistic creator or child of God? Starting with such alternative conceptions, we could choose different objective principles, including priority rules, via suitable procedures of construction.[70] We cannot yet answer this question, however: doing so requires an examination of Rawls's full theory of moral justification, to which we will turn in part 3 of the book.

Now that we have discussed the priority of the principles of justice over other normative concerns, we can turn to the questions of which principle(s) would be chosen from the OP and, if there are multiple ones, how they would be related to one another. Rather than discuss *why* the OP parties would choose Rawls's three lexically ordered principles—a question that will occupy us for much of the book's remainder—I will instead focus on describing these principles and their hierarchical ordering. In descending order of priority, the three principles are equal liberty (EL), fair equality of opportunity (FEO), and the difference principle (DP) (Rawls lists the last two in inverse order):

> **First principle** [equal liberty (EL):] Each person is to have an equal right to the most extensive total system of basic liberties compatible with a similar system of liberty for all.

---

68. KCMT 308, 319. Cf. CPrR 5:61–62 (also cited at TJ 28n16), where Kant describes empirical and pure practical reason and says that the latter is "the supreme condition of the former."
69. TJ 221. Davidson (1985, 49–51, 54, 57–59) places a special emphasis on the priority relations in Rawls's theory and by doing so ties Rawls's theory tightly to Kant's.
70. Rawls himself speculates that "average utilitarianism might be presented as a kind of constructivism"; see KCMT 323n1 and TJ §27.

Second principle Social and economic inequalities are to be arranged so that they are both:
  (a) [difference principle (DP):] to the greatest benefit of the least advantaged . . . , and
  (b) [fair equality of opportunity (FEO):] attached to offices and positions open to all under conditions of fair equality of opportunity.[71]

Rawls's three principles of justice are rules for fairly distributing social primary goods, and they are chosen by parties in the OP to best secure their three regulative interests, to which the social primary goods are means. There is a division of labor among the three principles with respect to which of these goods they distribute: EL allocates basic liberties; FEO allocates jobs, offices, and positions, along with their associated "powers and prerogatives"; and DP allocates income and wealth.[72] More precisely, EL equally allocates a set of rights, freedoms, etc. given by a list that Rawls calls the "basic liberties": they include "political liberty (the right to vote and to hold public office) and freedom of speech and assembly; liberty of conscience and freedom of thought; freedom of the person, which includes freedom from psychological oppression and physical assault and dismemberment (integrity of the person); the right to hold personal property and freedom from arbitrary arrest and seizure as defined by the concept of the rule of law" (TJ 53). As we shall see, the list of basic liberties—like the list of social primary goods more broadly—is not assembled by means of "a purely psychological, statistical, or historical survey"; rather, liberties are included on the list because they are strongly linked to the three regulative interests.[73] Given the absolute priority of EL over the other

---

71. TJ 266. This is Rawls's final statement of the three principles in *Theory*. For simplicity, I have left out the just savings principle (see TJ §§44–45). In response to criticisms by H. L. A. Hart, Rawls later changed EL's "most extensive total system" to "fully adequate scheme"; see JFPM 392 and PL 331–34.

72. FEO also (equally) allocates the nonbasic liberties of freedom of movement and free choice of occupation; see KCMT 313 and PL 228. The specified division of labor is apparent in the cases of EL and FEO—the social primary goods that they allocate are even mentioned in the principles themselves—but not in the case of DP. Rawls ties the DP to the idea of a social minimum income in *Theory*, however, so mine is a natural interpretation (TJ 244–45, 252; cf. JF 129–30). He does occasionally speak of the DP distributing other goods, though, such as education (e.g., TJ 86–87), and later refers to my interpretation of the DP as its "simplest form" (JF 59n26, 65). Finally, the social bases of self-respect—the last of the social primary goods—are secured by EL with the assistance of FEO and DP: see the self-respect argument for the priority of liberty (TJ 476–80).

73. KCMT 314. Rawls leaves many liberties off the list (e.g., "the right to own certain kinds of property (e.g., means of production) and freedom of contract as understood by the doctrine

two principles, "basic liberties can be restricted only for the sake of liberty."[74] This lexical priority is known as the Priority of Liberty.

FEO has two distinct components. First, FEO requires formal equality of opportunity or "careers open to talents": that is, it proscribes both arbitrary discrimination (on the basis of race, gender, etc.) and monopolistic privilege (including barriers to entry in labor markets) (TJ 62; DJ 141; JF 67n). Second, FEO demands substantive equality of opportunity: all citizens must have a fair chance to achieve advantaged social positions, regardless of their social circumstances (i.e., family background and class status). To achieve such fairness, the state must act to prevent "excessive accumulations of property and wealth" and supply "equal opportunities of education for all" (TJ 63). More specifically, the state will need to impose inheritance and gift taxes, limit the right of bequest, and subsidize education (whether directly through public schools or indirectly through vouchers, tuition tax credits, loans, etc.).[75] Moreover, "fair [equality of] opportunity [FEO] is prior to the difference principle [DP]" and consequently cannot be sacrificed for its sake; this lexical priority is known as the Priority of FEO.[76]

Finally, the DP requires that inequalities in income and wealth be to the "greatest benefit of the least advantaged." What exactly does this require? As a first approximation, Rawls argues that it requires maximizing a social minimum income: if we think of the least advantaged as the poorest members of society, then the way to make the least advantaged as well off as possible

---

of laissez-faire" [TJ 54]), presumably because he believes—perhaps incorrectly—that they lack a sufficiently tight connection to the three regulative interests.

74. TJ 266. These restrictions can occur in two varieties of cases: (1) "a less extensive [but still equal] liberty must strengthen the total system of liberties shared by all" (e.g., restrictions on majority rule to protect civil liberties) and (2) "a less than equal liberty must be acceptable to those with the lesser liberty" because the inequality would lead to better protection of their other liberties (e.g., giving more votes to the better educated on the assumption that they are more disposed to protect *everyone's* civil liberties) (TJ 266, §37). Under *nonideal* conditions, of course, basic liberties can be sacrificed for the sake of other social primary goods (TJ 54–55, 476, §39).

75. TJ 245; CP 141; JF 51, 161. The exact set of policies to be adopted in support of FEO will vary, of course, from society to society; it can only be determined for any given society by utilizing the four-stage sequence (§31).

76. TJ 77, 266. As with EL, FEO does allow inequalities of opportunity, but only if they "enhance the opportunities of those with the lesser opportunity" (TJ 266). Again, under *nonideal* conditions, fair opportunities can be sacrificed for the sake of more income and wealth for the least advantaged (PL 228, 363–64). On this point and FEO in general, see Taylor (2004), from which this paragraph is excerpted. Finally, in defining the Priority of FEO, Rawls notes that FEO is "lexically prior to the principle of efficiency and to that of maximizing the sum of advantages," but the priority of right already guarantees this: because FEO is a principle of right/justice, it must be prior to normative principles of the good, be they welfarist, perfectionist, or any other (TJ 266).

in terms of income is to make the social minimum income as large as possible by raising taxes (e.g., proportional income and/or expenditure taxes) until they reach a point where additional increases will in fact reduce revenues available for redistribution (due to disincentives to work, invest, etc. that result).[77] The problem with such a scheme, of course, is that the income subsidies necessary to bring everyone up to the social minimum will themselves generate disincentives for recipients, leading some to work little or not at all.[78] Rawls later suggests adding leisure time to the index of social primary goods to deal with this problem; the DP would then require us to maximize a social minimum index of income and leisure (JF 179; cf. Van Parijs 1995 and 2003, 216–18). As a practical policy matter, this change in the DP might require using workfare or wage subsidies instead of welfare grants scaled to income.[79] Whereas the function of FEO is to "eliminate the influence of *social* contingencies," like family and social class, on the grounds that "those with similar abilities and skills should have similar life chances" and job opportunities, the function of DP is to prevent *natural* contingencies—the distribution of these abilities and skills through a "natural lottery" of genes and early childhood socialization— from determining the distribution of income and wealth: Rawls considers all of these contingencies to be equally morally arbitrary (TJ 63–65, 87–89).

In later chapters I will (re)construct Rawls's Kantian defenses of these principles, but for the time being we can ask whether the principles themselves are particularly Kantian. As Rawls notes, his principles of justice are "analogous to categorical imperatives" because their validity "does not presuppose that one has a particular desire or aim"; rather, they simply hold in virtue of our "nature as free and equal rational beings."[80] Given their specific subject matter, however,

---

77. TJ 252; JF 59n26, 161. In other words, taxes for redistributive purposes should be set to maximize revenues and therefore the size of the social minimum income; we should increase (or decrease) them until we reach the top of the Laffer curve.

78. Rawls implicitly recognizes this problem in *Theory* when he speaks of maximizing "the total income of the least advantaged (wages plus transfers)": transfers may depress wages (due to labor disincentives), so total income is the proper maximand here, not transfers alone (TJ 245).

79. Rawls's later critique of welfare-state capitalism might seem to call my redistributionist interpretation of the DP into question (TJ xiv–xv; JF §§41–42). A careful reading of Rawls's comparison between welfare-state capitalism and property-owning democracy will indicate, however, that the DP will play the role that I have indicated—only that in the latter, because FEO is achieved and ownership of capital (human, physical, and financial) is more widespread, a principle that maximizes a social minimum index of income and leisure will require less redistribution than it would in the former. Cf. S. Freeman (2007a, 103–8).

80. TJ 222–23. Levine claims that Rawls's principles cannot be categorical because they are "conditioned by merely contingent ends; namely, the set of primary goods," but as I showed above, social primary goods are necessary, not contingent, ends because they support the three

they should be seen as analogous to garden-variety categorical imperatives rather than to The CI or its derivative metaprinciples, UPR and UPV, which due to their role in testing the validity of principles are more analogous to the OP than to its products. As for the specific content of these principles, Rawls's EL would surely pass muster with Kant's UPR, which has a strikingly similar structure, and Kant himself endorsed equal freedom of the pen as well as of religion, presumably because he believed that any principles of justice denying these freedoms would be inconsistent with the UPR.[81] In "Theory and Practice," for example, Kant argues that the idea of citizens as free, equal, and independent is implicit in the UPR (T&P 8:290; cf. MM 6:313-14). Independence permits active citizens to think of themselves as (and, if the idea of the original contract is realized, actually to become) colegislators who must consent to public laws; consequently, actual legislators must reject any public law as unjust that could not possibly be endorsed by a state's citizens—Kant calls this the "touchstone of any public law's conformity with right."[82] As he says later in the essay, however, citizens could never endorse a policy that prevented them from correcting rulers' errors through "freedom of the pen," because such a policy either (1) assumes ruler infallibility or (2) implies that when rulers do injure their citizens they really do them no wrong, as they have no duties to them and therefore do not have to be publicly accountable for their actions—a Hobbesian notion that Kant deems "appalling" (T&P 8:304). Therefore, policies contrary to freedom of the pen violate UPR.

The formal component of Rawls's FEO, which establishes bare "careers open to talents," would also pass muster with the UPR by similar reasoning. The idea of equality implicit in UPR is one of equality before the law: all subjects of a state have equal rights vis-à-vis other subjects and are equally susceptible to lawful coercion by the ruler, who alone is excepted from it (T&P 8:291). This implies that no subject can acquire a higher status than another except through a process equally available to others; as Kant puts it, "every member of a commonwealth must be allowed to attain any level of rank within it . . . to which his talent, his industry and his luck can take him," a policy which

---

regulative interests, which reflect our autonomy and cannot be set aside like discretionary subjective ends. See Levine (1974, 54-55, 61-62n12); cf. Johnson (1974, 63); Darwall responds also to these charges (1980, 337-39).

81. Kant endorses these freedoms at, among other places, WIE 8:36-38, 40-41, and MM 6:327-28.

82. T&P 8:294-97, 311 (realization of original contract); MM 314-15 (active/passive distinction).

obviously rules out all "hereditary prerogative" (e.g., nobility by birth) but which should also rule out other forms of arbitrary discrimination (T&P 8:292; cf. MM 6:329). Interestingly, Kant does not follow Rawls in endorsing anything like the second, substantive component of FEO or the DP; on the contrary, he says, "this thoroughgoing equality of individuals within a state . . . is quite consistent with the greatest inequality in terms of the quantity and degree of their possessions, whether in physical or mental superiority over others or in external goods" (T&P 8:291–92). Kant holds that once a state provides equal freedom and juridical equality for all of its citizens, any inequalities that subsequently arise trigger no claims of justice; thus, in Rawls's taxonomy, Kant is a classical-liberal defender of the "system of natural liberty" (TJ 57–58, 62–63).

Within Kant's defense of "careers open to talents," however, there is a foothold for Rawls and other liberal egalitarians to expand the claims of equality. Kant criticizes inherited status by noting that "since birth is not a *deed* of the one who is born, he cannot incur by it any inequality of rightful condition" (T&P 8:293). As we saw above, though, Rawls would argue that natural and social contingencies are all just a matter of lucky genetic, familial, and social draws at birth; therefore, it is as morally arbitrary to make job opportunities and income hinge upon these things as it is to make the unequal juridical status of nobles hinge on birth—and for precisely the same reasons. Rawls would accuse Kant of endorsing heteronomous principles here, ones that fail to abstract sufficiently from contingency and that therefore leave us politically hostage to the "alien causes" of natural law and existing social hierarchies. Just as Rawls describes Kant's moral theory as an attempt to "deepen" Rousseauean autonomy, so we can think of Rawls's political theory as an attempt to deepen Kantian equality.[83]

2. The Institutions of Justice

Rawls's principles of justice are to apply not primarily to individuals but instead to what he calls the *basic structure* of society, which is "the way in which the major social institutions distribute fundamental rights and duties and determine the division of advantages from social cooperation. By major institutions I understand the political constitution and the principal economic

---

83. TJ 225. Rosen (1993, 173–208), Kaufman (1999), and Guyer (2000, 262–86) have all argued that Kant's political writings, despite classical-liberal overtones, can be given a liberal-egalitarian reading.

and social arrangements. Thus, the legal protection of freedom of thought and liberty of conscience, competitive markets, private property in the means of production, and the monogamous family are examples of major social institutions" (TJ 6). We should understand that Rawls is not necessarily defending the structure or even the existence of these particular social institutions here: justice as fairness is consistent with both private and public ownership of the means of production, and Rawls's writings on the structure of the family became more radical and critical over time, thanks in part to criticisms offered by Susan Okin (TJ 242, 448; IPRR 595–601; Okin 1989). Rather, he is arguing that major social institutions should be the subject of justice because their effects "are so profound and present from the start": they strongly influence citizens' chances in life by being the overwhelmingly predominant distributors of social primary goods, which as we have seen are essential for the pursuit of the three regulative interests. Principles of justice must focus on reforming these institutions if the distribution of social primary goods is to reflect right; the decentralized actions of individuals and associations, though they can certainly influence this distribution as well, cannot begin to have the powerful structural effects on allocation that major social institutions can—and such effects are precisely what distributive justice requires, at least according to Rawls's justice as fairness.[84]

Rawls asserts that by focusing on the basic structure of society, his principles of justice "add in various ways to Kant's conception . . . [but] this and other additions are natural enough and remain fairly close to Kant's doctrine, at least when all of his ethical writings are viewed together" (TJ 222). There is, in fact, precious little daylight between Rawls and Kant on this issue. An examination of Kant's Doctrine of Right shows him applying his theory almost exclusively to the major social institutions: private property, contract, family, state, civil society, etc.[85] Thus, Kant himself seems to be treating the basic structure as subject, at least implicitly. Rawls's emphasis on Kant's general moral philosophy

---

84. Much ink has been spilled responding to G. A. Cohen (2000), who attacks the idea of the basic structure being the subject of justice. One straightforward response is to point out that, when *central structural features* of distributions are the focus, decentralized individual and associational responses will have little effect and are therefore a sideshow to the reform of major social institutions, which is "where the action is." Cohen recognizes and attempts to respond to such arguments in chapter 10 of his book. Furthermore, Rawls (at least in *Theory*) argues that his contract theory, properly extended, would have broader implications for individual behavior, including obligations of fairness and mutual aid (TJ §§18–19).

85. MM 6:260–70 (property); 271–76, 284–86 (contract); 276–84 (family); 311–42 (state); 325–30 (civil society: church, charitable institutions, nobility, slavery/serfdom).

rather than his political theory has led him to miss the essential similarity of their positions on the subject of justice.[86]

If we reform the major social institutions to make them consistent with these principles of justice, we will realize part of Rawls's ethico-political ideal: the *well-ordered society* (WOS). It is fully realized when "(1) everyone accepts and knows that the others accept the same principles of justice, and (2) the basic social institutions generally satisfy and are generally known to satisfy these principles" (TJ 4, 397). Publicity (discussed earlier) plays a central role in this definition, as does the justice of the basic structure itself; these same elements feature prominently in Kant's doctrine of right (for example, PP 8:348–60, 381–86). However, Rawls goes well beyond these merely political concerns to ethical ones when he says that "if men's inclination to self-interest makes their vigilance against one another necessary, their public *sense of justice* makes their secure association together possible. Among individuals with disparate aims and purposes a shared conception of justice establishes *bonds of civic friendship;* the general *desire for justice* limits the pursuit of other ends" (TJ 4–5; emphasis added). An affective attachment to the principles of justice and to one's fellow citizens can indeed be an aid to political stability, just as our capacity "to act from (and not merely in accordance with) the principles of justice," when suitably mature, helps us to resist the "inclination to self-interest" (KCMT 312; TJ §69). Rawls's first moral power and associated civic friendship take us into the ethical realm, though, at least for Kant: right deals merely with "the formal condition of outer freedom," that is, the sheer consistency of our actions with justice, but Rawls's notion of a sense of justice requires us to act "from" justice, that is, out of respect for it and our fellow citizens, which Kant would call virtuous; moreover, friendship for Kant is invariably an ethical ideal, as it involves "equal mutual love and respect" (MM 6:218–20, 380, 390–91, 469–73). Thus, Rawls is perfectly correct when he says that we should "think of the notion of a well-ordered society as an interpretation of a kingdom of ends" or (even more strongly) when he claims that "the principles regulative of the kingdom of ends are those that would be chosen in [the OP]" (KCE 264; TJ 226). In this light, Rawls's conviction that justice as fairness could be "extended to the choice of more or less an entire ethical system" appears more plausible and makes the WOS into a stepping stone towards a genuine

---

86. S. Freeman (2007b, 22) explores Rawls's relative neglect of what he saw as Kant's derivative political theory.

"ethical commonwealth."[87] The rich Kantian aspirations of Rawls's theory are rarely more evident than they are here.

3. The Psychology of Justice

As this description of the WOS makes clear, the full development of citizens' senses of justice not only stabilizes but also enriches social and political life; one of the ways that it does this is by promoting "an ethic of mutual **respect** and self-esteem" (TJ 225). As we saw earlier, the first moral power involves acting out of respect for humanity (both in ourselves and in others) and for the moral law itself (FH and FUL, respectively), and I argued that it must also include the idea of our self-authorship of moral law (FA). When we see ourselves as colegislators of moral law, we view our own failures to abide by it and to act from it with *shame*, because such failures reveal a lack of self-control and self-government, like animals of a "lower order . . . whose first principles are decided by natural contingencies."[88] On the other hand, the recognition that we and others can develop our capacity for autonomy leads us to self-esteem and a respect for our fellow men and their rights; it is this capacity, Kant says, that is "raised above all price" and that endows its possessors with dignity (GMM 4:434; used by Rawls at TJ 513). Rawls's understanding of self-respect and respect for others almost perfectly tracks Kant's own, as he himself recognizes and emphasizes. Kant says that although the moral law "humiliates self-conceit," it also leads to "self-approbation" when we recognize that "this constraint is exercised only by the lawgiving of [our] *own* reason"; that is, our exercise of autonomy, though it constrains our cupidity and humbles us, becomes a basis for self-esteem when we see it as an expression of the highest part of ourselves—our pure practical reason.[89] To see this capacity in others too leads to the mutual respect that is embodied in FH, which directs us to treat others as ends, never merely as means (GMM 4:429).

---

87. TJ 15, 115, 221, 226. S. Freeman (2007b, 22) makes special mention of this connection. Höffe (1984, 122–23) notes the ethical quality of Rawls's WOS but simply regards it as some kind of category mistake, failing to see that Rawls does not *intend* the WOS to be a merely juridical ideal, as his comparison with the kingdom of ends makes clear; see Levine (1974, 57) for a particularly crude misunderstanding of this comparison.

88. TJ 225; TJ §67. Rawls contrasts moral *guilt* and moral *shame*: the former arises when we violate the rights of others and tremble at the thought of their righteous wrath and revenge; the latter involves the additional thought that failure to respect the rights of others is a failure to ourselves—a failure of self-control and self-respect—that will call upon us the justified derision of others (TJ 225, 391, 423).

89. CPrR 5:71–82, 87; MM 6:402–3. On ethical duties of respect towards others, see MM 6:462–68.

Rawls relatedly speaks of the *good of the sense of justice*—the idea that "this disposition to be guided by the standpoint of justice accords with the individual's good," which Rawls calls "congruence."[90] Without congruence, justice might come to seem an alien imposition on one's plan of life, which given the second moral power is a freely chosen expression of one's deepest ends, values, and commitments. How can something that seems merely to constrain one's pursuit of the good actually accord with it or even be part of it? Two components of Rawls's congruence argument seem especially pertinent here. First, once we recognize our nature as free, equal, and moral beings, we will also realize that acting from principles that express our nature is a form of self-realization and therefore a key component of any rational plan of life. Second, maintaining a just society not only allows us to exercise the "widest regulative excellences of which each is capable" (i.e., the skills of self-government), which according to Rawls's Aristotelian principle is an intrinsic good, but also helps "encourage the diverse internal life of associations in which individuals realize their more particular aims," which is a value of Humboldtian social union.[91] Hence, pursuing justice allows us to realize our natures, our capacities, and our subjective ends, and thereby to further our plans of life. Rawls describes happiness, however, as the "successful execution . . . of a rational plan of life drawn up under . . . favorable conditions"; therefore, justice can be not just a good in itself but also a means to our own happiness (TJ 359).

The concept of congruence may seem foreign to Kant's moral philosophy, but in fact he develops a strikingly similar notion himself in the second *Critique*. As I noted above, Kant's idea of the complete good, which is the architectonic objective end of pure practical reason, combines perfect virtue with a proportionate happiness for all finite rational beings (CPrR 5:110–11). Kant thereby unites the supreme moral good, virtue—the highest expression of our pure practical reason—with the universal subjective good, happiness—the highest expression of our empirical practical reason—but does so in a way that maintains the absolute priority of the former over the latter: virtue acts as "the supreme condition . . . of all our pursuit of happiness."[92] We are thus assured that in our morally obligatory pursuit of the highest good we will not have to

---

90. The parts of the congruence argument are scattered throughout *Theory* but collected and summarized in TJ §86. Also see S. Freeman (2003a) for a comprehensive review of this argument.
91. TJ 463, 500–501; on the Aristotelian principle and Humboldtian social union, see TJ §§65 and 79, respectively.
92. Cf. GMM 4:393: "a good will seems to constitute the indispensable condition even of worthiness to be happy."

abandon hopes for our own and others' happiness. Rawls takes great pride in his attempt at "overcoming the dualisms in Kant's doctrine," including that between "reason and desire," our rational and sensuous selves, but Rawls's doctrine retains this particular dualism and seeks to transcend it in much the same way that Kant's does—leaving us with a final, unexpected affinity between their philosophies.[93]

V. Conclusion: Where Rawls and Kant Diverge

So far in this chapter we have focused on the similarities between Rawls's and Kant's respective Kantian constructivisms, but what are the differences? Some of the differences that Rawls himself emphasizes are more apparent than real. For example, Rawls maintains that, in contrast to Kant, the selection of principles in his procedure of construction is a "collective" one among a plurality of parties (TJ 226). He notes earlier, however, that we can "view the agreement in the original position from the standpoint of one person selected at random," so the practical effect of plurality is unclear.[94] Perhaps Rawls just means to highlight the fact that "everyone is to consent to these principles," but he is no different from Kant in this respect, who says in the fourth (FA) formulation of The CI that we should think of "*every* human will as a will giving universal law through all its maxims" (TJ 226; GMM 4:432 [emphasis added]). Rawls also claims that his theory applies only to a narrow subset of finite rational beings—human beings—whereas Kant "may have meant his doctrine to apply to all rational beings as such" (TJ 226). Strictly speaking, Kant does not think his moral doctrine applies to *infinite* rational beings ("holy wills") because their "volition is of itself necessarily in accord with the law," that is, they do not experience the moral law as a binding restraint and are therefore under no obligations or duties (GMM 4:414, 439). Kant does believe that his doctrine applies to all *finite* rational beings, not just to human beings, but because he implicitly defines finite rational beings as needy and vulnerable animals who seek their own happiness and always feel the moral law as a binding though self-authored restraint—even if they realize perfect virtue, like the

---

93. TJ 226-27; KCE 264; KCMT 304. Interestingly, Rawls mentions the relationship between virtue and happiness in Kant's system in an early paper (SJ 115) and discusses the complete good at LHMP 225-26, 313-19, arguing there that it is "foreign to Kant's constructivism" and a kind of Leibnizian corruption of his thought (316-17).

94. TJ 120-21. For a different perspective, see Laden (1991).

Buddha—it seems like a distinction without a difference, at least in the absence of evidence of finite rational beings who are different from human beings in ways relevant to morality.[95]

Two other differences mentioned earlier are worth revisiting, as they are more significant. First, Rawls notes that the scope of his theory is narrower than Kant's: Rawls's theory is a theory of justice only, whereas Kant's is a general moral theory, encompassing right as well as virtue (TJ 15; KCMT 339). As we have seen, though, Rawls's justice as fairness sometimes intrudes upon the ethical domain (e.g., his concepts of reasonableness and the WOS), and in *Theory* at least Rawls is hopeful that his procedure of construction can be extended so as to produce a comprehensive moral theory. *Theory* can be viewed, therefore, as Rawls's Doctrine of Right, with occasional forays into the ethical and hints of a future Doctrine of Virtue that is never delivered, for reasons I will discuss as the book progresses (TJ 15, §§18, 19, 51, 52). Second, Kant's constructivism is higher order than Rawls's: it offers metaprinciples like The CI and its components, the UPR and UPV, rather than specific political and ethical principles, and these metaprinciples are more closely analogous to Rawls's OP than to his principles of justice. Given Rawls's goal of justifying particular principles of justice, it is unsurprising he chose to build a less stratospheric theory, yet it remains distinctively Kantian. As I noted above, Rawls tries to deepen Kant's idea of political equality, but more generally he tries to derive concrete principles of justice using Kantian techniques, principles that provide better guidance in the (re)construction of major social institutions than Kant's broader imperatives.

The differences between Kant and the "Kantian period" Rawls that I have discussed up to this point are either minor or merely apparent, but one difference that fully emerges at the end of this period is a major one indeed: Rawls's fateful decision in "Kantian Constructivism" to ground his conception of persons in democratic culture rather than in practical reason, a decision that points the way to his later political liberalism. The discussion in this chapter so far has simply assumed that Rawls's Kantian conception of the person has priority over alternative conceptions (e.g., of persons as sensuous beings, artistic creators, or children of God), but Rawls needs to justify this conception and its priority, which he does in "Kantian Constructivism" by maintaining that

---

95. GMM 4:389. Hence, those who have criticized Rawls's Kantianism on the grounds that it applies only to human beings (e.g., Levine 1974, 55) would need to explain how *human* finite rationality differs from *other forms* of finite rationality, of which there are no examples of which we are (yet) aware. Kant himself ponders this question in his *Anthropology* (8:215).

it is already "implicit in the public culture of a democratic society" (KCMT 305). This justificatory method has its roots in *Theory*, where the idea of preexisting (democratic) consensus as a condition of moral objectivity is first mooted; however, it exists there side by side with a wholly different and even incompatible Kantian approach, which sees our "nature" as free and equal moral beings as being rooted in pure practical reason. In part 3 of this book I will provide a detailed review of Rawls's conflicted approach to justification in *Theory* and trace his decision to adopt what I earlier called a constructivist-*cum*-relativist method, which achieves its most fully developed form in *Political Liberalism*. I will also criticize Rawls's decision, despite the many compelling reasons he offers for it, because it fails to provide sufficient support for his Kantian conception of the person and therefore dangerously undermines the case for his three principles of justice—principles that he invested much time and energy in defending throughout his career and would presumably have been loath to abandon.

This last point may appear to be a non sequitur, however: even if *Political Liberalism*'s justificatory technique fails to support the Kantian conception of the person, can't the principles themselves be defended on alternative, non-Kantian grounds? In part 2 of this book, I show that they cannot, because their only successful defenses are Kantian in nature. To support this claim, though, I will need to reconstruct Rawls's arguments for these principles. Such reconstructions are required for two reasons: first, Rawls's defenses are often incomplete (priorities of right and liberty and the DP) or simply absent (priority of FEO); second, Rawls is frequently unaware how strongly these defenses rely upon his Kantian conception of the person, a backward linkage that is required by his Kantian constructivism, as we have seen.[96] By filling the gaps in his defenses and relating them back to his conception of the person, we will gradually become aware of how radical and radically Kantian this conception really is, an awareness that is hard to achieve until we have seen the role that it and its various components play in the process of justification. This radical Kantianism of his conception of the person and the defenses that rely upon it will prove to be the shoals on which a political-liberal defense of justice as fairness runs aground.

---

96. Rawls's failure to link these defenses tightly to his Kantian conception of the person is understandable: his most systematic defenses are to be found in *Theory*, but he did not fully develop his Kantian constructivism until nearly a decade later. Hence, one way to understand my reconstructions is that they try to retool *Theory* in light of "Kantian Constructivism in Moral Theory." I should point out that he begins such reconstruction work himself in "The Basic Liberties and Their Priority" (PL 289–371), originally published in 1982, towards the end of his Kantian period.

PART 2

Reconstructing Rawls

2

The Kantian Conception of the Person

I. Introduction

In chapter 1, I discussed Rawls's Kantian conception of the person and the way in which it is reflected in particular features of the OP. To recapitulate, Rawls conceives of persons as free and equal rational (i.e., moral) beings, with the moral quality being primary, the other two mostly derivative. As moral beings, we have the two moral powers of reasonableness (moral autonomy) and rationality (personal autonomy); to be more precise, competent adults possess the capacity to develop and exercise the two powers. Agents in the OP consider the development and exercise of these powers to be highest-order interests, which guide their selection of principles of justice and take absolute priority over other interests, including their higher-order interest in "protecting and advancing their conception of the good, whatever it may be" (KCMT 313).

As I will demonstrate over the next several chapters, this conception of the person—in its current form, at least—is inadequate to the task of grounding the chief features of Rawls's justice as fairness, namely, the lexical priorities and the DP. First, in order to ground the priority of FEO, this conception must be extended to include a third conception of autonomy—self-realization—as we shall see in chapter 5. Second, and perhaps more importantly, Rawls never explains how the two moral powers are related to one another (if indeed they are) or why rationality is deemed a *moral* power at all; Jeremy Waldron, for example, contends that there is "a discontinuity between moral autonomy and the pursuit of an individual conception of the good," one that threatens to make all principles of justice seem "alien . . . from the personal point of view."[1]

---

1. Waldron (2005, 308, 319). See, however, the congruence argument of *Theory* §86, which I discussed in chapter 1.

Thus, any adequate Kantian conception of the person must address the relationship between its constituent parts, whether it is taken to include two component conceptions of autonomy (as Rawls suggests) or three (as I shall claim below). To anticipate somewhat the arguments I will make in part 3: unless we can tie its component conceptions of autonomy and the lexical priorities they underwrite back to a Kantian conception of moral autonomy, we will be unable to give a solid foundation to justice as fairness as a whole, which must ultimately rest upon Kant's practical postulate of freedom as a necessary presupposition of finite rational agency.

Given the inadequacy of Rawls's conception of the person, I will extend and explicate it in this chapter so that it can ground the three priorities and the DP in chapters 3–6. This extended conception consists of three hierarchically ordered conceptions of autonomy (Kantian variants of moral autonomy, personal autonomy, and self-realization, respectively—see section III) linked together by both deductive and inductive methods. The first method (see section IV) utilizes a procedure analogous to Rawls's four-stage sequence to derive lower conceptions of autonomy from higher ones along with their associated plans and rules, while the second (see section V) constructs an ideal cognitive-developmental psychology, an epicyclic system using an iterative model of agency to explain the emergence of higher conceptions from lower ones. By revealing this tight relationship among the three Kantian conceptions of autonomy, which jointly constitute a unified Kantian conception of persons, I offer a Rawlsian theory of internal autonomy capable of bridging the gap between the practical postulate of freedom and the complex form of external autonomy yielded by justice as fairness, namely, the rights and powers that its principles support.[2]

As I shall show later in this chapter, this extension makes Rawls's conception of persons more methodically Kantian, that is, more consistent with Kant's own model of finite rational agency as it was presented early in chapter 1. In Kant's model, we ascend a ladder of necessitation from rules of skill and counsels of prudence (hypothetical imperatives) to commands/laws of morality

2. My distinction between internal and external forms of autonomy follows Alfred Mele's in the following passage: "The capacities involved in . . . autonomy are of at least two kinds, broadly conceived. *[external:]* Some are directed specifically at one's environment. Assuming some autonomy for Prometheus, he was considerably less autonomous bound than unbound; chained to the rock, he possessed only a severely limited capacity to affect his environment. *[internal:]* Others have a pronounced inner-directedness, their outward manifestations notwithstanding. Capacities for decision making and for critical reflection on one's values, principles, preferences, and beliefs fall into the second group" (Mele 2001, 144).

(categorical imperatives), including The CI, the metalaw of morality. Each step up this ladder is achieved by greater abstraction from contingency and is associated with an increasing legislative authority for the corresponding objective principles of choice. In parallel fashion, as we rise from self-realization and personal autonomy to moral autonomy in the extended Kantian conception of the person, we encounter conceptions of autonomy with an increasingly comprehensive authority and a correspondingly greater abstraction from "social, natural, and fortuitous contingencies" (JF 55). Though Kant would hesitate to label instrumental and prudential reasoning autonomous, I will argue that they, like the parallel concepts of self-realization and personal autonomy, deserve the label because they share key features with moral autonomy—at least if they are interpreted in an appropriately Kantian fashion.

Before beginning this extension of Rawls's conception of the person, I need to make two comments about my approach. First, I want to couch it within a larger context: the contemporary debate about the meaning of autonomy. Autonomy is a concept with many conceptions, and this bewildering conceptual variety has motivated efforts by some philosophers to construct relevant taxonomies, which offer distinctions between autonomy as a capacity and as an actual condition, between basic and ideal forms of autonomy, between moral and personal autonomy, and (as we have seen) between internal and external autonomy (see, e.g., Christman 2009, G. Dworkin 1988, Feinberg 1989, and Mele 2001). The unified Kantian conception of persons constructed in this chapter provides one way (though certainly not the only way) to interpret and relate the many conceptions of autonomy, both historical and contemporary, and therefore serves as a contribution to the larger debate. This being said, the three conceptions of internal autonomy offered in section II—moral autonomy, personal autonomy, and self-realization—are interpreted in specifically Kantian ways in section III prior to being assembled into a Kantian conception of persons. Although I believe that these interpretations are the best ways to understand the relevant conceptions, and argue so in section III, partisans of alternative interpretations will surely demur, insisting that my interpretations stretch these conceptions to the breaking point. All I really need to show for the purposes of this chapter, however, is that these are reasonable interpretations of these conceptions because they preserve their central features of authenticity, flourishing, etc. So long as this is true, the extended Kantian conception of persons can be seen as integrating what are usually considered unrelated or even antagonistic conceptions of internal autonomy.

Second, given the numerous ethical elements of Rawls's political thought and his evident aspirations in *Theory* toward a broader, moral form of Kantian constructivism (which I discussed throughout chapter 1), the extended Kantian conception of the person will engage issues of right and virtue, justice and ethics. Rawls himself, in describing a morality of principles (that stage of cognitive development in which moral autonomy first becomes possible), states that it "takes two forms, one corresponding to the sense of right and justice, the other to the love of mankind and to self-command," that is, to matters of right and virtue, respectively (TJ 419). Although I focus almost wholly on the political in this book, I want to extend Rawls's conception of the person in such a way that it could ground a reconstructed Rawlsian doctrine of virtue (which Rawls adumbrates in *Theory* §§18, 19, 51, and 52), should such a project ever prove of interest to other scholars.

II. Three Conceptions of Internal Autonomy

A. Moral Autonomy (MA → MA_K)

In its usual sense, moral autonomy (MA) involves having an operative sense of justice (see, e.g., TJ 41, 442; Johnston 1994, 72). Human beings have an unfortunate tendency, whether driven by the simplest physical desires or by the most elaborate plans of life, to encroach upon the legitimate claims of others. An effective sense of justice counters this natural tendency by giving us the ability to apply and act on moral principles; it enables us to limit the pursuit of our own interest out of a regard for the interests of other individuals and a desire to engage them in equitable cooperation. Having an effective sense of justice cannot be all there is to being morally autonomous, though. In fact, if individuals view the moral law as an alien imposition and the sense of justice that enables its application as a mere product of socialization reinforced through an internal sanction of guilt, they will likely come to see their sense of justice as a heteronomous burden that limits their freedom.[3]

Consequently, any complete theory of moral autonomy needs to answer certain questions about moral law's source and structure: from where does the

---

3. The murderer Raskolnikov in Dostoevsky's *Crime and Punishment* evinces this attitude on various occasions in the text. As we shall see, moral autonomy may conflict with personal autonomy, understood roughly as the pursuit of authenticity in accordance with a self-chosen plan of life.

moral law come, and what character does it have? All theories of moral autonomy have to locate the source of moral law in the moral agent himself—the word "autonomy" derives from the Greek terms *autos* (self) and *nomos* (law, convention) and thus literally denotes self-legislation—but what this means precisely and what its implications are for the form of the moral law are a matter of debate. Just as there are myriad conceptions of autonomy, both internal and external, so there are innumerable variants of moral autonomy, three of which I will discuss here.

One famous literary conception of moral autonomy is the existentialist one, found in the novels of Jean-Paul Sartre and Albert Camus.[4] For the existentialists, an authentic morality must be one autonomously chosen, and existentialist autonomy involves a radical denial of natural and social determinism: we are at all times completely free to choose in moral matters and otherwise. Furthermore, this freedom implies an absence of objective moral law (i.e., a law that holds across persons) because such a law would itself represent a variety of determinism. All moral claims are purely subjective, binding only on individuals who endorse them. Taken to its logical conclusion, existentialism would appear to imply that an individual's endorsement of a moral claim at time T would fail to bind him at time T + 1: personal identity may itself constitute a kind of determinism, one which we must be as free to overturn as that of objective moral law. Put slightly differently, existentialist moral autonomy looks like Kantian negative freedom absent the positive freedom, and it comes dangerously close to being lawless and therefore anomic rather than autonomous.

A conception of moral autonomy even more closely related to the Kantian conception is that of Jean-Jacques Rousseau. For Rousseau, the individual *qua* citizen attains moral autonomy when he aligns his particular will with the "general will" of his community, a will that is general with respect to its possessor (the body politic), its aim (the common interest), as well as its form (applying to all citizens equally and impartially). Such subordination might appear to be the very opposite of autonomy, but Rousseau contends that by participating in the collective authorship of law each citizen achieves a higher form of freedom: specifically, a positive freedom from lawless desire and personal dependence (Rousseau 1997, 53–54). The alienation of all rights to the sovereign people, a people of which each citizen is a colegislative part, enables that people to discipline itself, regularizing the unruly appetites of natural man

---

4. See, e.g., Sartre's *Nausea* and Camus's *The Stranger*. For a brief discussion of the existentialist conception of autonomy, see Hill (1989a, 94).

and overcoming the mutual degradations and status obsessions of social man. Rousseau would contemptuously reject the idea that we are only genuinely free when we act without restraint upon those desires planted in our breasts by nature or corrupt society, in which case we are not autonomous agents but mere conduits. We only achieve genuine freedom and moral autonomy when we author moral law collectively with our fellow citizens and enforce it with the full might of the social-contract state. Rousseau's moral autonomy is consequently not only collective in nature but also culturally specific, tied to citizenship in a particular state.[5]

The most influential conception of moral autonomy, central to this book, is the Kantian conception (MA_K). To review, autonomy for Kant is a characteristic of the will of finite rational beings such as ourselves, with an autonomous will having both negative and positive properties. Its negative property is *independence* from the "objects of volition" and other "alien causes" (GMM 4:440, 446). That is, an autonomous will must not be determined by contingent features of persons, such as our motives, ends, and capacities; this is what distinguishes pure practical reason, the source of the moral law, from empirical practical reason, which is in service to our idiosyncratic needs and wants. When thinking morally we must, as Kant says, "abstract from the personal differences of rational beings as well as from the content of their private ends" (GMM 4:433). The positive property of an autonomous will is its *self-legislative capacity*, the "will's property of being a law to itself" (GMM 4:447). If, as Kant claims, the will is a kind of causation, and all causation is law-governed, then a will that is independent from all "alien causes" must give law to itself. Moreover, the independence of an autonomous will from any contingent features of persons guarantees that any law flowing from it will be strictly general and universal in quality, which explains the shape of the first formulation of The CI ("act only in accordance with that maxim through which you can at the same time will that it become a universal law" [FUL]) (GMM 4:421, 446–47).

Contemporary Kantians like Rawls have similarly emphasized both independence from "natural contingencies and social accident" and self-legislation

---

5. Cf. Habermas (1996, 101–2): "[Rousseau] gives the idea of self-legislation more of an ethical than a moral interpretation, conceiving autonomy as the realization of the consciously apprehended form of life of a particular people. . . . He counts on political virtues that are anchored in the ethos of a small and perspicuous, more or less homogenous community integrated through shared cultural traditions." Rousseau's political theory might be understood as a constructivist-*cum*-relativist position and consequently bears some resemblance to political liberalism, at least as I shall interpret it in part 3 of the book. On this point, see Laden (2001, esp. 23–47).

as features of moral autonomy (TJ 225). Consider the following definition of moral autonomy from §40 of *Theory:* "A person is acting autonomously when the principles of his action are chosen by him as the most adequate possible expression of his nature as a free and equal rational being. The principles he acts upon are not adopted because of his social position or natural endowments, or in view of the particular kind of society in which he lives or the specific things that he happens to want. To act on such principles is to act heteronomously" (TJ 222). These principles of action can even extend beyond the realm of right into the realm of virtue, that is, they may not only require (on threat of sanction) particular actions/omissions but also stipulate that certain objective moral ends be adopted by conscientious moral agents (e.g., respect for the humanity of self and others [FH], leading to duties of physical self-perfection, beneficence, etc.). Though Rawls attempts to restrict the purview of his theory to matters of right, Kant extends his theory in exactly this way in his *Tugendlehre* or Doctrine of Virtue, and as I noted in section I, we will use this more comprehensive, orthodox definition of Kantian moral autonomy (TJ 15; MM 6:373–493).

What advantages, if any, does Kantian moral autonomy have over its existentialist and Rousseauean competitors? First, notice a commonality among these three conceptions of moral autonomy: each counsels detachment as a tool for achieving independence of judgment and for avoiding heteronomy. Without detachment, our judgments on moral matters will tend to reflect those of the society around us or simply cater to our natural, familial, or sectional interests; we will not legislate our own morality in such circumstances but rather act as a medium or channel for the demands of nature and culture—we may *feel* autonomous as we enact these demands, but the feeling is an illusion. In the existentialist rejection of conventional morality, the Rousseauean critique of particularity/partiality of will, and the Kantian call to abstract from contingencies, we find a similar insistence on avoiding determination by what Kant refers to as "alien causes."

The detachment achieved by existentialist and Rousseauean moral autonomy, though, is arguably incomplete. The existentialist takes pride in liberating himself from all objective moral laws—even ones legislated by his earlier selves—but ends in thraldom to the immediacy of his own impulses. His freedom from convention, his "authenticity," is purchased at a steep price: an even baser slavery to natural inclinations or, if these can be overcome, a completely lawless will and the eclipse of *nomos* by a protean *autos*. Existentialist moral autonomy is, in the end, either heteronomous or anomic. The Rousseauean conception, while certainly not anomic, is also liable to the charge of heteronomy. This charge may appear an odd one, as Rousseau's moral autonomy demands detachment from natural and social demands as a prologue to collective self-legislation. However, the general will is general only with respect to members of the sovereign, to the body of citizens; noncitizens, whether internal (women) or external (foreigners), do not participate in it. The general will therefore remains partial, lacking detachment from the particularity of gender and national culture. Thus, the existentialist and Rousseauean variants of moral autonomy fail on their own terms: they urge detachment as a means to independent judgment but remain mired in the heteronomy of nature and culture, thereby compromising the independence of that judgment.

By contrast, Kantian moral autonomy takes detachment to its logical conclusion without wholly abandoning the idea of (moral) law. Moral autonomy must not only be governed by law (*nomos*) but also be the expression of a genuine, unmediated self (*autos*) attained by abstracting from all contingent features of persons, including gender and national culture—which explains why Rawls considered Kant to be a "deepened" Rousseau (TJ 225). Of course, one might worry along with Michael Sandel that after all of this detachment and abstraction, there may be nothing we would recognize as a "self" left over (Sandel 1982, esp. 92–94). Relatedly, Joseph Raz is concerned that Kantian moral autonomy reduces "[self-]authorship to a vanishing point as it allows only one set of principles which people can rationally legislate and they are the same for all" (Raz 1986, 370n). These anxieties appear to motivate the next conception of internal autonomy, personal autonomy, which permits a thicker, more substantive conception of the self while still retaining elements of detachment, abstraction, and reflection. As I will argue in section III, though, the best interpretation of personal autonomy is one that incorporates moral concerns—specifically, those highlighted by Kantian morality.

B. Personal Autonomy (PA)

As the name implies, personal autonomy has a narrower scope than moral autonomy, as it focuses on individual plans of life and conceptions of the good rather than universally valid rules and objective ends. Personal autonomy is an ideal of creative self-authorship and the qualities of character necessary to support it, including especially authenticity, rationality, and self-control. Like moral autonomy, personal autonomy is interpreted in a variety of ways, but these different interpretations do not qualify as full-fledged conceptions of an overarching concept of personal autonomy; rather, they simply emphasize different features of what is in fact a unified concept.

Joseph Raz, for example, highlights the creative side of personal autonomy, especially in the following passage from *The Morality of Freedom:* "The ideal of personal autonomy holds the free choice of goals and relations as an essential ingredient of individual well-being. The ruling idea behind the ideal of personal autonomy is that people should make their own lives. The autonomous person is (part) author of his own life. The ideal of personal autonomy is the vision of people controlling, to some degree, their own destiny, fashioning it through successive decisions throughout their lives" (Raz 1986, 369). Raz sees the personally autonomous individual almost as an artist who molds and shapes not clay or granite but his own life. The image also captures the active rather than passive attitude of such an individual: he does not simply accept the imprint his life has been given by nature, his family, and his society, but seeks to remove it, improve it, or make it his own. Personal autonomy is not inconsistent with personal conservatism, though it does require us to reflect critically upon and consciously endorse the elements of our plan of life.

Rawls, on the other hand, emphasizes that personal autonomy (his second moral power of rationality) requires deliberative rationality. That is, when we reflect on our ends and our plans to achieve them we must reason in a way consistent with the principles of rational choice, including "the adoption of effective means to ends; the balancing of final ends by their significance in our plan of life as a whole; and the assigning of a greater weight to the more likely consequences" (KCMT 316; cf. TJ §§63–64). Such mental self-discipline is an essential complement to the free creativity stressed by Raz, as it gives coherence to our system of ends and makes their attainment more likely. Additionally, with Rawls as with Raz, the focus is on the process of deliberation rather than the outcome: a rational and self-critical stance towards one's own character, values, and aims is compatible with various ways of life, including immoral or simply degraded ones.[6] To sum up, we might think of Razian creativity as the *substance* of personal autonomy and Rawlsian rationality as its *form*.[7]

---

6. See, e.g., Raz (1986, 380) on the personally autonomous murderer.
7. By pairing Raz and Rawls, I do not intend to imply that there are no significant differences between them, even on the topic of personal autonomy. For example, Raz is more explicit than Rawls in listing and detailing the conditions of personal autonomy (viz. "appropriate mental

As noted above, personal autonomy requires certain qualities of character for its support. These qualities are usually seen as conditions of its exercise, sometimes as constituent elements, that is, parts of personal autonomy itself. John Christman (2009) identifies two classes of such conditions, which he calls *authenticity* and *competency* conditions, that neatly complement the two facets of personal autonomy stressed by Raz and Rawls. Authenticity conditions include "the capacity to reflect upon and endorse (or identify with) one's desires, values, etc." The self-authorship that is so prized by Raz requires just such a capacity to accept, revise, or reject personal commitments upon critical reflection; if we lack such a capacity, our lives will in effect be authored by others, such as parents and peers. Moreover, as Harry Frankfurt and Gerald Dworkin have argued, this capacity for reflective endorsement may suggest that our desires are hierarchical: Dworkin, for example, defines personal autonomy as "a second-order capacity of persons to reflect critically upon their first-order preferences, desires, wishes, and so forth and the capacity to accept or attempt to change these in light of higher-order preferences and values," where "higher-order" preferences "define their nature, give meaning and coherence to their lives."[8] Such hierarchical models of agents, which often arise in discussions of personal autonomy, will also play a central role in this chapter's extension of Rawls's Kantian conception of the person.

Competency conditions include "various capacities for rational thought, self-control, and freedom from debilitating pathologies, systematic self-deception, etc." Among these conditions would certainly be a capacity for deliberative rationality in Rawls's sense, for without the ability to balance competing ends and choose intelligently among the means to them, autonomy would likewise be impossible. Various forms of self-control (over belief, willing, action, etc.) are also key, as akratic tendencies undermine our ability both to formulate and to execute plans of life.[9] Though more extensive lists of enabling conditions

---

abilities, an adequate range of options, and independence"). He also embeds personal autonomy within a plural-perfectionist political theory very unlike justice as fairness, a theory that gives his understanding of personal autonomy much of its flavor, e.g., his insistence that "autonomy is valuable only if exercised in pursuit of the good," understood in a value-pluralist way. See Raz (1986, 372–78, 381, 395–99, 407–24).

8. G. Dworkin 1988, 20. Cf. Frankfurt 1988, 15, 19, and Bratman 2003. The central concern of Frankfurt's article is freedom of the will rather than personal autonomy (a term he never uses in it), but it is highly relevant to discussions of personal autonomy. Dworkin and Frankfurt's hierarchical agent models are extremely close to each other, though Dworkin's is more thoroughly and explicitly developed. For a discussion of Dworkin's views and a comparison with Frankfurt's, see Haworth (1991, esp. 129–30, 134); I return to them in section III of this chapter.

9. On this point, see esp. Mele (2001).

have been discussed, the twin conditions of authenticity and competency seem sufficient to support the creative and calculating features of personal autonomy, respectively, its unique pairing of bohemian and bourgeois qualities.[10]

As I suggested above, personal autonomy as it is normally understood is not only distinct from moral autonomy, neither implying nor being implied by it, but also potentially at odds with it. As David Johnston has pointed out, "a person could be morally autonomous without being in the habit of subjecting her own values and projects to critical appraisal. Similarly . . . it is possible to be personally autonomous without being morally autonomous," as would be the case with a reflective, rational, and self-controlled serial killer—Hannibal Lecter, for example.[11] The purely procedural quality of personal autonomy provides no assurance that resulting conceptions of the good or plans of life will be consistent with the moral law or any other substantive standard, for that matter. I will contend in section III that taking personal autonomy's proceduralism seriously drives one towards a moralized conception of personal autonomy, but for the time being one can sympathize with Onora O'Neill, who maintains that Kant and personal-autonomy theorists have "radically differing conceptions of action and autonomy" and argues in favor of "disentangling Kant's conception of autonomy from contemporary ones" (O'Neill 1989, 66, 75; cf. Hill 1989a, 92–95).

C. Self-Realization (SR)

The perfectionist concept of self-realization is not typically associated with autonomy. It has been defined by Joseph Raz as "the development to their full extent of all, or all the valuable capacities a person possesses," be they physical, emotional, intellectual, or moral (Raz 1986, 375). In the history of Western thought, at least, an externally given model has usually identified which faculties are valuable and, among these, which are to be given priority. Whether this model's source has been a specific cultural tradition (e.g., the heroic ideal of Archaic Greece, memorably illustrated in the epic poetry of Homer) or a natural teleology accessible via theoretical reason (e.g., the ideals of a good man and a good citizen developed by Aristotle, or even Karl Marx's "species

---

10. For a more extensive list of enabling conditions, see Feinberg (1989, 30–43).
11. Johnston (1994, 76–77); cf. Raz 1986, 380. Also see G. A. Cohen's "Mafioso" example in Korsgaard (1996b, 183–84), and G. Dworkin (1988, 29) and Feinberg (1989, 43–44) on personally autonomous servility and aggression.

being"), self-realization is not obviously consistent with autonomy on any usual understanding of that term.[12]

This said, John Stuart Mill arguably defended self-realization *as* a conception of autonomy.[13] Mill might seem an unlikely expositor of autonomy, strictly speaking, as he uses the word only once in his central writings, as a synonym for a state's independence.[14] However, Mill is an inspirational figure to countless personal-autonomy theorists, and the modern conception of personal autonomy unquestionably has its roots in his doctrine, especially in "On Liberty." In the third part of this essay, for example, Mill celebrates the "free development of individuality" and the selection of a distinctive "plan of life," ideas and turns of phrase that are later picked up and developed by Raz and Rawls (Mill 1998, 63, 65).

Mill puts much greater emphasis on the idea of development, though, than most theorists of personal autonomy. He quotes Wilhelm von Humboldt approvingly ("the end of man is . . . the highest and most harmonious development of his powers to a complete and consistent whole") and stresses that "he who chooses his plan for himself, employs all his faculties. He must use observation to see, reasoning and judgment to foresee, activity to gather materials for decision, discrimination to decide, and when he has decided, firmness and self-control to hold to his deliberate decision" (Mill 1998, 64–65). Unlike most defenders of self-realization, however, Mill does not rely upon an externally given model to determine which powers or faculties are to be developed: "It really is of importance, not only what men do, but also what manner of men they are that do it. Among the works of man, which human life is rightly employed in perfecting and beautifying, the first in importance is surely man himself. . . . Human nature is not a machine to be built after a model,

---

12. See MacIntyre (1984), esp. chaps. 10–12 on the virtues in heroic societies, ancient Athens, and Aristotle, respectively. Also see Aristotle (1958, esp. 101–6 [3.4]), and Elster (1985, 82–92) on Marx's ideal of self-actualization through free and creative work.

13. The extent of Mill's perfectionism is a matter of debate in the secondary literature: Haksar (1979, 233), for example, contends that Mill is a thoroughgoing perfectionist, while Gray (1996, 87–88) and Rawls (LHPP 311–13) defend him against this charge—though they admit that his theory has some perfectionist characteristics. Certain contemporary theorists, such as William Galston and Joseph Raz, can also be interpreted as liberal (and therefore pluralistic) perfectionists. See Galston (1991, esp. chap. 8) and Raz (1986, esp. chaps. 13 and 14).

14. Mill (1998, 428). The quotation is from *Considerations on Representative Government* (sec. XVI) and reads as follows: "Identity of language, literature, and, to some extent, of race and recollections, have maintained the feeling of nationality in considerable strength among the different portions of the German name, though they have at no time been really united under the same government; but the feeling has never reached to making the separate states desire to get rid of their autonomy."

and set to do exactly the work prescribed for it, but a tree, which requires to grow and develop itself on all sides, according to the tendency of the inward forces which make it a living thing."[15] Despite the Aristotelian imagery at the end of this quotation, Mill clearly sets himself apart from the rest of the self-realization tradition by seeing personal perfection as a matter of *individualized* self-development, the bringing of our distinctive powers to fruition in thought and action through our idiosyncratic plans of self-perfection; the value and priority of such powers is determined by choice, not by nature or culture. The whole point of individuals composing their own lives and being given the liberty to do so, from Mill's perspective, is that as a result they will perfect their various capacities and talents and thus become unique, fully developed human beings. Although Mill would plainly argue that what motivates his political commitment to self-realization and its preconditions is the greatest-happiness principle, his language suggests an aesthetic motivation, though perhaps it is only proximate: for example, he says that "it is . . . by cultivating and calling forth all that is individual in themselves that human beings become a noble and beautiful object of contemplation."[16] In other words, self-realizing agents effectively turn themselves into unique works of art, giving visual pleasure to themselves and others in the process.[17]

Self-realization as a conception of internal autonomy, be it Mill's variant or another, can easily come into conflict with the other two conceptions we have surveyed. The potential conflict with moral autonomy is the most obvious: plans of self-perfection, being the unrestricted creative output of diverse individual minds, may transgress ethical and even juridical duties. For example, competitive athletes may take performance-enhancing drugs in the pursuit of an ideal of physical perfection, violating both ethical duties (against self-mutilation, insofar as such drugs have long-term negative health consequences) and juridical ones (against consumption of drugs prohibited by sporting regulations and/or state legislation).[18] Less obvious, perhaps, is its potential tension with personal autonomy. Setting aside moral issues, perfectionist projects like that of the drug-taking competitive athlete may "crowd out" other valuable elements of a plan of life, including our interests in material comfort and meaningful relationships with friends and family.

15. Ibid., 66; cf. ibid., 69, and WIE 8:42: "the human being, *who is now more than a machine.*"
16. Mill (1998, 70); on Mill's idiosyncratic utilitarianism, see ibid., 15, 139–42.
17. Cf. TJ 376 (emphasis added): "take pleasure in [self-realizing activities] as *displays* of human excellence."
18. On self-mutilation as a violation of self-respect, see MM 6:423.

This last statement raises a question that I skirted above: what is the precise relationship between a plan of self-development and a plan of life? If these plans were nonoverlapping, then some simple reading could be given to the concept of conflict between them: more of one might very well demand less of the other—a sort of psychic zero-sum game. As I suggested at the end of the last paragraph, however, a more natural interpretation of the relationship is that a plan of self-development is merely one element of a plan of life. This interpretation raises at least three additional questions, though: (1) Isn't the "crowding out" problem above simply a redescription of the problem of balancing final ends, which is a task of deliberative rationality and thus wholly internal to personal autonomy? (2) If so, couldn't we generate subtypes of personal autonomy for each category of final ends—consumption autonomy, relationship autonomy, and so forth—that might conflict with one another? (3) If so, why is self-realization so special that it merits its very own conception of autonomy? I return to these questions in the next section, where I construct an alternative interpretation of self-realization that not only incorporates moral concerns but also explains why self-realization must be understood as a distinct and subordinate element of personal autonomy.

III. The Nature of the Hierarchy: An Extended Kantian Conception of the Person

Is there any way to interpret these three conceptions of internal autonomy so that, despite the obvious tensions and conflicts between them, they could be seen as internally related and, if so, what would such a relationship look like? If an internal or structural relationship among these three conceptions of autonomy could be developed, it would help to resolve these tensions and conflicts by indicating which conceptions (and applications of these conceptions) are to receive priority or greater weight in cases of inconsistency. In this section, I offer specifically Kantian readings of these three conceptions of internal autonomy and combine them into a unified and hierarchical Kantian conception of persons. As we shall see in the next section of this chapter, this conception of the person is less a hybrid version of internal autonomy than an "unpacking" of Kantian moral autonomy, which remains the dominant conception throughout.

The structural relationship among these conceptions could take many forms.[19] One might, for example, pick one conception as the dominant one and just resolve any conflicts in its favor. Apart from the problem of underdetermination (in the case of conflict between the two subaltern conceptions), this solution may give insufficient weight to the legitimate claims of the other two conceptions. All of these conceptions are compellingly defended on rather diverse grounds (e.g., detachment/impartiality, authenticity, flourishing, etc.); consequently, this approach appears to be too extreme and dismissive, failing to give due weight to our considered convictions. A less extreme but related solution would be a hierarchy, where lower-ranked conceptions would give way to higher ones in cases of conflict. Although this solves the problem of underdetermination, it would leave open concerns about justification: why should some conceptions invariably trump others? An even less extreme solution would be a kind of weighting scheme, with no conception receiving an infinite weight relative to another, though this would raise the problem of a common metric: how should "units" of these three conceptions be compared or even calculated? The very diversity of the grounds on which they are defended militates against such an approach. A hybrid solution may be possible (e.g., weighting in some cases, hierarchy in others), though it would of course inherit the problems of its component systems. Lastly, one might punt on structural ideals entirely and resolve conflicts on a case-by-case basis, relying upon individual judgment. Such an intuitionist approach is impractical, as we saw in chapter 1, but it is also inconsistent with two of the formal criteria of right, generality and publicity. Particular intuitions do not generalize across judges and cases—if they did, they would constitute applications of a principle, the possibility of which (at least with regard to foundational principles) is precisely what intuitionism rejects—and this lack of generalizability will hamper and perhaps cripple any attempt to make the reasons for the judgment publicly accessible.

Despite the difficulties involved in identifying such a structural relationship, the benefits of doing so would be substantial, as it would help us to resolve exactly the kinds of conflicts that were discussed above. Moreover, various theorists of autonomy have maintained that the myriad conceptions are not only distinct but also unrelated or very tenuously related; the identification of a structural relationship could lead to a revision of these assessments

19. See TJ §8 for a detailed discussion—one which informs my own in this paragraph—of different ways to resolve conflicts between competing principles.

by revealing an underlying unity to the concept of autonomy, at least within a Kantian framework.[20] A sufficiently powerful structural relationship might even suggest (as was the case with personal autonomy) that we are not dealing with different conceptions at all, but rather facets of a fully unified concept.

In this chapter, I will defend just such a structural relationship among Kantian readings of these three internal conceptions of autonomy. This hypothesized relationship will be hierarchical in at least two senses. First, the higher conceptions of autonomy will *constrain* the lower—that is, in cases of conflict between any two, the higher will prevail. More broadly, higher conceptions will serve a *guiding* function for lower ones, not only offering a framework within which lower ones must operate but also influencing their development in subtler ways. Second, lower conceptions of autonomy will in many cases be instrumental to (or even constitutive of) higher ones. That is, lower conceptions will sometimes be made to serve as means to the ends set by higher ones and more rarely will become integrated into higher ones, usually by coming to share the ends of the higher conceptions.

More specifically, I wish to propose a hierarchy of the three conceptions in which moral autonomy occupies the highest position, personal autonomy, the second, and self-realization, the third. *Kantian moral autonomy* (MA_K) will generate the moral law, which will be universally and unconditionally binding on all finite rational beings and will encompass matters of both right and virtue (i.e., requiring not only particular actions and omissions but also the adoption of particular ends). *Kantian personal autonomy* (PA_K) will produce a life plan that is subordinate to this moral law; whenever they conflict, the plan of life must give way. This plan of life may be instrumental to or even constitutive of the moral law: for example, a plan of life may serve the moral law (in a strictly negative way) by respecting rights, or it may in a real sense become part of the moral law by pursuing and being motivated by an objective moral end (e.g., beneficence performed out of respect for others' humanity). Lastly, *Kantian self-realization* (SR_K) will lead to the development of valuable skills and capacities; any such development plans must give way in cases of conflict with either plans of life or the moral law. Plans of self-development may again be instrumental to or even constitutive of plans of life and the moral

---

20. Gerald Dworkin (1988, 6) expresses skepticism about the unity of the underlying concept when he says that "it is very unlikely that there is a core meaning which underlies all these various uses of the term." Raz goes even further, as we saw in the subsection on moral autonomy (1986, 370n). I take issue with Raz's claim in Taylor (2005).

law; examples of the latter, constitutive kind of relation include cases where self-perfecting activities become elements of, not simply means to, a plan of life (e.g., physical exercise as an intrinsic good in one's plan of life rather than a mere means to health or status) or again where such activities are motivated by an objective moral end (e.g., intellectual self-improvement pursued out of respect for humanity in oneself).[21]

To describe this structural relationship is not to justify it, of course, and in the following two sections of the chapter I will defend not merely its unity and coherence but its psychological feasibility as well. Before doing so, however, I need to describe and defend its component parts, namely, specifically Kantian readings of moral autonomy, personal autonomy, and self-realization. I have already defended a Kantian reading of moral autonomy against two of its chief competitors (existentialist and Rousseauean readings) and will say more in its defense below. I want to focus, however, on Kantian readings of personal autonomy and self-realization. It is far from clear that moralized Kantian interpretations of these two internal-autonomy conceptions are possible, much less compelling, but I will argue that in fact these are the best interpretations of these conceptions on their own terms, that is, they offer the most persuasive and attractive readings of authenticity and autonomous flourishing, respectively. I conclude this section by considering how true to Kant the extended Kantian conception of the person really is.

A. Kantian Personal Autonomy (PA_K)

Given section II's definitions of Kantian moral autonomy (MA_K) and personal autonomy (PA), a truly Kantian personal autonomy (PA_K) would have to meet two apparently inconsistent criteria:[22]

1. it would need to be ultimately motivated not by idiosyncratic interests and passions but rather by pure practical reason, that is, motivated by *objective* reasons, which are universal in form, bind all finite rational beings, and provide a "unity to our lives" that may be lacking under the mere rule of nature and culture (Schneewind 1996, 290);

---

21. For more on beneficence and natural self-perfection, both of which are imperfect duties of virtue, see MM 6:386–88, 391–94, 444–46, 452–54.
22. This subsection reproduces much of Taylor (2005, 611–16).

2. it would need to make substantial room for *subjective* reasons (i.e., reasons specific to particular agents) in order to make self-creation or self-authorship a real possibility, for autonomy on the Kantian model threatens to reduce "[self-]authorship . . . to a vanishing point as it allows only one set of principles which people can rationally legislate and they are the same for all" (Raz 1986, 370n).

Is it even possible for a single conception of personal autonomy to meet both of these criteria, to be not only ultimately objective but also substantially subjective? I shall argue in this subsection that Kant offers just such a conception in his *Tugendlehre* or Doctrine of Virtue—specifically, in the form of certain imperfect duties of virtue to self (natural perfection) and others (beneficence).

First, however, I want to place these duties in context by briefly reviewing part of Kant's taxonomy of duties in his late moral philosophy (see figure 4, based on diagrams at MM 6:240, 398). Kant divides duties into duties of right and duties of virtue, which are distinguished by (1) the presence of *external enforcement* with respect to actions/omissions in the former and its absence in the latter and (2) the absence of a requirement to adopt particular *ends* in the former and its presence in the latter.[23] For example, the duty of noncoercion (proscription of murder, etc.) may be enforced by threat of punishment but does not require those who discharge it to have any particular end (e.g., the right of human beings) in mind when doing so, whereas the duty of respect (proscription of contempt, ridicule, etc.) may not be enforced by threat of punishment but does require those who fulfill it to have a particular end (namely, a recognition of the dignity of other human beings) in mind when doing so (MM 6:333–37, 462–68).

Duties of virtue are additionally subdivided into perfect and imperfect duties (of virtue).[24] Perfect duties of virtue require particular actions/omissions because these are so closely related to the adoption of particular ends, whereas imperfect duties of virtue allow latitude in the choice of actions/omissions so long as the end is still adopted. For example, respect is a perfect duty of virtue, as particular signs of disrespect (e.g., defamation) are to be avoided as simply inconsistent with the end of respecting the dignity of others; beneficence, on

---

23. MM 6:379–83. One can also discharge one's duties of right virtuously (i.e., meritoriously) if one makes "the right of humanity, or also the right of human beings, one's *end*" (MM 6:390–91).

24. On the distinction between perfect and imperfect duties in general, see MM 6:390–91. Also see Denis (2006).

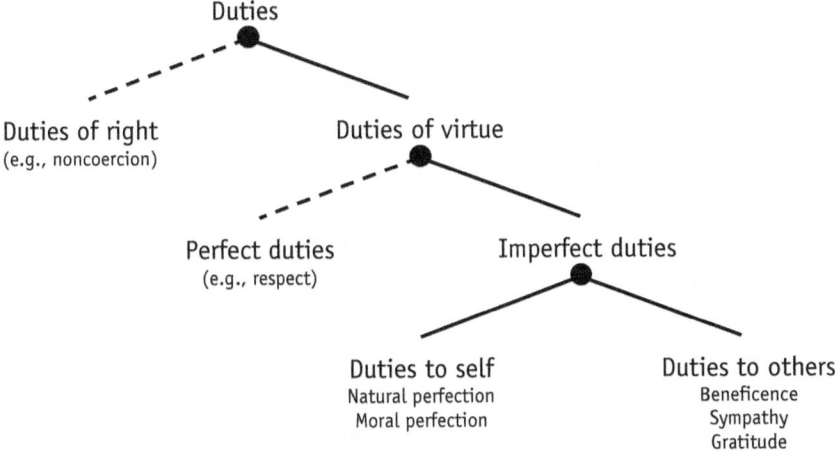

Fig. 4 Partial taxonomy of duties in Kant's late moral philosophy

the other hand, is an imperfect duty of virtue, because it requires no particular actions/omissions (e.g., giving fifty dollars to Habitat for Humanity) so long as the end of helping others is still adopted.[25] Finally, the imperfect duties of virtue are further subdivided into (imperfect) duties (of virtue) to self and others. The imperfect duties of virtue include duties to perfect oneself both naturally and morally and to love others in a practical manner through beneficence, sympathy, and gratitude.

Natural perfection of oneself requires cultivation of one's natural faculties and talents of body, mind, and spirit, both for its own sake and for the sake of myriad possible purposes, moral ones specially.[26] As noted in chapter 1, the capacity to set ends is what defines humanity; respect for humanity in our own person (dictated by the formula of humanity [FH]) therefore entails the development of this capacity along myriad dimensions.[27] Kant emphasizes, though,

---

25. MM 6:452–54. Though the duty of beneficence requires no particular actions, a *complete absence* of beneficent actions would be a violation of the duty (GMM 4:423, 430; MM 6:453). Also, all duties of right are perfect duties: one cannot impose an end by use of coercion, though one can use coercion to guarantee the performance or omission of an action (MM 6:390–91).

26. GMM 4:422–23; MM 6:386–87, 391–93, 444–47. Kant explicitly rules out the perfection of *others* as a duty: he says that perfection is "something that only the other himself can do," for unless the other himself sets it as an end, the cultivation of his talents will fail to be meritorious. Again, one can force actions but not ends, and only the free adoption of virtuous ends can earn merit (MM 6:386).

27. GMM 4:429–30; MM 6:391–93. For a different approach to justifying natural perfection as a duty see O'Neill (1989, 98–101).

that we have great discretion with respect to both *which* talents we should develop and *how much* we should develop them and that our occupational choice largely decides which set of skills we develop.[28] *Moral perfection* of oneself demands the nurturing of one's moral disposition, with the ultimate aim of purity, so that respect for moral law is sufficient incentive for discharging duty—a purity not to be attained in this life but rather in the next (CPrR 5:122–24; MM 6:386–87, 392–93, 446–47). Kant leaves little room for discretion here, though: he says that this duty is "narrow and perfect with respect to its object" and that one must therefore "strive with all one's might" for moral purity (MM 6:393, 446).

Practical love of others is related to willing, not feeling, as feeling cannot be commanded as a duty.[29] What must be willed here is a benevolent *conduct*, as given by duties of beneficence, sympathy, and gratitude. Like Kant, I will focus on the first. Beneficence is the duty to promote the happiness of others by making their (permitted) ends our ends as well and by then acting to advance those ends (MM 6:387–88, 393–94, 452–54). Kant says that "there is still only a negative and not a positive agreement with *humanity as an end in itself* unless everyone also tries, as far as he can, to further the ends of others" (GMM 4:430; also see Herman 1993, chap. 3; O'Neill 1989, 98–101). Respecting the rights of others, in other words, is a necessary but not a sufficient condition for respecting their humanity: if the capacity to set ends defines humanity, then we must help others to achieve their (permissible) ends in order to respect them fully. As was the case with natural perfection, we have a great deal of discretion regarding *how* and *to what extent* we fulfill our duty of beneficence. As Kant says, "the duty [of beneficence] has in it a latitude for doing more or less, and no specific limits can be assigned to what should be done"; we may, for example, refuse requests for help if we believe they will not advance the recipient's happiness or if they conflict with our "true needs" (MM 6:388, 393).

I can now return to my original claim, namely, that Kant implicitly offers us a conception of personal autonomy in his Doctrine of Virtue in the form of

---

28. MM 6:392, 445–46. On the precise nature of the relationship between natural perfection and occupation, see Taylor (2004, 342–43).

29. MM 6:401, 449. Kant rejects the idea of a duty of practical love towards *oneself*: the promotion of one's own happiness is at most an *indirect* duty and only insofar as its promotion is necessary to ward off poverty, pain, etc., as "great temptations to violate one's duty." That is, the promotion of one's own happiness is, from a moral point of view, only useful as a means to promote (adherence to) morality (MM 6:386).

two imperfect duties of virtue: natural perfection of oneself and beneficence towards others. We can see how these two duties constitute a conception of personal autonomy if we consider how they satisfy the two criteria for a Kantian conception of personal autonomy enumerated above. First, they are both *ultimately* motivated by objective reasons. As we have seen, the duties of self-perfection and the practical love of others follow from a respect for humanity as an end in itself, whether it lies in our own person or in the person of others, and humanity is an objective end of pure practical reason. These duties provide architectonic principles for a virtuous life that derive from our own capacity for moral autonomy and, as we shall see, help correct the anomic and heteronomous features of personal autonomy.[30]

Second, both duties allow subjective reasons to play a very substantial role. By leaving so much to discretion, these duties create a great deal of room for self-creation or self-authorship. A virtuous Kantian agent has enormous freedom to fashion his own plan of life—one reflecting his own idiosyncratic "tastes, opinions, ideals, goals, values, and preferences" (Feinberg)—while *at the same time* discharging his duties to perfect himself and advance the happiness of others (Feinberg 1989, 32). For example, self-perfection can be achieved through any number of different occupations, hobbies, and other personal projects that will often be *a* central if not *the* central focus of agents' plans of life. More often than not, advancing the happiness of others plays a similarly large role, whether it is achieved in intimate settings (e.g., through one's support for family, friends, and colleagues) or in more impersonal, institutionalized ways (e.g., gifts of cash and labor to organized charities). By choosing among these different means to (ultimate) objective ends, agents can fashion unique and satisfying lives for themselves—authentic lives of their own making but also lives having a moral point. In other words, the shape of such lives can be responsive to *subjective reasons* (e.g., choosing one occupation over another because of one's tastes and/or skills) without ceasing to be about *objective ends;* the pursuit of such ends validates or redeems supporting subjective reasons even if their origin is heteronomous. As Allen Wood says, "if I am a decent person, I will choose to give my life meaning by pursuing some set of ends that fall under the general description 'my own perfection' and 'the happiness of others.' Where that is so, morality *underwrites* our ground

---

30. In chapter 1's discussion of Rawls's "thin theory of the good" I showed how maxims contrary to beneficence and self-perfection could not be universalized and so were rejected by The CI (FUL) and our own pure practical reason.

projects, regarding them as morally meritorious" (Wood 1999, 328–29; cf. Reath 1989, 66–68).

None of this is meant to deny, of course, that Kantian agents may adopt merely subjective ends that are consistent with both right and the perfect duties of virtue. One example might be a certain type of consumption activity: although some kinds of consumption have a self-improving quality to them (e.g., reading challenging novels), others will lack this quality and thus qualify as merely subjective ends (e.g., reading the *Beetle Bailey* comic strip).[31] Kantian duties of virtue are not "maximalist," demanding that moral agents sacrifice all their merely subjective ends in order to perfect themselves and aid others. These concerns must play *some* role in the life of a virtuous agent, of course, but he can limit them without blame in order to pursue merely subjective ends, including especially his "true needs" (for food, clothing, shelter, companionship, etc.).[32]

Now that we have a Kantian conception of personal autonomy in hand, we can see how higher conceptions of autonomy guide and constrain lower ones in the Kantian conception of the person. MA_K *guides* PA_K through the *imperfect* duties of virtue to self and others: life plans must adopt humanity as an end and must therefore incorporate beneficence and natural self-perfection in an unspecified fashion. Discretion is wide with respect to how and to what degree the end is to be pursued, but adoption of the end itself is not discretionary. MA_K *constrains* PA_K through the *perfect* duties of both right and virtue: our life plans must not only hew to the demands of justice (e.g., by not violating the rights of others to their persons and possessions) but also avoid actions that show disrespect to ourselves or others (e.g., suicide, self-mutilation; slander, arrogance). No discretion exists with respect to these perfect duties, as their infringement automatically violates the freedom of others or the dignity of humanity.

What I have shown so far is that a genuinely *Kantian* personal autonomy is a possibility, that morality and authenticity can be combined without doing violence to either. I want to show, however, not only the possibility of a Kantian personal autonomy but its superiority *as* a reading of personal autonomy. This superiority derives from its unique capacity to solve two interrelated problems internal to personal autonomy—what I will call the *contingency* and

---

31. On consumption as a self-actualizing (but not self-realizing) activity, see Elster (1986, 103, 106).
32. MM 6:393, 432–33, 453. For a discussion of "true needs," see LHMP 173–76, 221, 232–34. On the larger issue of setting ends in a virtuous life, see Wood (1999, 325).

discontinuity problems—that threaten to turn personal autonomy heteronomous, even anomic. I will introduce these problems and develop their solution by way of an example that highlights the potential for tension between MA_K and PA: a personally autonomous thief, who has rationally reflected upon and endorsed his immoral way of life and pursued it with impressive self-control and dedication.

Let us begin with the problem of contingency. Suppose this thief learns from experience that he has a nontrivial feeling of regret whenever he steals. Upon reflection, he decides that this feeling is the heteronomous product of early childhood socialization, one inconsistent with his chosen way of life, his "practical identity" (Korsgaard 1996b, 115). He therefore decides to annihilate this inauthentic element of his personality, perhaps through immersion therapy (e.g., stealing exclusively from the poor for a period of time until he is inured to these feelings or they go away) or some other kind of psychological intervention. He has engaged in what Harry Frankfurt has called "identification and withdrawal": by assuming the reflective standpoint of the consummate thief—a position with which he passionately identifies—he is able to identify his feeling of regret as inauthentic and so begin to withdraw from his tacit accommodation of that feeling and even to root it out (Frankfurt 1988, 18).

In this example, I have simply described what it means to be personally autonomous: the personally autonomous individual does not passively accept features of his personality whatever their nature and source but seeks authenticity by identifying and trying to remove those features that are not consistent with his practical identity. If authenticity is the driving motivation behind personal autonomy, however, why should this kind of reflection and criticism stay targeted only at lower-order personality features? Can we not ask the same questions about practical identity itself? Suppose the thief were to reflect upon his identity *qua* thief—or put differently, upon his commitment to the character ideal and reflective standpoint of the consummate thief. He might discover that this commitment was *itself* heteronomous in origin, perhaps the product of family traditions and expectations (maybe his father and grandfather were thieves) and poor economic opportunities. Of course, he might come to endorse this identity even upon reflection—but then again, he might not. He might instead choose to reject it on grounds similar to those that led him to reject the feelings of regret.

Similar grounds, but by no means identical ones. When the thief reflects upon and maybe critiques his own identity, he must assume *another* practical identity, if only temporarily and as a hypothetical matter. He must step outside himself, detach himself from his fierce commitment to a particular way of life in order to assess it dispassionately. This process may be painful, just as it may have been painful for him to detach himself from his feelings of regret and assess them from a higher standpoint, but authenticity's writ knows no limits. What might this new standpoint be? Perhaps it is the more general standpoint of a consummate *criminal,* from which he can evaluate the advantages and disadvantages of a life of thievery versus, say, vandalism.[33] But wouldn't the appropriateness of this more encompassing standpoint itself be a fit object of reflection and even critique for reasons of authenticity? The criminal perspective was not randomly chosen after all.

This "regressive" quality of reflection in the service of authenticity has been discussed by Harry Frankfurt and Gerald Dworkin in their closely related expositions of hierarchical models of agency. Frankfurt describes it this way: "There is *no theoretical limit* to the length of the series of desires of higher and higher orders; nothing except common sense and, perhaps, a saving fatigue prevents an individual from obsessively refusing to identify himself with any of his desires until he forms a desire of the next higher order. The tendency to generate such a series of acts of forming desires, which would be a case of humanization run wild, also leads toward the destruction of a person" (Frankfurt 1988, 21; emphasis added). Dworkin presents it as part of a dilemma: "Either [acts of critical reflection] are themselves autonomous (in which case we have to go to a higher-order reflection to determine this, and since this process can be repeated *an infinite regress threatens*) or they are not autonomous, in which case why is a first-order motivation evaluated by a nonautonomous process *itself* autonomous" (Dworkin 1988, 19; emphasis added). Frankfurt defends against this infinite-regress threat by what can only be described as agential fiat: "When a person identifies *decisively* with one of his first-order desires, this commitment 'resounds' throughout the potentially endless array of higher orders. . . . There is no room for questions concerning the pertinence of desires or volitions of higher orders."[34] Dworkin, on the other

---

33. The thief might try instead to assess his thievery from an equally particular standpoint—say, that of a vandal—but adjudicating between these perspectives would presumably require a more general perspective, if only temporarily.

34. Frankfurt (1988, 21). Notice the similarity of this move to that of the moral realists, who close off certain lines of philosophical questioning by what appears to be mere "fiat": when they are questioned as to *why* we must do what moral first principles require, they simply declare them to be *"intrinsically* normative" (Korsgaard 1996b, 33–34, 40–42). See my discussion of realism in chapter 1.

hand, tries to sidestep the issue by emphasizing that he is not trying to analyze autonomous acts but rather autonomous people, *defined* simply as those who have an uncoerced second-order identification with their first-order desires. As he maintains, "there is no conceptual necessity for raising the question of whether the values, preferences at the second order would themselves be valued or preferred at a higher level" (Dworkin 1988, 19–20).

As we saw with the thief example above, however, there is indeed a need to raise such a question, a need internal to the concept of personal autonomy itself: authenticity. The essential question of authenticity—is this personal characteristic really, genuinely *me?*—may be asked of any relevant personal trait, be it as specific as a feeling or as general as a practical identity. One cannot therefore avoid the threat of infinite regress by either agential or definitional fiat.

How big a threat *is* infinite regress, though? Frankfurt and Dworkin seem to assume that ever-higher levels of reflection and criticism have no natural stopping point, but again the thief example suggests otherwise, as the regress there appears to be moving him in a certain direction: toward ever-higher levels of detachment and abstraction from contingency. The self-critical thief moved from a specific feeling to a cherished identity to a more general and hypothetical identity. This sequence tends unerringly toward a familiar stopping point, namely, the perfectly detached point of view obtainable by a Kantian moral agent in reflection, in which he abstracts from all "social, natural, and fortuitous contingencies" and by doing so attains the impartial authority to legislate for himself and others.[35] The universal principles of right and virtue authored from this point of view then constrain and guide our more particular plans of life, as we have seen. What all of this suggests is that taking personal autonomy's proceduralism seriously drives us inexorably toward a moralized understanding of such autonomy—namely, PA_K.

This leads us to the second problem, of discontinuity. Return for a moment to the thief's feelings of regret. Suppose the thief, rather than uprooting his feelings, instead abandons his way of life: he agonizes over the thought of wiping out such deeply held emotional commitments and in a flash of inspiration undergoes a Damascene conversion away from thievery and towards, let us suppose, dentistry. He goes almost discontinuously from being a personally autonomous thief to being a personally autonomous dentist. Everyone is no

---

35. JF 55. Compare this line of argumentation with my criticism of competitors to MA_K in section II of this chapter.

doubt familiar with conversions, if not of this particular type, then of a similar type, especially in the realm of religion and politics. One troubling aspect of these conversions from the viewpoint of personal autonomy is their vertiginous quality and their seeming lawlessness. The discontinuity in identity implied by such conversions can be radical, suggesting (as was the case with the existentialist conception of moral autonomy) the eclipse of *nomos* by a protean *autos*.

One advantage of PA_K as a conception of personal autonomy is that it can absorb such jarring tectonic shifts in the self while still providing an unbroken substratum of *moral* identity.[36] As J. B. Schneewind notes, such "natural disarray of the passions and desires is a given in Kant's ethics. Moral agency brings a kind of unity to our lives that prudential agency alone could never bring."[37] Moreover, as we have just seen, this moral agency is not alien to personal autonomy but is rather a necessary element of it, the result of working out the implications of a comprehensive commitment to authenticity. Thus, *Kantian* personal autonomy is not oxymoronic, but rather the consummation of the root concept and the solution to its internal problems of contingency and discontinuity.

B. Kantian Self-Realization (SR_K)

In my earlier discussion of autonomous self-realization, I suggested that the most natural interpretation of it was as an *element* of personal autonomy. Now that we have constructed PA_K, we can see (Kantian) self-realization as that component of PA_K dealing with personal perfection. SR_K is in effect PA_K with a restricted range of application: instead of dealing with the wide array of desires, values, ends, etc. that can serve as the raw materials for self-authorship, SR_K focuses on the development and possible perfection of our myriad skills and capacities, whether they are intellectual, physical, or spiritual. SR_K is effected by way of a plan of self-development, one that must overcome a variety of

---

36. In some cases, of course, individuals have a crisis of faith in morality itself; a lapse into moral skepticism breaks up the deepest supporting layer of PA_K. In the conclusion of the book, I offer a reconstruction of Kant's argument for the reasonableness of practical faith in our own freedom, which is the basis of a Kantian morality; ultimately this is the only case for being moral a Kantian can make to the moral skeptic—apart from prudential arguments, naturally.

37. Schneewind (1996, 290); cf. Korsgaard (1996b, 121): "our identity as moral beings—as people who value themselves as human beings—stands behind our more particular practical identities."

internal barriers (including akrasia, myopia, and risk aversion) to be successful.[38] This struggle against our natural inertial tendencies for the sake of self-perfection is as illustrative of our autonomy as the overarching struggles for authenticity and morality. Such a conception of autonomy still allows much scope for creativity—for instance, we must choose an array of skills to develop, allocate our time and effort across them, and decide upon techniques for their development—but it is narrower than its parent concept in having a unitary ultimate end: an ideal of personal perfection.

Partisans of nonautonomous readings of self-realization will no doubt object to the way that SR_K subordinates perfectionism to—or perhaps conflates it with—autonomy. Nevertheless, this conception is a completely valid interpretation of the original concept, retaining its focus on personal perfection and the conditions of human flourishing but incorporating those authenticity conditions associated with personal autonomy. Under SR_K, the character ideal that we pursue is chosen rather than imposed upon us by nature (e.g., Aristotelian or Marxist teleology accessible by theoretical reason) or culture (e.g., heroic ideal of Archaic Greece). At the same time, though, the end of personal perfection is not discretionary, as we saw in the previous subsection: we may be able to choose how and to what degree we cultivate our skills and abilities, but self-perfection as an end is dictated by MA_K, which guides PA_K (and therefore its component SR_K) on PA's own grounds of authenticity; as we have just seen, the ends of self-perfection and beneficence are not heteronomous impositions on PA but rather are implications of its central value. As I will discuss below and in chapter 5, this reading of self-realization is required to round out Rawls's Kantian conception of persons and ground the lexical priority of FEO, and it is tightly connected with the lowest rung of Kant's ladder of necessitation—rules of skill—in his own model of finite rational agency.[39]

I now return to a question I posed in the earlier discussion of autonomous self-realization: if SR_K is only a component of PA_K, why am I treating it here as a separate conception of internal autonomy? I suggested there and will now argue that SR_K has a special, subordinate status within PA_K owing to the unusual nature of its object, namely, our skills and capacities. Rawls would

---

38. On this point, see Elster (1986, 107–8).
39. All of this raises the question: to what extent is Rawls a perfectionist? His focus on the development and exercise of our two moral powers and his favorable comments about "ideal-regarding principles" (such as those of justice and perfection) versus "want-regarding principles" suggest a perfectionist streak; however, he viewed perfectionism as a maximizing teleological theory, basically unlike justice as fairness. See TJ 21–23, 26–27, 287, and Taylor (2005, 621–22).

classify these things as *natural* primary goods: like all primary goods, they are "things that every rational man is presumed to want [because they] normally have a use whatever a person's rational plan of life"; they are natural rather than social (like rights, liberties, opportunities, income, and wealth), however, for "although their possession is influenced by the basic structure, they are not directly under its control" (TJ 54). As examples of such primary goods, he gives "health and vigor, intelligence and imagination," physical and mental capacities that are in part given by nature (genetics; early childhood diet, exercise, and education) but also cultivated according to a rational plan of self-development in adult life.

Like social primary goods, our capacities act as resources for the achievement of ends in our plans of life: some of these capacities are tied to particular ends, but many more are generic in quality, such as those listed by Rawls; they are fungible, like money, capable of being used in the pursuit of a wide variety of ends. Unlike social primary goods, however, these resources are internal to the person: whereas social primary goods are possessions, natural primary goods are best regarded as part of our identity—they are something we *are* rather than something we *have*. Akin to moral law or those larger plans of life we follow, our plans of self-development and the skills on which they focus define us as persons; they partially constitute our character, which is why they are appropriately part of a theory of *internal* autonomy. Our capacities, in short, bridge two worlds: an outer world of social primary goods, which guarantee our external autonomy and serve as personal resources, and an inner world of moral laws and life plans, which motivate and regulate our use and development of personal resources, be they external or internal. Put another way, they serve as a kind of interface between internal plans and external resources: our mental, physical, and emotional capacities are what allow us to act upon things in the outer world in the service of our inner objectives. Their dual nature helps explain the special status of that facet of PA_K, SR_K, that has them as its object.

The preceding may explain why SR_K is a distinct, even special component of PA_K, but it does not explain why it is subordinate to PA_K's other components. To show why, let us begin by noticing that just as it would be heteronomous to sacrifice the integrity of our plan of life for the sake of additional external means to its achievement, so it would be heteronomous to do this for the sake of additional internal means. The difficulty here is not that self-development *as an end* may become too prominent a component of our plan of life (although this could become a moral failing if beneficence is wholly neglected as a result, for instance). After all, properly balancing all of the various ends of a plan of life (the physical and social pleasures, self-development, the happiness of others, etc.) is simply part of the task of personal autonomy. Rather, the problem is that self-development as a (mere) means to fulfilling ends in our plan of life may become overly prominent, and this is indeed a kind of heteronomy, one which threatens the integrity of our life plan by "crowding out" its other elements.

The source of this problem is again the dual nature of our capacities. Unlike money, for example, the capacities selected and nurtured by our plan of self-development can be final ends in our plan of life.[40] Like money, however, capacities can also be fungible, universal means for the pursuit of other ends, whether those capacities are generic physical and mental abilities like strength and wit, respectively, or psychological qualities like patience, diligence, focus, resolve, and self-control more generally. As such, they are liable to abuse in the form of a pathological overinvestment in their development. Some examples will help us identify the phenomenon in question:

1. As a (mere) means to competitive victory, athletes may endure grueling and even cruel levels of training and self-discipline to enhance their strength and endurance.
2. As a (mere) means to educational attainment, students may pour hundreds of hours into preparing for standardized tests, honing a particular set of intellectual skills.
3. As a (mere) means to romantic or professional success, men and women may sink staggering time, effort, and expense into (re)shaping their bodies in the pursuit of a demanding ideal of beauty.[41]

Obsessive attempts to accrue skills, talents, etc. as mere means to physical or social pleasure or the fulfillment of consumerist or status needs, for example, are pervasive phenomena that must be guarded against by the maintenance of hierarchy *within* PA_K; if not, other ends in our system of ends may be "crowded

---

40. For a discussion of the irrationality of pursuing money as an end, see Aristotle (1958, 26–27 [1.9]).
41. I do not want to deny that certain structural features of society—for example, the existence of so-called winner-take-all (WTA) markets, where large prizes go to only a handful of top competitors—can exacerbate this problem and that social reform may properly focus on changing such features. On WTA markets, see Frank and Cook (1996).

out" not due to personally autonomous balancing of our ends but rather to heteronomous fixation on accumulating means to particular ends, especially those given to us by nature (e.g., sex) and culture (e.g., status). Instrumentalism is a constant threat in commercial societies, and any theory of internal autonomy must tackle it not merely in its typical form—the sacrifice of personal and moral integrity for money—but also in the less noted form just outlined.

Now that we have a moralized Kantian conception of self-realization in hand and have shown its distinctness from and subordination to the other elements of PA_K, we should ask what advantages it may have over John Stuart Mill's alternative conception of autonomous flourishing, which we surveyed earlier. Despite the aesthetic-perfectionist qualities of his conception, Mill's underlying justification for it is utilitarian: just as he refuses to depend upon "the idea of abstract right, as a thing independent from utility," so he would refuse to regard aesthetic or perfectionist reasons as the *ultimate* grounds of his theory of individualized self-development; when Mill says that the self-realized individual becomes "more valuable" to himself and others, there is no doubt that he cashes out this value in terms of utility (Mill 1998, 15, 70). Insofar as Mill deems pleasure or desire to be a simple natural good, something intrinsically normative—and there is substantial evidence for this reading of Mill—his theory is a variety of moral realism and inherits the myriad problems of that approach, which I examined in chapter 1, including an inconsistency with even a weak, doctrinal notion of autonomy.[42] If Mill's utilitarianism could be reconstrued as constructivist, however, it might prove a worthy competitor to SR_K as an interpretation of autonomous flourishing.[43]

C. How Kantian Is the Extended Kantian Conception of the Person?

Before moving on to examine the coherence and even feasibility of this extended Kantian conception of the person, we should reconsider its Kantian provenance. To be specific, how does this extended Kantian conception relate to Kant's own model of finite rational agency, as laid out early in chapter 1? Notice that the three hierarchically ordered Kantian conceptions of autonomy

---

42. For evidence of Mill's moral realism, see Mill (1998, 163, 168–75 [chap. 4 of "Utilitarianism"]). On doctrinal versus constitutive versions of autonomy, see PL 98–100.

43. Rawls concedes that "utilitarianism might be presented as a kind of constructivism" (KCMT 323n1).

in this conception—namely, MA_K, PA_K, and SR_K—are paralleled by the three hierarchically ordered varieties of imperative in Kant's own model of finite rational agency: categorical commands of morality (including the metalaw of The CI), hypothetical counsels of prudence, and hypothetical rules of skill. Categorical commands of morality are simply the legislative products of a morally autonomous agent: when this agent has abstracted from all forms of contingency, there is nothing left to condition the laws that emerge from his legislative will (*Wille*, or what I called $Will_A$), and it will therefore yield completely unconditioned law, namely, the universal-law formulation of The CI (FUL), which can be used to test all proposed practical principles, including more particular laws of morality (e.g., proscriptions of physical coercion). A less abstracted legislative will generates counsels of prudence to offer guidance in our exercise of personal autonomy, and as I argued in chapter 1, personal autonomy—the second moral power of *rationality*—is intimately related to Kantian prudential reasoning.

The connection between rules of skill and self-realization is perhaps less obvious, and it will not be fully elucidated until chapter 5. For Kant, the rules of skill are technical imperatives: they determine not "whether the end [sought] is rational and good . . . but only what one must do in order to attain it. . . . Since in early youth it is not known what ends might occur to us in the course of life, parents seek above all to have their children learn *a great many things* and to provide for *skill* in the use of means to all sorts of *discretionary* ends" (GMM 4:415). Of course, once individuals have reached adulthood, they continue to develop these and other skills in the pursuit of their chosen ends, and this quest for excellence is the key element of self-realization. Kant also emphasizes, though, that the development of one's skills is a self-regarding duty (if an imperfect one): "as a rational being he necessarily wills that all the capacities in him be developed, since they serve him and are given to him for all sorts of possible purposes" (GMM 4:423). Thus, for Kant as for Rawls, self-realization is a moral imperative, and rules of skill are the tools that our legislative reason offers for this project of personal perfection, which is itself guided and limited by the tutelary authority of the moral law and a rational plan of life.

Kant goes on to note that these three varieties of imperative are "clearly distinguished by *dissimilarity* in the necessitation of the will" (GMM 4:416). Whereas the commands of morality bind rational agents unconditionally, counsels of prudence have force only in relation to a universal subjective end (namely, happiness), and the rules of skill constrain only insofar as agents actually will the ends to which these rules specify the means. Thus, a hierarchy exists among the imperatives: morality limits the pursuit of happiness, which in turn dictates the development of certain skills. A parallel hierarchical relationship holds among Rawls's three priorities, as I shall argue over the next three chapters: the priorities of right and political liberty (which are grounded in MA_K) are paramount; the priority of civil liberty (based upon PA_K) is next; while the priority of FEO (founded on SR_K) is last. Thus, while all three of these facets of autonomy are illustrative of our independence from natural and social contingency, the degree of their independence differs, and this dissimilarity motivates the hierarchical relationship among both them and the lexical priorities that they ground.

IV. The Coherence of the Hierarchy: A Three-Stage Sequence

In the previous section, I demonstrated that the three Kantian conceptions of autonomy that constituted the extended Kantian conception of the person were not only consistent with one another but also closely interrelated. SR_K was seen to be an element—albeit a distinct, subaltern one—of PA_K, and PA_K itself was shown to point towards MA_K as a result of its central value of authenticity. In this section, I want to contend that the connection among these three conceptions is even stronger than previously shown. Specifically, these three Kantian variations on the theme of internal autonomy are three "moments," so to speak, of the central Kantian insight, one I have mentioned several times in this chapter and the last: *along both intensive and extensive margins (i.e., force and scope), legislative authority varies directly with abstraction from contingency.*

Given the very abstract quality of this insight, I want to develop it a bit in the context of the thief example used in the last section. Recall that upon reflection the thief was alienated from his feeling of regret, judging it inauthentic and inconsistent with his heartfelt commitment to the character ideal of the consummate thief. Of what must his reflection consist, however? The thief must detach himself from his feeling of regret and consider it from a higher perspective, namely, that of the consummate thief. From that perspective, he may ask himself whether this is a feeling that he wants and, if he does not, set out to change it. Equivalently, he might set aside his knowledge of this feeling and simply ask himself what feelings he *qua* consummate thief should have about stealing; they will presumably be good feelings, and he will then recall his bad feelings, see they are at variance with the feelings he should have, and seek to change them. I bring up this second, more complex rendering of reflection to point out that abstraction from contingency can be read as abstraction from *knowledge* of contingent circumstances, like the thief's feelings of regret. If the thief sets aside his feelings, *even if only in thought,* he can achieve the detachment required by authenticity, and his judgments will acquire a new authority as a consequence. In summary, abstraction from knowledge of contingency here enhances authority of judgment, which is just the central Kantian insight in a personal-autonomy context.

The idea that our self-government might improve if we ignore certain seemingly relevant information may appear paradoxical: isn't more information always better, on the usual rational-choice grounds? The answer, maybe surprisingly, is no. We are used to thinking positively about ignorance in the context of justice—think of justice personified, blindfolded in order to guarantee impartiality—but parallel considerations come into play in other, more personal contexts. Think about a smoker who has had a friend hide his cigarettes as part of his effort to quit: would he be better off knowing their location or more self-governing as a result? More generally, laying aside knowledge (if only hypothetically) of contingent circumstances may aid autonomy by buttressing self-control and allowing deeper, more authentic commitments to prevail in judgment.[44]

I will apply these insights below by developing a three-stage sequence from which the three Kantian conceptions of autonomy can be derived. This sequence is a heuristic device that allows a conscientious agent to answer fully the practical Kantian question: what should I do (CPuR A805/B833)? To answer this question, the agent considers how he (or his representative) would choose under certain hypothetical circumstances. At the first stage of the sequence, the MA_K stage, the agent abstracts from all knowledge of contingency and from this position of full legislative authority chooses universal moral laws, binding

---

44. The advantages of *limiting* choice and/or information come up frequently in game-theoretic contexts. A general defending an island with his troops against great odds, for example, may neglect to tell them of a bridge offering an escape route, and this ignorance may be beneficial not only for the general but for the troops themselves: they might collectively prefer standing and fighting to the disorderly exodus that would ensue if they knew of the bridge. These advantages typically arise in situations where commitment and self-control are vital (e.g., Ulysses and the Sirens), as they clearly are for moral and personal autonomy.

with full force on him and all other finite rational beings. At the second stage, the PA_K stage, the agent gains knowledge of his higher-order preferences and natural talents but continues to abstract from all other knowledge of contingency; in it, he chooses a plan of life consistent with the moral law chosen in the previous stage, a plan that is prudentially binding only on him and those with similar characteristics. In the final, SR_K stage, the agent gains full knowledge and selects a plan of self-development consistent with the moral law and his plan of life; this plan is of even more limited force and scope. At every successive stage of the sequence, abstraction from knowledge of contingent circumstances lessens and legislative authority therefore declines along both the intensive and extensive margins.

This three-stage sequence is intended to be Rawlsian in spirit if not in letter. I will discuss below its similarities to (and important differences from) Rawls's own *four*-stage sequence, but I want to mention another, perhaps closer similarity here. In *Theory*, Rawls distinguishes between two ideal perspectives: the OP and deliberative rationality, which very roughly parallel the MA_K and PA_K stages here.[45] As Samuel Freeman remarks, "both perspectives are idealizations; neither takes individuals just as they are. Instead, *both artificially control the information available and constrain the judgments of those occupying these positions by normative principles:* by rational principles in judgments of one's good and reasonable principles constraining rational judgment in case of judgments of justice" (S. Freeman 2007a, 150–51; emphasis added). The similarity is striking, though Rawls admittedly states that the deliberatively rational agent "chooses in light of all the relevant facts"; as I shall soon show, the "relevant facts" at the PA_K stage include only those that are absolutely essential for choosing our rational plan of life, as further knowledge of our personal traits might heteronomously alter our choice of final ends and thereby subvert our prudential self-control.[46]

A. The Analogy with Rawls's Four-Stage Sequence

In *Theory* §31, Rawls develops the "four-stage sequence," a procedure for generating his three principles of justice and then applying them to social

---

45. On deliberative rationality and the (thin) theory of the good more generally, see TJ chap. 7.
46. TJ 366. Rawls also considers OP choice to be collective rather than individual (as with MA_K), but as I argued in the final section of chapter 1, this turns out to be a distinction without a difference.

institutions. The four stages and their associated principles, rules, etc. are as follows:

1. *Original position* → three principles of justice: EL, FEO, and DP (justice as fairness)
2. *Constitutional convention* → constitution (system of government; bill of rights)
3. *Legislature* → social and economic policies (distributive justice; economic efficiency)
4. *Judiciary/Administration* → court and bureaucratic decisions (applying legislation)

As one descends through this sequence, rules generated at prior stages constrain the later ones; additionally, the veil of ignorance is gradually lifted (i.e., more information becomes available to the relevant parties), allowing decisions to be more finely tailored without a loss of impartiality, thanks to the accumulation of prior constraints. The four-stage sequence brings justice as fairness to earth; it transmits the moral authority of the original position to properly structured institutions of government in particular (though idealized) liberal-democratic societies.[47]

In this section, I am using an analogous *three*-stage sequence to generate the hierarchy of conceptions of autonomy that I proposed above. I say "analogous," because there are several key differences between my sequence and Rawls's. First, my unit of analysis is the individual rather than the closed society of *Theory*. Whereas Rawls was interested in applying principles of social justice to social institutions, my concern will be rules to guide individual behavior, ranging from the very general (moral law) to the highly specific and idiosyncratic (plans of self-development). Our concerns will intersect, of course, at the highest level of generality (moral law/principles of justice) but diverge thereafter due to the different functions of the theories. Second, even at this highest level of generality there is some divergence in our concerns, because Rawls is focused mostly on matters of right—in particular, on social justice—whereas I am interested in issues of both right and virtue, that is, a comprehensive (Kantian) moral doctrine.[48] Third, the three stages of my sequence are

---

47. TJ 171–76; also see TJ 221–22, where the principle of participation preserves the equal representation of the original position in lower stages.
48. See TJ 15; I discussed in chapter 1 his numerous gestures in *Theory* towards a Rawlsian doctrine of virtue.

interpenetrating and mutually supporting, as we shall see in this section and the next, whereas Rawls's four stages are wholly unidirectional: later stages may be instrumental to the earlier ones by bringing their rules to fruition but will never be constitutive of them. Finally, while Rawls's sequence is designed to support one level of community—specifically, a national political community—my sequence supports potentially overlapping communities at each stage, from universal moral community to communities of plans to communities of skills/capacities, a feature of the theory that will be discussed in the final section of the chapter. (See figure 6 for a preview.)

These differences should not be allowed to obscure the fundamental similarity between the two sequences, however, a similarity that goes well beyond shared mechanics (e.g., the veil of ignorance, prior constraints, etc.). In both Rawls's sequence and my own, the authority of any given stage derives directly from *its abstraction from contingent features of societies or persons,* respectively. As we move through either sequence, abstraction gradually lessens with the lifting of the veil of ignorance, as would authority were it not for the accumulation of constraints from prior stages to buttress it. This connection between abstraction from contingency and legislative authority is a distinctively Kantian insight: the ability to give law to oneself hinges upon freedom from the influence of "objects of volition," as noted in the subsection on moral autonomy above; the negative property of an autonomous will, independence from contingency, is the foundation for its positive property, self-legislative capacity. A residual difference between our approaches, however, which is related to the difference in unit of analysis, is that while in Rawls's sequence successive stages are addressed to the same audience—a national political community—in mine the audience shifts, from all rational beings (moral-autonomy stage) to particular individuals and perhaps those who share their plans in various lower-level communities (personal-autonomy and self-realization stages). Thus, the authority of lower stages in my sequence is of a different, less comprehensive kind than the authority of the highest stage, which is moral authority proper.[49]

---

49. My general approach in this section—which is to use at the individual level a theoretical apparatus designed for use at the societal level—is similar in concept to that of Schapiro (1999); cf. Plato (1991, 45 [369a]). I offer one more analogy between the two sequences, discussed further below: just as the principles of justice are applied differently in different societies via the four-stage sequence, so the moral law is realized in different ways in different plans of life via the three-stage sequence (e.g., through diverse individual projects of self-perfection and beneficence).

Note that in both my three-stage sequence and Rawls's four-stage sequence, information is withheld at higher stages so that deliberation there will not be heteronomously corrupted. Take my thief example from earlier: at the PA_K stage, the thief would be unaware of his feelings about theft; he would choose a character ideal on the basis of his higher-order preferences and indelible natural talents alone. If he were made aware of these feelings at this stage, it might illegitimately influence his judgment, because these feelings (so long as they are capable of being changed) are not the constituents of his life plan but its proper object, something to be brought into conformity with his deeper commitment to an occupation. This is a condition of PA_K. In similar fashion, the constitutional-convention stage of Rawls's four-stage sequence selects a scheme of government, bill of rights, etc. in ignorance of a society's *existing* legislation, lest that knowledge corrupt the convention's deliberations (e.g., by allowing framers to infer the class structure and perhaps their own class interests). Existing legislation may very well be inconsistent with the constitution that is chosen, but that is a reason to reform the laws, not change the constitution. Hiding information has costs in both cases—it disallows minute tailoring of plans/constitutions to individual/societal circumstances and is therefore likely to prompt disruptive, even painful reform efforts—but the accompanying benefits outweigh them: authenticity in the first case, impartiality in the second.

In the remainder of this section I will step through the three stages of my sequence, from the top of the autonomy hierarchy to the bottom. The agent (or his delegate) will be faced with different information and rule constraints at each stage and tasked with producing principles or plans relevant to that stage. In this way the entire sequence of conceptions of internal autonomy with their corresponding products will be derived. Because my interest at this point is in internal rather than external autonomy, I will temporarily assume away all external concerns, including both legal and economic resources.[50] In chapters 3 through 6, however, I will reintroduce them, showing how the

---

50. Another external concern that is set aside here is social context, e.g., whether others share my goals, values, etc. Rather than assuming these concerns away, even temporarily, one might imagine doing the following instead: each individual, when (hypothetically) moving through the sequence, generates a *set* of plans of life and self-development in which each plan is contingent upon a specific social context and suite of legal and economic resources; when the veil is lifted, the corresponding plan is implemented. Allowing such contingency planning behind the veil would still generate the same sequence of internal autonomy conceptions—at least at the level of abstraction at which I am here operating—so I will instead proceed by temporarily setting aside such concerns.

Kantian theory of internal autonomy developed here must be accompanied by a parallel theory of external autonomy, namely, justice as fairness, which guides both the creation and reform of political and economic institutions with the aim of sustaining this internal autonomy.

B. Deriving Autonomy, Stage 1 (α): Kantian Moral Autonomy—Full Veil

At this stage, the agent (or delegate) has no knowledge of individuating characteristics, including personal talents, tastes, values, and ends; racial, gender, and national identity; age; etc. In the absence of such information, he achieves independence from the contingent features of his person, that is, the negative property of an autonomous will. Consequently, any principles he offers will be universal in form, because in the absence of individuating characteristics he is effectively choosing for/as everyone. If the agent is also told that he is choosing principles for finite rational beings—that is, for needy physical beings who possess the capacities for both pure and empirical forms of practical reason—such principles will address the maxims (for the pursuit of subjective ends) that beings of this sort will invariably propose. The archetype of principles of this sort is, of course, the FUL formulation of The CI, which was presented in the subsection on moral autonomy above.

The moral law that emerges after tracing out all implications of the categorical imperative encompasses matters of both right and virtue. In his *Metaphysics of Morals*, Kant formulates the architectonic principles of right and virtue and catalogues the various duties that flow from them, be they duties relating to private and public right (*Rechtslehre*) or the many perfect and imperfect duties to self and others that constitute virtue (*Tugendlehre*), many of which were detailed in the previous section (e.g., natural self-perfection, beneficence).[51] These duties require, in the case of right, particular actions/omissions under threat of sanction and, in the case of virtue, the adoption of certain objective ends, the most general one being humanity as an end in itself.[52] The moral law and its associated duties of right and virtue regulate the agent in all subsequent stages of the three-stage sequence; they act as constraints on his choice of plans of life and self-development, by not only prescribing or

---

51. For the universal principles of right and virtue, see MM 6:230 and 6:395, respectively.
52. *Perfect* duties of virtue to self and others also require particular actions/omissions (e.g., the prohibition of suicide and ridicule), but their violation is not punishable. See MM 6:422–24, 467–68.

proscribing particular courses of action but also guiding him to adopt particular objective ends.

C. Deriving Autonomy, Stage 2 (β): Kantian Personal Autonomy—Partial Veil

In the second stage, the veil is incompletely lifted, revealing a subset of the agent's distinguishing characteristics. The characteristics revealed are those consistent with a certain character ideal of personal autonomy: specifically, the ideal of the perfectly rational and self-controlled person.[53] That is, any characteristics of the individual that would potentially hinder rationality and self-control—for example, impatience, extreme risk aversion, poor impulse control, lack of focus and resolve, and irrational habits of thought (e.g., giving priority to the most proximate desire)—remain hidden from him. What is revealed to him are two general categories of personal information (in addition, of course, to the impersonal knowledge of the moral law from Stage 1): *higher-order preferences* and *natural talents*. Higher-order preferences are, as Gerald Dworkin defines them, those qualities of individuals that "define their nature, give meaning and coherence to their lives" (G. Dworkin 1988, 20). They could include occupational preferences, character ideals, commitments to projects of assorted kinds, the imperatives of ethical and religious doctrines consistent with the moral law, etc.[54] Natural talents are exceptional abilities and/or disabilities—whether they are intellectual, emotional, or physical—that act as robust, indelible contributions to or constraints on life-plan formation and execution. Thus, the term "natural" refers not to the origin of talents (though such origins are often natural in the genetic sense) but rather to their permanence or ineradicability.

The ideal of the perfectly rational and self-controlled agent is implicit in most discussions of personal autonomy. As I noted earlier, Rawls emphasizes

---

53. Alfred Mele constructs just such a model of an ideally self-controlled person over the course of the first half of his book *Autonomous Agents* (2001, esp. 13, 27–29, 94, 118–22). Mele maintains that perfect self-control is a necessary but not sufficient condition for personal autonomy; for his sufficient conditions (for compatibilists and libertarians, respectively), see 187, 220.

54. For Kant, the only kind of religion consistent with the moral law is one that is purged of both superstition and enthusiasm, i.e., the beliefs that we can redeem ourselves before God with cultish rituals (e.g., prayers, lighting of votive candles, participation in the Eucharist, etc.) and that we can directly perceive divine influence (e.g., grace, miracles, portents), respectively. Kant says that "apart from a good life-conduct, anything which the human being supposes he can do to become well-pleasing to God is mere religious delusion and counterfeit service to God" (Rel 6:170–75).

the part that deliberative rationality plays, just as John Christman highlights the so-called competency conditions of rationality and self-control. Such competency is not the whole of personal autonomy, of course: authenticity and creative self-authorship are arguably necessary conditions as well, and the partial veil should be arranged to reveal information required to make these qualities effective (e.g., knowledge of the genealogy of higher-order preferences, so that those produced by conditioning or equally strong forms of socialization can be targeted for critical scrutiny in the service of authenticity).[55]

Personal autonomy is realized, of course, through an individualized plan of life, one that integrates our various preferences, ideals, and commitments into a coherent, mutually consistent whole, aided or hindered by our indelible capacities. Knowledge of our higher-order preferences and natural talents is sufficient for the production of such a plan, as the former element provides the aims and standards, the latter the (partial) means to meeting them. Lower-order dispositions and modifiable capacities, on the other hand, are best regarded not as components of our plan of life but as its objects: the former are to be cultivated (e.g., a love of Bach) or pruned (e.g., a taste for cigars) as they help or hinder our plans, respectively, and the latter are likewise to be shaped for the benefit of our higher, more comprehensive ends. As we shall see in the next subsection, this self-fashioning with respect to our intellectual, emotional, and physical capacities is the distinctive task of self-realization.

Just as a plan of life will constrain the agent or his delegate in the next stage of the three-stage sequence, by limiting and directing his self-development, so the moral law constrains him in this stage and the next. Its prohibitions and prescriptions of action and its obligatory objective ends do more than place rough limits on the shape of his life: they profoundly influence not only his self-conception but also the way he frames and orders his pursuits. He sees himself first and foremost as a moral agent, not a prudential agent, and he organizes his higher-order preferences (at least insofar as he is virtuous) to advance the objective end of humanity, whether it is through self-perfection or the practical love of others. To the degree that humanity as an end comes to be his architectonic higher-order preference, his personal autonomy and plan of life become not just a means to but constitutive of his moral autonomy and the moral law, respectively.

---

55. See Mele (2001, 122) on the possibility that perfectly self-controlled agents might lack personal autonomy due to "mind control" or "brainwashing." Also see my earlier example of the thief, where I suggested that his attachment to a life of crime might be due to strong family influences.

D. Deriving Autonomy, Stage 3 (γ): Kantian Self-Realization—No Veil

In this last stage of the three-stage sequence, the veil is completely lifted and the agent or his delegate has all personal information revealed to him, including information about his lower-order dispositions and modifiable capacities. He is now moved by an idea of personal perfection and begins to select sets of skills to develop, to choose techniques for developing them, and to allocate time and effort across them—in short, he starts creating a plan of self-development in full knowledge of his personal characteristics. The skills to be developed are of many potential kinds, including intellectual (e.g., deliberative rationality), physical (e.g., coordination), moral (e.g., ethical judgment), emotional (e.g., impulse control), etc. In addition, many of these skills are properly considered metaskills, that is, skills necessary for the development of skills; among these are patience, diligence, focus, resolve, and self-control more generally. Full knowledge of oneself is absolutely essential in order to develop these skills and metaskills: without a complete inventory of our preferences, habits, and capacities, we would have no idea where to focus our efforts, what internal resources were at our disposal, and which characteristics would be most likely to act as stumbling blocks to self-development.

This lack of abstraction from the contingent features of our person clearly suggests that the independent authority of this stage will be quite limited. As noted earlier about Kantian self-realization, our own perfection requires that we clear many internal bars (e.g., akrasia, myopia, and risk aversion), and this effort is analogous to efforts to overcome our selfish inclinations for the sake of the moral law or to bring order and coherence to our often disorganized preferences, values, and ends for the sake of a plan of life. It is, in short, emblematic of our autonomy, though in a more limited sense than our struggles for the moral law and a plan of life. Consequently, the authority of this stage will be mostly derivative, coming from the moral law and plan of life that were formulated in previous stages and that constrain this one.

These higher-order guides will determine most, perhaps nearly all, of the self-realizing activities pursued by our hypothetical individual. The moral law requires that (virtuous) agents take their own self-perfection, both natural and moral, to be an end, and plans of life specify the skills to be so perfected, whether as a means to those plans (e.g., test-taking skills as a route to college admission) or as a constituent element of them (e.g., professional skills that possess both instrumental and intrinsic value). To the extent that we embrace the ends of higher stages as our own when we engage in self-realizing activities—either by perfecting skills out of respect for humanity in ourselves or by developing them as constituent elements of our plan of life—our self-realization "folds back," so to speak, into higher stages, acquiring their enhanced authority. Otherwise, such activities have either secondary authority as instruments in the service of those higher ends or whatever very limited authority they possess in their own right *qua* self-realizing activities.

We have now progressed through the three stages of the sequence and have seen how the hierarchical relationship among the three Kantian conceptions can be elaborated and justified in a deductive fashion. Each stage can be seen as a more restricted, less authoritative version of the previous one. MA_K is the dominant conception, and its law compels all finite rational beings; its unrestricted authority derives from its abstraction from every contingent feature of persons. PA_K is the secondary conception, and its associated plan of life compels merely the person in question (or maybe those with similar characteristics) due to its lesser degree of abstraction, one that hides only knowledge of lower-order dispositions and modifiable capacities; its authority is augmented to the extent that it discharges duties of right and virtue and adopts humanity as an objective end. SR_K is the tertiary conception, and its associated plan of self-development has little independent authority due to the complete absence of abstraction; it gains authority through its service to and adoption of the superior ends of moral and personal autonomy. We can also see how these three stages are interpenetrating and mutually supporting: higher stages restrict and shape lower ones, while lower ones serve and can even be constitutive of higher ones.

V. The Feasibility of the Hierarchy: An Ideal Cognitive-Developmental Psychology

The first explication of hierarchy was a top-down derivation; this one, on the other hand, will be a construction from the bottom up, starting with SR_K and building to PA_K and then MA_K. It will tell an idealized story of our cognitive development and the gradual emergence of a moral sense. By means of the repeated application of a simple model of agency (figure 5), it will show how higher conceptions of autonomy grow out of lower ones until the highest conception, moral autonomy, is ultimately reached. Whereas the previous explanation presented lower conceptions of internal autonomy as restricted, more particularistic versions of higher ones, this one will see lower conceptions as psychological building blocks for higher ones, with moral autonomy as a kind of capstone.

This ideal cognitive-developmental psychology is simply a reconstruction of the one that Rawls himself presents in chapter 8 of *Theory*. Rawls creates there a three-stage theory of moral development in the rationalist tradition of Rousseau, Kant, and Mill, but most especially of Jean Piaget and Lawrence Kohlberg, who are renowned for their psychological stage theories (TJ 402–5). The purpose of Rawls's theory is to demonstrate how members of a well-ordered society might come to acquire a sense of justice, which is a necessary condition for the feasibility and stability of his overall theory of justice (TJ 398). His psychological theory is thus best considered a supplement to, not a substitute for, the defenses of justice as fairness presented in part 1 of *Theory:* he just wants to show that justice as fairness is psychologically viable; were it not, its recommendations would carry little weight. Similarly, one should view the justification of this section not as freestanding but rather as supplementary to the more orthodox, Kantian justification described in the previous section: it suggests the psychological feasibility of the hierarchy, showing how it could emerge through a highly idealized stage theory of cognitive development.

One might question the need to show the psychological feasibility of a conception of the person, such as the extended Kantian one proposed here. "Ought" implies "can," so if any moral theory proves incapable of being followed, it would appear to have no function outside the genre of utopian literature (CPrR 5:125). However, internal autonomy is not morality itself but rather its ground, as we shall see in chapters 3–6, so it is not obvious that the psychological infeasibility of the ground would invalidate the morality on which it is based. Still, if morality is relative to a conception of the person and if we cannot achieve or at least approach that conception, it is difficult to see what *relevance* that morality has to us, even if we are capable of obeying it. Recall that constructivists believe that any normative concept "refers schematically to the solution of a practical problem" and that our conception of ourselves (our "practical identity") "both embodies the problem and serves as an aid in finding the solution" (Korsgaard 1996b, 115; 2003, 99). Thus, if the extended Kantian conception of persons does not apply to us, because it is impossible for us, then the morality based upon it is in effect a solution to a problem we do not face; it would then be a valid morality for a different species of being with the right set of problems, but not for us. Showing the psychological (near) feasibility of the extended Kantian conception of persons is therefore a necessary condition of its relevance to us; if it is not psychologically feasible, then this entire book is an exercise in exomorality.

My reconstruction of Rawls's three-stage cognitive-developmental psychology (which is itself merely his interpretation of the stage theories of Piaget and Kohlberg, whom I will at times cite below) shares with his theory its three-stage form, which models the progress from lower to higher forms of moral understanding and culminates in a fully developed moral sense, that is, moral autonomy. My theory will differ from Rawls's, however, in two key ways. First, my three stages will focus on the evolution of the three associated forms of autonomy and the development of the complex set of skills necessary for their exercise. Whereas Rawls explores only moral autonomy and its gradual development over his three stages, I will additionally examine personal autonomy and self-realization (along with their preconditions), which serve as the building blocks of moral autonomy and with it constitute the extended Kantian conception of persons—a conception that is necessary to underwrite the three lexical priorities and the difference principle, as we shall see in chapters 3 through 6. Second, the ascent through my three ordered stages is internally driven by a simple agency model, as I will soon show. The same ascent through Rawls's stages, though, is externally driven by ever more inclusive forms of social interaction: his first stage (morality of authority) arises in the family, the second (morality of association) in extrafamilial groups like schools and sport teams, and the third (morality of principles) in the larger political society (see TJ §§70–72, 75). If external concerns like social context and legal/economic resources are to be set aside for the time being, as I indicated in the last section, then some internal motor such as the agency model will be needed to drive the ascent through the three stages of the autonomy hierarchy. By such means, I will be able to construct a theory of internal autonomy from the ground up, without reliance on external props that in effect assume what needs to be proven: namely, that there is an underlying and natural progression through psychological stages that well-ordered families, associations, and political societies are morally obligated to support.

These last comments raise several questions about the status of this reconstructed stage theory that I should address before proceeding. First, am I claiming that my three-stage theory is strictly necessary for the realization of the hierarchical Kantian conception of the person? No, as there may be alternative psychological paths to the same destination. I simply want to argue that *in principle* the Kantian conception could be realized in this way and that there is nothing in the psychological literature that absolutely rules out this possibility.[56] This raises a second question: is it really true that the cognitive-developmental literature does not rule out stage theories of this description or similar (such as those of Rawls, Piaget, and Kohlberg)? Rawls points out that the research in this area is "rather speculative," and scholarly opinion in the psychology community is in fact divided over the explanatory power of stage theories in general and those of Piaget and Kohlberg in particular (TJ 399, 403n6). These stage theories have been extensively tested, however, and I can fairly characterize the results as follows: although several adjustments have been required, these theories have held up reasonably well, and my own reconstruction of Rawls's stage theory takes into account the critical empirical findings.[57] Lastly, is my use of moral psychology different not only in letter but also in spirit from Rawls's own? No, because Rawls himself says that although "we want the psychological account of moral learning to be true and in accordance with existing knowledge," it will not have the precision of a scientific theory, nor will it be immune from other faults common to philosophical adaptations of such theories (TJ 404-5). Only if such defects deliver fatal blows not only to my particular stage theory but also to any other theory (stage or otherwise) that might support the extended Kantian conception of the person will its psychological feasibility be seriously called into question.

In the remainder of this section, I will first develop a rudimentary model of agency with four conceptual stages: *self-reflection, abstraction, self-criticism/*

---

56. For completeness, I should note that there may be alternative psychological paths to *different* destinations as well, i.e., to the realization of non-Kantian conceptions of the person. If the Kantian conception takes priority over others, as I will demonstrate by the end of this book, then these alternative paths should be avoided on moral grounds.

57. Laura Berk's highly influential textbook on child development examines the relevant literature (2003, 485-87, 490-93, 497-98). She says that "follow-up research indicates that Piaget's theory accurately describes the general direction of change in moral judgment [and also that] much evidence confirms Piaget's conclusion that moral understanding is supported by cognitive maturity, gradual release from adult control, and peer interaction," and she notes that "like Piaget's cognitive stages, Kohlberg's moral stages are loosely organized . . . [although] less mature moral reasoning is gradually replaced by more advanced thought" as people age (485-86, 491). Given these findings, my own three-stage theory will allow for the gradual development of autonomy as well as ongoing interaction among the different levels of autonomy; I make no counterfactual assumption of "clean breaks" or unidirectionality from one stage to the next. Stage theories have certainly come in for sharp criticism by Flanagan (1991, chap. 5) inter alia; Gilligan (1982) has offered an influential feminist critique of Kohlberg's theory in particular. It would be accurate to say, though, that these critiques have led at most to the modification rather than abandonment of existing stage theories.

distancing, and *self-discipline/self-control*. The model is iterative: each repetition of it moves the agent upward toward higher stages of autonomy, from self-realization to personal autonomy and finally to moral autonomy. I will (re)describe each of these stages along the way, showing how each one not only builds upon and incorporates previous ones but also marks the development of an increasingly sophisticated set of intellectual, physical, and emotional powers. In the chapter's final section, I will recap and discuss both of the justifications of hierarchy and describe how this hierarchy can support many potentially overlapping communities at each level or stage (figure 6).

A. An Iterative Model of Agency with Four Conceptual Stages

The first stage in my agency model is *self-reflection*. It implies the idea of consciousness and involves the treating of one's own actions, thoughts, and even identity as potential objects of investigation. Self-reflection is the essential starting point for conscious (as opposed to reflexive) efforts to affect these objects.[58] Though self-reflection may lead to theoretical questions (e.g., do I exist?), my focus here will be on practical questions. Three such questions will be of particular interest and will be carried through the following stages: (1) What am I doing? (action); (2) Why am I doing it? (thought/justification); and (3) Who am I? (identity).

The second stage, following closely on the heels of the first, is *abstraction*. To abstract is to go beyond the concrete and immediately sensible through analysis and synthesis. Abstraction helps us to address practical questions/topics, including the three just listed. For example:

1. Action
    a. Analysis: components of action (e.g., a golf swing)
    b. Synthesis: integration of movement (e.g., dribble to layup: score in basketball)
2. Thought/justification
    a. Analysis: stages of argument (e.g., premises of syllogism)
    b. Synthesis: coherence of images (e.g., splashes of color: mosaic)

---

58. Piaget writes about "reflective thought" too and links it to abstraction (my second stage): "with formal operations [i.e., reflective thought] there is even more than reality involved, since the world of the possible becomes available for construction and since thought becomes free from the real world" (1950, 151).

3. Identity
    a. Analysis: taxonomy of desire (e.g., dimensions of taste in literature)
    b. Synthesis: ideal of character (e.g., courage, patience, fortitude, etc.: heroism)

Analysis and synthesis allow us to see how our objects of investigation are composed of smaller elements and are themselves elements of larger objects. By revealing connections such as these, abstraction makes it easier to grasp what we are doing, why we are doing it, and who we are.

Self-reflection and abstraction prepare the way for the third stage: *self-criticism* and the *distancing* that often follows from it. When we reflect upon our actions, thoughts, and identity, we may become dissatisfied with them for any number of reasons: for example, they may fail to achieve certain ends, or meet certain standards, or be consistent with one another. To apply tests such as these to ourselves is to engage in self-criticism. When the application of these tests leads to disappointment, we may become alienated from the problematic elements and try to remove or distance ourselves from them. For example, when our actions fail to achieve an end, we are often frustrated by our ineptitude; when we find our arguments to be fallacious, we generally reject our erroneous reasoning; and when we discover that some of our desires are not consistent with one another (e.g., the desire for good health and the desire to smoke), we commonly become alienated from a subset of them.[59]

The distancing and alienation that frequently result from self-criticism directly motivate the fourth and final stage: *self-discipline* as a technique leading to *self-control* as a character trait. By disciplining ourselves through training, games, behavior modification, etc., we can hopefully achieve powers of self-mastery that will allow us to alter, eliminate, or simply avoid problematic elements of our actions, thoughts, and identity. For example, by practicing our movements we can achieve coordination and gracefulness (physical self-control); by exercising our minds with puzzles we can become more consistent and coherent reasoners (intellectual self-control); and by aversion therapy or similar techniques we can learn to resist and even eliminate untoward desires (affective self-control).[60]

---

59. Piaget similarly argues that "reflective thought" requires "a sort of detachment from one's own point of view or from the point of view of the moment" (1928, 71).
60. See Berk (2003, 502–6) for a review of the psychological literature on the development of self-control in children.

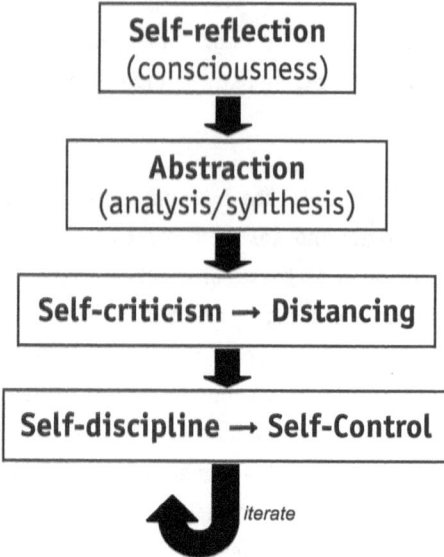

Fig. 5 Model of agency

Again, this four-stage model of agency, running from self-reflection to self-control, is an *iterative* one. That is, we repeat this process over time with diverse sets of issues; sometimes we revisit old concerns, and sometimes we break fresh ground. This iterative process is progressive, however, in that it takes place in a context of increasing self-control along numerous dimensions. Thus, when issues are revisited, they are typically revisited at ever higher levels of refinement or complexity: for example, a physical coordination issue raised at an early age (e.g., the ability to walk) will probably look very different from a coordination issue raised at a later age (e.g., the ability to play hopscotch). As we shall see, the progressivity of this iterative model of agency (summarized in figure 5) drives the ascent through the hierarchy of internal-autonomy conceptions, an ascent that culminates in moral autonomy.

B. Constructing Autonomy, Stage 3 (γ): Self-Realization

We begin with a person early in life, as he is moving through the initial iterations of the agency model presented above.[61] This person is largely amoral,

---

61. The phrase "early in life" does not necessarily mean "at a young age," though it usually will. "Early in life" means at a low level of development, immediately preceding Stage 3 (self-realization). The developmentally disadvantaged may not reach this point until later in life, if ever.

though responsive to immediate stimuli (e.g., corporal punishment) that enforce moral behavior. His ends are selected mostly by nature and to a lesser extent by his family and society; he engages in free choice with respect to means and perhaps intermediate ends but not to final ends, which are chosen for him. Finally, he enjoys a kind of "preprogrammed" pleasure when he attains his ends (e.g., sensual pleasure).[62]

During these initial iterations the person begins to develop a repertoire of basic skills and capacities that enable him to achieve his immediate, usually given ends. These include

1. basic motor skills: suppression of reflexes, hand-eye coordination, etc. (*physical self-control*)
2. rudimentary instrumental reasoning skills: discerning means to ends; seeing the stages needed to reach an objective; short-term planning abilities, including both strategy and tactics; etc. (*intellectual self-control*)
3. crude emotional and motivational skills: for example, the ability to overcome impatience through tricks of imagination (e.g., pretending that desirable objects are something else) or distraction games (e.g., counting or singing)[63] (*affective self-control*)

The development of such skills marks the *initial* entry of the person into the self-realization stage of the hierarchy. His attainment of various useful capacities and metacapacities not only makes his immediate ends more reachable but also lays the foundation for developing ever more refined and complex capacities in the future, including whole classes of capacities that are at first mostly undeveloped (e.g., moral capacities).

The reason I highlighted the word "initial" above is to prevent a likely misunderstanding: even as the iterations of the agency model continue and the person advances to ever higher levels of the autonomy-conception hierarchy, he revisits the self-realization stage throughout this climb to develop the complex and varied skills necessary to operate at higher stages. The system I am envisioning is *epicyclic* in nature: a continuous cycling of the agency model generates an ascent of the autonomy-conception hierarchy that is itself cyclic,

---

62. Cf. Rawls's "Morality of Authority" (TJ §70). Also see Berk (2003, 485, 488–89) on Piaget's and Kohlberg's stages of "heteronomous" and "preconventional" morality, respectively.
63. On children's techniques for delaying gratification, see Mischel (1996) and Mischel and Baker (1975).

as lower stages are constantly revisited from higher ones. In other words, movement in the hierarchy is not unidirectional, because lower stages continue to see developmental activity even as higher stages are achieved; moreover, that very developmental activity makes higher stages reachable.

A mountaineering analogy may be helpful at this point. Think of a mountain climber as a continuously cycling agency model, moving through an iterative process of eating, sleeping, etc. The climber's ultimate goal is to scale a peak like Mount Everest, and in order to do this he must establish not only base camps but also advance camps at which he can acclimate himself to the lower air pressure and temperature at higher elevations. These camps are like the stages in our hierarchy, as he moves back and forth between higher camps (where he acclimates himself) and lower camps (where he restocks supplies, rests, and trains), a process that culminates in reaching the peak. The metaphor is inexact, of course: it fails to capture the qualitative differences among the stages in the autonomy-conception hierarchy, and it suggests incorrectly that the process ends when moral autonomy is first achieved. Still, it does manage to capture many of the complexities of the proposed epicyclic system.

C. Constructing Autonomy, Stage 2 (β): Personal Autonomy

Now observe this same person later in life. He is largely motivated by an instrumental, conventional morality, one that is sensitive to the long-term consequences of transgression on his reputation and plan of life. His ends, even his final ones, are now subject to autonomous revision, rejection, and adherence; though they may still be strongly influenced by his family and society, they are no longer insulated from the force of self-criticism. Finally, he has acquired the ability to take refined pleasure (e.g., pride) in the achievement of his overall plans.[64]

This transformation of the person from a clever animal to a personally autonomous agent is made possible through the development of certain higher-order skills and capacities, especially cognitive ones. They include

1. the ability to reason about final ends, values, ideals, etc. (*noninstrumental reasoning*)

---

64. Cf. Rawls's "Morality of Association" (TJ §71). Also see Berk (2003, 484–85, 489) on Piaget's and Kohlberg's stages of "autonomous" and "conventional" morality, respectively.

2. the ability to develop both a plan of life and associated conception-dependent desires (e.g., the desire to be a self-authoring agent); this ability includes powers of integration, cultivation, and culling as applied to the higher-order preferences just listed[65] (*advanced managerial and planning skills*)
3. an effective hierarchy of motivators, that is, the ability to restrain lower-order preferences for the sake of higher ones, such as those involving projects, occupations, or character ideals; this hierarchy may entail the use of various tricks (e.g., giving ourselves rewards for completing various stages of projects) to overcome our natural inertial tendencies, including laziness and myopia (*advanced self-discipline and self-control*)

Such developmental activity at the self-realization stage enables the creative self-authorship of the personal-autonomy stage and partially relaxes the holds of nature, family, and society. The activities these skills make possible—integration of higher-order desires, long-range planning, and sophisticated forms of self-control—constitute a higher, more demanding conception of autonomy than self-realization.

As we saw earlier, however, skills and capacities developed at the self-realization stage can be much more than mere means to formulating and carrying out a plan of life; they can also be the constituent elements of such a plan. The development of professional skills and athletic abilities, for example, can be an important part of a plan of life as well as a means to financial security and status, respectively. That is, such development can be an end in itself, even pursued solely for its own sake. Just as personal autonomy and its associated plan of life limit and direct self-realization, so self-realization can be a means to and even constitutive of personal autonomy. In this way lower stages in the hierarchy become building blocks for higher ones.

Like the self-realization stage, the personal-autonomy stage will be revisited for a variety of reasons. Future iterations of the agency model, for instance, will raise new problems for one's current plan of life (including dissatisfaction with one's identity) and force revisions of it. Better understanding of one's moral obligations in the moral-autonomy stage, whether regarding duties of right or duties of virtue, may necessitate changes in one's plans as well. There could also be instances of "feedback," where a skill initially developed as a

---

65. See Rawls's discussion of conception-dependent desires at PL 83–85.

mere means to a plan of life grows to be a constituent element of it, leading to corresponding changes in one's plan of life and even reinforcing efforts to develop the skill in question. All of these possibilities illustrate the idea of an epicyclic system, where ascent of the hierarchy (driven by a forever-cycling agency model) occurs simultaneously with (re)visits to lower levels and further developmental activity there.

D. Constructing Autonomy, Stage 1 (α): Kantian Moral Autonomy

Consider this person still later. His reasoning and action are now morally autonomous, and he is able to criticize not just his own plan of life and its associated conception-dependent desires but even conventional morality itself. His ends are now circumscribed by a self-legislated moral law, one including objective rules and objective ends, right and virtue. Just as his plan of life brought lower-order desires to heel for the sake of higher-order ones, so the moral law makes his higher-order desires subordinate to a highest-order conception-dependent desire: the desire to act according to those principles that are, as Rawls put it, "the most adequate possible expression of his nature as a free and equal rational being" (TJ 222, 417). Associated with this highest-order desire are a rightful pride in moral freedom, respect for humanity and the moral law, and shame in slavery to either natural desires or convention.[66]

This further transformation of the person from a self-authoring prudential agent to a self-legislating rational being is made possible by the cultivation of the most complex and demanding skills a person can possess, including

1. a greatly refined faculty for self-criticism with respect to ends, values, desires, etc. that makes possible perfect distancing (if only in thought), that is, an ability to imagine ourselves shorn of all of our individuating characteristics and to consider what kind of law would be generated from this Archimedean point of pure practical reason (*perfect distancing and legislative capacity*)
2. an ability to recognize and submit to the authority of this autonomous law, to see that in obeying it we liberate ourselves fully from mere determination by genetic, familial, and social forces and take direction

---

66. Cf. Rawls's "Morality of Principles" (TJ §72). Also see Berk (2003, 489–90) on Kohlberg's stages of "principled" or "postconventional" morality.

instead from the highest, best part of ourselves (*rational respect and obedience*)
3. highly developed intellectual and emotional self-control: the internalization of self-given norms, a capacity for impartiality and even a cool detachment from our own interests, a facility at using certain mental tricks (e.g., imagining ourselves in the position of another person or of a Smithian "impartial spectator") to gain such detachment, etc. (*moral self-discipline and self-control*)

As suggested earlier, the achievement of moral autonomy is not a once-and-for-all affair: we must continually refine and reinforce these skills and capacities by revisiting the self-realization stage in order to perfect our moral autonomy, a goal too demanding perhaps to be attained in this life.[67]

The task of morally perfecting ourselves demands returns to the personal-autonomy stage as well. As we become more morally autonomous, we will start to recognize that elements of our plan of life are inconsistent with the moral law (e.g., because they use subtle forms of coercion or deception) and must therefore be eliminated or modified. Moreover, as our admiration for moral law deepens and our respect for humanity grows, we will reconceive many of the elements of our plan of life. For example, while we might continue on the same career path as we develop moral autonomy, our reasons for staying on it will extend beyond income, status, and other subjective reasons to include the objective reason of self-perfection. When we reorient our life plan in this way, we elevate it from a mere instrument of the moral law (which it is if it only conforms to it outwardly) to an integral part of it as well as an instantiation of virtue.

VI. Conclusion: A Hierarchy of Communities

Figure 6 depicts the justificatory strategies of sections IV and V, with Roman numerals standing for distinct individuals, Greek letters for different stages of the hierarchy, and two-way arrows for the justificatory strategies themselves. When outward-pointing, the arrows represent the three-stage sequence described in section IV: by raising Rawls's veil of ignorance (i.e., by abstracting

---

67. On immortality as a postulate of pure practical reason, see CPrR 5:122–24.

less from the contingent features of persons), we can derive the lower stages of the hierarchy from the higher ones while simultaneously generating their associated rules and plans. When inward-pointing, they represent the ideal cognitive-developmental psychology of section V: the three stages are here part of an epicyclic system, where the iterations of an agency model (figure 5) allow ever higher stages of the hierarchy to be reached—though not without repeated visits to lower stages. I have combined these inward- and outward-pointing arrows into two-way arrows to emphasize that the three stages of the hierarchy are both interpenetrating and mutually supporting: higher stages provide abstract models for the lower ones, constrain and guide their development, and at times incorporate them; lower stages assist the higher ones by serving as building blocks for them, instantiating their purposes, and on occasion becoming part of them.

I noted toward the beginning of section IV that this hierarchy of autonomy conceptions supports potentially overlapping communities at each stage. The highest stage, however—moral autonomy—supports one and only one universal, comprehensive community of all finite rational beings. This community unites humanity under a single moral law, which provides a basis for all valid systems of justice and ethics.[68] As Kant says, existing political communities (e.g., nation-states) and ethical communities (e.g., religious congregations) are the incomplete realizations of the universal political and ethical communities foretold by the moral law.[69] Humanity has a duty to work toward such universal communities; otherwise, our current institutions will become the endpoints rather than the way stations of social evolution (Taylor 2010).

The second stage, personal autonomy, supports many overlapping communities of plans. Individuals may belong to a host of educational, philanthropic, recreational, religious, and ethnic organizations whose members share common sets of ends, projects, values, character ideals, etc. and whose memberships may intersect in various ways. Unlike the universal political and ethical communities toward which all human beings must labor, membership in communities

---

68. Similarly, Cicero maintains that "true law is right reason in agreement with nature; it is of universal application, unchanging and everlasting; it summons to duty by its commands, and averts from wrongdoing by its prohibitions. We cannot be freed from its obligations by senate or people, and we need not look outside ourselves for an expounder or an interpreter of it. And there will not be different laws at Rome and at Athens, or different laws now and in the future, but one eternal and unchangeable law will be valid for all nations and all times" (1994, 211). For a discussion of Stoic influence on Kant, see Nussbaum (1997).

69. On universal political community, see MM 6:352–55; on universal ethical community, see Rel 6:115–24.

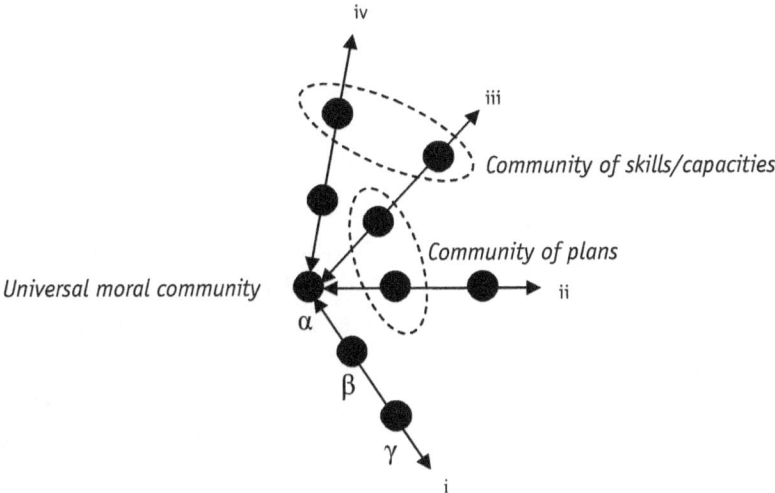

Fig. 6 Hierarchy of communities

of plans is strictly discretionary, though our duties of virtue (such as self-perfection and the practical love of others) are often best discharged in such settings. When such community adopts and is motivated by moral ends (e.g., true religious community, whose purpose is the ethical improvement of its congregants), it can become not just a means to but a part of universal moral community.[70]

The third stage, self-realization, also supports many intersecting communities of skills and capacities. Membership is similarly discretionary, but their purview is generally narrower; some examples are test-prep organizations (intellectual capacities), therapy groups (emotional skills), and workout clubs (physical abilities). When the skills such organizations support are not just means to but constitutive of their members' plans of life (e.g., karate clubs), they effectively become communities of plans, bridging the two lower levels of community; when the skills are pursued for objective reasons (e.g., physical self-perfection), they may bridge all three.

I emphasize the hierarchy's ability to support these different levels of community because the focus until now has been unrelentingly individualistic. Perhaps not many people would argue that a methodological and normative

---

70. Rel 6:100–102. How should liberal-democratic nations be classified? They share some traits of universal political community (e.g., republicanism, partial submission to international norms), but their exclusivity and reliance upon nonuniversal bonds of solidarity (e.g., shared language and political history) make them like communities of plans.

individualism is intrinsically hostile to community. Here at any rate it underwrites it, even motivates it, as cooperation with others who share our values and ends is one condition of the effective exercise of autonomy. We can now begin to see why a full theory of autonomy will have to address external conceptions of autonomy as well (e.g., rights to free association and speech), as such conceptions provide a framework for some communities to flourish and rule out other kinds of community entirely (e.g., totalitarian political communities). The next four chapters, in fact, will demonstrate how the lexical priorities of right, liberty, and FEO and the DP provide the necessary external conditions for the development and exercise of the three hierarchically ordered forms of autonomy that together constitute the extended Kantian conception of the person. These external, institutionalized forms of autonomy also underwrite a special kind of liberal political community, one with necessarily universal aspirations, as I shall argue in the conclusion to the book.

3

The Priorities of Right and Political Liberty

I. Introduction

The priority of the right over the good is a central feature of Rawls's doctrine of right and one of its most Kantian elements. Because it has been the target of strong criticism, especially by communitarians, I will briefly review Rawls's definition and justification of it, arguing that once we augment Rawls's conception of the first moral power so that it includes a capacity for moral autonomy, the priority of right flows readily from it (see, e.g., Sandel 1982). Such an extension is both required by the structure of Rawls's constructivism and implied by a Kantian understanding of reasonableness.

The major focus of this chapter, however, will be the priority of political liberty. The next chapter, which examines the priority of other basic liberties, might seem a more natural place for a discussion of it, as Rawls himself defends basic liberties as a group and leaves them unranked within the first principle. Nevertheless, I have chosen to discuss political liberty and its priority together with the priority of right because both, I shall argue, are grounded in our reasonableness, whereas the other basic liberties and their priority are grounded in our rationality. Rawls appears to recognize this foundational difference in *Political Liberalism* but fails to see its implications. I will reconstruct Rawls's defense of the intrinsic good and lexical priority of political liberty as an institutional expression of our moral autonomy in the domain of right. His defense as it currently stands is radically incomplete, and his other, predominantly instrumental defenses are seriously and probably irremediably flawed.

One striking implication of defending political liberty's priority on these grounds is the hierarchical relationship thereby created between the political and civil liberties, with the former taking lexical priority over the latter. This result straightforwardly contradicts Rawls's claim that these two classes of basic liberties are "of equal weight . . . with neither externally imposed on the other," so the account I propose below is frankly revisionist (PL 412). I intend to show, however, that this suggested hierarchical relationship is the only defensible interpretation of Rawls's theory, being directly implied by the similar relationship between the reasonable and the rational, that is, between the two conceptions of moral and personal autonomy discussed in the previous chapter.

II. The Priority of the Right over the Good

A. Definition

Before offering a definition of the priority of right, I need to explain Rawls's distinction between teleological and deontological moral theories. He defines *teleological* theories as those in which "the good is defined independently from the right, and then the right is defined as that which maximizes the good" (TJ 21–22). The good that teleological theories attempt to maximize can take many different forms: if it is understood as "the realization of excellence in the various forms of culture," then the theory is perfectionist; if it is understood as pleasure, then it is hedonistic; etc.[1] In short, there are at least as many teleological theories as there are maximizable conceptions of the good, including efficiency (allocative and/or productive), welfare, piety, glory, etc. However the good is understood, though, teleological moral theories treat right and principles of justice as mere tools to maximize it. Whatever moral value they have is derivative, and they may therefore be violated when doing so would better promote the good than obedience would.[2]

Rawls defines a *deontological* theory, on the other hand, simply as a nonteleological theory, that is, "one that either does not specify the good independently of the right, or does not interpret the right as maximizing the good. . . . Justice as fairness is a deontological theory in the second way" because it does not maximize the good but does define it independently of the right (e.g.,

---

1. TJ 22. For Rawls's critiques of the teleological theories of utilitarianism and perfectionism, see TJ §§5–6, 27–28, 30 and TJ §50, respectively.

2. I will skip over many well-known complications here, including the fact that developing a very strong disposition to obey rules of justice may best promote the good, even if it leads one to obey rules in certain cases where violation would have been ideal. For a discussion of this and related issues in the utilitarian context, see Smart and Williams (1973, 42–57).

individual conceptions of the good are defined independently from the right, though they must subordinate themselves to it and may even incorporate it).[3] Many kinds of deontological theories exist (e.g., Rossian intuitionism), but justice as fairness is an especially extreme form in terms of its treatment of the good.[4] As Rawls notes, justice as fairness does not merely fail to maximize the good but completely subordinates it to the right: "In justice as fairness one does not take men's propensities and inclinations as given, whatever they are, and then seek the best way to fulfill them. Rather, their desires and aspirations are restricted from the outset by the principles of justice which specify the boundaries that men's systems of ends must respect. We can express this by saying that in justice as fairness *the concept of the right is prior to that of the good*. . . . The priority of justice is accounted for, in part, by holding that the interests requiring the violation of justice have no value. Having no merit in the first place, they cannot override its claims" (TJ 27–28; cf. KCMT 319; PL 173–76, 195–200). Unlike teleological moral theories, justice as fairness does not allow the principles of justice to be overridden for the sake of efficiency, welfare, perfection, etc.; in short, right takes lexical priority over the good—however it is defined—in Rawls's deontological theory.

As Rawls notes, such priority is a distinctive feature of *Kantian* deontological theories (KCMT 317, 319; TJ 28n16). In a striking passage of the second *Critique,* Kant argues that the moral duties legislated by our own pure practical reason must serve as "the supreme condition" of our prudential pursuit of the good (understood here as happiness), lest we remain mired in "mere animality" (CPrR 5:61–62; cf. T&P 2:282n). This priority is also implied by what Rawls has called the "lexical priority . . . of a good will" in Kant's theory: as the good will is simply a will in conformity with and motivated by a self-legislated and universal moral law, its priority over other, contingent goods (e.g., "talents of mind" like wit, "qualities of temperament" like courage, "gifts of nature" like happiness, complements to a good will such as moderation and self-control, etc.) implies the priority of morality.[5] As noted in the first chapter, Kant's conception of morality includes both the legal and the ethical, so his characterization of morality as the "supreme condition" constraining our pursuit of happiness entails the priority of right (as well as virtue) over the good (MM 6:205, 230, 395).

---

3. TJ 26. On the last parenthetical point, see my chapter 1 discussion of the so-called congruence argument as well as S. Freeman (2007a, 71–72).

4. See Rawls's discussion of intuitionism in TJ §7, esp. pp. 35–36.

5. LHMP 156; GMM 4:393–94, 402. I return to this point below when discussing the priority of right's justification.

Before moving on to justification of the priority of right, I should point out that this rule already includes Rawls's "priority of justice over efficiency and welfare," which he separately defines in the final statement of his two principles of justice: "the second principle of justice [i.e., FEO plus DP] is lexically prior to the principle of efficiency and to that of maximizing the sum of advantages" (TJ 266). If right is lexically prior to the good, then by implication the principles of right are prior to efficiency and welfare, which are just two conceptions of the good. Rawls makes this point himself on a different occasion: "the principles of justice . . . are lexically prior . . . to claims of the good. This means, among other things, that the principles of justice . . . cannot . . . be overridden by considerations of efficiency and a greater net balance of social well-being" (KCMT 319). Therefore, there is one priority rule too many in justice as fairness, and the priority of justice over efficiency and welfare should be dropped as superfluous.

B. Justification

The priority of right is relatively simple to justify within the context of Rawls's Kantian-constructivist theory. Begin with the first moral power, reasonableness, which is the capacity for a "sense of justice," that is, "the capacity to understand, to apply and to act from (and not merely in accordance with) the principles of justice," at least to a "certain minimum degree" (TJ 442; KCMT 312; cf. PL 19). As Rawls suggests, his conception of moral autonomy, which he calls "full autonomy," incorporates this understanding of reasonableness: "by affirming the first principles that would be adopted in [the OP] and by publicly recognizing the way in which they would be agreed to, *as well as by acting from these principles as their sense of justice dictates* . . . citizens' full autonomy is achieved."[6] I argued in chapter 1 that Rawls's conception of reasonableness should be enlarged to include this capacity for (Rawlsian) moral autonomy. The main reason for this extension is as follows: unless this capacity is part of Rawls's conception of moral persons, of which the OP parties are aware via their highest- and higher-order interests, they will be unable to conceive of its realization in the well-ordered society made possible by their choice

---

6. KCMT 315 (emphasis added). Kant's conception of moral autonomy incorporates Rawls's own conception in turn, because it is both broader (including virtue as well as right) and higher order (generating a metaprinciple of morality, The CI, rather than principles of morality themselves). See my chapter 1 discussion of these points.

of principles of justice; also, their highest-order interest in the development and exercise of the first moral power must include an interest in realizing self-legislation, as only if their highest-order interest is augmented in this way will OP parties be suitably motivated to select political principles (e.g., the democratic principle of equal political participation) that will enable citizens to attain full autonomy.[7] Rawls seems to endorse this reading himself when he says that "the sense of justice [is] the desire to act in accordance with the principles *that would be chosen in the original position*" (TJ 275; emphasis added).

Another way to spot the need for an expanded conception of reasonableness is to see that for a Kantian, at least, acting reasonably is simply the same as acting for the sake of autonomous moral law—a point to which Rawls himself alludes in §86 of *Theory*. As Kant shows in section I of the *Groundwork*, to act reasonably is to act with a good will, that is, to act not only in conformity with duty but also for the sake of duty or with duty as the immediate motivation. Kant goes on to declare, however, that to act strictly from duty is to act without regard either to any motives other than duty itself or to any ends that the discharge of duty might advance. This leaves nothing but the *form* of duty, which is law-like; thus, Kant says that "duty is the necessity of an action from respect for law" (GMM 4:400). To what kind of law, then, is duty linked? Rather telegraphically, Kant says, "Since I have deprived the will of **every impulse that could arise for it from obeying some law,** nothing is left but the conformity of actions as such with universal law, which alone is to serve the will as its principle, that is, *I ought never to act except in such a way that I could also will that my maxim should become a universal law.* Here mere conformity to law as such, **without having as its basis some law determined for certain actions,** is what serves the will as its principle, and must so serve it, if duty is not to be everywhere an empty delusion and a chimerical concept" (GMM 4:402; emphasis added). The move to FUL is too quick here, but we can unpack Kant's meaning. Kant seems to associate an "impulse" (i.e., inclination) to obey a law only with *particular* laws for *particular* actions. For example, we might discharge a duty of beneficence, which directs us to aid people in need, out of a sympathetic impulse. Since we are abstracting from all such inclinations, however, we are also (by implication) abstracting from all *particularity* in law, and a law that is in no way particular must be universal. But what does it mean for an agent with a good will, who chooses all of his maxims "from duty,"

---

7. On Rawls's principle of participation and its limits, see TJ §§36–37. I will elaborate on this claim below.

to choose such maxims consistent with universal law as such? If we think of maxims themselves as being (subjective) laws, and universality as being a characteristic, then a conscientious agent must choose maxims that are fit to be universal laws—but this is simply FUL. For Kant, therefore, to act reasonably (i.e., with a good will) is to test proposed maxims using FUL.

As we saw in chapter 1, however, to adopt such a principle and to use it for screening maxims is to attain the highest form of moral autonomy: all other imperatives involve residual heteronomy (by including the motives, ends, and other characteristics of persons and even the subject matter of particular laws), but The CI in all its formulations abstracts away from these, so agents attain full moral autonomy by making it determinative in their choices. Rawls himself makes reference to this Kantian connection between reasonableness and autonomy: "the sense of justice . . . reveals what the person is, and to compromise it is not to achieve for the self free reign but to give way to the contingencies and accidents of the world" (TJ 503). That is, the first moral power is emblematic of our will's ability to "be efficient independently of alien causes *determining* it," which in conjunction with the objective lawfulness of all causality yields autonomy of the will.[8] Expanding the definition of reasonableness to encompass Rawlsian moral autonomy is therefore required in a Kantian understanding of the first moral power, which Rawls manifestly adopts, at least during what I earlier called his "Kantian period."[9]

Now that I have expanded reasonableness to encompass Rawlsian moral autonomy (i.e., full autonomy), we can readily show that this capacity implies the priority of the right over the good. Just as for Kant the morally autonomous will is governed first and foremost (though not exclusively, of course) by The CI, so for Rawls the fully autonomous citizen is governed first and foremost by principles of justice. Full autonomy requires that we act upon those principles we would choose in a situation (namely, the OP) that reflects our freedom from social, natural, and fortuitous contingencies. To compromise these principles of right for the sake of our plan of life, plan of self-development, or lower-order desires would be to sacrifice our moral autonomy for what is properly

---

8. GMM 4:446. For further discussion, see chapter 1.
9. Evidence for this claim can be found throughout Rawls's writings of this period, especially in *Theory* §40 ("The Kantian Interpretation of Justice as Fairness"), where he maintains that "by *acting from* these [autonomous political] principles persons express their nature as free and equal rational beings. . . . For to express one's nature as a being of a particular kind is to act on the principles that would be chosen if this nature were the decisive determining element" (TJ 222; emphasis added).

subordinate—namely lesser conceptions of autonomy (personal autonomy or self-realization) or purely heteronomous impulses. Rawls expresses this sentiment well in the following passage from *Theory* §86: "The desire to express our nature as a free and equal rational being can be fulfilled only by acting on the principles of right and justice as having first priority. . . . It is acting from this precedence that expresses our freedom from contingency and happenstance. Therefore in order to realize our nature we have no alternative but to plan to preserve our sense of justice as governing all other aims. This sentiment cannot be fulfilled if it is compromised and balanced against other ends as but one desire among the rest. It is a desire to conduct oneself in a certain way above all else, a striving that contains within itself its own priority" (TJ 503). Notice the key role played here by Rawls's Kantian conception of the person: the lexical priority of right hinges on his particular understanding of "our nature," which is that of a "free and equal rational being" who can achieve self-legislation only by abstracting away from "contingency and happenstance" in his selection of principles of justice. Whether such a radical conception of the person is implicit in our democratic culture or rather in our moral consciousness (as a result of pure practical reason, as Kant would have it) is a question to which I will return in part 3.

III. The Priority of Political Liberty

A. Definition

Rawls says that "the principle of equal liberty, when applied to the political procedure defined by the constitution, I shall refer to as the principle of (equal) political participation. It requires that all citizens are to have an equal right to take part in, and to determine the outcome of, the constitutional process that establishes the laws with which they are to comply" (TJ 194). A right to equal political participation is effected through a set of basic liberties, both core and auxiliary, with the protection of the former's "fair value." The core liberties are the rights to *vote* and *hold public office:* each citizen is to have one vote equal in weight to that of others (which requires certain institutional features, such as electoral districts with equal numbers of electors), and he must have at least formally equal access to state elective offices, membership in political parties, positions in the civil service, etc. (TJ 53, 196). The auxiliary liberties are those that are needed to support the core political liberties, without which their exercise would be ineffective and perhaps even futile: these include the rights to *free political speech and assembly*, which enable citizens to persuade, plan, and mobilize for political purposes (PL 309, 340–63). Finally, the core political liberties need to have their "fair value" guaranteed: formal equality is inadequate if citizens are to have a genuinely equal chance to "determine the outcome of . . . the constitutional process that establishes the laws." The concept of fair equality of opportunity must therefore be incorporated into Rawls's first principle of justice in order to assure that "those similarly endowed and motivated [will] have roughly the same chance of attaining positions of *political* authority irrespective of their economic and social class."[10] Doing this will involve, inter alia, the public financing of political parties and campaigns, public support for political debate (e.g., subsidies for both political advertising and public-affairs programming), and state efforts to prevent the concentration of property and wealth, all of which are needed to preserve a level political playing field and prevent the democratic political process from being hijacked by powerful special interests.[11]

Before discussing the priority of these political liberties, I should point out that Rawls has been strongly criticized (e.g., by Jürgen Habermas) for making the political liberties subordinate to other liberties—including liberty of conscience and freedom of the person—which are thereby "withdrawn from the reach of democratic self-legislation" (Habermas 1995, 129). As I will show in more detail below, Rawls already privileges the political liberties in several ways vis-à-vis the civil liberties (e.g., by protecting their "fair value" and emphasizing their "distinctive place" among the basic liberties), contra Habermas (PL 327). More fundamentally, however, Rawls emphasizes that constitutional guards on the civil liberties are themselves a product of "democratic self-legislation" via the "people's constituent power" to create and reform constitutions; once the structure of Rawls's four-stage sequence is taken into account,

---

10. TJ 197. Only the fair value of the core political liberties is protected; other liberties are not treated in this "special way" (PL 327). I will discuss the reasons for this treatment—and whether it goes far enough—later in the chapter.

11. TJ 198–99. Notice how protecting the fair value of core political liberties greatly complicates the structure of justice as fairness. For example, socioeconomic concerns that were seemingly relegated to the second principle are now seen to be addressed (at least in part) by the first principle. Moreover, Rawls argues that some auxiliary political liberties such as free political speech may need to be restricted (or "regulated," to be more precise) in order to preserve the fair value of the core political liberties (PL 356–63).

one can see that "the liberties of the moderns are subject to the constituent will of the people" by means of the popular ratification of prior restraints on regular legislation (e.g., the Bill of Rights).[12] Liberal constitutionalism is not necessarily in tension with popular sovereignty, at least so long as constitutions themselves require democratic endorsement.

The priority of the political liberties, like all other priorities in justice as fairness, is of the strongest kind: lexical (or lexicographic) priority. (See the appendix to this chapter for a primer on lexical priority.) At least under ideal conditions, political liberty cannot be traded off for the sake of FEO, DP, or even (as I shall argue below) civil liberties including liberty of conscience, freedom of the person, freedom of nonpolitical speech and press, etc., regardless of the rate of exchange.[13] Political liberties can only be restricted or regulated for internal reasons, including the protection of political liberty itself. For example, *unequal voting rights* might be justifiable if such inequality better protected the other political liberties of those with fewer voting rights. One way to flesh out this example is as follows: suppose that education were strongly correlated with civil libertarianism and that plural voting based on education were adopted (i.e., more education, more votes); this could lead to a better protection of everyone's *political* speech and association rights, and because these rights are key supports for the core political liberties, those with fewer votes might be net gainers *even in terms of their political liberty*.[14] Similarly, a *lesser extent of political liberty* (for example, in the legislative stage through constitutional constraints such as the division of powers, judicial review, a written bill of rights, etc.) may protect political liberty itself, especially if unmitigated majoritarianism can undermine itself and become a threat to the very practice of democracy.[15] Only for these reasons, and not for reasons associated

---

12. PL 403-9. Much hinges, of course, on the nature of the ratification procedure that imposes such constraints, which must itself be sufficiently democratic—as Rawls himself recognizes (PL 406, 433-34). For an explanation of Rawls's four-stage sequence, see TJ §31.

13. Many complications arise here, to which I will return below. For example, certain facets of freedom of the person can reasonably be seen as auxiliary political liberties: without basic protections from arbitrary arrest, for instance, one's ability to participate in politics might be crippled—especially if one's political opponents can arrange such arrests. However, other facets of freedom of the person (e.g., the right to engage in consensual sexual activity) are much more difficult to construe in this way.

14. See TJ 203-5. I am not arguing that such an example is plausible, but only that it has the *right form* to excuse the inequality, as its justification is strictly internal to political liberty.

15. For example, the cycle of regimes in book 8 of Plato's *Republic* suggests that direct, majoritarian democracy has a tendency to devolve into tyranny (1991, 240-49 [562a-569c, esp. 563d-e and 566e]). Cf. TJ 197, 200-203.

with merely civil liberties, FEO, or DP, can political liberty be regulated, restricted, or sacrificed.[16]

B. Justification

Because lexical priority is such a strong form of priority—indeed, it is the strongest form possible—its justification is especially difficult. In this section, I will show that some of Rawls's arguments for political liberty and its lexical priority fail (either in whole or in part) because of a common error: Rawls's belief that once he has shown the instrumental value of political liberties for some essential purpose (e.g., guaranteeing political stability), he has automatically shown the reason for their lexical priority. I will hereafter refer to this belief—that the *lexical* priority of the political liberties can be inferred from the *high* priority of interests they serve—as the "inference fallacy." Other arguments fail because, although the interest in question has the needed priority, political liberties are not *requisite* for its protection but merely *strongly contributory* towards it.

Lexical priority is such a stringent condition that a special form of justification will turn out to be necessary for its defense. However, one of Rawls's arguments for the intrinsic value of political liberties has the required form: it justifies the lexical priority of the political liberties by arguing that *they are necessary for the realization of an interest that itself has lexical priority*—namely our overriding interest in the development and exercise of our capacity for moral autonomy. As stated, though, the argument has several weaknesses, but these can be readily corrected, leaving a justification for the priority of political liberty that is directly connected to Rawls's hierarchical Kantian conception of the person.

1. Instrumental Defense I: Protecting Nonpolitical or Civil Liberties

At numerous places in Rawls's writings, he distinguishes between the political liberties (core and auxiliary) and the nonpolitical or civil liberties, including liberty of conscience as well as freedom and integrity of the person—those liberties, in short, that are necessary for our pursuit of a conception of the good

---

16. They also cannot be limited for the sake of the various conceptions of the good, but this follows from the priority of right rather than the priority of political liberty, strictly speaking, because the latter is an *internal* priority, one that contributes to the ordering of the various elements of justice as fairness. However these internal elements of right are arranged, though, they always as a group have lexical priority over the good—see the previous section.

and the plan of life that realizes it.[17] Rawls makes note of (but tries to avoid endorsing) the claims of classical liberals such as Benjamin Constant and Isaiah Berlin that the former liberties are mostly, if not entirely, means to protect the latter.[18] Rawls effectively develops this line of argument himself in *Theory* §37, however, and notes in *Political Liberalism* that "even if [Constant/Berlin's instrumentalist] view is correct, it is no bar to counting certain political liberties among the basic liberties and protecting them by the priority of liberty. For to assign priority to these liberties they need only be important enough as essential institutional means to secure the other basic liberties under the circumstances of the modern state" (PL 299).

For example, with respect to core political liberty, Rawls argues that "we should narrow or widen its extent up to the point where the danger to liberty from the marginal loss in control over those holding political power just balances the security of liberty gained by the greater use of constitutional devices" such as the division of powers, judicial review, etc. (TJ 202). This argument is explicitly instrumentalist: political liberty is a means to civil liberty, and the determination of its extent is a matter of benefit/cost analysis, where the benefits and costs are measured in terms of the protection of civil liberties rather than in a socioeconomic currency. Rawls suggests similar instrumentalist arguments for the inequality of political liberties: he says that John Stuart Mill's proposal for plural voting at least has the "required form" if he believed the inequality to be to the benefit of those with the lesser political liberty, where the benefit is to be measured in terms of the "larger security of their other liberties . . . [such as] equal liberty of conscience or liberty of the person."[19] Again, political liberty is seen as a means to civil liberty, such that when the latter requires inequality or restriction of the former, the former must give way.

This argument for the political liberties and their priority is undoubtedly a powerful one, because as Rawls suggested in the passage quoted above, the "loss in control over those holding political power" has historically been one

---

17. TJ 176–77, 195, 201–2, 205, 217; PL 4–5, 206, 299. Rawls refers to the nonpolitical or civil liberties as "the other freedoms that, so to say, define the intrinsic good" of citizens (TJ 205). I will reconstruct Rawls's defense of these liberties and their lexical priority in the next chapter.

18. TJ 177n, 195, 202n; PL 4–5, 206, 299. Rawls criticizes Habermas for ascribing a purely instrumentalist view to him (PL 404n39). Interestingly, Constant did now hew to a purely instrumentalist line himself: he notes the intrinsic value of the political liberties at the end of his famous speech to the Athéné Royal (Constant 1988, 326–28).

19. TJ 204–5. This argument was originally presented in J. S. Mill's *Considerations on Representative Government*, chap. 8 ("Of the Extension of the Suffrage").

of the primary causes of violations of civil liberties, as any review of communist and fascist dictatorships of the twentieth century will show. Does this argument justify the *lexical* priority of the political liberties, however, such that no trade-offs for the sake of socioeconomic benefits can be entertained? (It obviously does not justify it vis-à-vis the civil liberties, because as we have just seen the protection of them can excuse the violation of political liberties in some cases, which are therefore not lexically prior to them.) *Only if it is the case that the political liberties are necessary to, rather than just strongly contributory towards, the protection of civil liberties.* If they are necessary to such protection, then the lexical priority of the civil liberties over other social primary goods (which will be defended in the next chapter) secures their own priority by implication: the sacrifice of political liberties for the sake of socioeconomic benefits will lead to less protection of civil liberties if they are, as stipulated, necessary conditions, but such a lessening of protection is inconsistent with the lexical priority of the civil liberties over these other social primary goods.

Such a tight connection between political and civil liberties seems implausible, however. For example, suppose that in democratic elections 10 percent of the population were *randomly* selected and given the right to vote, whereas the other 90 percent were disenfranchised. If the selection process were truly random, then the reform would be unlikely to threaten civil liberties: expectationally, at least, the same interests would be represented, so there is little reason to think that politicians would be unleashed to violate the liberties of all or part of the population. The cost savings (in terms of the saved opportunity cost of time involved in voting, etc.) might be significant. Would such an exchange of political liberty for socioeconomic benefits be ruled out by the instrumental argument for the priority of the political liberties? So long as civil liberties were protected just as well under the new scheme, it is difficult to see why it would fail to pass muster. Even if reforms of this sort were to diminish protection for civil liberties, so long as compensating expenditures could be made to return us to the previous level of protection (e.g., diverting some of the savings into legal advocacy for the disenfranchised) the instrumental argument would have to allow the diminution of political liberty.[20]

---

20. A detour through microeconomic theory might be helpful here. Suppose that several kinds of inputs (e.g., political liberties and their priority, the division of powers, judicial review, etc.) can be utilized to produce one output, namely the protection of civil liberties. So long as these inputs can be substituted for one another, none is strictly necessary for the production of

The lesson here—to which I will return below—is that even if the interest to be protected by political liberties (e.g., civil liberties) has the requisite lexical priority, the priority of political liberties will not be justified by implication unless they are strictly necessary for such protection. If they are merely strongly contributory towards such protection, then other means of protection can potentially be substituted for them; if such substitution leads to socioeconomic gains while maintaining the level of protection, the political liberties will not receive lexical priority through the instrumental argument. This suggests a more general problem with instrumental arguments for lexical priority: they have to assume an absence of substitute means to attain the desired end, an assumption that is difficult (though perhaps not impossible) to sustain in practice. As we shall see, the only persuasive argument for the lexical priority of core political liberties turns out to be one that focuses on their *intrinsic* value.

2. Instrumental Defense II: Guaranteeing Just Legislation

As I noted above, Rawls puts great emphasis on protecting the "fair value" of the political liberties: unless steps are taken to level the political playing field (through limits on inequality of wealth, public financing of political parties and electoral campaigns, etc.), political equality will be effectively subverted because the rich will gain disproportionate influence over time (TJ 197-99; PL 327-30, 356-63, 407). Rawls suggests at several points in his writings that the reason such inequality is undesirable is that it will lead to unjust class legislation: those with disproportionate political influence, the wealthy, will use their power to create and defend laws that serve their interests in ways inconsistent with justice as fairness (e.g., legislation favoring creditors and landlords over borrowers and renters, respectively) (TJ 198; PL 327-28, 330). The priority of right requires that law be made consistent with the first principles of justice, using the four-stage sequence as a heuristic, with interests contrary to justice receiving no weight in legislative decision making, so Rawls's demand that the political liberties and their fair value be given lexical priority seems

---

the output: we can maintain output (i.e., stay on the same isoquant) when one input is reduced by just increasing the level of one or more of the other inputs. In order for them to be strictly necessary, we must be facing a production technology like the Leontief production function, which is characterized by no substitutability across inputs (i.e., elasticity of substitution equal to zero). In this case, reduction of an input (e.g., political liberty) will *necessarily* reduce output (e.g., the protection of civil liberties). I think one would be very hard pressed to make the case that there are no substitutes for political liberty in the production of civil-liberty protection. For a discussion of the Leontief production technology, see Varian (1992, 4-5).

prima facie defensible, given the weight of the moral interest at stake here and the evident role political equality plays in securing it.

Nonetheless, we can ask the same question here that we did above: if alternative, possibly cheaper means exist to create and defend just legislation, then the priority of political liberty and its fair value may not be sustainable, at least on instrumental grounds. Suppose, for example, that the redistribution and public financing needed to defend political liberty's fair value were rather expensive—a plausible supposition—and cheaper means to just law existed. We might imagine small reductions in efforts to maintain fair value with compensating measures to secure "justice-neutrality," such as greater investment in publicity and transparency, so that unjust laws are likelier to be identified and resisted. If these compensating measures were (at the margin) less expensive than efforts to maintain fair value but just as effective in securing just legislative outcomes, then the lexical priority of political liberties and their fair value over socioeconomic concerns could not be sustained. Again, the priority of political liberty seems to depend here upon questionable, contingent empirical claims about the strict necessity of political liberty for achieving admittedly important public ends.

3. Instrumental Defense III: Advancing Conceptions of the Good

In "The Basic Liberties and Their Priority" (Lecture VIII of *Political Liberalism*), Rawls takes yet another approach to defending the lexical priority of political liberties, this one based on the instrumental role they play in advancing our conceptions of the good. His argument here is addressed to agents in the OP, who are merely *rationally* autonomous, so its instrumentalism is appropriate: he assumes that political liberty is a means to develop the first moral power and that this power is in turn viewed "solely as a means to a person's good" (PL 315, 332, 334–35). To be more specific, Rawls offers the following multistage argument: (1) the priority of political liberty is necessary for the development of the first moral power; (2) this power is necessary for social cooperation; (3) such cooperation is necessary for the realization of our conceptions of the good; and therefore (4) the priority of political liberty is justified. To complicate things further, Rawls proceeds to make this general argument in a number of specific ways—namely with respect to the goods of stability, a well-ordered society (WOS), and self-respect. I will discuss Rawls's self-respect arguments for the priority of liberty in the next chapter and therefore focus here on the two remaining variants.

In the stability variant, Rawls points out the "great advantage to everyone's conception of the good of a . . . stable scheme of cooperation" and then maintains that his theory of justice is "the most stable conception of justice . . . and this is the case importantly because of the basic liberties and the priority assigned to them" (PL 316; cf. TJ §76). As one can see from the general version of this argument I presented above, a sort of "sequential necessity" is at work here, which means that the argument is not only vulnerable at each stage (for the same reasons as the other instrumental defenses) but also multiplicatively vulnerable, so to speak: weaknesses at one stage exacerbate those at others, and weaknesses exist at several stages of this argument. First, though social stability is certainly important for the advancement of our conceptions of the good, we cannot reasonably ascribe the lexical priority to it that would be necessary to make this argument work. For instance, high rates of economic growth, which commonly lead to labor dislocation and endanger social stability by increasing income inequalities, also enhance wealth and provide greater resources to citizens for pursuing their conceptions of the good. At the margin, therefore, parties in the OP might be well advised to trade off some political liberties (say, those of the poor, who are most likely to object politically to income inequalities) for the sake of faster economic growth *even with the attendant reduction in social stability*—at least insofar as the trade-off was reasonably expected to work to the long-run advantage of the poor.[21] So even if political liberty were strictly necessary for social stability, one could not derive its lexical priority from the high but defeasible priority of the stability interest it supports, as this would be an example of the inference fallacy.

Second, political liberty is unlikely to be strictly necessary for social stability. Even if we set aside examples in which alternative supports for social stability can replace political liberty at the margin in a way that maintains social stability and yields socioeconomic gains, surely there are cases where constraints on political liberty can *directly* enhance social stability. Germans, for example, require a political party to get at least 5 percent of the popular vote

---

21. I am assuming here that economic growth "lifts all boats," to use John F. Kennedy's language, but that it lifts some boats much faster than others, so that even if the poor benefit (perhaps greatly) from such growth, the rich benefit even more, and such inequalities often generate resentment. Such growth may be consistent with the DP, of course, so long as any attempt to reduce the inequalities attending growth would ultimately leave the poor with even less. See TJ 68 (on DP-consistent inequality) and 263–64 (on John Maynard Keynes's argument that "inequalities in wealth and authority" might be justified if they redound to the benefit of the working class in the long run).

in order for it to receive an allocation of seats in the Bundestag; this proviso was explicitly designed to keep small radical parties out of the legislature—an understandable goal, given their historical experience of such parties (especially in the Weimar Republic) and the threat they can pose to social stability (see Palmer 1997, 201–2, 211). The proviso, however, effectively (albeit partially) disenfranchises radical voters of both the Left and Right; in short, it trades off the political liberty of some for the sake of a social stability that benefits all. But if the priority of political liberty is not strictly necessary for social stability, and if such stability itself lacks lexical priority, then the larger argument is placed in grave jeopardy.

In the WOS variant, Rawls makes use of the Humboldtian idea of social union, declaring a well-ordered society to be a "social union of social unions," one that combines and harmonizes its smaller, component organizations in order to create a more systematic social good; he goes on to assert that the "principles which secure the basic liberties . . . [are] the best way to establish the comprehensive good of social union" (PL 321–23; also see PL 204 and TJ §79). This variant is somewhat more complex than the first, as the "comprehensive good of social union" seems to be not only a means to, but also a component of, people's individual conceptions of the good. Nevertheless, the same criticisms offered for the first variant apply to the second. Rawls does not explain here why the good of social union is of such overriding importance that it can never be sacrificed for the sake of other social goods (e.g., high economic growth) that are also critical to advancing our conceptions of the good—therefore making it vulnerable to the inference-fallacy objection—nor does he explain why political liberty is strictly required for, rather than just strongly contributory towards, the good of social union. In the absence of arguments for these rather strong claims, we must conclude that the instrumental case for the lexical priority of political liberty has not—and perhaps cannot—be made.

4. A More Promising Path: Defending the Intrinsic Value of Political Liberty

Rawls has insisted, in response to contrary claims by Jürgen Habermas, that not all of his defenses of (the priority of) political liberty are instrumental, and he directs us to two parts of his writings where he says that noninstrumental defenses are offered.[22] Rawls suggests at least three overlapping but incomplete

---

22. PL 404n39. He directs us to TJ 205–6 and PL V:7 (201–6). (He actually says PL V:6 [195–200] in the footnote, but this must be a mistake, because the indicated section has little

defenses of the priority of liberty there. One, a self-respect argument, I will again postpone examining until the next chapter.[23] The second, a WOS argument, is simply an intrinsic-value version of the one I discussed above, addressed to citizens rather than agents in the OP; the criticisms I offered there apply just as strongly when the WOS is seen as an element of, rather than simply a means to, our individual conceptions of the good.[24]

This leaves the third defense, which is incomplete as stated but is also considerably more promising than the others. Rawls says that "the exercise of the two moral powers is experienced as a good. . . . Part of the essential nature of citizens . . . is their having the two moral powers which root their capacity to participate in fair social cooperation," including the *political* collaboration that creates the legal framework within which smaller social unions work.[25] As I shall show, this argument has approximately the right form: we must ground the priority of political liberty in the development and exercise of the moral powers (especially the first moral power), which are good for citizens *given their nature as persons*. Unfortunately, it has at least three limitations as Rawls presents it.[26] First, his argument is not expressly about the political liberties and their priority but rather about the more general "good of political society." Second, by saying that the exercise of the moral powers "may be an important good . . . for many people," he qualifies his claim so much that he makes it seem as if it applies only (or perhaps chiefly) to people with a certain conception of the good, for example a civic-humanist one for which "taking part in democratic politics is seen as the privileged locus of the good life."[27] Finally, he bases this argument on the Aristotelian principle, which motivates cultivation

---

connection with the political liberties, whereas PL V:7 is entitled "The Good of Political Society" and fits the description offered in the footnote.)

23. PL 203; cf. TJ 205, where he speaks of the need to "enhance the self-esteem . . . of the average citizen [and] his awareness of his own worth," etc.

24. PL 204; cf. TJ 205, where he argues that political liberty enhances the "moral quality of civic life" and "lays the foundations for civic friendship and shapes the ethos of political culture."

25. PL 202–3; cf. TJ 205–6, where he suggests that citizen exercise of political liberty can support "the development of his intellectual and moral faculties," enabling him "to be guided by some conception of justice and the public good rather than by his own inclinations."

26. I should hasten to add that Rawls clearly did not intend for this argument to be free-standing; rather, he saw it as a component of the larger WOS defense I have already criticized. My purpose in separating it out will soon be clear.

27. PL 206. The original footnote that referenced this section as presenting a noninstrumental defense of the political liberties confirms this interpretation, as Rawls says there that they play "a significant or even a predominant role in the lives of many citizens engaged in one way or another in political life" (PL 404n39).

of myriad skills of social cooperation, rather than on the first moral power. This decision is consistent with and may even explain the prior limitation because of the principle's pluralistic understanding of perfection: the excellences appropriate for some may not be so for others.[28]

These limitations can be readily overcome, however, by a reconstruction of this argument that justifies the lexical priority of political liberties by demonstrating that *they are necessary for the realization of an interest that itself has lexical priority*—to wit, our overriding interest in the development and exercise of our capacity for moral autonomy, which is the highest, authoritative conception of autonomy. This reconstruction begins with my argument above (in the justificatory section on the priority of right) that the first moral power, reasonableness, should be expanded to include full autonomy, which is Rawls's version of moral autonomy. This expanded version of the first moral power implicitly contains an ideal of equality: so long as one has the potential to act out of respect for self-legislated principles of justice to a "certain minimum degree," one is recognized to have moral personality and therefore qualified for citizenship along with all other similarly constituted beings, which should include every competent adult (TJ 442; PL 19). Some, of course, will have especially acute senses of justice that qualify them for special offices (e.g., judicial ones) in the basic structure of a WOS, but this is consistent with the preceding claim of basic equality (KCMT 333).

This equality, rightly understood, is *colegislative:* as Rawls says, "all view themselves as equally worthy of being represented in any procedure that is to determine the principles of justice that are to regulate the basic institutions of society. This conception of equal worth is founded on their equally sufficient capacity (which I assume to be realized) to understand and to act from the public conception of social cooperation" (KCMT 333). As this suggests, co-legislative equality is conceived at the outset as merely a *hypothetical political liberty,* a right to be represented in the OP, where parties reflect upon and choose principles of justice. Kant captures this idea of our hypothetical colegislation of the moral law in the fourth (FA) formulation of The CI, which is "the principle of every human will giving universal law through all its maxims," with such law serving as the ground for "a systematic union of rational beings," that is, "a kingdom of ends" (GMM 4:432–33).

---

28. PL 203n35. See TJ §65 for a discussion of the Aristotelian principle; on its pluralism, see TJ 377–78, 387–88.

Hypothetical political liberty in the first stage of Rawls's four-stage sequence becomes *actual political liberty* in the second, constitutional stage. As Rawls explains in a key passage, "Justice as fairness begins with the idea that where common principles are necessary and to everyone's advantage, they are to be worked out from the viewpoint of a suitably defined initial situation of equality [the OP] in which each person is fairly represented. The principle of participation transfers this notion from the [OP] to the constitution as the highest-order system of social rules for making rules. . . . *The constitutional process should preserve the equal representation of the [OP] to the degree that this is practicable*" (TJ 194–95; emphasis added). In other words, Rawls sees actual political liberty as *effecting* hypothetical political liberty and (by implication) moral autonomy, providing them both with an institutional medium for growth and expression. Just as moral autonomy can be understood on Kantian grounds as the legislation of morality for a kingdom of ends, so in the context of right it can be understood as participation in republican self-government, whether directly (as a legislator or a bureaucrat crafting laws or regulations, respectively) or indirectly (as a voter judging and choosing between the legislative programs of parties and candidates). Through such participation, as Rawls rightly notes, we can "enlarge [our] intellectual and moral sensibilities" and exercise them in the creation of fair and impartial law for our society (TJ 206). Political liberty, however, is not just a means to the development and utilization of our capacity for moral autonomy, but in some sense *is* that capacity expressed in political-institutional form. Descending from the first stage of the four-stage sequence greatly complicates the exercise of moral autonomy, of course, because we move from the unanimity of the OP to the plurality of constitutional and legislative process. In it, competing perspectives and interpretations of foundational political principles necessitate features absent from the OP, whose univocality is assured by the veil: majority rule, layers of representation, procedural rules, etc.[29] Still, this moral autonomy effected under conditions of plurality echoes that modeled via the OP and aspires to an ideal of collective political self-legislation, one in which accord is approached not through devices like the veil but by systematic efforts to overcome sectional and sectarian interests and thereby to achieve impartiality in lawmaking.

Kant forges this same link between actual and hypothetical political liberty in his works, seeing in republican self-government an admittedly imperfect

---

29. On the univocality of the thickly veiled OP, see TJ 120.

manifestation of moral autonomy. First, consider how he derives the universal principle of right (UPR), which is meant to govern the choice of principles of justice and subsequent legislation, from the formula of universal law (FUL).[30] The UPR is simply a restricted version of the FUL, one that is appropriate for the realm of right: it applies only to the *form* (not the intention) of actions affecting *others* (not oneself) via a *conflict* of wills (not a coincidence of them, as with charity) (GMM 4:421; MM 6:230). Briefly, the UPR carves out a set of mutually consistent action-spaces for individuals, where consistency is guaranteed by means of universal justice, which coordinates potentially conflicting actions and polices boundaries; it translates the idea of maxim-consistency, which FUL insists upon in the ethical realm, into the language of right.

Kant implicitly performs a parallel derivation of actual political liberty from hypothetical (embodied in the FA). He extends his idea of colegislation of the moral law by all finite rational beings to the realm of politics, initially in a hypothetical sense alone: in "Theory and Practice," for example, he sees each citizen as a "colegislator" of a "basic law" or "original contract" (i.e., the social contract), which is considered *"only an idea* of reason" (T&P 294–95, 297). In "Perpetual Peace" and the *Rechtslehre,* though, he goes even further by extending it to regular lawmaking, saying that "the legislative authority can belong only to the united will of the people," by which he means that the "active" republican citizens should have an "equal right to vote within this constitution" for their "deputies (in parliament)."[31] Through their legislative representatives, the citizenry exercise full authority over war, taxation, and even the executive himself, whose powers may be restricted or removed entirely by them (PP 8:350; MM 6:317, 325, 345–46). The collective political self-legislation thereby achieved is meant to be an analogue of the morally autonomous creation of legislation for a kingdom of ends and an arena for the exercise and development of our moral sensibility, just as the public sphere is for our intellectual sensibilities.[32] Kantian republicanism translates FA into the language of right.

---

30. FUL says "act only in accordance with that maxim through which you can at the same time will that it become a universal law," whereas UPR says "any **action** is right if it can **coexist** with **everyone's freedom** in accordance with a universal law, **or** if on its **maxim** the freedom of choice of each can coexist with everyone's freedom in accordance with a universal law" (GMM 4:421; MM 6:230 [emphasis added]).

31. MM 6:313–15, 319, 341. He explains the active/passive citizens distinction at MM 314–15 and T&P 8:295–96, which is designed to exclude from the franchise citizens in a dependent position due to employment or familial relations.

32. For further discussion of the nature and limits of Kantian republicanism, see Taylor (2006).

If actual political liberty effects moral autonomy for Rawls and Kant (as was just argued) and if moral autonomy is lexically prior to the other conceptions of autonomy (as was argued in chapter 2), then *the political liberties are lexically prior to the nonpolitical/civil liberties,* whose supports are to be found either in personal autonomy (i.e., the second moral power of rationality; see chapter 4) or in self-realization (which requires the nonbasic liberties of free movement and choice of occupation; see chapter 5). Because nonpolitical or civil basic liberties are themselves lexically prior to FEO and the DP, as I will maintain in the next chapter, the political liberties are prior to them as well by transitivity. In correcting the three drawbacks to Rawls's third argument for the intrinsic value of political liberty, we have thus constructed a persuasive justification for the priority of political liberty that ties directly to Rawls's hierarchical Kantian conception of the person and avoids the apparently irremediable weaknesses of the instrumental defenses.

5. Is the Proposed Defense a Fair Reading of Rawls?

Before reviewing the textual support for this reconstructed justification of the priority of political liberty, we must first consider a powerful objection to it drawn from Rawls's own texts. In responding to Habermas's claim that he subordinates political to civil liberties—or, to use the language of Constant, that he subordinates the liberties of the ancients (which protect collective or public autonomy) to those of the moderns (which secure private autonomy)—Rawls says the following about the relationship between political and civil liberties and between the two moral powers on which they are respectively grounded: "The ancient and the modern liberties are co-original and of equal weight *with neither given pride of place over the other.* The liberties of both public and private autonomy are given side by side and *unranked* in the first principle of justice. These liberties are co-original for the further reason that both kinds of liberty are rooted in one or both of the two moral powers, *respectively* in the capacity for a sense of justice and the capacity for a conception of the good. As before, *the two powers themselves are not ranked* and both are essential aspects of the political conception of the person, each power with its own higher-order interest."[33] If Rawls's claims here are correct, then my reconstruction above is

---

33. PL 413 (emphasis added). Strictly speaking, the "higher-order interest" at the end of the quotation should read "highest-order interest," as the development and exercise of the two moral powers are *highest-order* interests in the OP, whereas the realization of a determinate conception of the good is merely *higher-order* (KCMT 312–13).

simply wrong: in order for the political liberties to take priority over the civil liberties, moral autonomy (first moral power) must take priority over personal autonomy (second moral power), but Rawls denies both priority relations here by saying these liberties and powers are "unranked" with respect to each other. As I will show, however, these claims cannot be supported within the context of his theory and are contradicted by his own writings.

First, Rawls says that "the reasonable and the rational are complementary ideas . . . each connects with its distinctive moral power, respectively, with the capacity for a sense of justice and the capacity for a conception of the good" (PL 52, 104). Neither the reasonable nor the rational can be fully understood or defended in the absence of the other: the latter provides the ends, the former the constraints on their pursuit. If agents had no conceptions of the good to advance, there would be no point to either social cooperation or the principles of justice that frame it. If agents had no sense of justice, they would constitute a "nation of devils," intelligent and perhaps even prudent beings but not moral beings of the kind we are studying; their interactions, while possibly lawful and harmonious through good institutional design, would mask their lack of inner worth, and we would be tempted to say with Kant (and Rawls) that without a sense of justice "there is no longer any value in human beings living on the earth."[34]

Second, Rawls places a special emphasis on the way in which the reasonable frames and limits the rational. He argues that "rational agents . . . are *subject* to certain appropriate conditions and these conditions will express the reasonable" (PL 52; emphasis added). That is, the prudential pursuit of conceptions of the good must take place within the bounds established by impartial rules of justice, which are promulgated and ratified through the first moral power. As he says more strongly elsewhere, "the Reasonable *subordinates* the Rational because its principles limit, and in a Kantian doctrine *limit absolutely,* the final ends that can be pursued" (KCMT 317, 319; emphasis added). The reasonable and its principles are lexically prior to the rational and its ends, at least in a Kantian theory like justice as fairness.

Third, Rawls suggests that the political liberties are grounded in the first moral power and that several civil ones (e.g., liberty of conscience, freedom of association generally) are grounded in the second.[35] Combining these three

---

34. MM 6:332; LP 128. The "nation of devils" language is from PP 8:366.
35. PL 334–35. I reconstruct Rawls's defense of these groundings both above and in chapter 4.

points, we must conclude that for Rawls, at least, the first moral power (reasonableness) and its allied political liberties frame and absolutely subordinate the second moral power (rationality) and its associated civil liberties. Priority does not preclude complementarity, but the simple fact that the reasonable cannot be imagined without the rational cannot call into question the former's absolute priority over the latter in a Kantian theory. Kant recognized happiness as the universal subjective end of finite rational beings such as ourselves, but he also thought it subordinate to the demands of our ethico-political vocation, and the same relationship of priority holds between their respective institutional conditions, Rawls's claims to the contrary notwithstanding (CPrR 5:25, 61–62).

In the course of disposing of this objection, we have seen that my reconstructed defense of the priority of political liberty over civil liberties draws at least implicit support from Rawls's texts. Is there any *explicit* support for it, however? In his "Reply to Habermas," Rawls says quite explicitly that "the four-stage sequence fits, then, with the idea that *the liberties of the moderns are subject to the constituent will of the people.* Put in terms of that sequence, the people . . . are making a judgment at the stage of the constitutional convention" about the form and protection of civil liberties (for example, through written bills of rights and judicial review) (PL 406; emphasis added). This suggests that the political liberties exercised at the constitutional stage take a certain priority over the civil liberties accorded protection in it; the seeming priority of civil over political liberties in Rawls's theory, which so exercises Habermas, is an illusion that results from focusing exclusively on the *legislative* stage, where the democratic will is indeed constrained by protections of civil liberties ratified *by that same will* in the prior, constitutional stage.[36]

Further (if less direct) support is provided by Rawls's insistence that political liberty must be treated "in a special way" and has a "distinctive place . . . in the two principles of justice" (PL 327). Its special status is demonstrated in

---

36. Rawls is less than clear about whether explicit constitutional provision (in the form of a bill of rights) has to be made to protect various basic liberties: at one point in *Political Liberalism* he says that "basic liberties of liberty of conscience and freedom of association are properly protected by explicit constitutional restrictions," but later in the book (in his "Reply to Habermas") he appears to backtrack, saying that "justice as fairness . . . allows—but does not require—the basic liberties to be incorporated into the constitution and protected as constitutional rights" (PL 338, 405). Perhaps the "properly" in the first quotation should be read as allowing but not mandating incorporation, but the surrounding text suggests otherwise. Basic liberties can, of course, be successfully protected in other ways (e.g., through unwritten legislative traditions and norms), as the British experience suggests.

part by the fact (discussed earlier) that, unique among the basic liberties, its fair value is protected: Rawls incorporates a brand of FEO into the first principle to guarantee that "those similarly endowed and motivated [will] have roughly the same chance of attaining positions of *political* authority irrespective of their economic and social class" (TJ 197; more generally, see TJ 197–99 and PL 327–31). Rawls additionally suggests that "a liberty is more or less significant depending on whether it is more or less essentially involved in, or is a more or less necessary institutional means to protect, the full and informed and effective exercise of the moral powers" (PL 335). As I argued earlier, the political liberties are tightly connected to the exercise of the first moral power, which indicates the great and perhaps overriding significance of these liberties—a point that Rawls himself makes when he notes that even "political speech," an auxiliary political liberty, "may be regulated in order to preserve the fair value of the [core] political liberties" (PL 357; more generally, see PL 356–63). These points imply that political liberty should at least receive greater weight than other liberties; whether that weight should be infinite vis-à-vis these other liberties, as lexical priority requires, is another matter, but the reconstructed priority defense I offered above provides reasons why it should.

One other important concern that might be raised in response to my reconstruction is that Rawls is openly hostile to civic humanism of the Arendtian or Rousseauean sort (which contends that human beings' "essential nature is most fully realized in a democratic society in which there is widespread and vigorous participation in political life") and that my elevation of core political liberty over other liberties is a civic-humanist move.[37] To respond simply by noting the different, Kantian provenance of my priority defense or by pointing out as Rawls does that "the principle of participation applies to institutions [and] does not define an ideal of citizenship [or] lay down a duty requiring all to take an active part in political affairs" would be insufficient, though. Even if my priority defense just establishes, on Kantian grounds, that political rights (not duties) have a preeminent status, the fact remains that this defense hinges upon the overriding importance of developing our capacity for moral autonomy, that political life provides the necessary setting for its exercise and enhancement, and that the failure to do so is a political vice. My

---

37. PL 206. For example, Rawls's rejection of the idea that political liberty serves to "make the individual master of himself" seems to be directed at Rousseau, who says "moral freedom . . . alone makes man the master of himself; for to be governed by appetite alone is slavery, while obedience to a law one prescribes to oneself is freedom," where such self-legislation is achieved politically by means of the general will (TJ 205; Rousseau, *Social Contract*, bk. 1, chap. 8).

priority defense consequently has civic-humanist implications for the good life. What this result highlights is that a coherent defense of the most distinctive features of justice as fairness requires a comprehensive Kantian moral doctrine, and its comprehensiveness is precisely what the later Rawls rejects as inconsistent with the legitimate stability required of a political conception of justice. I cannot address this concern here, important as it is, but I will return to it in a systematic way in part 3.

C. Implications

1. The Role and Priority of Auxiliary Political Liberties

As I argued above, the core political rights of voting and holding public office not only provide an institutional setting for the exercise of moral autonomy but also effect or embody its practice—to deliberate over, author, and ratify just laws simply *is* morally autonomous action in the realm of right—and just as this conception of autonomy is lexically prior to the others so its institutional incarnation is lexically prior to other institutional protections. The auxiliary political liberties derive their own priority from the role they play in supporting the core political liberties; as Rawls says, "certain basic liberties are *indispensable* institutional conditions once other basic liberties are guaranteed; thus freedom of thought as well as freedom of association are necessary to give effect to . . . the political liberties" (PL 309 [emphasis added]; cf. PL 335). They may be regulated or even restricted if they come into conflict with the core liberties for some reason (e.g., campaign advertising as a form of free political speech may be regulated if it erodes the fair value of the political liberties), but they are assured lexical priority over other, nonpolitical basic liberties that are instead based on personal autonomy (second moral power) (PL 356–63).

The core political liberties do not operate in a vacuum: in order to be fully and effectively exercised, they need a variety of institutional supports. Some of these supports were discussed in the context of maintaining the "fair value" of core political liberties, including limitations on the inequality of wealth, public financing of political advertising, parties, and campaigns, etc.; these supports are designed primarily to maintain substantive equality in political power. The auxiliary political liberties, on the other hand, are less about equality than effectiveness: in their absence, it would be difficult if not impossible to imagine the meaningful exercise of political power.

These liberties fall into two general categories. The first category, including freedom of political thought, speech, press, and assembly, is *directly* supportive of the core political liberties. Because the function of political liberty is to allow expression of moral autonomy in the context of right, its priority implies that essential institutional means for such expression themselves take priority, and the freedoms just described are such means. In order to assess the justice of various legislative proposals or to construct them oneself, one must be free to think as well as to consider the opinions of others—especially the critical opinions of others—whether they are expressed in person or through the media. Moreover, given that political autonomy is achieved (if at all) under conditions of plurality, the means must be available to coordinate with others, whether on actions or beliefs, through discussion, debate, organization, mobilization, etc., and this is possible only if freedom of association is protected. The writing and authorization of autonomous political law is inevitably a public enterprise, one requiring the conscientious involvement of all citizens (or at least their chosen representatives), so institutional means including free speech and assembly must be available to help citizens realize collective self-legislation.

The second category of auxiliary political liberties is *indirectly* supportive of the core political liberties. It includes, inter alia, "freedom of the person [psychological and physical integrity] . . . ; the right to hold personal property and freedom from arbitrary arrest and seizure as defined by the concept of the rule of law" (TJ 53). These liberties work in tandem to establish minimal psychological and physical security, without which exercise of core and direct-auxiliary political liberties will be crippled or even rendered otiose. Ancient Athenians' legal customs, for example, may have undermined their democracy by distracting politically active citizens, forcing them to invest time and effort in avoiding ostracism (i.e., a decade of exile) and fighting easily filed but frivolous suits for impiety, etc. (see Davies 1993, 110–11). As I will show in the next chapter, these liberties play a similar role in protecting the exercise of personal autonomy.

A question that instantly arises here, given my earlier critique of instrumental defenses of the priority of political liberty, is the following: to what extent are the auxiliary political liberties *strictly necessary* ("indispensable," as Rawls puts it) for the support of the core ones? If they are not, then it might be worthwhile in certain cases to trade off auxiliary political liberties for lower goods (e.g., civil liberties, FEO, etc.), so long as support for the core liberties can be maintained by compensating measures—but if this is so, then the auxiliary liberties do not have priority. The possibility and desirability of such trade-offs appear to vary across the two categories of auxiliary goods. The directly supportive auxiliary liberties do seem to have the requisite necessity, at least along some dimensions. Consider, for example, the case of free political speech. Some controls on speech (e.g., the so-called time, place, and manner regulations, such as bans on campaign advertising by megaphone on residential streets at three in the morning) appear unobjectionable, because compensating measures are easily imagined (e.g., making alternative venues available or providing additional subsidies for advertising), so along these dimensions free political speech is not strictly necessary and therefore does not have lexical priority. Other controls, however, lack this feature and are therefore forbidden by the priority of political liberty. For example, content restrictions disallowing speech that makes certain claims (e.g., Holocaust denial) or addresses certain topics (e.g., bestiality) permanently place out of bounds certain realms of public debate. No compensating measures are possible here apart from the removal of the restrictions, because they simply cut off political discussion and thus the possibility of critique and judgment in regard to the banned claims and topics—but this possibility is required for broad moral autonomy in the realm of right, and attempted compensating measures that buttressed discussion regarding *other* claims or topics would simply miss the point.[38]

Defending the strict necessity of the indirectly supportive auxiliary liberties is admittedly more difficult. Some *minimal* provision of psychological and physical security is surely required for the morally autonomous exercise of political power: for example, a high probability of death or arbitrary arrest and torture at the hands of political opponents or their operatives is impossible to square with it. This being said, it is difficult to establish how much beyond an uncontroversial minimum is strictly necessary for the effective exercise of core political liberty without knowing more about the society in question. Would restrictions on personal property of the sort found in a commune, for instance, necessarily infringe upon effective exercise? What about predictable and egalitarian violations of bodily integrity, such as compulsory blood-donation or kidney-donation programs? Beyond the establishment of a basic minimum of

---

38. See Rawls's discussion of the distinction between "regulating" and "restricting" basic liberties, especially with respect to speech, at PL 295–98, 336. One might think it is possible to engage in critique and judgment *without* such discussion, but as Kant rightly asks, "how much and how correctly would we *think* if we did not think as it were in community with others to whom we *communicate* our thoughts, and who communicate theirs to us!" (WOT 8:144).

psychological and physical security and its priority by parties in the OP, little else could probably be determined about the required extent of such auxiliary liberties until later in the four-stage sequence.

2. Practicing the Priority of Political over Civil Liberty

If my reconstructed defense of the priority of political liberty is correct, then the core and auxiliary political liberties require not just high but infinite weight vis-à-vis nonpolitical liberties, whether basic or nonbasic (e.g., the FEO-associated nonbasic liberties of free movement and free choice of occupation). What would such priority look like in practice, that is, in what kinds of cases would civil liberties have to be sacrificed to political ones? A full answer to this question would require use of Rawls's four-stage sequence, and the details would consequently vary somewhat with time and place.[39] However, I can at least offer some tentative examples in a contemporary American context, the first a free association example and the second a free speech one, both dealing with issues of gender.

Civil freedom of association might in some cases undermine the fair value of the political liberties, for instance, as in the case of a major civic association that excludes people on the basis of gender: freedom of association militates in favor of allowing the organization to do so, as it is private and voluntary, and control over its own membership is essential to the advancement of its members' shared values and ends; the fair value of political liberties, on the other hand, militates against it, as exclusion from such associations may make it more difficult to develop leadership and communication skills, build useful personal connections, and otherwise assemble politically relevant capacities and contacts.[40] If the political liberties take priority over merely civil liberties, as I have argued, then the associational rights of the civic organization's members must give way to the need for substantively equal political liberty, and the organization must adopt some kind of gender-neutral membership policy

---

39. One example of this occurs in Rawls's discussion of economic institutions: market economies are mandated by justice as fairness, but different varieties of ownership schemes for non-human productive resources (e.g., market socialism versus decentralized capitalism, or Rawls's "property-owning democracy") can be consistent with it, depending "in large part upon the traditions, institutions, and social forces of each country, and its particular historical circumstances" (TJ 242; also see TJ xiv–xvi, TJ §42, and JF 135–40).

40. This example is loosely based on the Supreme Court case *Roberts v. United States Jaycees*, 468 U.S. 609 (1984). For a discussion of this case, see the contributions to Gutmann (1998). Much hinges, of course, on whether there are reasonably comparable alternative venues for developing such skills, etc.

as a consequence. This result would not be assured if we gave the political liberties high as opposed to infinite weight vis-à-vis civil liberties.

Civil freedom of speech is generally understood to include the protection of pornography, if not obscenity.[41] Suppose, however, that pornography commonly objectifies women and that by doing so it reinforces male power and female subordination; further suppose that such patriarchy is inconsistent with political equality and fails to support the fair value of the political liberties.[42] If these suppositions are correct, then there might be grounds for regulating pornography so that such objectification is minimized or eliminated: political liberty takes lexical priority over mere civil liberties, so when they conflict the latter must give way to the former.[43]

I want to make clear that I am not necessarily endorsing the arguments presented in either this example or the prior one. Rather, I am suggesting that they at least have the *right form* to be taken seriously by justice as fairness. By contrast, arguments that urge limits on civil liberties of association or speech on the ground that they reinforce gender inequalities and lead to a

---

41. Obscenity is generally distinguished from pornography, which the *American Heritage Dictionary* defines as "the presentation of sexually explicit behavior, as in a photograph, intended to arouse sexual excitement." The Supreme Court in *Miller v. California*, 413 U.S. 15 (1973), defined obscenity, which is not constitutionally protected speech, according to three criteria: "(a) whether the 'average person, applying contemporary community standards' would find that the work, taken as a whole, appeals to the prurient interest . . . ; (b) whether the work depicts or describes, in a patently offensive way, sexual conduct specifically defined by the applicable state law; and (c) whether the work, taken as a whole, lacks serious literary, artistic, political, or scientific value." Needless to say, these guidelines have been inconsistently applied (by the Supreme Court as well as other courts) due to the extreme ambiguity of the terms used ("contemporary community standards," "patently offensive," "prurient," "serious . . . value," etc.).

42. See the various essays in MacKinnon (1987), especially "Francis Biddle's Sister," for a defense of similar claims. It is noteworthy that the Supreme Court has decisively rejected the idea that pornography can be banned merely on the basis that it objectifies women and as a consequence effectively discriminates against them: see *Hudnut v. American Booksellers Assn., Inc.*, 475 U.S. 1001 (1986).

43. One counterargument might go as follows: in order to assess regulations that propose to eliminate objectification in pornography, citizens would need access to examples of objectifying pornography, in order for them to make an informed judgment about the appropriateness of the regulations; moreover, because in a democratic society such regulations are always subject to revision, such examples would have to be remain accessible to all citizens on a permanent basis—which suggests that the need to preserve free *political* speech would undercut efforts to ban such pornography, at least in any systematic way. Perhaps this is an example (like campaign advertising) where auxiliary political liberties can come into conflict with core ones, in which case the former would have to give way. However, I suspect that the problem cannot be resolved so easily, at least not in this case, because the object to be regulated is precisely what needs to be discussed politically, yet the regulation itself would subvert such discussion. The problem arises (insofar as it is a problem) because in a democracy citizens are not just subjects but also sovereigns; therefore, we cannot solve the problem by simply limiting access to examples of objectifying pornography to an elite cadre of legislators, as that would itself be antidemocratic.

violation of *nonpolitical* FEO do not have the right form, as basic liberties (whether political or civil) have lexical priority over FEO. I will postpone until the next chapter a more general discussion of the practical meaning of the priority of all basic liberties, political and civil, over FEO and the DP.

I will conclude by noting that a particular strand of First Amendment interpretation gives priority to political speech, association, etc. over civil varieties. This strand comes in both strong and weak forms. Robert Bork's writings on the First Amendment offer an example of the former: for instance, in one article he argues that the *only* function of constitutional protections of speech is political—namely, to support democratic self-government (Bork 1971, 23, 26, 32). Harry Kalven's writings, on the other hand, serve as an example of the latter, weak form: he concedes that the First Amendment protections of speech and association may have nonpolitical functions, but like Bork he asserts that the political function is key (Kalven 1964, 208). Some variety of this weak form might be a natural approach to First Amendment interpretation if judges were guided by the priority of political liberty, at least as I have reconstructed it.

3. Does Lexical Priority Create "Black Holes"?

One worry that has been raised with respect to lexical priority, whether of political liberty or of any other feature of justice as fairness, is that it creates a kind of "black hole" for resources. For example, given that political liberty requires various resources for its exercise, and given that it has infinite weight relative to other resource uses (e.g., civil liberty, FEO, the DP, conceptions of the good), all available resources should be drawn into support for political liberty: whenever there is a conflict over the use of resources between political liberty and something else, political liberty will win, each and every time, until all resources have been effectively conscripted by it.[44] The two other, inferior priorities of civil liberty and FEO also have such "black hole" tendencies, but because they are beneath the priority of political liberty, they too have their resources sucked into the vortex. Everything is apparently within the event horizon of political liberty, which may be a cause for celebration in some political-theory circles if true.

Such a celebration would be premature, however, because Rawls, though friendlier to the deliberative democrats than is usually supposed (or so I have indicated here), is not *that* friendly. Were justice as fairness a maximizing

44. This concern is raised with respect to the lexical priority of FEO by Arneson (1999, 81–82) and Pogge (1989, 169).

theory, the lexical priorities would create a pecking order of maximands, with the highest (political liberty) indeed consuming all resources. However, as I showed early in the chapter, justice as fairness is a deontological rather than a teleological theory and "does not interpret the right as maximizing the good," the good in this case being our interest (pursued by OP agents guided by the Thin Theory of the Good) in the development and exercise of our first moral power.[45] As Rawls repeatedly states, the moral powers need only be developed "to a certain minimum degree. . . . Nothing beyond the essential minimum is required"; thus, there is no requirement to maximize our capacity for moral autonomy—or our capacities for personal autonomy and self-realization (TJ 442; PL 19). Rawls does suggest that justice as fairness shares some features with perfectionism—a teleological theory—including its tendency to "encourage certain traits of character, especially the sense of justice," but nowhere does he suggest that such traits should be maximized, whatever that would look like (TJ 287). The "black hole" worry is therefore revealed to be a red herring.

4. Transitions to Democracy:
What (if Anything) Is Prior to Political Liberty?

Rawls states on numerous occasions that the priority of the basic liberties, including the political liberties, holds only under "reasonably favorable conditions," that is, under conditions that allow them to be "effectively exercised" or "established"; they may rightly be restricted if these conditions are absent, but "only to the extent that [such restrictions] are necessary to prepare the way for the time when they are no longer justified."[46] His description of "reasonably favorable conditions" has varied over time and texts: in *Theory*, he says they entail improved "conditions of civilization" as well as "certain social conditions and [a] degree of fulfillment of needs and material wants," whereas in *Political Liberalism*, he says they require "citizens' basic needs be met" and encompass "social circumstances . . . determined by a society's culture, its traditions and acquired skills in running institutions, as well as its level of

---

45. TJ 26–27. Justice as fairness, as we shall see in chapter 6, does maximize one thing: a social minimum index of income and leisure for the least advantaged. However, this form of maximization raises no "black hole" worries, as there is a natural stopping point for such maximization, namely index equality.

46. TJ 54–55, 132, 217–18, 474–76; PL 7, 297. Full compliance is required in addition to reasonably favorable conditions in order for the priority rules associated with the special conception of justice to come into play—see TJ 54–55, §39.

economic advance (which need not be especially high)."⁴⁷ One red thread running through nearly all of these attempts to define the concept is an emphasis on economic conditions. This raises the following question, which Rawls himself effectively poses: could political liberty be restricted for the sake of economic growth, if by doing so "reasonably favorable conditions" were created for the full and effective exercise of the political liberties themselves?

This question might justifiably appear an odd one to ascribe to Rawls, not just because of his theory's robust commitment to democracy (which I have, if anything, reinforced above), but also because he seems to explicitly rule out such trade-offs between political liberty and economic growth in his texts. In *Theory*, for example, Rawls asks us to "imagine . . . that people seem willing to forego certain political rights when the economic returns are significant" and says that such a trade-off would be banned by the priority of liberty— *except under "extenuating circumstances," that is, when "reasonably favorable conditions" have not been met* (TJ 55). This casts in a different light Rawls's similar claim in *Political Liberalism* that "the equal political liberties cannot be denied to certain social groups on the grounds that their having these liberties may enable them to block policies needed for economic efficiency and growth": if efficiency and growth were necessary to create reasonably favorable conditions for the exercise of political liberties and the denial of such liberties to "certain social groups" helped accomplish this end, then it might be justifiable for the very reasons suggested by Rawls (PL 294–95).

Of course, the possibility of such a case being made within the context of his (nonideal) theory depends on showing, inter alia, that economic efficiency and growth can help to establish reasonably favorable conditions for the full and effective exercise of political liberty and that the restriction of political liberty along particular dimensions can encourage economic efficiency and growth. On the first point, Rawls's discussion of the fair value of political liberties suggests that sizable economic resources may be needed to finance political parties and campaigns, support political debate through subsidies for political advertising and public affairs programming, etc. (TJ 198–99). More generally, citizens need sufficient leisure and money in order to discuss and participate in public affairs

---

47. TJ 132, 476; PL 7, 297. As Rawls says in *The Law of Peoples*, "great wealth is not necessary to establish just (or decent) institutions" (LP 107). Rawls is more explicit here than elsewhere about how to transition to "well-ordered societies" (i.e., decent or liberal societies): see LP §15, especially the discussion of the three guidelines for the duty of assistance (LP 106–12). Unfortunately, the transitions he has in mind are to generically well-ordered societies, not liberal democracies, so what he has to say is not especially relevant to my concerns above.

and to acquire journals, books, and other forms of mass media that cover politics. By making sufficient resources available for these purposes, improved economic efficiency and growth of per capita income can indeed help to establish reasonably favorable conditions for the full and effective exercise of the political liberties.

The second point is harder to make, but many passages in *Theory* point the way forward. For example, Rawls's brief discussion of John Maynard Keynes suggests a useful illustration of growth-enhancing limits on political liberty.[48] Keynes argued that the economic inequality that existed prior to World War I made possible a massive accumulation of capital (due to the rich's low marginal propensity to consume) and that this rise in the capital stock ultimately redounded to the benefit of the working class by increasing the marginal productivity of their labor (see Keynes 1920, 18–22). Had the working classes been politically empowered in the nineteenth century, however, this accumulation might not have taken place: redistributive taxation might have taken money from the class most likely to save and given it to the one most likely to spend, thus drastically reducing the century's extraordinarily high level of reinvestment. Denying the vote to the working classes for the sake of economic growth, which is blatantly inconsistent with the priority of political liberty, might be justified under certain historical circumstances as a way of generating conditions needed for the effective exercise of *everyone's* political liberties.

Could anything beyond property qualifications for voting or similar oligarchical strictures (albeit temporary, transitional ones) be justified with such an argument? At another point, Rawls says that "perhaps Burke's unrealistic account of representation had an element of validity in the context of eighteenth century society. . . . At that time unequal political liberty might conceivably have been a permissible adjustment to historical limitations" (TJ 217). As Hanna Pitkin remarks in *The Concept of Representation* (which Rawls himself cites at this point), Edmund Burke's concept of representation was highly elitist and inegalitarian. Burke believed that society should encourage the development of a "natural aristocracy" to govern in the national interest, which was to be discovered by means of rational parliamentary debate rather than by consultation with one's constituents. Pitkin points out the antidemocratic

---

48. TJ 263–64. Rawls uses Keynes's remarks to illustrate the belief that "inequalities in wealth and authority . . . may be justified if the subsequent economic and social benefits are large enough," though Rawls's focus here is just savings.

implications of his position: "Elections are merely a means of finding the members of a natural aristocracy, and presumably any other method of selection would be as acceptable if it were equally efficient at picking them. Burke himself at times suggests that some other process of selecting the elite might be superior. . . . Representation here becomes a synonym for good government, which is why Burke can maintain that 'the king is the representative of the people; so are the lords; so are the judges. They are all trustees for the people.' Representing is trusteeship, an elite caring for others."[49] For Burke, then, nondemocratic forms of government—from unelected legislatures to hereditary monarchies—can still be genuinely representative and hence consistent with the national interest. In the context of the current discussion, this national interest might include concern for economic growth. Thus, the transitional limits on political liberty that might be entertained within Rawls's (nonideal) theory could include not only a restricted franchise but also strictly nondemocratic forms of rule.

These remarks raise the question of how political elites, whether in a restricted-franchise or even nondemocratic regime, could be motivated to promote economic efficiency and growth. The problem of motivating elites certainly occupied Rawls, who wrote of "the danger to liberty from the loss in . . . control over those holding political power" (TJ 202). During his only other discussion of Burke in *Theory*, Rawls offers some reasons why a "governing class with pervasive hereditary features" might rule in the national interest: "Political power should be exercised by men experienced in, and educated from childhood to assume, the constitutional traditions of their society, men whose ambitions are moderated by the privileges and amenities of their assured position. Otherwise the stakes become too high and those lacking in culture and conviction contend with one another to control the power of the state for their narrow ends. Thus Burke believed that the great families of the ruling stratum contribute by the wisdom of their political rule to the general welfare from generation to generation" (TJ 264). Whether these virtues Burke ascribes to the *ancien riche* would lead them to promote economic reform, especially the encouragement of economic growth, is another question entirely. Much depends upon the progressiveness of aristocratic culture and the sense of duty these

---

49. Pitkin (1967, 171–72). As she emphasizes, the "elitist, ratiocinative representation of the whole nation" is but one element of Edmund Burke's concept of representation, which includes a distinction between "actual" and "virtual" representation and a concern for the "accurate reflection of popular feelings" as well (185). Rawls's one other discussion of Burke in *Theory* suggests, however, that the first element is his primary focus (TJ 264).

rulers have to advance the long-run interests of their subjects, including their ultimate interest in democratic self-government.

Kant grappled with many of the same issues in his political and historical writings. Not unlike J. S. Mill, he believed that the transition to a representative democracy would take place under the enlightened rule of an absolute monarch, one who would lead his people from a state of minority (i.e., the inability to think for oneself without the guidance of another) to complete intellectual and political self-government. The monarch would discharge this task by maintaining public order, protecting civil liberties, including freedom of the press, promoting (or at least not hampering) public education, and steadily ceding legislative power to representative institutions on matters of war, taxation, etc. Finally, he would be motivated to take these actions—which are wholly contrary to his long-run interests—by the exigencies of geopolitical competition: in order to strengthen his society for such competition and secure the financing that he needs for military campaigns, he would slowly have to enlighten and empower his own people. Though each step in this process would be in the short-run interest of the monarch, it would lead to his political disempowerment in the long run, turning him into a limited, constitutional monarch constrained by a democratic legislature.[50]

Some have ascribed views of this sort to Rawls himself. Don Habibi, for example, quotes Mill regarding the legitimacy of absolutism in dealing with barbarians "provided the end be their improvement, and the means justified by actually effecting that end"; he claims in the associated footnote that "John Rawls defended the denial of liberty along similar lines" in *Theory*.[51] Such a claim goes too far, though. Rawls's nonideal theory is so sketchily developed that it is simply not possible for us to know how he would have responded to the kinds of arguments I offered above, much less to those offered by Mill. These arguments may have the right form to work within the context of Rawls's nonideal theory, and they may be suggested by certain things that Rawls says, but we cannot ascribe them to Rawls himself with any confidence. Even so, a Rawlsian nonideal theory must be developed to provide policy guidance in these matters, and my musings above are intended merely as a first, highly tentative step in that direction.

---

50. For a detailed discussion of Kant's theory of democratic transitions, see Taylor (2006). This summary paragraph was taken from p. 557 of the article.

51. Habibi (1999, 136, 144). Habibi references TJ 132; the Mill quotation is from *On Liberty* (Mill 1998, 15).

IV. Conclusion

Many political theorists have criticized Rawls for subordinating democracy to liberalism, public to private autonomy, or the liberties of the ancients to those of the moderns. This criticism is understandable: as Josh Cohen points out, *Theory* "does not tell us much about the politics of a just society. . . . This relative inattention to democracy—to politics more generally—may leave the impression that Rawls's theory in some way denigrates democracy, perhaps subordinating it to a conception of justice that is defended through philosophical reasoning and is to be implemented by judges and administrators insulated from politics"; he associates this view of Rawls with such scholars as Benjamin Barber, Bonnie Honig, Michael Walzer, and Sheldon Wolin (J. Cohen 2003, 86, 131n1). A similarly prominent critic of Rawls, Jürgen Habermas, has made related observations, as we have seen: he says of Rawls's theory that its "two-stage character . . . generates a priority of liberal rights which demotes the democratic process to an inferior status. . . . The rigid boundary between the political and the nonpublic identities of citizens . . . is set by basic liberal rights that constrain democratic self-legislation, and with it the sphere of the political, from the beginning, that is, prior to all political will formation" (Habermas 1995, 128–29).

Like Cohen, I think that Rawls can be successfully defended against such criticisms. As I showed above, Rawls makes "the liberties of the moderns . . . subject to the constituent will of the people" during the process of constitutional ratification, and he recognizes the "distinctive place" of political liberty by protecting its fair value—a status unique among the basic liberties—and by favoring it when it conflicts with other basic liberties, including those (e.g., political speech) that usually support it (PL 327, 406). Additionally, as this chapter's revisionist account of the priority of political liberty suggests, a case can be made within the context of Rawls's theory for the lexical priority of core political liberty (namely, the rights to vote and hold public office) over other basic liberties. Though Rawls maintains that the "liberties of both public and private autonomy are given side by side and unranked in the first principle of justice," I have shown that this position cannot be sustained and that a persuasive case based on the first moral power can be made for the intrinsic good and lexical priority of political liberty as an institutional expression of and support for our moral autonomy in the realm of right (PL 413). Far from elevating liberalism over democracy, Rawls is best understood as elevating democratic practice over other concerns, not for the civic-humanist reasons of an Arendt or a Rousseau but rather for impeccably Kantian ones.

Appendix: A Primer on Lexical Orderings

A "lexical" (i.e., lexicographic) ordering is, in brief, a dictionary ordering. For example, suppose that every political order could be characterized by a unique five-letter word, and further suppose that each letter in this five-letter word stood for a particular desirable political value and that the rank of the letter assigned indicated the degree to which that value was attained (where "A" indicates that the value is wholly achieved and "Z" that it is not achieved at all). Consistent with Rawls's justice as fairness, I will make the first three letters represent the basic liberties, fair equality of opportunity, and the difference principle, respectively; the last two will symbolize efficiency and perfection of character in turn. Now consider the following three political orders: AARON, AZURE, and BABEL. Table 1 places them in lexical order.

Table 1 A lexical ordering

Basic liberties	Fair equality of opportunity	Difference principle	Efficiency	Perfection of character
A	A	R	O	N
A	Z	U	R	E
B	A	B	E	L

Thus, AARON is socially preferred to AZURE, which is socially preferred to BABEL. For our purposes, the chief thing to note about this lexical social-preference ordering is that AZURE is socially preferred to BABEL, despite the fact that a move from AZURE to BABEL would leave fair equality of opportunity perfectly achieved (A) rather than completely unachieved (Z). Why doesn't this reverse the ordering? Because in a lexical ordering, earlier letters take priority over later letters: A is higher than B in the basic liberties column, so AZURE beats BABEL. In other words, no gain in a later letter (e.g., fair equality of opportunity) can ever justify a loss in an earlier letter (e.g., basic liberties). Lexical priority is thus the strongest priority available.

4

The Priority of Civil Liberty

I. Introduction

Chapter 3 focused on political liberties, that is, those basic liberties, both core and auxiliary, that serve as institutional expressions and supports of our moral autonomy in the domain of right. The core political liberties are the rights to vote and hold public office, and the auxiliary political liberties include free political thought, speech, press, and assembly as well as minimal protection at least for psychological and physical integrity. I will turn in this chapter to civil or nonpolitical liberties, that is, those basic liberties that serve as either direct or indirect institutional buttresses for our personal autonomy. Civil liberty incorporates nonpolitical "freedom of speech and assembly; liberty of conscience and freedom of thought; freedom of the person . . . ; the right to hold personal property and freedom from arbitrary arrest and seizure."[1] This distinction between the political and civil liberties has been a consistent feature of Rawls's political thought.[2] Although he asserts that these two classes of basic liberties are "of equal weight . . . with neither externally imposed on the other," I showed in the last chapter that political liberties take priority over civil ones in cases of conflict (PL 412). In this chapter, though, I set

---

1. TJ 53. The line of demarcation between political and nonpolitical basic liberties is not as clean as I imply here. For example, insofar as one's plan of life involves ambitions for high office, the political liberties can act as supports for one's personal autonomy. Moreover, insofar as one's plan of life takes account of our political duty to participate in collective self-legislation, it becomes an expression of moral autonomy, and in a sense the nonpolitical liberties that support the autonomous formation of this plan support moral autonomy in turn—at least in this case. I am, of course, just redescribing the mutual support of the three hierarchically ordered stages of the extended Kantian conception of the person that I defined and defended in chapter 2.

2. TJ 176–77, 195, 201–2, 205, 217; PL 4–5, 206, 299. Rawls calls the civil or nonpolitical liberties "the other freedoms that, so to say, define the intrinsic good" of citizens (TJ 205).

aside the internal priority relation between the two sorts of basic liberties and concentrate on the priority of basic liberties in general, and civil liberties in particular, over other concerns: the priority of liberty regards the basic liberties as paramount and forbids their sacrifice for the sake of efficiency, utilitarian and perfectionist ideals, or even other principles within justice as fairness (namely, FEO and the DP), regardless of the size of the benefits that might obtain as a consequence of such sacrifice.

Two examples will illustrate the force of this priority vis-à-vis the two inferior principles of justice. Suppose that a law is proposed to punish (maybe only with fines) advocacy of racially and sexually bigoted doctrines on the grounds that their spread would hinder the implementation of FEO: the dissemination of such doctrines in a population—especially among employers—may hamper the matching of people and their talents with appropriate jobs in the basic structure. Such a law would clearly violate the priority of liberty, as liberty can be sacrificed only for the sake of liberty, and would therefore be ruled out.[3] Now suppose that a law is offered to punish advocacy of ascetic or antimaterialist doctrines (e.g., the teachings of Jesus in the Gospels) on the grounds that their widespread adoption would effectively undermine the DP's mandate: were such ideas to gain in popularity, economic trade and production would likely diminish and fewer resources would therefore be available to redistribute to the least advantaged members of society. Again, if EL is lexically prior to the DP, such a law must be rejected.

The priority of liberty has always played a central role in Rawls's political theory. Rawls notes that "the force of justice as fairness would appear to arise from two things: the requirement that all inequalities be justified to the least advantaged [the DP], and the priority of liberty. This pair of constraints

---

3. The allowable sacrifices of liberty for liberty can take several forms. First, some basic liberties might be sacrificed for the sake of others: for example, free political speech (in the form of campaign expenditures) may be curtailed in order to protect the fair value of core political liberties—see chapter 3. Second, a basic liberty may be limited for its own sake: for example, so-called time, place, and manner regulations on political speech may help to preserve the value of political speech itself by making its exercise across persons mutually consistent (by means of, say, *Robert's Rules of Order*)—see PL 341. Third, a basic liberty may be *temporarily* sacrificed if such sacrifice is a condition for its own eventual effective exercise: for example, core political liberties might be sacrificed if this were necessary to increase GDP and thereby make adequate economic resources available for their effective exercise—see chapter 3 and below. This last variety of sacrifice falls under the rubric of nonideal theory, discussed in TJ §39. David Reidy has suggested to me that punishment of the advocacy described above might be defended on such grounds; he used the compelling framework developed in Reidy (2002) to do so. I have responded to this possibility in a separate paper.

distinguishes it from intuitionism and teleological theories" (TJ 220). As we shall see, its importance in his work has if anything increased over time. Part of the reason for this greater prominence is Rawls's growing ambivalence about the other distinctive elements of his political theory, especially the lexical priority of FEO and the DP.[4] In the absence of the former element, the priority of liberty would be the chief thing preventing the special conception of justice from collapsing into the general conception, in which all social primary goods (and presumably those interests they support) are lumped together. Rawls is deeply opposed, however, to the notion that "all human interests are commensurable, and that between any two there always exists some rate of exchange in terms of which it is rational to balance the protection of one against the protection of the other," and anything short of lexical priority for the basic liberties would countenance such trade-offs under certain circumstances (PL 312).

This central component of justice as fairness has been criticized in a long line of articles, including contributions by Kenneth Arrow, Brian Barry, Ricardo Blaug, Norman Daniels, Joseph DeMarco and Samuel Richmond, H. L. A. Hart, Russell Keat and David Miller, and Henry Shue (see Arrow 1973; Barry 1973a; Blaug 1986; Daniels 1989a; DeMarco and Richardson 1977; Hart 1989; Keat and Miller 1974; Shue 1975). All these authors have found Rawls's defense of the priority of liberty deficient in some respects, and many of them have been sharply critical of the very idea of lexical priority for basic liberties: Barry considers it "outlandishly extreme," while Hart deems it "dogmatic" (Barry 1973a, 276; Hart 1989, 252; also see Arneson 2000, 240–41). In section II of this chapter, I will review Rawls's three arguments for the priority of liberty in *Theory* and argue that two of them do indeed fail (either in whole or in part) because of two types of error, both of them discussed in chapter 3. One is Rawls's conviction that once he has shown the instrumental value of the basic liberties for some essential purpose (e.g., securing self-respect), he has automatically shown the reason for their lexical priority. I will again refer to this conviction—specifically, that the *lexical* priority of the basic liberties can be inferred from the *high* priority of the interests that they serve—as the "inference fallacy." The other kind of error arises because though the interest in question may have the necessary priority, the basic liberties are not *requisite*

---

4. On his ambivalence towards the priority of FEO, see JF 163n44; on his ambivalence towards the DP, see TJ xiv.

for its protection but merely *strongly contributory* towards it. As we saw in the last chapter, lexical priority is such a stringent condition that a special form of justification will be necessary for its defense.

As I will also demonstrate, though, Rawls's third argument for the priority of liberty does not commit either of these two errors. This defense, which I will call the hierarchy argument, suggests that the priority of liberty flows immediately from a certain conception of free persons. Unfortunately, the argument as presented is radically incomplete, leaving a number of important questions unanswered. In section III, therefore, I present a partial reconstruction of the hierarchy argument, showing that it can offer a compelling and attractive defense of the priority of liberty. This reconstruction explains the highest-order interest in rationality, justifies the lexical priority of all civil liberties, and reinterprets the threshold condition for the application of the priority of liberty. What had perhaps previously seemed a peculiarly disproportionate concern for the civil liberties is shown to follow quite naturally from the extended Kantian conception of the person.

II. Three Arguments for the Priority of Liberty in *Theory*

In this section, I will examine Rawls's three arguments for the lexical priority of liberty found in the revised edition of *Theory*.[5] In the first of these three, which I will label the self-respect argument, Rawls maintains that the priority of the (equal) basic liberties is needed to secure equal citizenship, which is itself a prerequisite for self-respect. In the second, which I will call the equal liberty of conscience argument, Rawls argues that the integrity of our religious beliefs (and, by extension, of our moral and philosophical ones) is of such importance that liberty of conscience (and, by extension, other basic liberties) must be given lexical priority. Finally, in what I will refer to as the hierarchy argument, Rawls maintains that the lexical priority of the basic liberties is justified by the lexical priority of a particular interest that they protect—namely, our interest in choosing our final ends under conditions of freedom. I will argue that the first and second arguments suffer from the two errors discussed above (although the second can be given a narrow interpretation that rescues

---

5. Rawls presents an additional argument in the first edition of *Theory* (542–43) but retracts it in *Political Liberalism* (PL 371n84) because it is inconsistent with one of his other arguments for the priority of liberty (namely, the Hierarchy Argument).

it from the charge) but that the third argument avoids them and can therefore serve as the basis for a reconstructed defense of the priority of liberty.

A. The Self-Respect Argument

In §67 of *Theory*, Rawls says that self-respect is "perhaps the most important primary good": without it, we will doubt our own value, the value of our plan of life, and our ability to carry it out, and we will therefore be susceptible to the siren call of "apathy and cynicism."[6] In §82 of *Theory*, as a prelude to the self-respect argument, he goes on to note how self-respect is tightly linked to status, that is, to our positions in social hierarchies. Because even a just society will be characterized by various kinds of inequalities (e.g., income differentials) that might erode the self-respect of the poorly ranked, any society concerned with securing self-respect for all of its citizens must affirm equality of status along a key dimension. Rawls believes political equality, or "equal citizenship," can serve this purpose, especially when socioeconomic inequalities are kept within reasonable bounds by "just background institutions" reflecting FEO and the DP.[7]

What is required for "equal citizenship," however? Rawls contends that equality in the provision of basic liberties is a necessary condition for equal citizenship and that such equality therefore provides a secure ground for self-respect: "the basis for self-respect in a just society is the publicly affirmed distribution of fundamental rights and liberties. And this distribution being equal, everyone has a similar and secure status when they meet to conduct the common affairs of the wider society" (TJ 477). Rawls persuasively argues that citizens in a just society could never consent to less than equal basic liberties, as "this subordinate ranking in public life would be humiliating and destructive of self-esteem" (TJ 477). A status inequality explicitly defined and enforced by the state would likely have a more devastating effect on self-respect than a socioeconomic inequality that emerges via a process merely superintended by the state. A self-respecting citizenry thus requires equal basic liberties. I summarize this multistage argument in figure 7.

Up to this point, Rawls has said nothing about the priority of the basic liberties; rather, he has focused exclusively on their equal provision. Only at

---

6. TJ 386. See PL 318–20 for a later version of the Self-Respect Argument.
7. TJ 478. There are other determinants of self-respect, of course, some of which are private and idiosyncratic (e.g., indelible psychological traits resulting from early childhood socialization).

The Priority of Civil Liberty   157

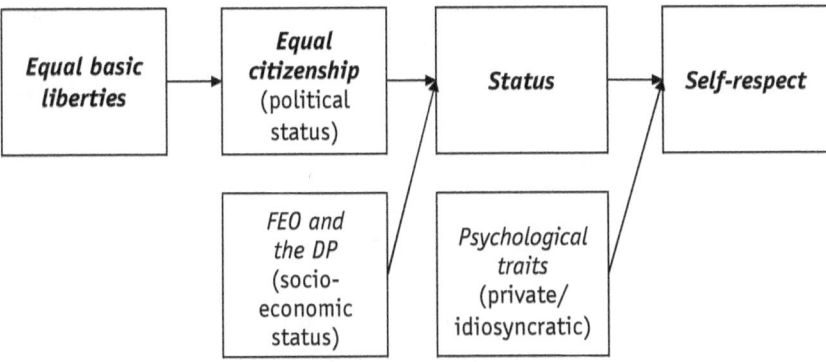

Fig. 7 The self-respect argument

the end of his main presentation of the self-respect argument does he mention the priority of liberty: "When it is the position of equal citizenship that answers to the need for status, the precedence of the equal liberties becomes all the more necessary. Having chosen a conception of justice that tries to eliminate the significance of relative economic and social advantages as supports for men's self-confidence, it is essential that the priority of liberty be firmly maintained" (TJ 478). This passage provides a superb illustration of what I earlier called the "inference fallacy": Rawls tries to derive the lexical priority of the basic liberties from the central importance of an interest that they support—in this case, an interest in securing self-respect for all citizens. Without question, the self-respect argument makes a very strong case for assigning the basic liberties a high priority; otherwise, socioeconomic inequalities might reemerge as the primary determinants of status and therefore self-respect. What it does not explain, however, is why lexical priority is needed. Why, for instance, would minor restraints on the basic liberties threaten the social basis of self-respect, so long as they were equally applied to all citizens? One example might be punishing Holocaust denial for the sake of political stability. Such a restriction would involve no subordination and, being very small, would be unlikely to jeopardize the central importance of equal citizenship as a determinant of status.[8]

8. To put this in OP terms: the *possibility* of beneficial trade-offs like the one mentioned would be known to parties in the OP (though they would be unaware of such historical details, of course); given this possibility, they would assign high but not lexical priority to the basic liberties, which *might* permit such trade-offs to be made were they to present themselves at the constitutional and/or legislative stages of the four-stage sequence (TJ §31). As I note in chapter 8, merely high priority might still lead to the constitutional practice of civil libertarianism,

Even if such minor restrictions were ruled out as too risky, we would still need to ask why self-respect is of such overwhelming importance that its social basis, an equal distribution of the basic liberties, must be given lexical priority. As noted above, Rawls maintains in §67 of *Theory* that self-respect is "perhaps the most important primary good," but he does not explain why this particular primary good should trump all others. As we shall see in the third subsection, the only way to justify something as strong as lexical priority for the basic liberties is to justify lexical priority for the interest they support, that is, assigning of such weight to an interest that it cannot be traded off for any other interest, no matter how high the rate of exchange. Securing self-respect for all citizens might be such an interest, but Rawls's arguments do not show why.

Before continuing on to Rawls's second defense of the priority of liberty, I would like to mention one other criticism of the self-respect argument. Unlike the ones offered above, this is an external rather than internal criticism. Rawls implicitly assumes in this argument that political and socioeconomic statuses are the only (or at least the predominant) kinds of status and thus the two rival supports for self-respect (cf. Shue 1975, 199). Other supports for self-respect are imaginable, however, and may be capable of maintaining it even in the face of cruel political and socioeconomic inequality. Medieval Christendom, for instance, offered a uniformly distributed basis for self-respect despite its vast inequalities in liberty and wealth: the equally inclusive love of God.[9] Rawls might very well respond that this belief does not apply (widely) in modern liberal-democratic societies, but even if this were true, his reply would signal the historical contingency of his argument. Rawls becomes more comfortable with such contingency after his so-called political turn, of course, but I will argue in part 3 that such comfort is ultimately unwarranted.

B. The Equal Liberty of Conscience Argument

In §26 of *Theory*, Rawls contends that free persons have certain "fundamental interests" that they must secure through the priority of liberty:

---

which would disallow such trade-offs due to a fear of legislative overreach and even abuse, but this constitutional analogue of the lexical priority of liberty would be exposed to shifts in the "calculus of social interests" due to its grounding in a nonlexical priority of liberty (TJ 4). For more details, see chapter 8's discussion of the possibility of a "utilitarian" civil libertarianism.

9. An earlier version of this criticism can be found in Barry (1973b, 48–49).

> I assume that the parties [in the OP] view themselves as free persons who have *fundamental aims and interests* in the name of which they think it legitimate for them to make claims on one another concerning the design of the basic structure of society. The *religious interest* is a familiar historical example; the interest in the integrity of the person is another. In the original position the parties do not know what particular forms these interests take; but they do assume that they have such interests and that the basic liberties necessary for their protection are guaranteed by the first principle. *Since they must secure these interests, they rank the first principle prior to the second.*[10]

Later, in *Theory* §33, Rawls further develops this argument with respect to the religious interest, among others. He explains the importance of this interest and the equal liberty of conscience that protects it as follows: "The parties [in the OP] must assume that they may have moral, religious, or philosophical interests which they cannot put in jeopardy unless there is no alternative. One might say that they regard themselves as having moral or religious obligations which they must keep themselves free to honor. . . . They cannot take chances with their liberty by permitting the dominant religious or moral doctrine to persecute or to suppress others if it wishes. . . . To gamble in this way would show that one did not take one's religious or moral convictions seriously, or highly value the liberty to examine one's beliefs."[11] We might view this argument as simply another illustration of the inference fallacy: Rawls tries to derive the lexical priority of equal liberty of conscience from the fundamental importance of the interest it supports—namely, an interest in examining and subscribing to certain philosophical, moral, and religious beliefs. The central importance of this interest is insufficient, however, to establish the lexical priority of the liberty that supports it: one might "highly value" this interest yet still endorse small sacrifices of equal liberty of conscience and the interest it protects if such sacrifices were necessary to advance other highly valued interests. Only if the interest had lexical priority over all other interests could such trade-offs be categorically ruled out.

---

10. TJ 131 (emphasis added). See PL 310–12 for a later version of the Equal Liberty of Conscience Argument.
11. TJ 180–81; cf. Hart (1989, 252): "It might be said that any rational person who understood what it is to have a religious faith and to wish to practice it would agree that for any such person to be prevented by law from practicing his religion must be worse than for a relatively poor man to be prevented from gaining a great advance in material goods through the surrender of a religious liberty which meant little or nothing to him."

We can interpret Rawls's argument in another way, though. The passages just quoted are larded with the language of compulsion: "must secure," "cannot put in jeopardy," "cannot take chances," etc. Also, when discussing the same issue in §82 of *Theory*, Rawls says that "in order to secure their unknown but particular interests from the original position, they [OP parties] are led, *in view of the strains of commitment* (§29), to give precedence to basic liberties" (TJ 475; emphasis added). Perhaps Rawls's argument here is best understood as follows: the parties in the original position, given their general knowledge of human psychology, must avoid committing to political principles whose outcomes they might not be able to accept; political principles that place fundamental interests (such as the religious interest) at even the slightest risk, by refusing lexical priority to the liberties that protect them, make the strains of commitment intolerable.

This argument seems especially powerful with regard to the religious interest. Religious persons have faith that their religious duties (e.g., acceptance of a creed, participation in certain ceremonies, etc.) are divinely mandated and that a failure to abide by these commitments may lead to divine retribution, even eternal damnation. If the parties in the original position agree to anything less exacting than the lexical priority of equal liberty of conscience, they may emerge from behind the veil of ignorance to discover that their own religious beliefs and practices have been put in jeopardy by discriminatory legislation and that they are psychologically incapable of abiding by such legislation due to an overriding fear of supernatural punishment.

This strains-of-commitment argument provides strong support for the lexical priority of equal liberty of conscience as applied to religion. Does it, however, extend to philosophical and moral commitments as well, as Rawls claims in §33 of *Theory*? Although one can point to a few important historical examples of people who were either incapable or unwilling to abide by laws that discriminated against their philosophical and moral beliefs (e.g., Galileo and Socrates), these cases are celebrated precisely because of their rarity: religious martyrs are far more common than philosophical or moral ones, as we have become uncomfortably aware in the wake of September 11 and with the spread of suicide bombing as a tactic of Islamic terrorists. Therefore, the strains-of-commitment argument, if it applies to moral and philosophical beliefs at all, is less compelling than in the case of religious belief.[12]

12. Rawls might reply here that reactions to strains of commitment can take both strong and weak forms and that the power of my examples derives from only considering the strong form.

What of Rawls's additional claim in §33 of *Theory* that "the reasoning in this case [i.e., equal liberty of conscience] can be generalized to apply to other freedoms, *although not always with the same force*" (TJ 181; emphasis added)? In some cases, this claim seems justified. Consider, for instance, Rawls's own example of "the rights defining the integrity of the person" (mentioned along with liberty of conscience in §39) (TJ 217; cf. TJ 53, 131). If something less than lexical priority for these rights were agreed to by the parties in the OP, they might again come out from behind the veil of ignorance to discover that their fundamental interest in bodily integrity had been jeopardized by legislation implementing, for example, compulsory live-donor organ harvesting or some radically egalitarian "slavery of the talented" for the benefit of the poor (e.g., heavy head taxes)—legislation that they might be hard pressed to obey. In other cases, though, this strains-of-commitment argument appears less compelling, as Rawls himself admits in the above quotation. Consider, for example, freedom of speech. Were freedom of speech given less than lexical priority, would the speech-curbing laws that might result lead to intolerable strains of commitment? Perhaps, though the not insubstantial variation in such legislation across stable liberal democracies (e.g., laws that check pornography, obscenity, Holocaust or Armenian-genocide denial, advocacy of race and religious hatreds, etc.) suggests otherwise. Even laws that would violate *core* protections of *political* speech on virtually anyone's understanding—for instance, restrictions on advocacy of the peaceful nationalization of industry—might not cause unbearably severe commitment strains. Parties in the OP, aware of the possible benefits of allowing such restrictions (for, say, political stability or solidarity), would be unlikely to tie the hands of agents in later stages of the four-stage

---

The strong form is for us to become "sullen and resentful," leading perhaps to "violent action in protest against our condition," while the weak form is for us to become "withdrawn and cynical," unable to "affirm the principles of justice in our thought and conduct. . . . Though we are not hostile or rebellious, those principles are not ours and fail to engage our moral sensibility" (JF 128). So Rawls might admit that violent resentment is indeed more probable in the religious case but still argue that cynical withdrawal is a real possibility in all of them. One can admit the force of this reply, though, and still point out that the *overall* strains in the religious case (strong plus weak) are more severe than in either the philosophical or moral cases (weak only), and this is all that I need for the above critique to do its work. All principles of justice will create *some* strains, however minor, so the strains-of-commitment argument must be understood only to rule out candidate principles that would generate especially severe, even intolerable strains—and principles that deny lexical priority to liberty of religious conscience qualify, as the long and bloody history of European Christianity amply demonstrates. Many thanks to Samuel Freeman for pressing me on this important point.

sequence by assigning infinite weight to these liberties vis-à-vis other social primary goods—at least for the reasons given here.

In summary, the strains-of-commitment interpretation of the equal liberty of conscience argument provides strong support for the lexical priority of certain basic liberties (e.g., religious liberty and the rights protecting integrity of the person) but weaker support for others (e.g., moral or philosophical liberty of conscience and freedom of speech). This result may not be especially surprising: there is no reason why the psychological strains of obeying laws that encroach upon fundamental interests should be same for each of these interests—some interests, after all, might be more fundamental than others. Hence, this interpretation of the equal liberty of conscience argument cannot by itself provide the desired support for the priority of liberty. What is needed is a defense of the priority of liberty that can justify the lexical priority of *all* basic liberties, not merely the subset whose violation creates intolerable commitment strains. Fortunately, Rawls's third argument for the priority of liberty points the way towards such a defense.

C. The Hierarchy Argument

Rawls initially presents the hierarchy argument in §§26 and 82 of *Theory*. He begins in §26 by distinguishing what he calls a "highest-order interest" from the fundamental interests that I discussed in the last subsection and by linking the former to the priority of liberty:

> Very roughly the parties [in the OP] regard themselves as having a *highest-order interest* in how all their other interests, including even their fundamental ones, are shaped and regulated by social institutions. They do not think of themselves as inevitably bound to, or as identical with, the pursuit of any particular complex of fundamental interests that they may have at any given time, although they want the right to advance such interests. . . . *Rather, free persons conceive themselves as beings who can revise and alter their final ends and who give first priority to preserving their liberty in these matters.* Hence, they not only have final ends that they are in principle free to pursue or to reject, but their original allegiance and continued devotion to these ends are to be formed and affirmed under conditions that are free. (TJ 131–32; emphasis added)

Rawls identifies here what he later calls a "hierarchy of interests" for free persons. Our highest-order interest (or that of our OP representatives) is in shaping our other interests, including our fundamental ones, under conditions of freedom, which we therefore assign "first priority"; this interest is identical to the highest-order interest in the development and exercise of our second moral power of rationality (KCMT 312). Our fundamental interests, including both our religious interest and our interest in integrity of the person, come second; they are best regarded as components of the higher-order interest in "protecting and advancing [our] conception of the good," as fundamental interests are likely to be preconditions or even constituents of these conceptions (KCMT 313). Rawls spells out the implications of the above passage more clearly in §82: "Thus the persons in the original position are moved by a certain *hierarchy of interests*. They must first secure their highest-order interest and fundamental aims (only the general form of which is known to them), and this fact is reflected in the precedence they give to liberty; the acquisition of means that enable them to advance their other desires and ends has a subordinate place" (TJ 476; emphasis added). Thus, the lexical priority of the basic liberties over the other social primary goods ("means that enable them to advance their other desires and ends") can be justified by a hierarchy of interests: the highest-order interest in choosing our ends in freedom takes lexical priority ("they must first secure . . .") over an interest in advancing those ends—an interest that is secured by FEO and the DP, which provide various kinds of resources (jobs, income, etc.) for this very purpose.

In short, the hierarchy argument tries to justify a hierarchy of goods (basic liberties over other social primary goods) with a hierarchy of interests (a highest-order interest in free choice of ends over an interest in advancing those ends). Notice how this argument deftly avoids the inference-fallacy objection: by asserting the *lexical* priority of our highest-order interest in the free choice of ends, Rawls is able to defend the lexical priority of the basic liberties that are its indispensable support. The hierarchy argument seems to be a promising approach to justifying the priority of liberty.

This argument also serves as one of the key defenses of the priority of liberty in *Political Liberalism*.[13] Rawls argues there that our highest-order interest

---

13. PL 312–14, 335. As I mentioned earlier, *Political Liberalism* contains versions of the Self-Respect Argument (PL 318–20) and the Equal Liberty of Conscience Argument (PL 310–12) as well. It also deploys variants of the Stability Argument (PL 316–18) and the Well-Ordered Society Argument (PL 320–23), which I discussed in chapter 3. Though Rawls does not try to assess the

in the development and exercise of rationality—both as a means to our conception of the good and as a constituent of it—must be supported by a set of basic liberties, including liberty of conscience and freedom of association. Apart from noting that liberty of conscience allows us to "fall into error and make mistakes" and thereby learn and grow as rational actors, Rawls spends little time connecting the basic liberties to this highest-order interest, nor does he really explain the underlying hierarchy of interests.

Several important questions therefore arise at this point. First, what is the exact nature of this highest-order interest, and why are some basic liberties crucial for its support? Second, what justifies the asserted hierarchy of interests? To put the question more sharply: does the hierarchy argument simply kick the problem of defending the priority of liberty up one level of abstraction (from goods to interests) without actually solving it?[14] Third, are there goods other than the basic liberties that are indispensable buttresses for our highest-order interest (e.g., literature comparing religious faiths, which is surely necessary for *intelligent* "free exercise"), and, if so, does this fact undermine the hierarchy argument? Rawls does not adequately address any of these questions, yet they must be answered for the hierarchy argument to be considered a full success.

In the next section, I show that all of these questions can be answered within the context of Rawls's political theory. To do so, however, I must draw upon the resources of chapters 1–3 in order to show that the highest-order interest in the free choice of ends follows naturally from the Kantian moral autonomy Rawls endorses in *Theory* §40, that the civil liberties are essential institutional supports for this interest, and that the priority of liberty becomes effective only if sufficient material means are available to sustain our exercise of rationality.

III. A Kantian Reconstruction of the Hierarchy Argument

A. Rationality as a Form of Autonomy

In chapters 1 and 2, I demonstrated the foundational role that Kantian moral autonomy plays in Rawls's conception of the person: the first moral power of

---

"relative weights" of the various grounds he offers for the priority of liberty, he does suggest that those "connected with the capacity for a conception of the good are more familiar, perhaps because they seem more straightforward and, offhand, of greater weight"; the Hierarchy Argument is one such ground (PL 324).

14. For a similar line of criticism, see Fehige (2000, 265).

reasonableness illustrates our "independence from natural contingencies and social accident" and equips us for political as well as ethical self-legislation; consequently, the development and exercise of both this power and the second moral power of rationality are highest-order interests of agents in the OP, guiding them in their selection of principles of justice (TJ 225). I also maintained in chapters 2 and 3 that the first moral power and its legislative products frame and limit the second moral power and its associated plan of life and conception of the good—Rawls's claims to the contrary notwithstanding (PL 413). This raises the question of precisely how the first and second moral powers (or, in the language of chapter 2, moral and personal autonomy) are related to one another and, specifically, whether the latter can even qualify as a conception of autonomy. I addressed this issue in chapter 2, demonstrating that personal autonomy can be derived from, and serve as a building block for, moral autonomy; thus, the second moral power is rightly reckoned a facet of autonomy and analogous to the first moral power. This relationship is vitally important because it justifies the asserted hierarchy of interests and the corresponding hierarchy of social primary goods.

B. Civil Liberties as Indispensable Supports for Rationality

In order to advance the reconstruction of the hierarchy argument, we must now answer the following question: how does this highest-order interest in rationality and its preconditions justify the lexical priority of the basic liberties over other social primary goods, as called for by the priority of liberty? I have already shown in chapter 3 why political liberty (i.e., the subset of basic liberties, both core and auxiliary, that serve as institutional expressions and supports of our moral autonomy in the domain of right) deserves such priority over not only FEO and the DP but also nonpolitical or civil liberties. So the question should be properly narrowed to: how does this interest in rationality and its conditions justify the lexical priority of civil liberties over FEO and the DP? Briefly, it justifies such priority because these civil liberties are indispensable conditions for the exercise of rationality, which is why our agents in the OP "give first priority to preserving [our] liberty in these matters" (TJ 131–32). If OP parties were to sacrifice civil liberties for the sake of lower social primary goods (i.e., the "means that enable them to advance their other desires and ends"), they would be sacrificing their highest-order interest in rationality and thereby failing to express their trustors' nature as autonomous beings (TJ 476, 493).

A concise examination of the civil liberties enumerated by Rawls will indicate why they are necessary conditions for the exercise of rationality.[15] Civil freedoms of speech and assembly, liberty of conscience, and freedom of thought are *directly* supportive of the creation and revision of plans of life: without secure rights to explore ideas and beliefs with others (be it in person or through various media) and consider these at our leisure, we would be unable to make informed decisions about our conception of the good. Freedom of the person (including psychological and bodily integrity), as well as the right to personal property and immunity from arbitrary arrest and seizure, are *indirectly* supportive of rationality, as they create stable and safe personal spaces for purposes of reflection and communication, without which the free design and revision of plans of life would be compromised if not crippled. Even minor restrictions on these civil liberties would threaten the highest-order interest in rationality, however slightly, and such a threat is disallowed given the absolute priority of this interest over lower concerns. Note also that lexical priority can be justified here for all civil liberties, not just a subset of them (as was the case with the strains-of-commitment interpretation of the equal liberty of conscience argument).[16]

As I mentioned in chapter 3 with regard to auxiliary political liberties, in order for these civil liberties to be truly indispensable, it must be the case that no compensating measures can be taken to sustain our exercise of rationality if we trade off civil liberties for lower goods; else, the civil liberties lack the requisite priority. The possibility and desirability of such trade-offs seem to vary across the two categories of civil liberties. The directly supportive civil liberties are indeed indispensable, at least along some dimensions. Civil free speech, for example, is consistent with so-called time, place, and manner restrictions because compensating measures, like additional funding for relevant media or other forums, are possible. However, it is inconsistent with content controls because such controls, by hindering the discussion of certain topics, reduce our ability to make informed judgments about them and thereby illicitly restrict our exercise of rationality; any compensating measures that might be proposed would either have to subvert the original control or aid discussion of other, uncontrolled topics, but the latter approach would be beside the

---

15. This list of civil liberties is drawn from diverse sources, including TJ 53, 177, 202, 205, 217, and PL 5, 299, 335.
16. This conceptual distinction between directly and indirectly supportive civil liberties is drawn from PL 335.

point, as a broad conception of rationality requires that all topics at least be *open* to discussion.[17]

The indirectly supportive civil liberties, on the other hand, are more difficult to defend as indispensable, as compensated trade-offs would surely be possible under some circumstances. For example, a small increase in the probability of arbitrary arrest (the result of, say, a money-saving reduction in criminal-procedural protections) might be made "rationality neutral" with an across-the-board boost to media subsidies—assuming, of course, that this increased probability of arrest were uncorrelated with one's selection of discussion topics. Still, as was the case with indirectly supportive auxiliary political liberty, a *minimal* provision of psychological and physical security is surely required for personally autonomous creation and revision of plans of life: for example, the continual, looming threat of violent death due to civil unrest or unchecked criminality would make the full exercise of rationality difficult, even if various compensating measures were taken. Beyond mandating a basic minimum, though, parties in the OP are not really in a position to say much more (due to the possibility of compensated trade-offs) and must consequently defer to the judgment of those later in the four-stage sequence, who will know more about their particular societies and therefore be in a better position to judge such trade-offs.

One problem with both the reconstructed hierarchy argument and its original version, as I implied at the end of the last section, is that goods other than the civil liberties are necessary to support our highest-order interest in rationality. For example, while freedom of speech is indeed essential for the creation and revision of plans of life, so are those material goods that make this freedom effective, including assembly halls, street corners, megaphones, soapboxes, etc.; much the same could be said of other civil liberties. One potential solution to this problem would be to redefine the priority of liberty so that it maintained the lexical priority of civil liberties over other goods *only when those goods were not needed to uphold the highest-order interest in rationality*. I offer a more elegant solution in the following subsection, though, a solution that

---

17. One might think that increased depth could compensate for reduced breadth or—to use a shooting analogy—that greater precision could compensate for reduced accuracy (due to the bias introduced by content controls). Any such imposed bias, however, is inconsistent with autonomy: all parameters of a discussion, including especially its scope, must be revisable *from within* for a discussion to be considered autonomous; no amount of aid can erase the stain of the original intrusion, which taints all subsequent discussion and forever colors any revisions to life plans that result. Content controls are wholly analogous to the heteronomous incursion of nature or convention into moral reasoning.

has the added advantage of elucidating the meaning of Rawls's threshold condition for the application of the priority of liberty.

C. An Interpretation of the Threshold Condition for Applying the Priority of Liberty

Rawls notes on several occasions in *Theory* that the priority of liberty comes into effect only when certain conditions are realized. For example, he begins *Theory* §82 with the following observation:

> I have supposed that if the persons in the original position know that their basic liberties can be effectively exercised, they will not exchange a lesser liberty for greater economic advantages (§26). It is only when social conditions do not allow the full establishment of these rights that one can acknowledge their restriction. The equal liberties can be denied only when it is necessary to change the quality of civilization so that in due course everyone can enjoy these freedoms. The effective realization of all these liberties in a well-ordered society is the long-run tendency of the two principles and rules of priority when they are consistently followed under reasonably favorable conditions. (TJ 474–75; cf. Mill 1991, 46–53, 85–93, 345–65)

His other discussions of the threshold condition in *Theory* provide little additional information, though later in §82 he adds a "degree of fulfillment of needs and material wants" to the social conditions that must be met before the priority of liberty can come into effect.[18]

Rawls's description of the threshold condition can be interpreted in at least three different ways, each of which is inclusive of (and therefore more stringent than) the ones preceding it:

1. *Formal threshold:* Before the priority of liberty can apply, a society must have achieved a level of wealth sufficient for it to maintain a legal

---

18. TJ 476; cf. TJ 54–55, 132, and PL 7. He later adds that "these conditions are determined by a society's culture, its traditions and acquired skill in running institutions, and its level of economic advance (which need not be especially high), and no doubt by other things as well" (PL 297). Finally, he discusses these conditions a little in *The Law of Peoples* §15, especially with respect to the three guidelines for assistance to "burdened societies" (LP 106–12).

system with courts, police, etc. that can define and protect the basic liberties of citizens within the bounds of the rule of law.
2. *Weak substantive threshold:* Before the priority of liberty can apply, a society must have achieved a level of wealth sufficient for it to allow its citizens to engage in the meaningful *formation* of life plans. For example, citizens must have access to media, public forums, and schools and must have sufficient leisure time to make use of these resources and reflect on their plans.
3. *Strong substantive threshold:* Before the priority of liberty can apply, a society must have achieved a level of wealth sufficient for it to allow its citizens to engage in the meaningful *advancement* of life plans. For example, citizens must have access to professional training, start-up funds for businesses, grants for artistic, literary, and scientific projects, etc.

Two implications of the reconstructed hierarchy argument are clear. First, at least the formal threshold must be met before the priority of liberty can apply: the priority of liberty would be meaningless in a society that could not even establish the basic liberties themselves due to social and economic conditions. All arguments for the priority of liberty, including the reconstructed one on offer here, must take feasibility into account. Second, the strong substantive threshold must be ruled out. Once the weak substantive threshold is met, the highest-order interest in rationality can be fully satisfied, as all of its necessary conditions (including the civil liberties and any other social primary goods essential for its exercise) are then in place. Any threshold more stringent than this one, including the strong substantive threshold, in effect sacrifices the civil liberties and the highest-order interest they protect for the sake of advancing, not forming, our plans of life, but such a sacrifice is ruled out by the reconstructed hierarchy argument. In summary, no threshold less stringent than the formal one or more stringent than the weak substantive one can be justified by this argument for the priority of liberty.

Now consider the choice between the formal and weak substantive thresholds: can the reconstructed hierarchy argument justify violations of the priority of liberty if needed to move society to a level of wealth where the formation of life plans is meaningful? Once we recognize that the only function of the civil liberties is to advance our highest-order interest in rationality, the answer becomes clear: if the violation of the civil liberties is the best means to advance the interest that they serve, then the priority of liberty can be temporarily set aside. To insist upon the imposition of the priority of liberty under such circumstances would be to fetishize the civil liberties. I thus conclude that the reconstructed hierarchy argument requires a weak substantive threshold for the application of the priority of liberty.

Note how this interpretation of the threshold condition solves the problem discussed at the end of the last subsection. Rather than modifying the definition of the priority of liberty, we can simply stipulate that its implementation be delayed until all social primary goods necessary for the advancement of the highest-order interest in rationality can be made available. Once this threshold is reached, however, civil liberties can no longer be sacrificed for lower social primary goods. Thus, the reconstructed hierarchy argument, in addition to offering a strong defense of the priority of liberty, clarifies the meaning of the threshold condition for its application.

We have now completed the reconstruction of the hierarchy argument. At the end of the last section we asked a number of questions about the original argument, all of which have now been answered. We have explicated the highest-order interest in preserving both rationality and the conditions of its exercise, which include civil liberties first and foremost. We have seen that the exalted position that this interest holds in our hierarchy of interests is justified by rationality's intimate connection to Kantian moral autonomy. Finally, we have learned that the contribution of social primary goods other than civil liberties to this highest-order interest does not weaken the argument for the priority of liberty but rather strengthens our understanding of the threshold condition for its application.

IV. Conclusion:
Implications for the American Practice of Civil Libertarianism

This reconstructed hierarchy defense of the priority of liberty has significant implications for American-style civil libertarianism, especially as reflected in First Amendment jurisprudence. Consider, for example, two strands of such jurisprudence: the line of Establishment Clause cases starting in the 1960s and the string of "incitement" cases ending in *Brandenburg v. Ohio* (1969). The U.S. Supreme Court initiated stricter enforcement of the Establishment Clause of the First Amendment ("Congress shall pass no law respecting an establishment of religion") in the early 1960s under the leadership of Chief Justice Earl Warren.

A long line of decisions—including *Engel v. Vitale* (1962), *Abington School District v. Schempp* (1963), *Stone v. Graham* (1980), and *Wallace v. Jaffree* (1985)—gradually eliminated most religious content from public school instruction. Mandatory school prayers, Bible readings, postings of the Ten Commandments, and voluntary school prayers were successively found unconstitutional. State laws either banning the teaching of evolution or mandating the teaching of "creation science" in public schools were also overturned. Finally, in *Lemon v. Kurtzman* (1971), the court promulgated a strict three-prong test for determining the constitutionality of policies challenged under the Establishment Clause. This test has been used, inter alia, to overturn laws offering supplementary salaries to parochial school teachers and other forms of economic aid to parochial schools.

The string of "incitement" cases, dealing with the punishment of persons who advocate illegal conduct, begins with *Schenck v. United States* (1919). In this case, Justice Oliver Wendell Holmes articulated his famous "clear and present danger" test for incitement, which established a low threshold for the punishment of people advocating illegal conduct (in this case, resistance to the draft during wartime). A succeeding series of cases that modified this threshold (both up and down) culminated in the 1969 decision of *Brandenburg v. Ohio*, which established an extremely high threshold for punishment of incitement: "the constitutional guarantees of free speech and press do not permit a State to forbid or proscribe advocacy of the use of force or of law violation except where such advocacy is directed to inciting or producing imminent lawless action and is likely to produce such action." In practice, this decision has effectively ended punishment for incitement, thoroughly insulating those who advocate violence—even revolutionary violence.[19]

What characterizes both of these lines of cases is the evolution of an uncompromising devotion to liberal neutrality: in the Establishment Clause cases, the Court sought to bar states from using their authority over minors to promote religious belief, whereas in the "incitement" cases, it in effect legalized the advocacy of sedition and other forms of lawless violence. What could justify such extremism in defense of (basic) liberty, both civil and political? The Supreme Court itself has offered a variety of justifications, but the kind most

19. For a history of the "incitement" and Establishment Clause decisions by the Supreme Court, see Stephens and Scheb (1988, 406-13, 510-17) and Steamer and Maiman (1992, 307-8, 336-37, 387-90, 393-427). The incitement cases find a rough parallel in the history of "seditious libel," which was effectively eliminated as a category of crime by *New York Times v. Sullivan* (1964).

likely to succeed is one that is based upon the inviolability of individual autonomy in matters of belief—like the justification provided by the reconstructed hierarchy argument.[20] Only this kind of justification can provide a secure and permanent defense of the basic liberties against all political contingencies. All other justifications (such as the utilitarian one I offer in chapter 8) are ultimately held hostage to what Rawls calls "the calculus of social interests": because they are not founded on the lexical priority of liberty (at the level of political principle [OP] rather than constitutional practice [constitutional and legislative stages]), their defense of political and civil liberty is always contingent on various historical conditions, such as the likelihood of legislative overreach or abuse, the character of the political culture, and the attractiveness of trading off basic liberties for some highly valued social good (e.g., solidarity or stability) (TJ 4; TJ §31). The reconstructed hierarchy argument for civil liberty and the reconstructed intrinsic-value argument for political liberty from chapter 3 do not hinge on such empirical circumstances: they offer robust defenses of the basic liberties that (at least when "reasonably favorable conditions" obtain) secure them and those highest-order interests that they protect—namely, the development and exercise of personal and moral autonomy, respectively—from the depredations of eudaimonism and political expediency.[21]

---

20. Vincent Blasi has identified at least three Supreme Court justifications in the speech context—namely, individual autonomy, the "marketplace of ideas" (i.e., competitive diversity), and political self-government (Blasi 1977, 521).

21. I should note in closing that there may be other available defenses of the lexical priority of liberty as a first-order political principle, to be chosen in the OP and implemented at the constitutional and legislative stages through civil libertarianism. Thomas Scanlon, for example, defends a "Millian Principle" based on the inviolability of individual autonomy in matters of belief, which (like the priority of liberty) rules out content controls and other forms of state intervention that trade off certain political and civil liberties for social goods like stability. See Scanlon (1972).

5

The Priority of Fair Equality of Opportunity

I. Introduction

The final statement of Rawls's second principle of justice reads as follows:

> Social and economic inequalities are to be arranged so that they are both:
> (a) [difference principle (DP):] to the greatest benefit of the least advantaged . . . , and
> (b) [fair equality of opportunity (FEO):] attached to offices and positions open to all under conditions of fair equality of opportunity.[1]

As discussed in chapter 1, FEO has two distinct components, namely, formal EO (i.e., "careers open to talents") and substantive EO (which compensates for the social contingencies of family and class). Moreover, "fair [equality of] opportunity is prior to the difference principle" and cannot be sacrificed for its sake (TJ 77, 266). Such priority may seem unnecessary: under what possible conditions would sacrificing FEO be to the "greatest benefit of the least advantaged," especially given that one of its goals is to "even out class barriers" (TJ 63)? Rawls suggests "it might be possible to improve everyone's situation [including the least advantaged] by assigning certain powers and benefits to positions despite the fact that certain groups are excluded from them. Though access is restricted, perhaps these offices could still attract superior talent and encourage better performance." As an example, Rawls offers (but does not endorse) the claims of Burke, Hegel, and others that "some sort of hierarchical social structure and a governing class with pervasive hereditary

---

1. TJ 266. For simplicity, I have left out the just savings principle (see TJ §§44–45).

features are essential for the public good" (TJ 73, 264; also see Williams 1962, 125–29; Lessnoff 1971, 75–76).

Though these claims are no doubt of historical interest, they might not seem particularly compelling, leaving us still wondering whether the lexical priority of FEO is in fact superfluous. However, we do not need to rely on an example as extreme as this one in order to recognize the possibility of conflict between FEO and the DP. For example, securing FEO through educational subsidies could be exceedingly expensive, as a disadvantaged family and class background may make it challenging to bring a student up to a level of competence, much less excellence, at any given task. Might it not be to the "greatest benefit of the least advantaged" to focus educational subsidies instead on those (often socially advantaged) students for whom such investment would offer the highest rate of return and then tax them for the benefit of the poor? Rather than fighting a costly and possibly futile battle against family and/or class privilege, we might instead put such privilege to work for the least advantaged among us through redistributive taxation. This thought appears to animate Rawls's concept of "natural aristocracy," a kind of institutionalized *noblesse oblige,* and it is precisely what FEO's priority rules out as illegitimate.[2] Thus, maybe contrary to our first impression, FEO's lexical priority has real bite: *the least advantaged cannot trade off their fair opportunities to achieve office and position for the sake of greater monetary benefits.*

Not surprisingly, this priority rule has been roundly criticized by many people, including Larry Alexander and Richard Arneson (Alexander 1985; Arneson 1999; also see Pogge 1989, 161–96). Alexander appears perplexed by the strength of the rule, believing that it fetishizes our status as producers; moreover, he worries that FEO may become a "black hole" for economic resources due to its lexical priority.[3] Similarly, Arneson contends that "enabling all individuals to have real opportunities for job satisfaction, educational achievement, and responsibility fulfillment is not plausibly regarded as a justice goal that trumps all other justice values and should be pursued no matter what the social cost" (Arneson 1999, 99).

Perhaps due to these criticisms, Rawls himself began to express doubts about the lexical priority of FEO late in his life. Consider the following footnote

---

2. TJ 57, 64–65. Rawls's concept of "natural aristocracy" combines the DP with merely formal equality of opportunity.

3. Alexander (1985, 198, 202–3, 205–6). On FEO as a "black hole," also see Arneson (1999, 81–82) and Pogge (1989, 169).

(apparently written sometime in the early 1990s)[4] from JF: "Some think that the lexical priority of fair equality of opportunity over the difference principle is too strong, and that either a weaker priority or a weaker form of the opportunity principle would be better, and indeed more in accord with fundamental ideas of justice as fairness itself. At present I do not know what is best here and simply register my uncertainty. How to specify and weight the opportunity principle is a matter of great difficulty and some such alternative may well be better."[5] This latter-day ambivalence prompts the following question: what does Rawls's original defense of the lexical priority of FEO look like? We thus arrive at one of the most puzzling lacunae in all of his work. Apart from a single passing discussion (to which I will turn shortly), he fails to offer *any* justification for this priority rule. He defines the priority of FEO, illustrates it, etc., but never gives us an argument for it. This gap in his theory is made all the more surprising by the almost obsessive care he takes in defending (with multiple arguments) the other major priority rule internal to justice as fairness, the priority of liberty (see TJ §§26, 33, and 82; PL Lecture VIII).

Over the following pages, I attempt to defend Rawls against both his critics and his own doubts by speculatively reconstructing his argument for the lexical priority of FEO, building not only on the few clues he provides but also on other resources found in TJ, including especially the Aristotelian principle (in TJ §65) and the Humboldtian concept of social union (in TJ §79). Moreover, I show that this reconstruction can be defended against the criticism that it commits Rawls to a substantive conception of the good, thereby jeopardizing the priority of right in his theory. As we shall see, this reconstituted argument for the lexical priority of FEO strengthens the case for justice as fairness as well as having controversial implications for public policy.

II. Reconstructing Rawls's Defense of the Priority of FEO

Before starting my reconstruction, I should say a few words about method. Any attempt to reconstruct someone else's argument should hew as closely as

---

4. E-mail correspondence with Erin Kelly, editor of JF (April 14, 2003).
5. JF 163n. There is some textual evidence (admittedly indirect) in TJ suggesting that Rawls noticed Alexander's criticisms. For example, one passage in the *original* edition of TJ (p. 87) that was sharply criticized by Alexander (1985, 199–200)—who felt it implied that FEO would never conflict with the DP—is missing in the *revised* edition (TJ 76). Alexander is never explicitly mentioned, however, anywhere in Rawls's writings.

possible to their own words, methods, concepts, and (insofar as we can discern them) intentions. As I reconstruct Rawls's defense of the priority of FEO, his own words on the subject (which are few and vague, as we shall see) will provide a rough guide. I will fill in the details using methods and concepts drawn from his own writings. Where interpolation or extrapolation is needed to advance the argument, it will be carefully discussed and defended. The final product of this effort should at the very least not be inconsistent with the spirit of Rawls's work; with luck, it will reflect his intentions and fit into the rest of his theory with a minimum of strain.

In light of the last chapter's reconstruction of Rawls's hierarchy argument, one orthodox Rawlsian way to justify the lexical priority of FEO over the DP (and therefore the lexical priority of fair opportunities to attain office and position over income and wealth) would be to justify the lexical priority of the *interest* that FEO supports over the consumption interest supported by the DP. What sort of interest might this be? Rawls identifies it during his one very brief discussion of the priority of FEO and its defense:

> I should note that the reasons for requiring open positions are not solely, or even primarily, those of efficiency. . . . [The priority of FEO] expresses the conviction that if some places were not open on a basis fair to all, those kept out would be right in feeling unjustly treated even though they benefited from the greater efforts of those who were allowed to hold them [as was the case with "natural aristocracy"]. They would be justified in their complaint not only because they were excluded from certain external rewards of office but because they were debarred from experiencing the **realization of self** which comes from a **skillful** and devoted exercise of **social** duties. They would be deprived of one of the main forms of human good.[6]

Rather than concentrating on the interest in the "external rewards of office" (including salary and prestige), which after all bears a strong resemblance to the consumption interest supported by the DP, I want to focus attention instead on the interest in "the realization of self" that the holding of offices

---

6. TJ 73 (emphasis added). This account of FEO's priority may help explain Rawls's position on the distribution of educational resources: "resources for education are not to be allotted solely or necessarily mainly according to their return as estimated in productive trained abilities, but also according to their worth in enriching the personal and social life of citizens, including here the least favored" (TJ 92).

and positions makes possible. If it can be shown that this interest is so important as to be lexically prior to the consumption interest, then the priority of FEO will have been justified on orthodox Rawlsian grounds. Rawls's description of self-realization as "one of the main forms of human good" suggests that such an approach may be a promising one.

In order to demonstrate the importance of our interest in self-realization, though, we must first determine of what self-realization consists. Rawls says that realization of self comes from "a *skillful* and devoted exercise of *social* duties." This skeletal explanation can easily be fleshed out by an examination of the Aristotelian principle (in TJ §65), which motivates the achievement of increasing virtuosity, and of the concept of social union (in TJ §79), which provides the context for the development of such virtuosity.[7] In the course of doing so we will see why and in what way Rawls believes that self-realization trumps mere consumption.

A. The Aristotelian Principle

Rawls defines the Aristotelian principle in the following way: "other things equal, human beings enjoy the exercise of their realized capacities (i.e., their innate or trained abilities) and this enjoyment increases the more the capacity is realized, or the greater the complexity." Enjoyment of this increasing virtuosity at any given activity is counterbalanced, though, by "the increasing strains of learning as the activity becomes more strenuous or difficult" (TJ 374, 376). This trade-off between the benefits and burdens of virtuosity at any given task influences how we will allocate resources (such as time and effort) across tasks when effecting our plan of self-development: "Every activity belongs to some chain. The reason for this is that human ingenuity can and normally will discover for each activity a continuing chain that elicits a growing inventory of skills and discriminations. We stop moving up a chain, however, when going higher will use up resources required for raising or for maintaining the level of a preferred chain" (TJ 378). Notice that in allocating resources the trade-off is between virtuosity at different activities, *not* between virtuosity and consumption. In fact, Rawls only speaks of our tendency to virtuosity being overridden when it comes into conflict with justice itself or when various psychological tendencies (e.g., risk aversion or time preference) inhibit it (TJ 376–78). (I will

---

7. Alexander speculates that the lexical priority of FEO might be defended using the Aristotelian principle but does not attempt such a defense himself (1985, 205–6).

revisit these two exceptions below, the first in subsection D, the second in section III.)

The importance of this tendency and its ramifications for institutional design are spelled out in the following passage, which is rich with implications for a defense of the priority of FEO: "The tendency postulated [i.e., the Aristotelian principle] should be relatively strong and not easily counterbalanced. I believe that this is indeed the case, and that in the design of social institutions a large place has to be made for it, for otherwise human beings will find their culture and form of life dull and empty. Their vitality and zest will fail as their life becomes a tiresome routine" (TJ 377). The social duties attached to offices and positions provide valuable and (as we shall see) unique opportunities for the exercise and improvement of our abilities. FEO and its priority can be seen as creating and protecting institutional space for the use of our skills and guaranteeing resources (including especially educational ones) to make their utilization effective. Consumption cannot substitute for self-realization through the skillful discharge of social duties for the very reasons alluded to in this passage: only increasing virtuosity can prevent life from becoming "dull and empty," whereas ever-increasing consumption—though perhaps initially satisfying, especially where basic needs have yet to be met—has a tendency to become a "tiresome routine" itself, with titillation giving way to boredom and jadedness in an endless series of addictive cycles (TJ 379).

I should immediately note that Rawls never explicitly makes such a claim about the lack of substitutability between self-realization and consumption. I am extrapolating here, but such an extrapolation is necessary to advance the argument: unless self-realization is of such a nature that consumption can never substitute for it, we will be unable to defend the priority relation between the respective social primary goods (fair opportunities for office and position versus income and wealth) that support them. Moreover, this extrapolation is consistent with many of Rawls's other statements about consumption. For instance, during his defense of the DP, Rawls contends that a "person choosing [according to the maximin rule] has a conception of the good such that he cares very little, if anything, for what he might gain above the minimum stipend that he can, in fact, be sure of by following the maximin rule"; this comparative indifference to consumption beyond a "satisfactory minimum" is consonant with (though it certainly does not imply) the above claim about substitutability.[8]

---

8. TJ 134–35. Rawls also says in PL that "were the parties [in the OP] moved to protect only the material and physical desires of those they represent, say their desires for money and wealth,

I think these considerations militate in favor of *provisionally* accepting such a claim in order to see whether the reconstructed defense of FEO's priority, taken as a whole, is compelling and broadly consistent with Rawls's overall theory.

Before moving on to consider why the Aristotelian principle should be linked to offices and positions in the basic structure of a just society, we should consider another objection to the argument thus far. The idea of making the Aristotelian principle the foundation for a defense of FEO's priority might be criticized on the grounds that, as a merely factual premise, the principle has no moral force and cannot do the normative work that I wish it to do. That is, the Aristotelian principle is, as Rawls often stresses, a "psychological law" or "natural fact," a description of an evolved human tendency with obvious adaptive features (TJ 375-76). To argue from this innate disposition towards virtuosity to a political principle that encourages and protects it is no more valid, so the criticism goes, than to argue from our innate disposition towards violence to a political principle that endorses blood feuds and factional warfare.

This criticism may lose its force, however, if its own premise is challenged: perhaps the Aristotelian principle, despite Rawls's assurances, is something more than a mere "psychological law." Few readers of TJ would question the moral role that autonomy plays in Rawls's theory; in sections 40 and 78, human autonomy is represented as the very ground of the moral law. Yet the *form* of its depiction, both there and elsewhere, is always factual in character: thus Rawls speaks of our *"nature* as free and equal rational beings" as well as of our observable capacities both for a conception of the good and for a sense of justice, which for Rawls are the constitutive elements of autonomy.[9] So Rawls often clothes his normative premises in factual language; therefore, his use of such language when he describes the Aristotelian principle does not necessarily rob it of moral force. Given the import of this premise in defending a central element of Rawls's justice as fairness, I believe we are justified in ascribing to it more than merely factual significance.

---

for food and drink, we might think that the original position modeled citizens' heteronomy rather than their rational autonomy. But at the basis of the parties' reliance on primary goods is their recognition that these goods are essential all-purpose means to realize the higher-order interests connected with citizens' moral powers and their determinate conceptions of the good" (PL 76). As I will show in section III, self-realization can be understood as a *third* moral power whose development and exercise OP agents should treat as a highest-order interest; I laid most of the groundwork for this claim in chapter 2.

9. TJ 222, 442, 452, 455 (emphasis added). Thus Rawls asserts that "these claims [about human moral capacities] depend solely on certain natural attributes the presence of which can be ascertained by natural reason pursuing common sense methods of inquiry" (TJ 442n).

B. Social Union

Throughout his discussion of the Aristotelian principle, Rawls constantly highlights the social context within which we develop our myriad skills. The increasing virtuosity of our fellow citizens, for example, is a good for us, as their exercised talents may help us to advance our own ends, may inspire us to similar forms of excellence, or may simply be a source of pleasure when they are publicly exercised. Such virtuosity can be developed and displayed in any number of social settings, including even games and other forms of play (TJ 373–77).

This last observation raises the following important question: why would the Aristotelian principle bear any special relationship to offices and positions in the basic structure, as required by the proposed defense of the priority of FEO? In order to understand this connection, we must first examine the Humboldtian idea of social union, discussed by Rawls in section 79. As Rawls notes there, individual men and women have neither the time nor the requisite inborn potentials to achieve all the possible forms of human excellence. They are forced to specialize, cultivating some skills and allowing others to lie fallow, as guided by a plan of self-development. Luckily, though, they can participate in and enjoy the complementary excellences of their fellow citizens via social cooperation in the pursuit of shared ends. Rawls's example of the symphony orchestra provides a nice illustration of these points: individual members of an orchestra may lack the time and/or ability to learn to play (or play well, at least) all or even most instruments in an orchestra, but they can specialize by training themselves on one or a few instruments and then collaborate with others in an orchestra to produce music, thereby sharing in the complementary excellences of their fellow musicians in the pursuit of a common goal (TJ 458–59n).

Now, as Rawls notes, such social unions can take many forms, many of which are not properly thought of as part of the basic structure of society, which is the subject of justice. So, for example, friendships, chess clubs, art associations, churches, etc. may be important examples of social unions, but membership in them would generally not be regulated by FEO. What then distinguishes those social unions that are part of the basic structure—governments, private and public corporations, universities, NGOs, and so forth—from social unions more generally? What makes them distinct (inter alia) is that the offices and positions associated with them require a major and usually dominant commitment of time and energy and act as the primary sources of livelihood for those who hold them. The social duties associated with these offices and positions and the rich repertoire of skills necessary to discharge them will consequently become a central focus of the lives of the officeholders, especially their pursuit of virtuosity. Such centrality is the source of the special connection between the Aristotelian principle and the offices and positions of the basic structure, and it explains why FEO is of such overwhelming importance: fair access to these positions is by far the most important way—though certainly not the only way—to help citizens achieve the excellences of which they are capable, because through it natural talents are matched to social settings where they can best be refined, exercised, and shared with others.[10]

C. Indispensability and "Black Holes"

I suggested in chapter 2 that developing and exercising our capacity for self-realization is properly considered the third highest-order interest of our agents in the OP, because this capacity is a third facet of our autonomy, reflecting our independence from natural, social, and fortuitous contingencies—though obviously in a weaker way than the other two facets, moral and personal autonomy. I will further develop these claims below, in section III, but there is already reason to believe that this interest and its institutional expression (FEO) has the necessary lexical priority over the consumption interest and its expression (DP); provision of fair opportunities for office and position therefore takes absolute priority over the provision of income and wealth. A lexical ordering of social primary goods must be grounded on the lexical ordering of those interests that they protect, as we discovered in chapters 3 and 4 with respect to the priorities of political and civil liberty, respectively.

As in those chapters, though, we must ask whether FEO is genuinely indispensable to the pursuit of this highest-order interest: might not compensated sacrifices of FEO be possible, ones that would maintain support for the development and exercise of our capacity for self-realization while generating certain additional benefits (e.g., cost savings)? If so, then FEO lacks the needed lexical priority. To check this possibility, let us consider the formal and substantive components of FEO separately. Recall that *formal* equality of opportunity demands "careers open to talents," that is, it prohibits arbitrary discrimination (on grounds of race, gender, etc.) as well as monopolistic privilege (barriers to entry in labor markets, especially "closed shop" unionism and exclusionary

---

10. Deciding *which* social unions to include in the basic structure may best be delayed until a post-OP stage (TJ §31).

occupational licensing) (TJ 62; DJ 141; JF 67n). Such openness is to be achieved, Rawls says, through the protection of two nonbasic liberties: free movement and free choice of occupation (PL 228). As with political and civil basic liberties, these nonbasic liberties can be sacrificed in certain ways without jeopardizing the interest they are designed to secure. For instance, temporary restrictions on free movement due to the requirements of a quarantine can be compensated by travel vouchers for use after it ends; this trade-off would leave the quarantined citizens' capacities for self-realization unaffected, assuming that job opportunities lost during quarantine can be offset by enhanced opportunities to search for distant jobs after quarantine. Other sacrifices are ruled out, though, because just compensation is simply impossible. This would be true of restrictions on movement and choice of occupation that systematically bias the creation and revision of plans of self-development. Consider, for instance, the example of apartheid (be it in South Africa or the Jim Crow South), which limited movement and choice of occupation on grounds of race. Such a system, by making location and occupation largely a function of irrelevant personal characteristics, forced victim self-development along the narrow conduits defined by law and social convention, indelibly biasing and distorting the plans made in response. These restrictions are the FEO analogues of content regulations on speech and press: no amount of additional assistance can erase the bias—it only speeds progress along those paths predefined by those with power, whereas the autonomous creation and revision of plans of life or self-development requires that those paths be defined and chosen by agents themselves.[11]

Substantive equality of opportunity, on the other hand, is designed to neutralize the effect of family and class on occupational choice, allowing natural talents to be properly matched to the offices and positions in the basic structure where they can be best developed. (A division of labor exists between FEO and the DP: the former strives to neutralize the effects of *social* contingency, while the latter tries to minimize the effects of *natural* contingency, i.e., the genetic draw.) If this neutralization, which is a necessary condition for self-realization, is to take place, all those biases in the creation and revision of self-development plans caused by family and class inequities must be

---

11. Such bias need not be the (central) intention of those who impose such restrictions in order to be illegitimate. For example, exclusionary licensing generally results from the self-interested political lobbying of occupational groups (e.g., physical therapists), but because such licensing has the *reasonably foreseeable effect* of biasing creation and revision of plans of self-development (by needlessly locking qualified parties out of professions for the benefit of cosseted incumbents) it is an unacceptable infringement of free choice of occupation.

eliminated by appropriate legislative action, such as educational and business subsidies, limits on bequest, inheritance taxes, etc., which "level the playing field" and therefore allow genuinely autonomous self-development to take place. Any residuum of social inequality "tilts the playing field" and distorts plan formation: a disadvantaged family and class background, for example, if left uncorrected, may cause agents to rule out particular occupations (e.g., white-collar jobs) and related forms of training (e.g., a college education) from the start. Whereas in the apartheid case the narrow conduits along which victim self-development was directed were both designed and reinforced by the state, in this case the conduits are maintained by state *inaction*, a passivity that allows the heteronomous influence of social contingency to constrain occupational planning. As a result, the development and exercise of the capacity for self-realization will be warped in ways that cannot be counterbalanced; as with the apartheid case, additional aid (e.g., to help working-class youth obtain the vocational training to which their class status has destined them) simply speeds progress along predefined paths—except that here, the "definition" is provided not by malevolent political forces but by impersonal and unplanned socioeconomic processes.

I noted in the introduction to this chapter that critics of the lexical priority of FEO have worried about the possibility of it becoming a "black hole," drawing in all economic resources (Alexander 1985, 203, 205; Arneson 1999, 81–82; Pogge 1989, 169). Given the priorities of political and civil liberty, however, it cannot pull in resources needed for them. Moreover, as I argued in chapter 3, the three moral powers of reasonableness, rationality, and self-realization must only be developed "to a certain minimum degree . . . nothing beyond the essential minimum is required" (TJ 442; PL 19). There is certainly no demand to maximize their development, whatever that might look like, so there is consequently no threat of all economic resources being consumed in an insatiable quest for maximal self-realization. Finally, as I shall argue in the next subsection, insofar as basic consumption needs (e.g., food, shelter, clothing) are preconditions of the *effective* development and exercise of our capacity for self-realization, the lexical priority of FEO must give way to them.

Nevertheless, given the severe demands of substantive equality of opportunity— namely, that all family and class inequalities be neutralized—one might reasonably expect that relatively little income and wealth will be left over for distribution to the least advantaged. In short, the DP may have to be largely sacrificed to the requirements of FEO. What is the chance of this occurring? It is difficult to answer this question in the abstract. Much depends upon how homogeneous and/or egalitarian the family and class institutions of the society in question are, which is something we cannot know at the level of the OP. The implications of emerging from behind the VI to discover you are in Norway versus India will obviously be very different: although both cases will engage nonideal theory, it would probably be safe to say that full implementation of the DP would have to be delayed for some time in India, as the lion's share of available resources would have to be committed to overcoming the caste system.[12] One feature of FEO that might reduce the strain on the social resource base is that inequality of opportunity is allowable so long as those with fewer opportunities are better off *in opportunity terms* than they would be in a position of equality; this exception is similar (in spirit at least) to the DP's allowance of deviations from the equal-income benchmark if it is to the financial advantage of the least advantaged (TJ 130–31, 265). Perhaps allowing this kind of inequality would encourage ambitious families to push their children harder, generating in the long run more resources for the provision of better job opportunities to the least advantaged. This is all quite speculative, of course, but such flexibility in FEO makes it more likely that it could be met at a reasonable cost, that is, with resources left over for implementation of the DP.[13]

D. A Threshold Condition for the Application of the Priority of FEO

Earlier I mentioned that the pursuit of virtuosity might legitimately be overridden if it conflicted with justice itself. For example, the priority of liberty would prevent the state from banning paeans to consumerism if its purpose in doing so were to prevent citizens from being distracted from self-improving

---

12. The Indian case raises a difficult issue for nonideal theory: what if there is no path to FEO out of a religiously based caste system that does not involve abolition of the family and/or radical forms of state-mandated religious reform, at least on a temporary basis? Such policies might create intolerable strains of commitment, and if so the applicability of the lexical priority of FEO to such societies would have to be called into question. (See TJ 448.)

13. Rawls seems to suggest at two points in *Theory* that the DP "reduces the urgency to achieve perfect equality of opportunity. . . . We are more likely to dwell upon our good fortune now that these differences are made to work to our advantage, rather than to be downcast by how much better off we might have been had we had an equal chance along with others if only all social barriers had been removed" (TJ 265, 448). As I noted in the introduction to this chapter, though, this is a defense of Rawls's "natural aristocracy," not of FEO: to permit opportunity advantages for the socially privileged on the grounds that they will make better use of them and thereby create surplus income to be redistributed to the poor is to institutionalize noblesse oblige. This is one step short of democratic equality (TJ 64–65).

activities. In other words, EL is prior to FEO, but FEO might be overridden, and its priority postponed, for reasons internal to the principle as well. For instance, Rawls notes that "the Aristotelian Principle characterizes human beings as importantly moved not only by the pressure of bodily needs, but also by the desire to do things enjoyed simply for their own sakes, **at least when the urgent and pressing wants are satisfied**" (TJ 379; emphasis added). Rawls recognizes here that the pursuit of virtuosity has preconditions, at least for limited physical beings such as ourselves: we cannot effectively hone our skills when we are racked by cold, thirst, hunger, or other such afflictions. Thus, the priority of FEO would have to be relaxed if relaxation of this sort were necessary to allow the accumulation of sufficient income and wealth to make the pursuit of virtuosity itself feasible.

This last example raises a larger question: under what conditions does the lexical priority of FEO come into effect? Rawls explicitly addresses this issue in PL, drawing a parallel between his first and second principles of justice: "The notion of fair equality of opportunity, like that of a basic liberty, has a central range of application which consists of various [nonbasic] liberties [such as free choice of occupation and freedom of movement] together with *certain conditions under which these liberties can be effectively exercised.* . . . Just as in the case of basic liberties, I assume that this range of application can be preserved in ways consistent with the other requirements of justice, and in particular with the basic liberties" (PL 228, 363-64; emphasis added). In the case of the basic liberties, these conditions include an unspecified level of social, legal, and economic development (especially a modicum of material comfort). Something similar is evidently intended for FEO: adequate sociopolitical and material resources must be available before the priority of FEO goes into effect, where "adequate" means whatever level is necessary for the liberties associated with FEO to be "effectively exercised" (TJ 54-55, 132, 474-76; PL 7, 297; LP 106-12).

Given what Rawls has said on this subject, we can speculatively reconstruct the nested set of thresholds for the application of the lexical priorities of liberty and FEO. Begin with his general conception of justice, within which "all social values—liberty and opportunity, income and wealth, and the social bases of self-respect—are to be distributed equally unless an unequal distribution of any, or all, of these values is to everyone's advantage" (TJ 54-55). This general conception presumably applies to all societies below a certain level of development. Once the requisite level of social, legal, and economic progress has been reached, however, the priority of liberty comes into play; given the lexical priority of EL over FEO, an increasing social resource base must first be used to secure the priority of liberty.[14] As the resource base continues to grow, though, a point is eventually reached where the priority of FEO comes into effect, and the special conception of justice can then be fully implemented. This speculative reconstruction, like the one at the close of chapter 3, suggests that Rawls's nonideal theory may provide more guidance than has been usually assumed; I will return to this point in the chapter conclusion.

III. The Priority of FEO Versus the Priority of Right?

An important question now arises: does the commitment to self-realization that I argue is implicit in the lexical priority of FEO simultaneously commit Rawls to a substantive conception of the good for its defense, thereby jeopardizing the priority of right in his theory? Arneson asks much the same question and answers it as follows: "Within Rawls' theory, which eschews any social evaluation of people's conceptions of the good, there does not seem to be a basis for affirming that the goods of job satisfaction and meaningful work trump the goods that money and other resources distributed by [the DP] can obtain. From the different perspectives afforded by different and conflicting conceptions of the good, individuals will differ on this question. . . . For some, work satisfaction and entrusted responsibility fulfillment may loom very large; for other individuals, quite other goods are crucial" (Arneson 1999, 98–99). Interestingly, Rawls's own criticisms of moderate perfectionism for being inconsistent with the priority of right may militate against my proposed defense of the priority of FEO: he says that the "criteria of excellence are imprecise as political principles, and their application to public questions is bound to be unsettled and idiosyncratic, however reasonably they may be invoked and accepted within narrower traditions and communities of thought" (TJ 286, 290). The perfectionism of Rawls's privileging of the pursuit of excellence through office and position is extremely weak and pluralistic compared to, say, Nietzsche's perfectionism. Nevertheless, it is initially unclear why the overriding importance

---

14. Rawls argues that "the case for certain political liberties and the rights of fair equality of opportunity is less compelling [than the case for "liberty of conscience and the rights defining integrity of the person"]. . . . It may be necessary to forgo part of these freedoms when this is required to transform a less fortunate society into one in which all the basic liberties can be fully enjoyed" (TJ 217). However, if my arguments in chapter 3 are sound, political liberties must be secured before either civil liberties or the nonbasic liberties of FEO.

ascribed to self-realization through work is any less "unsettled and idiosyncratic" than that ascribed by Nietzsche to creating and elevating *Übermenschen* for the sake of artistic and military prowess (see Nietzsche 2006, esp. "The Greek State").

Might there be some way for Rawls to respond to these criticisms and to show that the priority of FEO and the priority of right are in fact consistent? One possible response, which we discussed in chapter 2, is that just as reasonableness and rationality are aspects of our autonomy and emblems of our independence from natural and social contingencies, so is our capacity for self-realization. Because autonomy is the very ground of the moral law in Rawls's doctrine of right, this response may rescue him from the charge of inconsistency.

Rationality's task of designing and implementing a plan of life requires the utilization of external resources, including especially the generic, liquid form of such resources, money. But there is a middle term, so to speak, between a plan of life and the external resources needed for its realization: *internal* resources, including skills, drive, and self-discipline. As I noted above, self-realization is solely concerned with cultivating such resources in accordance with a plan of self-development, just as rationality is focused on organizing and culling desires. Moreover, like rationality, self-realization may be impeded by refractory animal impulses. As Jon Elster has noted, akrasia, myopia, and extreme risk aversion can act as barriers to the development of internal resources: creating such resources in ourselves is initially painful (hence akrasia and myopia as barriers) and not guaranteed to succeed (hence risk aversion as a barrier) (Elster 1986, 107–8). So self-realization is in large part a struggle against these natural inertial tendencies, as Rawls himself intimates, and our success at it is as emblematic of our autonomy as the struggle of rationality against untoward desires (TJ 376–77).

I do not intend to suggest here, of course, that people develop their skills only as a way to advance their life plans. As Rawls emphasizes, "the Aristotelian Principle characterizes human beings as importantly moved . . . by the desire to do things for their own sakes" (TJ 379). That is, the perfection of one's skills can be not only a means to, but also constitutive of, one's plan of life, as I emphasized in chapter 2. For example, the professional and occupational ideals that play a substantial role in self-realization can at times become elements of our conceptions of the good. Such duality should not present a problem: virtuosity, like health, is both good in itself and good for what it makes possible.

As I also noted in chapter 2, these three facets of autonomy—reasonableness, rationality, and self-realization—are paralleled by the three hierarchically ordered varieties of imperative in Kant's own model of finite rational agency: categorical commands or laws of morality (including the metalaw of The CI), hypothetical counsels of prudence, and hypothetical rules of skill (GMM 4:415–19; also see Paton 1947, 89–96). The connections between reasonableness and morality and between rationality and prudence were the foci of chapters 3 and 4, so I shall limit myself to explicating the third of these connections, that between self-realization and skill. In the midst of chapter 2, I pointed out that while Kant's rules of skill are merely technical imperatives, the development of our skills is a moral imperative, namely, a self-regarding imperfect duty: "as a rational being he necessarily wills that all the capacities in him be developed, since they serve him and are given to him for all sorts of possible purposes" (GMM 4:423). Kant elsewhere maintains that "the capacity to set oneself an end—any end whatsoever—is what characterizes humanity," and because the third formulation of The CI (the formula of humanity) insists that we "use humanity, whether in [our] own person or in the person of any other, always at the same time as an end, never merely as a means," the failure to develop our capacity to set ends is a failure to respect humanity in ourselves.[15]

What is the nature of this capacity, however, and how is it to be developed? This capacity to realize "all sorts of possible ends" is to be cultivated via the development of the three "natural powers" that constitute it: those of "spirit, mind, and body" (MM 6:392, 444). The first two involve capacities for theoretical and practical reasoning, while the last involves physical capacities (such as longevity, strength, endurance, resistance to disease, etc.), which can be developed through gymnastics and medicine (MM 6:445; cf. Plato 1991, 82–87 [403c–408e]). Recall from chapter 2 the complex of skills and metaskills that were to be achieved through a plan of self-development, not simply moral, intellectual, emotional, and physical skills but also the metaskills (patience, diligence, focus, resolve, and self-control) that were necessary to develop them. This is the subject matter, as it were, of self-realization, and the three "natural powers" that Kant identifies are simply an alternative description of this complex.

15. MM 6:392; GMM 4:429. Also see Korsgaard (1996a, chap. 4) and Wood (1999, 120): "Preserving and respecting rational nature means preserving and respecting it in all its functions, not merely in its moral function of giving and obeying moral laws. Furthering rational nature requires furthering all the (morally permissible) ends it sets, not merely the ends it sets in response to duty."

Kant repeatedly emphasizes the imperfection of our duty of self-development: it is simply an "ethical . . . duty of wide obligation"; consequently, we may exercise discretion along both the extensive and intensive margins of choice, that is, with respect to which skills we develop and how much we develop them, respectively (MM 6:392). A plan of self-development is merely a decision by a self-realizing agent to develop particular skills to specified degrees, whether for their own sake or for the sake of larger prudential or moral goals. Interestingly for our purposes, Kant associates this kind of planning with a "human being's choice of [his] occupation":

> Which of these natural perfections should take precedence, and in what proportion one against the other it may be a human being's duty to himself to make these natural perfections his end, are matters left to him to choose in accordance with his own rational reflection about what sort of life he would like to lead and whether he has the powers necessary for it (e.g., whether it should be a trade, commerce, or a learned profession). For, quite apart from the need to maintain himself . . . a human being has a duty to himself to be a useful member of the world, since this also belongs to the worth of humanity in his own person, which he ought not to degrade. (MM 6:392, 445–46)

Thus, Kant—like our reconstructed Rawls—seems to see the employment context as the primary arena for self-realization, the institutional space that allows us to develop our myriad intellectual and physical skills for public purposes. We have now come full circle, concluding with a deeply Kantian justification for Rawls's laconic claim that the violation of FEO's priority would hinder "the realization of self which comes from a skillful and devoted exercise of social duties" (TJ 73; emphasis added).

IV. Conclusion

I have argued in this chapter that the lexical priority of FEO can be successfully defended against its critics, despite Rawls's own doubts about it. Using the few textual clues Rawls leaves, I speculatively reconstructed his defense of it, showing that it is grounded on our interest in self-realization through work. This reconstructed defense made use of concepts already present in TJ, including the Aristotelian principle (section 65), which motivated the achievement of increasing virtuosity, and the Humboldtian concept of social union (section 79), which provided the context for the development of such virtuosity. I also showed that this commitment to self-realization, far from violating the priority of right in Rawls's theory, stems directly from his underlying support for autonomy, which is the very foundation of the moral law in his doctrine of right.

Alternative defenses of FEO's lexical priority are no doubt possible. For example, one implication of this priority is that eliminating *social* inequalities (i.e., those arising from family and class privilege) is infinitely more important than counterbalancing *natural* inequalities (i.e., those arising from differences in ability and ambition) (TJ 63–65, 73–78). Thus, one might be able to provide a basis for the lexical priority of FEO by arguing that social inequalities are infinitely worse than natural inequalities. Why might this be so? Perhaps social but not natural inequalities keep us from being full and equal participants in the basic structure of a well-ordered society or cause special injury to the self-respect of those denied fair opportunities, owing to the fact that social inequalities seem more a product of conscious human action and even human design than natural inequalities. Thus, the social dependency implicit in Rawls's idea of "natural aristocracy" might be deemed infinitely more degrading than the natural dependency that is arguably implicit in the DP itself, which makes the income of the least advantaged dependent in large part on (properly motivated) able and ambitious people.[16]

Without denying the promise of such alternatives, I do want to emphasize two advantages of the self-realization defense. First, it is clearly based in Rawls's text, as I noted at the beginning of section II. When Rawls contends that those denied fair opportunities would be "debarred from experiencing the realization of self which comes from a skillful and devoted exercise of social duties," he seems to be indicating his preferred way of defending FEO's lexical priority. We are not bound, of course, to follow Rawls's lead, but given his own words and the way the resulting self-realization defense fits neatly within his theory, a certain deference may be apt. Second and more importantly, the self-realization defense was shown in section III to spring from the same underlying commitment to autonomy that ultimately grounds the priorities of right

---

16. Many thanks to Debra Satz and Tamar Schapiro for pushing me to consider such alternatives.

and liberty. This defense thus serves as a constituent element of a unified, autonomy-based defense of the three priorities in justice as fairness. Other approaches to defending the priority of FEO would likely lack this coherentist justification.

Whichever approach to defending the priority of FEO that we ultimately decide to take, we must still ask: why is its defense so important? Given Rawls's admission that the argument for the DP is "unlikely ever to have the force of the argument for the two prior principles," most of the power and distinctiveness of justice as fairness would appear to derive from the internal priorities of liberty and FEO (TJ xiv; cf. TJ 220). Therefore, a persuasive defense of FEO is a vital support for his theory, the distinctiveness of which would otherwise depend mostly, if not exclusively, on the defense of the priority of liberty. But the implications of a compelling defense of FEO's lexical priority extend much further than this. Though the United States has obviously failed to provide either fair opportunities or a decent social minimum for its own citizens, its relative emphasis on the former (especially in the form of subsidies for higher education) may draw support from the priority of FEO: the decision to commit resources to state colleges and universities, subsidized student loans, etc., rather than to broader financial support for the poor, may be partially justified by the modest perfectionism of the self-realization defense.[17] This same perfectionism might also militate against the strongest forms of affirmative action, as I have argued elsewhere (Taylor 2009). Thus, far from being an obscure and poorly motivated companion to the priority of liberty, the priority of FEO is arguably its peer in terms of its importance to justice as fairness and the controversiality of its policy implications.

---

17. The United States has the fifth-highest level of postsecondary enrollment in the world (82% of the relevant age group), behind only Finland (90%), South Korea (90%), New Zealand (86%), and Sweden (84%) (*Economist* 2008, 78). The United States' noncompliance is clearly nonideal (TJ §39), but *given* the noncompliance, FEO's resource demands should trump those of the DP.

6

The Difference Principle

I. Introduction

Rawls says in *Theory* that "the force of justice as fairness would appear to arise from two things: the requirement that all inequalities be justified to the least advantaged, and the priority of liberty (TJ 220)." The difference principle (DP), which proclaims that "social and economic inequalities are to be arranged so that they are . . . to the greatest benefit of the least advantaged," consequently plays a central role in his political theory (TJ 266 ["final statement of the two principles of justice"]). As I argued in chapter 1, the DP requires that a social minimum index of income and leisure be maximized. Unlike what Rawls later calls the "simplest form" of the DP, which maximizes social minimum income, the fuller version includes leisure as well to prevent the labor disincentives that would emerge in a simple guaranteed-income system; as a practical policy matter, the inclusion of leisure would increase the attractiveness of workfare and wage subsidies (e.g., Earned Income Tax Credit).[1] For the sake of simplicity and familiarity, though, I will use "social minimum income" as shorthand for "social minimum index of income and leisure" throughout the chapter. Moreover, when discussing the DP or alternatives to it (e.g., the

---

1. TJ 245, 252; JF 59n26, 65, 161, 179; cf. Van Parijs (2003, 216–18). Another way to explain the inclusion of leisure is as follows. The point of maximizing the social minimum income is to maximize the minimum consumption bundle; however, by including only income we implicitly leave out one item from this bundle, leisure, which is not acquired through the direct expenditure of income but rather through reductions in labor that themselves reduce total income. Thus, two individuals with the same income do not necessarily have the same consumption bundle, because one of them (say, Rawls's Malibu surfer [JF 179]) might have more leisure time than the other. To account for this, leisure must be added to the index. To maintain a money metric, leisure might be translated into income using the average wage rate of unskilled workers as a crude measure of the opportunity cost of time to the least advantaged (TJ 84).

restricted-utility principle), I will always assume that the case for EL, FEO, and their priority has already been established.

The secondary literature on the DP is large and varied, and one might reasonably wonder whether there is anything left to say about it.[2] In this chapter, though, I will focus on a topic that is largely undeveloped within this literature: the Kantian-constructivist justification of the DP. I will show that Rawls's most promising defense of the DP—that sketched in *Theory* §26—can be filled out using Kantian-constructivist methods and that his later defenses of the DP are not very compelling (as he himself seems to recognize), due in part to their abandonment of Kantianism. The persuasiveness of this Kantian reconstruction of the §26 defense calls into question Rawls's latter-day ambivalence (discussed in the chapter conclusion) about the place of the DP in justice as fairness.

Before beginning this critique and reconstruction, I should note that I am offering a luck-egalitarian reading of the DP: maximizing social minimum income is an attempt to compensate for certain unchosen and consequently undeserved natural inequalities, especially inequalities in native ability and ambition.[3] I believe that this interpretation can be supported by many passages in Rawls's texts (especially parts of TJ §17). Moreover, the reconstructed defense I offer, which depends upon this luck-egalitarian interpretation, coheres well with the best justifications for the other central principles in Rawls's theory, which were examined in the preceding three chapters. Other interpretations are possible—and in some cases even plausible—but addressing them here would take me beyond my principal task: adding the final element to a unified, autonomy-based defense of the essential doctrines of justice as fairness, namely, the lexical priorities of right, liberty (both political and civil), and FEO as well as the DP.[4] If the reconstituted defense of the DP that I provide here is found persuasive, then the luck-egalitarian interpretation of the DP upon which it relies will itself gain plausibility.

---

2. Some of the more famous contributions are Barry (1973b), G. A. Cohen (2000), J. Cohen (1989), Nozick (1974), Pogge (1989), Van Parijs (1995, 2003), and Waldron (1993). For a thorough list, see S. Freeman (2003b, 537–39).

3. R. Dworkin (2000) defends a kind of luck egalitarianism, criticized by both Anderson (1999) and Scheffler (2003).

4. Scheffler (2003), for example, opts for a citizenship-based rather than luck-egalitarian reading of Rawls's DP. Also see S. Freeman (2007a, 122), who admits the DP may be seen as a higher-order, Paretian sort of luck egalitarianism.

II. Rawls's *Theory* §26 OP Defense of the DP: An Interpretation and Kantian Reconstruction

Why should OP agents select the DP over other distributive principles? In §26 of *Theory*, Rawls begins to provide a persuasive answer to this question, but it needs to be better developed. His argument there, which consists of four steps, can be summarized as follows:

1. The DP is the maximin rule among distributive principles.
2. The maximin rule for choice under uncertainty is rational when three conditions obtain.
3. These three conditions obtain in the OP.
4. Therefore, parties in the OP should select the DP as their distributive principle (TJ 132–35; JF 97–100).

Before spelling out the details of this argument, I should first explain the maximin rule. There are many decision rules that could be used under conditions of risk and uncertainty, all of which fall somewhere along the spectrum depicted in figure 8, running from most risk averse on the left to most risk loving on the right. These rules generally use objective or subjective probability estimates. Maximin and maximax (and other "maxis," like maximed [maximize the median]) do not, though: a maximin (maximax) rule makes the decision that maximizes the minimum (maximum) payoff. Consider table 2, in which *payoffs* (in dollars, utility, etc.) are determined both by an agent's *decisions* and by *circumstances* beyond his control—though perhaps not beyond his ability to predict. Which decision should an agent make here? If the agent is using a maximin decision rule, he will choose D_3, as it offers the best *worst* outcome (13); if using maximax, on the other hand, he will choose D_2, as it offers the best *best* outcome (22). Notice that these decisions do not depend on the probabilities of the circumstances, so long as each circumstance has a positive probability (i.e., it is possible).[5] Given these two definitions, the DP is clearly

---

5. By contrast, a risk-neutral decision rule—which just maximizes the agent's expected payoff: $\max_k \sum_i p_i P(D_k, C_i)$—will yield different decisions for different probability distributions over the circumstances. For example, if $p(C_1) = 0.2$, $p(C_2) = 0.4$, and $p(C_3) = 0.4$, then D_2 will maximize the expected payoff (14.8 versus 14.6 for the other two). If $p(C_1) = 0.8$, $p(C_2) = 0.1$, and $p(C_3) = 0.1$, on the other hand, D_3 will maximize it (13.4 versus 4.4 for D_1 and 3.7 for D_2). The agent will choose D_1 if using maximed, however, as it offers the best *median* outcome (16). Also note that this example provides far more information (about payoff structures, etc.) than would be available behind the VI.

maximin   risk neutrality   maximax

Fig. 8 Decision rules under uncertainty

Table 2 Payoff matrix

Decisions	Circumstances (mutually exclusive and exhaustive)		
	C_1	C_2	C_3
D_1	1	16	20
D_2	0	15	22
D_3	13	14	16

the maximin rule among distributive principles: it selects the income distribution that has the highest *minimum* income.

This establishes Step 1 of Rawls's argument. Moving on to Step 2, we need to determine the conditions under which it would be rational to use the maximin rule—in this context, the DP. Rawls argues that if the following *three* conditions obtain, the DP is rational to use:

Condition 1: "a knowledge of likelihoods is impossible, or at best extremely insecure."

Condition 2: "the person choosing has a conception of the good such that he cares very little, if anything, for what he might gain above the minimum stipend that he can, in fact, be sure of by following the maximin rule."

Condition 3: "the rejected alternatives [among decision rules] have outcomes that one can hardly accept. The situation involves grave risks" (TJ 134; cf. JF 98).

Condition 1 is in some sense the most straightforward of the conditions but also, as we shall see, rather controversial. If individuals have no basis for making reliable calculations of probabilities (in this case, probabilities of achieving different income levels), then they must use maximin or some other maxi rule, because all the other decision rules require probability estimates that are unavailable here by supposition (Barry 1973b, 91). Condition 1 clears the field of all contenders but the maxis. (I will show below that allowing *subjective* probability estimates does not change this conclusion.)

Conditions 2 and 3 together explain why maximin is preferable to other maxi rules. These two conditions are depicted graphically in figure 9. On the x-axis we have income, while on the y-axis we have utility, understood here as the degree of life-plan realization, which is consistent with Rawls's comments on the admissibility of *constructed* utility functions in the argument for justice as fairness.[6] The utility function $U(I)$ depicts Conditions 2 and 3 in the limit: the person's (ideal) preferences are such that he cares nothing about income above the threshold α (Condition 2) and suffers a catastrophic loss of utility below the threshold (Condition 3).[7]

Given these conditions, it would be rational to choose maximin over other maxi rules. Because all incomes over the threshold offer the same level of utility, maximizing the median, maximum, or other nonminimum income has no point.[8] Maximizing the minimum income, on the other hand, has a very important point: because any income below the threshold is disastrous, a truly rational person would want the lowest income to be as large as possible given

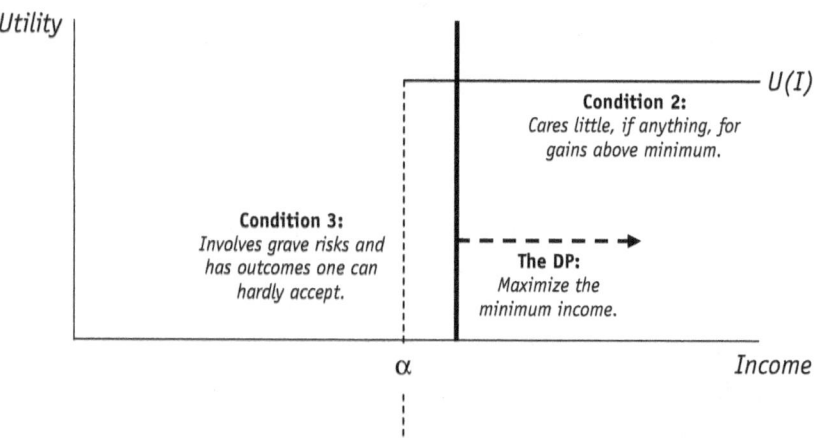

Fig. 9 Depicting Conditions 2 and 3

---

6. As Rawls notes, a utility function is "but a mathematical expression that encodes certain basic features of our normative assumptions" and entails no commitments to utilitarianism as a doctrine (JF 107). In this case, the utility function represents the degree of life-plan realization or, from the OP perspective, regulative-interest fulfillment.

7. Compare my graph to Rawls's graph at JF 108. I will discuss a key difference between the two momentarily.

8. Maximizing the median income is a poor proxy, incidentally, for maximizing expected or mean income (which can only be done with probability estimates): the median and mean are only equal in symmetric distributions, such as the normal distribution, but income is never symmetrically distributed—it is invariably right-skewed, so that the mean is above the median, by an amount that varies spatiotemporally and is therefore unknown behind the VI.

the radical uncertainty about income realizations; even if the maximized minimum income remains below the threshold, maximizing it will minimize the gap between it and the threshold and thereby minimize the possibility of catastrophic utility loss.

This establishes Step 2 of Rawls's argument. Before we move on to Step 3, however, we should stop to consider a few key features of Step 2. First, notice that no assumptions were made about the choosing agent's preferences regarding risk. The choice of maximin, in other words, is not dependent on any "special psychology" of the choosing agent apart from the three conditions themselves; as Rawls notes, "it is the fundamental nature of the interests the parties must protect, and the unusual features of the [choice setting], that support the use of the maximin rule" (JF 107). The threshold α—which I will sometimes refer to as the *basic-needs threshold*—also plays a key role in the argument: if basic needs are not met, catastrophic utility loss ensues; if they are met, on the other hand, then additional income does nothing to increase utility. In later writings, Rawls tends to equate this threshold with the social minimum itself, which he calls a "highly satisfactory" and "guaranteeable level" (JF 99–100). By doing so, though, he conflates two things that should be kept distinct: (1) the threshold below which utility drops precipitously and (2) the social minimum income that can be declared "highly satisfactory" only in reference to such a threshold and the ideal structure of preferences that it represents.[9] Rawls's hostility to the idea of such a threshold seems to hinge on his belief that it must be interpreted as "natural" and "nonsocial," but this does not follow: the threshold can instead be based on specific essential interests (e.g., the three regulative interests of the parties in the OP), the minimal satisfaction of which might necessitate a particular amount of income.[10] I believe that the real reason for Rawls's hostility is his belief that by accepting such a

---

9. Two complementary examples will show that the threshold and the social minimum should be kept distinct. First, in a society of *workaholics*, the maximized social minimum income would be rather high—taxes would have little effect on productivity and could therefore be large, raising a lot of revenue for redistribution—so it is implausible to think that reducing this social minimum slightly (i.e., not maximizing it) would involve "grave risks" (Condition 3). Second, in a society of *workaphobes*, the maximized social minimum would be quite low—taxes would discourage productivity and would therefore have to be kept small, raising little revenue for redistribution—so it is implausible to think that someone receiving it would care "very little, if anything, for what he might gain above the minimum stipend that he can, in fact, be sure of by following the maximin rule" (Condition 2). The threshold and the social minimum must therefore be conceptually decoupled, contra the later Rawls.

10. JF 100n21; cf. J. Cohen (1989, 733–34) and his discussion of the "natural threshold interpretation (NTI)," which was first suggested by Barry (1973b, 97).

threshold argument he would undermine his case for the DP; I will address this concern when discussing objections to Condition 3 below (see JF 120; cf. J. Cohen 1989, 732).

To complete Step 3, we need to show that these three conditions hold in the OP. Rawls maintains that Condition 1 obtains by virtue of the thick VI: because "the parties have no basis for determining the probable nature of their society, or their place in it . . . they have no basis for probability calculations" (TJ 134; JF 101–2). To make objective estimates of the probabilities of different income levels being realized, parties would need at least some information about themselves and about income distributions under alternative economic systems, but this kind of personal and historical information is excluded by the thick VI, which allows only general scientific information as well as knowledge of the Thin Theory of the Good. As we have seen, in the absence of such reliable estimates, parties will be forced to rely upon one of the maxi rules.

As for Condition 2, Rawls says very little in its defense, other than to reiterate in various ways the claim that once a "satisfactory minimum" is achieved "there may be, on reflection, little reason for trying to do better."[11] Why would OP parties ascribe this variety of asceticism to those whom they represent, however? The highest-order interests in developing and exercising the two moral powers might imaginably be satisfied at a certain income level, as Rawls usually speaks of "sufficient" development of these powers entitling individuals to equal justice (e.g., TJ 442 and KCMT 333). Why would the higher-order interest in a particular conception of the good be so satisfied, however? Cohen tries to provide an explanation in the following passage: "while the parties represent individuals who do care about getting more than the minimum (because they prefer more primary goods to less), they must act to ensure that positions are acceptable. *Since getting to an acceptable position is much more important than getting past that position, [Condition 2] obtains*" (J. Cohen 1989, 732n18; emphasis added). But this is simply a non sequitur: that an agent cares "much more" about getting to a minimum than getting beyond it does not imply that he "cares very little" about getting beyond it—in terms of the graph above, the fact that the utility function is steeper at α than beyond implies only that it is shallow*er*, not shallow, beyond α. The absence of any defense of Condition 2 is a serious weakness in Rawls's argument to which I will return when

---

11. TJ 135; JF 99–100: "quite satisfactory," etc. Also see TJ 258: "beyond some point [wealth] is more likely to be a positive hindrance, a meaningless distraction at best if not a temptation to indulgence and emptiness."

dealing with objections to these three conditions below; I will show there that a defense of this condition tied to Rawls's own conception of the person (as Kantian constructivism requires) is possible.

Condition 3, on the other hand, is relatively easy to defend within the context of the OP. Rawls says that distributive principles other than the DP "may lead to institutions that the parties would find intolerable" and may leave people in positions "they could not accept" (TJ 135; JF 103). The strains of commitment, in other words, would be too extreme. Why? Due to the reasons that I discussed in chapter 1: some ends must be willed because of either duty (e.g., developing and exercising the two moral powers) or finitude (e.g., enough food, water, and shelter for survival, which is a condition for all other willing), and achieving these ends to a sufficient level will require certain minimal resources, including income. Any distributive principle that fails to provide a level of income sufficient to meet these basic needs would generate intolerable strains of commitment. In the OP, parties would be aware (thanks to their knowledge of the social and natural sciences as well as the Thin Theory of the Good) that a basic-needs threshold of this description exists—they might not know its *level* (a point to which I will return below), but they would recognize it or its equivalent, such as a basic-needs *range* where the utility function is steep but not vertical. Hence, Condition 3 should hold in the OP.

This completes Step 3 and, in combination with the previous steps, Step 4 as well. If the three conditions obtain in the OP, as Rawls argues, then rationality demands that agents there use maximin as a decision rule, but maximin in this distributive context is simply the DP. Therefore, it is rational for agents in the OP to choose the DP, and Rawls has shown by way of the OP that a radically egalitarian distributive principle follows from a Kantian conception of the person. As I indicated above, however, the three conditions that justify the use of maximin and therefore the DP are themselves controversial. Thus, over the remainder of this section I will consider some of the more powerful objections to these conditions, in terms of both their ability to support the use of maximin and their relevance in the context of Kantian constructivism.

A. Objections to Condition 1

As we saw above, Condition 1 plays a key role in the argument for the DP, reducing the field of candidate decision rules to only the maxis. Moreover, this condition is closely related to Rawls's Kantian conception of the person: Condition

1 is brought into play by a thick VI, which deprives OP parties of any information that would enable them to make a heteronomous choice and therefore allows them to choose from a position of negative freedom, one independent of the "alien causes" of natural and social contingency.[12] As Rawls notes, the choice setting created by a thick VI is one of uncertainty, not risk: there exists no "*objective* evidential basis for estimating probabilities, for example, relative frequencies, or actuarial tables, or the relative strengths of the various propensities of things (states of affairs) that can affect the outcome" (JF 106; emphasis added). Therefore, radical uncertainty rules out all but the maxi rules, as indicated.

One might object, however, that the impossibility of objective probability estimates does not imply the impossibility of *subjective* ones. Rawls recognizes this problem, and in later work he admits that his position that probability estimates "must be based on at least some established facts or well-supported beliefs about the world" would not be endorsed by a "general subjectivist (or Bayesian)" interpretation of probability (JF 101). In *Theory*, he discusses the problem at some length and concedes that there is a subjectivist approach to assigning probabilities in the OP: "The construction of the individual's prospect depends at this stage solely upon the principle of insufficient reason. This principle is used to assign probabilities to outcomes in the absence of any information. *When we have no evidence at all, the possible cases are taken to be equally probable.* Thus Laplace reasoned that when we are drawing from two urns each containing a different ratio of black to red balls, but we have no information as to which urn we are faced with, then we should assume initially that the chance of drawing from each of these urns is the same" (TJ 146; emphasis added). Rawls objects to the use of such techniques in the OP on the grounds that the decision is simply too important to be made with such thin information and that because we are choosing not just for ourselves but for our descendants as well we should be even "more reluctant to take great risks," but these grounds appear to invoke the kind of risk aversion that Rawls claims is absent from his version of the OP (TJ 146; JF 106-7). Rawls's later discomfort with Condition 1 leads him to downplay its importance: he worries that it "raises difficult points in the theory of probability that so far as possible we want to avoid" (JF 101).

---

12. KCE 265; GMM 4:446. See chapter 1 for a detailed discussion of the Kantian provenance of Rawls's thick VI.

Condition 1 is essential, however, to making Rawls's argument for the DP work: if this condition is even slightly relaxed so as to allow subjective probability estimates to be used, then the entire spectrum of decision rules is available, and under these circumstances (as we shall see later) the choice of maximin may not be robust to more liberal readings of Conditions 2 and 3. If Rawls hopes to salvage his argument for the DP, he must somehow hold his ground. Fortunately for him, a subjectivist approach to probability offers no serious threat to his argument—at least if we interpret his argument as I have done above. Suppose we allow OP parties to use the principle of insufficient reason, assigning equal likelihoods to all possible income realizations and thereby employing a continuous uniform distribution.[13] In order to employ such a distribution for making probability estimates of particular income levels (or, better, certain ranges of income), OP parties must set lower and upper bounds for this distribution, which are its only two parameters. A lower bound might be set at zero (assuming that no social system consistent with the other two parts of justice as fairness would allow citizens to start in a position of receivership) or at a certain social minimum (assuming a distributive principle is being considered that sets a specific lower bound on the income distribution).[14] Where would the upper bound be set, however? None of the usual conceptions of distributive justice set a *specific* upper bound on income. Many effectively limit upper incomes by imposing income-dispersion constraints or perhaps by making the top income a fixed multiple of the bottom one, whatever it may turn out to be, but these differ from setting a specific upper bound.[15] Without specifying an upper bound, we simply cannot use the continuous uniform distribution in making probability estimates—it is undefined

---

13. The uniform distribution is also called a "rectangular" distribution because of the shape of its probability density function (pdf). A continuous uniform distribution has a constant positive probability within a specified range [a, b] and probability zero outside that range. Its pdf is $P(x) = 1/(b - a)$ for $a \le x \le b$ and zero for all other x; its cumulative distribution function (cdf) is $D(x) = (x - a)/(b - a)$ for $a \le x \le b$, zero for $x < a$, and one for $x > b$.

14. Of the "traditional conceptions of justice" Rawls considers in *Theory* §21, only a subset of the mixed conceptions set a specific social minimum—to wit, B.2.(a) and B.3.(a) (TJ 107). Even the DP falls short on this count: it simply directs us to maximize the minimum, without specifying what that minimum will be—something it cannot do unless we sweep aside the VI or make it thinner.

15. One could of course imagine a distributive principle that, among other features, set very specific lower and upper bounds on the income distribution, including the degenerate case where the bounds were identical (i.e., income must be equal and set at a specific level). In this case alone could a uniform distribution be employed to make probability estimates for incomes or ranges of income lying within these bounds.

in this case—and are again left with a choice among the maxi rules, which do not require such estimates.[16]

Thus, the relentless logic of a thick VI prevents OP parties from making any probability estimates, be they objective or subjective, and they are consequently in no position to weigh their prospects under different distributive principles—they simply lack the information to make such comparisons. *Given the other two conditions, the choice of the DP follows ineluctably from the radical uncertainty of the OP*, an uncertainty intended to reflect our freedom from all varieties of natural and social contingency as well as our capacity for moral autonomy. Rawls's late decision to deemphasize this condition is consequently a partial retreat from a thorough grounding of this defense upon a Kantian conception of the person.

B. Objections to Condition 3

Before discussing Condition 2, which may be the most controversial condition, we should first consider objections to Rawls's use of Condition 3, as these objections will play a role in the later discussion of Condition 2. As I noted above, the third condition assumes the existence of a basic-needs threshold (or range) below which catastrophe results, leading to unbearable strains of commitment. This threshold results from both duty and finitude: below certain levels of income, agents will be incapable of discharging essential obligations (e.g., developing their moral powers to a degree sufficient for moral personhood) or meeting basic physical needs (e.g., enough food, water, shelter, etc. for survival). Being scientifically informed and motivated by a Thin Theory of the Good, parties in the OP will be aware of the existence of such a threshold if not its level.

Rather than disputing the existence of such a threshold, a critic might instead suggest that the DP is not the only principle of justice capable of keeping individuals above it. Consider, for example, what the later Rawls calls the "principle of restricted utility," which is just the principle of average-utility maximization constrained by a "suitable social minimum."[17] (In order to make

---

16. Trying to solve this problem by drawing the upper bound b itself from a continuous uniform distribution would just compound the problem: how would we determine *this* distribution's lower and upper bounds?

17. JF 120. This principle is equivalent to mixed conception B.3.(a) at TJ 107 and M2 at J. Cohen (1989, 728). Rawls retracts the specific criticism of B.3.(a) found at TJ 278–79 in JF 127–28n47, having been persuaded of its unsoundness by Waldron (1993). Cf. Barry (1973b,

this principle genuinely comparable to the DP, I will substitute income for utility in it, making it instead a principle of constrained average-*income* maximization—though I will still refer to it by Rawls's preferred name.)[18] If this social minimum were set at or above the basic-needs threshold, the principle of restricted utility would prevent catastrophic losses in welfare and would at least be no worse a choice overall than the DP—as would any other distributive principle possessing a "suitable social minimum," assuming the other two conditions held.

Rawls in his later writings recognizes this problem and considers it to be so acute that he largely abandons the kind of defense I have been reconstructing in this section: he concedes that the principle of restricted utility could deal with Condition 3 just as well as the DP, and because he no longer wants to put much weight on Condition 1, he pursues a justificatory strategy relying almost entirely on Condition 2, which I will discuss below (JF 120; cf. J. Cohen 1989, 732). Rawls is too hasty in coming to this conclusion, however, and I will argue that the DP has advantages over the principle of restricted utility in dealing with the third condition. First, notice that the success of any principle claiming a suitable social minimum hinges on its awareness of the location of the basic-needs threshold: at what level of income does utility take its catastrophic plunge? Given that the exact location of this threshold is likely to vary widely depending upon a variety of natural and social conditions (geography; climate; individual characteristics; economic, social, and political progress; etc.) and given that these conditions are completely hidden from parties in the OP by the thick VI, parties are again faced with radical uncertainty—this time regarding the location of the threshold—and are therefore unable to select a *suitable* social minimum or any distributive principle making use of one.[19]

102-3): "there seems to be no case for saying, in the [OP], that the society should be bound by the maximin distributional constraint once there is a possibility of getting everyone past the threshold."

18. This substitution allows us to dispose of certain obvious criticisms of the principle, such as Rawls's worries about its "indeterminacy" and Cohen's concerns about complexity (JF 126-27; J. Cohen 1989, 745). Given the motivation of parties in the OP, the (reconstructed) principle is clearly attractive: if more social primary goods are better, then maximizing average income is prima facie desirable so long as disastrously low incomes can be avoided.

19. As Cohen says, "it is implausible that rationality and human nature do combine to yield a definite threshold that is uniform across people and circumstances" (J. Cohen 1989, 734). Unfortunately, he also concludes that the existence of a basic-needs threshold would mean that "Rawls's argument [for the DP] is transparently wrong" (ibid.). As we have just seen, however, combining the existence of such a threshold with radical uncertainty about its location *strengthens* Rawls's argument, especially vis-à-vis its closest contender, the principle of restricted utility.

Only the DP is well suited to deal with uncertainty about the location of the threshold: it maximizes minimum income and consequently minimizes the probability that it will fall short of the threshold, whatever it turns out to be in different contexts.

The critic could reply, however, that setting the exact level of a suitable social minimum is a job best postponed until a later stage of Rawls's four-stage sequence.[20] In *Theory* §31, Rawls suggests that at the legislative stage "the second principle comes into play [and] the full range of general economic and social facts is brought to bear"; at this third stage of the sequence, enough is known about a society's "natural circumstances and resources, its level of economic advance and political culture" to determine the basic-needs threshold and set a suitable social minimum (TJ 172–73, 175). If this is where the second principle (or any proposed substitute) "comes into play" anyway, why could parties in the OP not adopt the principle of restricted utility with the understanding that the exact level of the suitable social minimum would be determined in the legislative stage, where all of the information relevant to pinpointing the basic-needs threshold will be revealed?

Recall that one of the formal constraints on alternative principles of distributive justice is *ordering:* a principle must "impose an ordering on conflicting claims . . . based on certain relevant aspects of persons and their situation which are independent from their social position, or their capacity to intimidate and coerce."[21] As Rawls says of the principle of restricted utility, though, its own "concept of the minimum is vague in that the guidelines it suggests do not specify a very definite minimum"; its vagueness raises the worry that it will fail to provide adequate guidance even in the legislative stage, when "general economic and social facts" are made available (JF 129). The worry arises because the meaning of "basic needs" is quite flexible even when full information is at hand: we might all agree on the existence of a basic-needs threshold, recognize the factors that produce it (duty, finitude, etc.), and have access to the relevant socioeconomic facts that help to determine its level, but we could and likely would still disagree substantially about its location.

Similar problems might seem to arise with respect to Rawls's other principles, but never to this degree. The equal basic liberties, for example, may need to be balanced against each other and otherwise regulated, a task better suited

20. Many thanks to Chad Van Schoelandt for pointing this out to me.
21. TJ 116. Rawls famously says here that "to each according to his threat advantage is not a conception of justice."

for a later stage in the sequence, but as Rawls notes, "it is often perfectly plain and evident when the equal liberties are violated," so the first principle can be expected to provide a fair degree of guidance for political actors (TJ 174; PL 331–40). Rawls also points out, however, that the situation is different with respect to "economic and social policies," which are dependent upon "speculative political and economic doctrines and upon social theory generally"; consequently, FEO and DP's guiding functions may be somewhat more limited (TJ 174). Much hinges on the socioeconomic principles in question, however, and there is good reason to think that the principle of restricted utility will provide much less guidance than the DP. Maximizing the social minimum income can certainly produce a great deal of disagreement in implementation. Because the aim is relatively clear and objective, though, the path to achieving it is less likely to produce dispute: socioeconomic policies can be tinkered with in Popperian piecemeal fashion over time to see which are the best at raising the minimum income, which is in principle measurable.[22] The task of setting a social minimum so as to meet "basic needs" is quite different and more open to dispute, as I suggested above: although many of the determinants of a basic-needs threshold are relatively clear and objective, the manner in which they determine the location of this threshold can be understood only through "speculative" and controversial doctrines and theories; consequently, even the aim here is unclear, and people are likely to hold widely varying opinions about it and about the level of income that would secure it.[23]

Because we assume OP parties to be familiar with human psychology and the principles governing political behavior, however, we can also assume that they will see the likely outcome of this vagueness with respect to the meaning of "basic needs" and a "suitable" social minimum. Recall that the principle of restricted utility has two components: an average-income maximand and a

---

22. One way of measuring it would be to examine the average (net) wage rates for unskilled labor, using occupational categories and wage statistics created by a politically independent agency (e.g., the U.S. Bureau of Labor Statistics).

23. The same kind of ambiguity discussed here might appear to arise in Rawls's theory with respect to ownership of the means of production, as he suggests that "the theory of justice does not include these matters . . . [which hinge] in large part upon traditions, institutions, and social forces of each country, and its particular historical circumstances," and upon (one might add) social-scientific disagreements about the comparative egalitarian tendencies of property-owning democracy and liberal socialism (TJ 242; cf. Roemer 1994). But even in this case, the DP provides clearer guidance than the principle of restricted utility: tinker with ownership regimes in an attempt to make the minimum income as large as possible. Again, because the objective is relatively clear, the means to achieve it are less obscure, or at least could be made so through systematic political experimentation with the structure of property rights.

suitable-social-minimum constraint. Average income can be defined relatively precisely, and the principle's primary goal is to make it as big as possible; a "suitable" social minimum is very difficult to pin down, on the other hand, and its role in the principle is merely one of a brake on maximization. In the battle between a (comparatively) sharply defined maximand and a fuzzy constraint, the winner should not be in doubt, not just due to human psychology—we tend to like the readily quantifiable and to warm to objectives more than constraints—but for another reason as well.[24] Even with the most strenuous efforts to protect the fair value of the political liberties, it will inevitably be the case that those with higher incomes will exert greater influence in political affairs, and the restricted-utility principle's maximand is of much greater interest to such citizens than its constraint. Even if these citizens have been properly politically socialized and are wholly devoted to their society's principles of justice, the fuzzy quality of the constraint will allow class bias to play a (perhaps subconscious) role. To paraphrase Pat Moynihan, the tendency will be to "define adequacy down" for the sake of higher average incomes, and ambiguity in the position of the basic-needs threshold will only make matters worse. As a result of all this, we can claim with some confidence that the principle of restricted utility is likely to fail the ordering condition (or is at least much more likely to fail it than the DP is) and to allow political conflicts to be decided in a way not sufficiently independent of natural and social contingencies.

Before moving on to the objections to Condition 2, I would like to discuss briefly another approach to giving special priority to the interests of the least advantaged, one that depends quite strongly on Condition 3: prioritarianism. Derek Parfit, the most prominent prioritarian, describes the "priority view" as the belief that "benefiting people matters more the worse off these people are"; this belief is grounded on the intuition that there is something specially objectionable about the situation of the "badly off: those who are suffering or those whose basic needs have not been met" (Parfit 1997, 212–13). Parfit is clearly tying priority for the least advantaged to Condition 3 here. Insofar as

---

24. The argument here is a bit intuitive, I realize, so I rely upon the reader's familiarity with the phenomenon. Those who work in research universities know the consequences over time of the following directive: maximize research productivity (measured in quality-weighted journal articles or books) subject to a constraint of "adequate" teaching performance. A less parochial example: maximize per capita GDP subject to a constraint of "adequate" quality of life or environmental conditions. (Thanks to the development of contingent-valuation surveys, wage/price hedonics, and travel-cost methods, however, some dimensions of environmental quality have graduated from fuzzy constraints to relatively sharply defined maximands—see A. Freeman [1993].)

the argument for the DP relies upon a similar intuition, this argument can be thought of as a species of prioritarianism.

I want to stress the word "species," however, because prioritarianism in its most general form—the form described by Parfit—cannot defend the DP without additional assumptions, namely, Conditions 1 and 2. Unless radical uncertainty is introduced via Condition 1, whether in the form of uncertainty over income or the location of the basic-needs threshold, priority for those "badly off" might be effected by something short of maximization, such as simply eliminating severe suffering or meeting basic needs. Unless (near) indifference to income above the basic-needs threshold is introduced via Condition 2, priority for the least advantaged might reasonably be sacrificed for the benefit of those better off: as Parfit admits, "this priority [for the worse off] is not, however, absolute. . . . Benefits to the worse off could be morally outweighed by sufficiently great benefits to the better off" (213). Only if we can maintain that the latter benefits are of little or no moral value can we defend maximization. It is to this controversial, largely undefended claim that I now turn.

C. Objections to Condition 2

As we have seen, so long as Conditions 1 and 3 hold without qualification—that is, there is extreme uncertainty about both income realizations and the location of the basic-needs threshold, below which utility drops precipitously—the DP can see off its competitors, including close ones like the principle of restricted utility, with or without the help of Condition 2. The first condition eliminates all contenders but the maxi rules, while the third condition makes maximin the only rational choice among them. The relevance of these conditions in the OP is guaranteed by the thick VI (a reflection of our negative freedom), the circumstances of justice (indications of our finitude), and lastly the Thin Theory (especially the highest-order interest in the development and exercise of our two moral powers), all of which originate in Rawls's Kantian conception of the person. In short, this justification for the DP is not only persuasive but also has impeccable Kantian-constructivist credentials.

If this is the case, then why do we need to think at all about the second condition or any objections to it? The need arises because this argument for the DP may not be robust to modest relaxations of the three conditions. For example, suppose that someone objected to the extreme reading of these conditions I have given so far, on the ground that they are not implications of a

Kantian conception of the person, and hence suggested a more qualified reading. An alternative interpretation might involve (1) lowering the VI enough to make *subjective* probability estimates possible, (2) admitting conceptions of the good that take a *modest* interest in income gains above the basic-needs threshold, and (3) turning the basic-needs threshold into a range with a *shallower* slope. In terms of figure 9, these changes would involve making the slope of the utility function shallower below α and steeper above α, generating an obtuse angle between the two segments. If these modifications were made, the superiority of the DP over close challengers like the principle of restricted utility would be called into question. Subjective probability estimates could be used to calculate expected income under the restricted-utility principle, for instance, and the relaxation of the second and third conditions would make mistakes in setting a suitable social minimum less costly and the benefits of maximizing average income more pronounced. The calculations would be complex and speculative, owing to the difficulty of estimating maximized minimum incomes, average incomes, etc. in what would still be an information-poor environment. Nevertheless, the results could no longer be guaranteed to support selection of the DP.

Under these circumstances, Condition 2 can play an important though auxiliary role. The closer the second condition is to holding in its most extreme form, the less likely it is for the DP to be trumped by the principle of restricted utility, *ceteris paribus*. If the benefits to be had from income realizations above the basic-needs threshold are small or nonexistent, then the gains to be achieved from maximizing the average rather than the minimum income will be correspondingly small or nonexistent, making the principle of restricted utility less attractive vis-à-vis the DP. The defense of Condition 2 is consequently a kind of "argument in the alternative," designed to shore up support for the DP when the pertinence of Conditions 1 and 3 (at least in their most extreme forms) is challenged.

The defense of Condition 2 in the context of the OP is quite challenging, however, as the condition itself is rather controversial, and Rawls and his interpreters have provided little support for it or its role in the OP, as I noted above. Given the three regulative interests that motivate OP parties, especially their higher-order interest in "protecting and advancing their conception of the good as best they can, whatever it may be," they would appear well motivated to acquire income beyond that necessary to secure the basic needs of those whom they represent (KCMT 313). Rawls maintains nevertheless that "the person choosing has a conception of the good such that he cares very little, if anything, for what he might gain above the minimum" (TJ 134). Why would the OP parties ascribe this kind of asceticism to their unknown trustors? As Rawls implies in both *Theory* §33 and other places, OP parties are well aware of the vast diversity of conceptions of the good that are adopted and pursued in the world, and they must also be aware that some of them (e.g., those of Western yuppies) place a very high value on material goods, the acquisition of which requires income far exceeding that needed to meet basic needs.[25] If this is so, then universal ascription of asceticism by the parties seems difficult if not impossible to support.

Recall, however, that OP parties presume that their trustors' conceptions of the good and associated plans of life have already been subjected to rational critique through the second moral power—a presumption that may be counterfactual.[26] Perhaps, then, we can read Rawls's claim in the following way: parties in the OP select principles of justice to advance their three regulative interests, including their higher-order interest in protecting and advancing a *rational* plan of life, and such a plan would place little to no value on income beyond the basic-needs threshold. Thus, the fact that many existing plans of life *do* place great value on such surplus income should not move OP parties, who select principles on a presumption of rationality. This restatement of the claim, while perhaps initially more plausible, nevertheless begs the question, what is irrational (or at least questionably rational) about placing substantial value on what I will hereafter refer to as "surplus income"?

In order to answer this question, we must move well beyond Rawls's texts, but hopefully in a way that Rawls himself would find congenial. The three interrelated answers to this question that I will survey are each incomplete and problematic, but the third can be connected to Rawls's Kantian conception of the person, and taken together they have a certain joint plausibility. They are best seen not as a complete reply but perhaps as a prolegomena for future research on one.

---

25. OP parties would presumably have access to a list of traditional conceptions of the good (like the list of traditional conceptions of justice Rawls presents at TJ 105–6). Otherwise, they would be unable to make strains-of-commitment judgments, which are assumed by the Equal Liberty of Conscience Argument for the priority of liberty, for example: without knowing that some conceptions of the good may be deeply religious in nature, how could OP agents assess the potential strain caused by opting for a low priority for religious liberty? (See the discussion of this argument in chapter 4.)

26. See my chapter 1 discussion of the supposedly heteronomous character of OP agents' higher-order interest.

First, Rawls associates happiness with "successful execution ... of a rational plan of life," so if surplus income were indispensable to life plans, we might reasonably expect increases in it to be correlated with greater happiness (TJ 359). A growing body of social-scientific literature, however, finds no correlation between surplus income and happiness: the only time greater income appears consistently to increase self-reported, subjective well-being is when basic needs remain unmet.[27] If this is true, and surplus income does little or nothing to promote the realization of plans of life and subsequent happiness, then its pursuit might indeed be called irrational. Rawls notes that one of the principles of deliberative rationality is "the adoption of effective means to ends"; if surplus income is an ineffective means to the universal subjective end of happiness, then its pursuit is an irrational obsession or fetish—or, in Kant's more measured language, simply imprudent (KCMT 316; GMM 4:415–19).

This mere outline of an argument is open to a wide array of objections, the most obvious one being the controversial quality of the social-scientific research upon which it relies.[28] I want to focus on another objection, however, that is perhaps more germane in this context: subjective satisfaction may not be the best understanding of what Rawls means by "happiness," and it may consequently not correlate particularly well with life-plan realization. Rawls's own conception of happiness is objective rather than subjective: it is not grounded upon subjective feelings but upon the objective circumstances of a person's life, including both "successful execution of a rational plan ... [and] sure confidence supported by good reasons that ... success will endure" (TJ 481; see TJ §§63, 83 more generally). Rawls thus emphasizes that even "saints and heroes" are happy if their life plans are successful, presumably even when they entail enormous sacrifice or suffering (TJ 482–83). Some plans that involve great subjective dissatisfaction—such as the striving, ambitious, restless lives of high-achieving individuals in the arts, sciences, business, and politics—may nonetheless be happy on Rawls's understanding. This suggests a potential problem with reliance on the social-scientific literature: just because

---

27. For a survey of this literature, see Layard (2005); also see Kahneman et al. (2006).

28. Needless to say, the idea that subjective well-being is uninfluenced by income beyond the basic-needs threshold runs counter to the entire thrust of modern neoclassical economics. I might add that academics should always be a little wary of such theories, as they play to their natural biases: by choosing academia, they have already revealed a willingness to trade off income for certain nonpecuniary benefits (e.g., autonomy, security, etc.), so any theory that takes a sour-grapes approach to the pecuniary rewards of highflyers will seem credible if not obvious to academics.

surplus income fails to correlate with subjective measures of well-being does not necessarily imply that it fails to correlate with objective measures, however suggestive the first correlation might be.

Regardless of how much weight we ultimately decide to put on this kind of argument, we will certainly have to think more carefully about how surplus income affects life-plan realization itself as opposed to the subjective or objective well-being that may flow from it. The second case for the irrationality of surplus-income pursuit does just this. Suppose that life plans have a major comparative element in the following sense: the success of my life plan relies upon the failure of other people's life plans, as would be the case with various forms of status competition. If status depends in large part upon income and what income can buy, then given the zero-sum quality of status competition, people are likely to overinvest time and effort in the acquisition of income; in other words, they will take part in a counterproductive "arms race" of surplus-income acquisition for the sake of income and consumption status.[29] Rawls himself, during his discussion of envy, criticizes this preoccupation with relative standing as "collectively disadvantageous."[30] If the craving for surplus income is jointly irrational for this reason, there may be good reason for OP parties to discount it in selecting principles of distributive justice, because they are effectively choosing for all persons and so would take such interactive effects into consideration.

Even if this argument were correct, it would not justify wholly discounting the desire for surplus income, because many if not most plans of life are not entirely comparative in this sense, and there are other, noncomparative reasons for wanting surplus income. Only the rare individual is completely preoccupied with status, and at least some of the desire for income exceeding basic needs can be traced to noncomparative elements of life plans. For example, a person interested in climbing Mount Everest out of love of nature, desire for adventure, a concern for developing and exercising various intellectual and physical skills and capacities, romanticism, etc. will require a lot of income and leisure to do so; thus, even a wholly noncomparative desire for mountaineering experience can motivate the pursuit of surplus income. Still, to the extent that

---

29. For recent work by economists on this subject, see Dupor and Liu (2003) and Hopkins and Kornienko (2004).

30. TJ 124–25; also see TJ §80 as well as MM 6:458–59. Interestingly in this context, in a 1998 letter to Philippe Van Parijs, Rawls describes the United States as having "a civil society awash in a meaningless consumerism" (Rawls and Van Parijs 2003).

some of the desire for surplus income is a result of status competition, a degree of discounting in the OP could likely be justified.

The two arguments presented so far have a certain amount of plausibility—the first is at least suggestive of the futility of surplus-income pursuit, whereas the second indicates that some such pursuit is collectively irrational—but neither can be readily linked back to Rawls's Kantian conception of the person, as Kantian constructivism prefers.[31] The third argument therefore tries to construct a more explicitly Kantian justification for discounting the pursuit of surplus income, one that works in tandem with the second argument. To start off, consider what Kant says in the *Groundwork* about the good will, which is an expression of our moral autonomy:

> Even if, by a special disfavor of fortune or by the niggardly provision of a stepmotherly nature, this will should wholly lack the capacity to carry out its purpose—if with its greatest efforts it should yet achieve nothing and only the good will were left (not, of course, as a mere wish but as the summoning of all means insofar as they are in our control)—then, like a jewel, it would shine by itself, as something that has its full worth in itself. *Usefulness or fruitfulness can neither add anything to this worth nor take anything away from it.* Its usefulness would be, as it were, only the setting to enable us to handle it more conveniently in ordinary commerce or to attract to it the attention of those who are not yet expert enough, but not to recommend it to experts or determine its worth.[32]

Thus, our incapacity to carry out the moral law in practice does nothing to detract from the worth of a good will: the fruitless good will still has its full worth, so long as we use "all means . . . in our control" to discharge our duty. We saw in chapter 2, however, that personal autonomy, which is charged with the critical (re)formulation and execution of a plan of life, can be seen as a facet of the Kantian conception of autonomy, as it also involves abstraction

---

31. The second argument has some relation, of course, insofar as Rawls's discounting of envy is connected to his idea that individuals are self-respecting and "have a secure sense of their own worth" apart from their positions in status hierarchies, at least in a well-ordered society (TJ 125; also see TJ §81).
32. GMM 4:394 (emphasis added). Rawls similarly speaks of moral autonomy as acting "from (and not merely in accordance with) principles of justice," i.e., acting with a good will (KCMT 312).

from contingency and to that extent obtains whatever authority it has. If so, then we might be able to say something analogous about plans of life and the *personally* autonomous wills that review, (re)create, and realize them: the fruitlessness of a personally autonomous will can do nothing to detract from its worth; even if we fail to carry out our plan of life (in whole or in part) due to some kind of incapacity or lack of means, the personally autonomous will retains its full value, so long as we conscientiously try to achieve the plan.

An example may be helpful here. Suppose we autonomously develop a plan of life that includes mountaineering as a major component and that we do so for the reasons I listed earlier, including some reasons that may be moral in quality (e.g., developing and exercising the various intellectual and physical skills and capacities required for mountaineering and thereby fulfilling imperfect duties of self-perfection). Incapacity may prevent us from carrying out our plan at all (e.g., an accident leading to physical disability), or a lack of means may limit our ability to carry it out to its fullest extent (e.g., income and leisure sufficient for an assault on Ben Nevis but not Mount Everest). Nevertheless, the purity of the plan and the manner in which it arose—through a personally autonomous will—guarantees that it will retain its full value as a reflection of such a will, even it remains largely or wholly fruitless.

If this is true, then (rational) individuals may be relatively unconcerned about reductions in surplus income: the purity and value of their plans can be maintained even in the face of such setbacks by simply scaling back their application—climbing Ben Nevis rather than Mount Everest, for example. Their conscientious commitment to mountaineering remains unaffected, as does the worth of their plans and of the personally autonomous wills that gave birth to them. The type of asceticism that Rawls has OP parties ascribe to rational trustors—having them care little or not at all about income above the minimum, as required by Condition 2—might then be justifiable on a certain Kantian conception of the person.[33]

The virtue of this argument, in addition to its Kantian provenance, is the way it works in tandem with the second argument: while the second argument shows the irrationality of surplus-income pursuit as a means to comparative

---

33. I want to emphasize that this is a *Kantian* argument, not one that Kant (or Rawls) would necessarily endorse. Kant is obviously very concerned with the consequences of moral action. Our duty to respect and realize the moral law in this world can, as Kant shows, be reconceived as a duty to promote the highest good, the architectonic end of pure practical reason (CPrR 5:109–11). The realization of *this* end, at least, cannot be a matter of indifference.

life-plan components, the third calls into question this pursuit even as a means to noncomparative components. A potential problem with the argument is that it seems almost too successful: if plans of life can be costlessly scaled down in the way I have suggested, then why would agents of this description care about social primary goods at all? For various reasons, however, there may be limits to the downward scalability of life plans, two of which I will mention here. First, as we have already seen, the basic-needs threshold places an ambiguous lower bound on such scalability: a certain level of income may be needed to achieve sufficient progress towards ends made unavoidable by finitude, duty, etc. Second, the imperfect duties of virtue (especially beneficence and natural self-perfection), which are morally required, may necessitate at least minimal commitments of resources. Given their imperfection, however, which involves a "latitude for doing more or less," they should not lead to violations of the third condition: the scale of our beneficence or self-perfection is again a matter of discretion, so long as we make a conscientious effort consistent with our "true needs," which we are left to gauge.[34]

This concludes my discussion of objections to the three conditions and their relevance in the context of the OP. As we have seen, each of the objections can be dealt with in a more or less satisfactory manner, thereby strengthening Rawls's *Theory* §26 defense of the DP. If Conditions 1 and 3 hold in the OP in their most extreme form, the DP can successfully defeat its challengers, including even its close cousin, the principle of restricted utility—and all this with or without the assistance of Condition 2. Even if the extreme versions of the first and third conditions cannot be sustained in the OP context, the DP still stands a good chance of success if the second condition can be shown to obtain to a high degree, and in this subsection I have given three arguments to this effect that, while individually problematic, are jointly persuasive if not convincing. Finally, this reconstructed defense is tightly connected to Rawls's Kantian conception of the person, as required by Kantian constructivism, and can therefore take its rightful place alongside the defenses of the three lexical priorities of right, liberty (political and civil), and FEO.

---

34. MM 6:391–94. To say that the desire for surplus income is irrational or (more weakly) questionably rational is not to say that it is without its uses. In a nonideal-theory context, such desires might be quite serviceable, even worthy of (temporary) promotion, as they might encourage greater productive efforts, more risk taking, etc., and thereby help to bring about the economic preconditions of justice as fairness. (See my nonideal-theory discussions in chapters 3, 4, and 5, as well as the economic writings of Adam Smith and John Stuart Mill.)

III. Rawls's Other Defenses of the DP: A Cascade of Failures

As I noted above, Rawls never fully developed his *Theory* §26 defense of the DP, and in his later writings he abandoned this defense in favor of others. In this section, I will review all of Rawls's alternative defenses of the DP, from his informal defense in *Theory* §13 and his Kantian defense in *Theory* §29 to his reciprocity, stability, and publicity defenses in *Justice as Fairness*.[35] I will show that: (A) his informal defense fails because the equal-income moral benchmark upon which he builds this defense is anything but a "widely accepted yet weak premise" and cannot be *immediately* derived from his Kantian conception of the person; (B) his Kantian defense fails due to its implicit reliance on the informal defense and its unpersuasive ascription of instrumentalism to alternatives to the DP, such as the principle of restricted utility; and (C) his reciprocity defense fails because it is a restatement of the unsuccessful informal defense, thereby inducing failure in the stability and publicity arguments, which are parasitic upon it.

A. The Informal, Non-OP Defense of the DP in *Theory* §13

Rawls maintains that the DP, which maximizes the social minimum income and therefore redounds to the greatest advantage of the *least* advantaged, can be "reasonably expected to be to *everyone's* advantage" (TJ 53, 57; emphasis added). This claim is counterintuitive, to say the least: why would middle-class and wealthy citizens be advantaged by the DP, which appears tailor-made to advantage the least advantaged at their expense? Rawls defends his claim in §13 of *Theory*, arguing that the DP is to everyone's advantage so long as the following four conditions hold:

> Condition 1: *Equality of income* is the moral benchmark.
> Condition 2: Any movements away from equality must be *sequential, incremental,* and subject to a *universal veto*.
> Condition 3: Income expectations across classes must be *close-knitted,* that is, any changes in the income expectations of one class must produce changes in the income expectations of all others.

---

35. *Informal:* TJ 65–73, JF 61–64; *Kantian:* DJSA 167–69, TJ 156–57; *publicity, reciprocity, and stability:* JF 119–30.

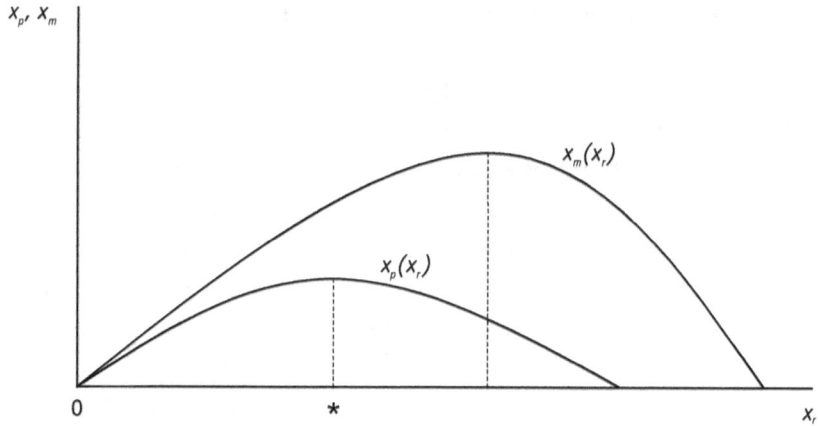

Fig. 10 Depicting Conditions 1–4

> Condition 4: Income expectations across classes must be *chain-connected*, that is, increases in the income expectations of any particular class must be linked to increases in the income expectations of all wealthier classes.[36]

Figure 10 offers a three-class example in which all four conditions hold and the DP is therefore chosen. The three classes are the poor, middle class, and rich; the incomes of their representative members are given by x_p, x_m, and x_r, respectively. The incomes of the poor and middle class are functions of the income of the rich, and they meet Conditions 3 (no flat spots) and 4 (the income of the middle class peaks after the income of the poor does). Starting from the moral benchmark of equal incomes (Condition 1) at the far left, sequential and incremental movements away from equality will pass muster until the poor exercise their veto at * (Condition 2), which maximizes their income and therefore satisfies the DP.[37]

---

36. *Condition 1:* TJ 69–70, 130–31; *Condition 2:* TJ 70, 131; *Conditions 3 and 4:* TJ 69–72. I offer two comments on Condition 2, which is a modification of Rawls's own (implicit) condition. First, we can think of the veto as being universal only so long as Condition 4 holds; if it fails to hold, then a universal veto will not necessarily lead to the DP being selected (TJ 70). I make the veto universal to reflect the ideals of symmetry and reciprocity that Rawls himself finds so compelling. Second, any movements away from inequality must be sequential and incremental to eliminate all bargaining advantage; otherwise, those with such an advantage may be able to make take-it-or-leave-it offers that violate the DP. I will elaborate upon these points shortly.

37. Compare with figures 9 and 10 at TJ 71. I depict incomes being equal (at the far left) at zero, on the assumption that perfect income equality can only be achieved through confiscatory

Conditions 3 and 4 are essentially empirical assumptions and difficult to evaluate, though the former is likely to hold: because the incomes in question are those of *representative* members of social classes, changes in one are indeed likely to be associated with changes in the others.[38] I will focus instead on Conditions 1 and 2, the normative assumptions. Condition 1 carries almost the entire weight of the argument: nearly all that is needed to get from Condition 1 to the DP is a weak Paretian assumption (Condition 2) that deviations from equality that benefit all classes (or that benefit one or more but fail to injure any) are allowable.[39] Thus, any assessment of Rawls's informal defense of the DP has to center on the role and status of Condition 1.

Before examining Condition 1, however, I should first note that it is unclear how much weight Rawls wants to put on this informal defense of the DP, at

---

taxes that eliminate any incentive for labor, etc. The reasons that the relaxation of any one of these conditions (with the others holding to their full extent) may lead to problems are as follows for each condition:

Condition 1: If the starting point is anywhere to the right of *, the poor will immediately veto, resulting in a set of incomes that violate DP. Given that x_p could peak anywhere over the range of x_r, the only way to ensure the choice of the DP is to make equal incomes at the far left the starting point.

Condition 2: Depriving the poor of their veto will result in the selection of a point to the right of *. Moreover, if moves need not be incremental, one party (e.g., the rich) might have enough bargaining power to make a take-it-or-leave-it offer to the right of * but to the left of x_p's right intersect with the x-axis, which would be accepted by all parties but violate the DP. Less radical bargaining-power asymmetries could obviously lead to violations as well.

Condition 3: For example, if x_p were to plateau rather than peak, it is unclear which end of the plateau the DP would pick: an "egalitarian" DP would pick the left end (no inequalities but those that improve the income of the least advantaged), whereas a "Paretian" DP would pick the right end (any inequalities but those that make the least-advantaged worse off). Both are reasonable interpretations of the DP and can be supported by Rawls's text. (Compare TJ 68 ["egalitarian"] with TJ 69 ["Paretian"], for instance; see Van Parijs [2003, 205–8] for further discussion.)

Condition 4: If x_m were to peak to the left of *, the middle class would exercise its veto before * were reached, violating the DP.

38. Rawls briefly considers a lexical difference principle to handle violations of Condition 3 but thinks such violations will be infrequent (TJ 72). As for Condition 4, Rawls assumes rather optimistically that "within a just social scheme a general diffusion of benefits often takes place," so that policies that improve the income of the least advantaged are likely to improve those of all classes (TJ 71–72). Counterexamples to this "trickle-up" theory are easy to devise: redistributive policies, for example, will often improve incomes at the bottom at the expense of those further up.

39. Additional assumptions in Rawls's theory make it more likely that such "Pareto-improving inequalities" can occur: the idea that incentives for the more advantaged might be necessary to encourage greater efficiency and innovation that redound to the benefit of the least advantaged, ruling out envy as a motivator in a well-ordered society, etc. (TJ 68, 124–25; cf. JF 63).

least in *Theory*. Rawls stresses at the beginning of chapter 2 (where the informal defense is presented) that his aim there is "to explain the meaning and application of the principles," not to justify them, a task that is assigned instead to chapter 3 (where the §26 OP defense is presented) (TJ 47; also see TJ §20). Indeed, after recapitulating the informal defense at the beginning of §26, Rawls recognizes the need to "argue for [the DP] more systematically" and thus proceeds to sketch his OP defense, which emphasizes the deductive side of reflective equilibrium (TJ 132; cf. JF 82, 133). One might therefore view the informal defense as less of a defense of the DP than an explication of it: it reveals how the DP is both Paretian and egalitarian, "a natural focal point between the claims of efficiency and equality," without necessarily justifying it (JF 123).

I mention this as a possible interpretation because it is hard to see the informal defense as a genuine justification for the DP, at least as Rawls understands the idea of justification. Can we, for example, consider Condition 1 to be one of the "widely held but weak premises" with which reflective equilibrium begins (TJ 16)? This appears implausible: the ideal of perfect income equality is neither "weak" nor "widely held," at least outside the circle of radical egalitarians. Can we think of it instead as an immediate *implication* of such premises, for example the ideal of persons as both free and equal? Rawls seems to favor this interpretation himself: he says that "since the parties in the original position are symmetrically situated and know . . . that the principles adopted will apply to citizens viewed as free and equal, they take equal division of income and wealth . . . as the starting point" (JF 123; cf. J. Cohen 1989, 747).

His position here can be fleshed out by recalling that Rawls sees society as a "cooperative venture for mutual advantage," that is, a system for the joint production of social primary goods that every capable adult member of the society takes part in, and as Derek Parfit writes, "when goods are co-operatively produced, and no one has special claims, all the contributors should get equal shares" (TJ 4; Parfit 1997, 209). Of course, one might instead say that in a productive setting the contributors will have "special claims" proportionate to their unequal contributions, but as Amartya Sen points out, "if production is an interdependent process, involving the joint use of different resources, it is not generally possible to separate out which resource has produced how much of the total product" (Sen 1985, 15; Rawls makes a related point at TJ 271). Except perhaps under special conditions (e.g., constant returns to scale), a marginal-productivity critique of equal claims cannot get off the ground. Given this fact, the idea that equal participants have presumptively equal claims appears plausible.

A question now arises, however: equal participants in such a scheme have presumptively equal claims *to what?* (Or as Sen might ask, "equality of what?" [1992, chap. 1].) One possibility, suggested by Rawls and Parfit above, was equal claims to the *fruit* of the joint labor of the participants. There are a number of other possibilities, though. A somewhat fanciful example: the participants might instead have equal claims to *lottery tickets* for the probabilistic dispersal of said fruit; this would guarantee *ex ante* but not *ex post* equality of outcome and would be attractive if the participants were risk loving. Another, less fanciful example: the participants might have equal claims to the *opportunity to compete* for said fruit in the marketplace; that is, their status as equal participants would entitle them to a fair opportunity (i.e., "equal prospects . . . for everyone similarly motivated and endowed") to battle for their share of the joint product (TJ 63).

This last example is not merely less fanciful: it is Rawls's precise position with respect to offices and positions in the basic structure of society, social primary goods among the "fruits" of joint production. He does not start with a hypothetical equal division of offices and positions but rather with the idea of a fair competition for such positions, a process to which all citizens should have equal access. Thus, Rawls's own derivation of FEO demonstrates that he does not believe that the equal division of social primary goods is an immediate implication of his conception of the person. As I showed in chapter 1, classical liberals such as Kant contend that the same logic that Rawls applies to offices and positions should be applied to income and wealth: for them, an important implication of the ideal of free and equal persons is that there should be an open-ended contest for such social primary goods, which explains their intense hostility to all forms of caste, nobility, and the like—they arbitrarily exclude or disadvantage some persons in socioeconomic competition (e.g., T&P 8:291–92).

I point this out not in order to support the classical-liberal position but to suggest that the liberal conception of persons as free and equal has no *immediate* implications for the distribution of income—or at least none that would be generally acknowledged as such. By presuming that it does, Rawls moves quickly but unconvincingly to the DP, arriving at it on the cheap, so to speak, in contravention of his own constructivist methodology. Rawls's

Kantian constructivism begins, as I have emphasized, with "widely held but weak premises" that are reflected in a procedure of construction that generates principles of justice, principles that may be rather challenging to our considered convictions. The obliqueness of the process reflects both the great complexity and the contested nature of the relationship between premises and conclusions in political philosophy. To short-circuit this process as Rawls does in his informal defense is to avoid conversation with the very group that Rawls most needs to convince: those who could never accept the equal division of income as a premise or see it as an immediate implication of human equality.

What is most impressive about the OP defense of the DP that Rawls adumbrates in §26 of *Theory* is the way that it starts with an initially attractive conception of persons, teases conditions from this conception that do not transparently predispose parties towards the DP, and then shows how these conditions lead them inexorably to choose the DP. Its very indirectness is a triumph of the constructivist method. The informal defense of the DP, on the other hand, is in too much of a hurry to reach its conclusion, which causes it to plant controversial moral claims in the middle of the OP. A striking example of this occurs when Rawls is summarizing his informal defense at the beginning of §26: asking that we "consider the point of view of anyone in the original position," Rawls maintains that "since it is not *reasonable* for him to expect more than an equal share in the division of social primary goods, and since it is not rational for him to agree to less, the sensible thing is to acknowledge as the first step a principle of justice requiring an equal distribution" (TJ 130; emphasis added). But an OP party is not characterized by reasonableness: guided by his three regulative interests, he seeks to maximize his bundle of social primary goods in a rationally autonomous fashion and is entirely unconcerned with whether his bundle is bigger than those of others. The §26 defense shows that *even under these conditions* the party will still choose the DP—a remarkable finding, and one that has at least some hope of persuading those who are not already radical egalitarians, unlike the informal defense, which contents itself with preaching to the choir.

B. The Kantian Defense of the DP in *Theory* §29

Whatever Rawls's original intent was with respect to the informal defense of the DP, he clearly intends the Kantian defense to provide a justification for the DP; indeed, it is to be found in a section of *Theory* entitled "Some Main Grounds for the Two Principles of Justice."[40] Rawls begins this defense by citing Kant's FH formulation of The CI ("so act that you use humanity, whether in your own person or in the person of any other, always at the same time as an end, never merely as a means") and saying that he will "freely interpret it in the light of the contract doctrine" (GMM 4:429; TJ 156). His argument is encapsulated in the following passage: "The difference principle interprets the distinction between treating men as a means only and treating them also as ends in themselves. To regard persons as ends in themselves in the basic design of society is to agree to forgo those gains which do not contribute to everyone's expectations. By contrast, to regard persons as means is to be prepared to impose on those already less favored still lower prospects of life for the sake of the higher expectations of others" (TJ 157). The first thing to notice about this argument is its strong dependency upon the informal defense: it appears addressed to citizens rather than parties in the OP (who do not have the kind of moral motivation mentioned), and it implicitly relies upon an equal-income moral benchmark, which provides a baseline against which credits or debits to "everyone's expectations" or to "prospects of life" for the "less favored" are to be tallied. Consequently, it inherits most of the problems associated with that defense.

A more general difficulty, however, is its ascription of instrumentalism ("treating men as means only") to all principles that fail to maximize the income of the least advantaged, including mixed conceptions such as the principle of restricted utility. Given that this principle respects not only the priorities of liberty and FEO but also the idea of a decent social minimum meeting basic needs of citizens, Rawls's implication that it must treat citizens as "means only" is uncompelling. In fact, this same accusation can be turned more convincingly against the DP itself. In effect, the DP makes of society a giant monopsonist with respect to the natural talents and ambitions of the advantaged, squeezing every drop of redistributive value out of them consistent with preserving incentives, defraying training and educational expenses, etc.[41] When Rawls suggests that the DP is in effect "an agreement to regard the distribution of natural talents as a common asset," talents that are embedded

---

40. TJ §29, specifically 156–57; also see DJSA 167–69 for an earlier version.
41. JF 63; cf. J. Cohen (1989, 740), who does not take seriously the advantaged's complaints regarding the DP.

in actual persons, it is hard not to see the DP's instrumentalism, its treatment of the advantaged as "means only" to the higher income expectations of the disadvantaged.[42]

Rawls, of course, has a convincing response to this objection: the language of "common assets" is intended to be metaphorical only. Rawls emphasizes that "it is persons themselves who own their endowments: the psychological and physical integrity of persons is already guaranteed by the basic rights and liberties that fall under the first principle of justice," and even instruments of redistribution that may be highly effective in eliciting greater effort from the advantaged (e.g., a "head tax on natural assets") are banned if they entail a "drastic infringement upon freedom" (JF 75 [and JF §21 more generally]; SRMC 231). Thus, the constraints on redistribution imposed by the priority of liberty, inter alia, prevent the DP from being interpreted as a purely instrumentalist principle; it must be evaluated in the context of its sister principles and their lexical priorities. A similar argument would surely apply, though, to the principle of restricted utility, which is not only constrained by the very same sister principles but also moved by respect for humanity in assuring that basic needs are met.[43] Rawls's charge of instrumentalism would probably prove effective against *unrestricted* utilitarian principles, but it cannot be used against the principle of restricted utility and perhaps the other mixed conceptions without bringing the DP itself under suspicion.[44]

Rawls might admit all this but continue to insist that anything short of the reciprocity that is reflected in the DP, which only allows inequalities that benefit all, is instrumentalist and treats the least advantaged as "means only," but, as we have seen, whatever power this claim has derives wholly from that of the informal defense and would therefore be persuasive only to those already enamored of radical economic egalitarianism. Once again, Rawls is in too much of a hurry to get to his point. This is not to say, of course, that a Kantian defense of the DP is infeasible—far from it. The reconstructed §26 defense of the DP has impeccable Kantian credentials: Rawls's Kantian conception of the person grounds each of the three conditions in that defense, especially the first one. What that defense showed, however, is that a Kantian justification for the DP must be based upon a rich conception of the person as

---

42. This leads Nozick (1974, 228) to wonder "whether any reconstruction of Kant that treats people's abilities and talents as resources for others can be adequate."
43. Rawls himself seems to recognize this last point at JF 128–29.
44. See Rawls's list of mixed conceptions at TJ 107; cf. J. Cohen (1989, 728).

an element in a procedure of construction, not upon more generic claims about treating people as ends rather than mere means.

C. The Reciprocity, Stability, and Publicity Defenses of the DP in *Justice as Fairness: A Restatement* §§34–38

In *Justice as Fairness: A Restatement,* Rawls largely abandons the *Theory* §26 defense of the DP and instead restates and expands arguments first made in *Theory* §29.[45] The central claim of these interlinked defenses in *Justice as Fairness* is that the DP reflects the ideal of reciprocity: it allows inequalities only if they "work effectively to improve everyone's situation starting from equal division" (JF 123). However, these are simply Conditions 2 and 1 from the informal defense of the DP, respectively, so the reciprocity defense is just a restatement of it (as Rawls himself suggests) and all of my previous criticisms apply in full.[46] As I will now show, the other two defenses from *Justice as Fairness,* the stability and publicity defenses, are parasitic on the reciprocity defense, so its failure induces their own.

The stability defense, which relies upon the idea of "strains of commitment," argues that it is easier for the most advantaged to deal with the strains of adhering to the DP than it is for the least advantaged to deal with the strains of adhering to the principle of restricted utility (JF 125–27; for a definition of "strains of commitment," see TJ 153). Rawls says that under the DP the most advantaged are "most likely to be discontent . . . violate the terms of cooperation, or . . . urge renegotiation" in order to secure more income than the DP allows them. He asserts, however, that their interest in greater income will (or at least can) be counterbalanced by other reasons—all three of which explicitly depend upon the ideal of reciprocity embodied in the DP. First, politically socialized citizens in a WOS conceive of themselves as free, equal, and engaged in "mutually advantageous social cooperation" with their fellow citizens; consequently, they will want principles that govern their society to reflect "an appropriate idea of reciprocity," that is, that idea embodied in the DP (JF 125–26; cf. JF §35.3). Second, more-advantaged citizens in

---

45. JF xvii; see his discussions of publicity, finality, stability, self-respect, etc. as grounds for the DP (TJ 153–56).
46. At JF 123–24, during his explanation of the reciprocity defense, Rawls reviews the informal defense of the DP, even making use of the diagram at JF 62 that he had earlier used to explain that defense.

particular will realize that they are already benefited by "social, natural, and fortuitous contingencies" as well as by the opportunity the DP provides to better themselves so long as the least advantaged are also helped; thus, in a spirit of reciprocity they will only support those inequalities that "improve the situation of others," as the DP requires (JF 55, 126; cf. JF §16). Finally, stable constitutional arrangements require "mutual trust and the cooperative virtues," and public understanding that the three types of contingencies just mentioned will be dealt with "only in ways that advance the general good" encourages trust and cooperation; because the DP embodies just such an ideal of reciprocity, it will check self-serving political activities by the most advantaged and thereby contribute to the maintenance of a stable constitutional order (JF 126; cf. JF §33).

Thus, the strains of adhering to the DP should be manageable for the most advantaged, or at any rate more manageable than the strains of adhering to the restricted-utility principle are for the least advantaged. Rawls explains why their strains of commitment will be so extreme under this principle in the following passage:

> In asking the less advantaged to accept over the whole of their life fewer economic and social advantages . . . for the sake of greater advantages . . . for the more advantaged, the principle of utility asks more of the less advantaged than the difference principle asks of the more advantaged. Indeed, asking that of the less advantaged would seem to be an extreme demand. The psychological strains that may lead to instability are bound to be greater. For as a principle of reciprocity, the difference principle rests on our disposition to respond in kind to what others do for (or to) us; while the utility principle puts more weight on what is a considerably weaker disposition, that of sympathy, or better, our capacity for identification with the interests and concerns of others. (JF 127)

Rawls admits that the restricted-utility principle, by setting a sufficiently high social minimum, might be able to remove the "high" strains of sullenness and resentment that can cause "violent action in protest," but that it would be incapable of ameliorating the "low" strains of a cynical withdrawal that is politically passive but incapable of genuine affirmation of the principle (JF 128; cf. Waldron 1993, 262–63).

Rawls's claim here about the relative strains confronting the least and most advantaged is entirely dependent upon his specific interpretation of reciprocity: the most advantaged can accept the DP, despite its economic costs to them, because it alone among the distributive principles can embody reciprocity; similarly, the least advantaged will necessarily bristle at the implications of the restricted-utility principle because it is not reciprocal in the specific way that the DP is. Is the DP the only way to instantiate reciprocity, however? As our discussion of the Kantian defense of the DP indicated, the principle of restricted utility is strongly egalitarian with respect to liberties, opportunities, and an income adequate to meet basic needs; income inequalities that benefit some are allowed only on the condition that the enumerated benefits are secured for all. The principle of restricted utility thus embodies a different but very closely related conception of reciprocity.[47] Rawls would no doubt respond that this conception is inadequate because it fails to start from the moral baseline of income equality, against which all proposed inequalities must be measured, but as we saw in the subsection on the informal defense of the DP, this baseline qualifies neither as a "widely held but weak premise" nor as an immediate implication of such a premise; accordingly, neither it nor any argument that depends upon it—such as the stability defense—is likely to be compelling outside radical-egalitarian circles.[48]

A similar criticism can be leveled against the publicity defense. Rawls reiterates here that any admissible principle of justice must meet the criterion of full publicity, that is, the principle, the beliefs upon which it is based, and its full justification must be capable of being publicly known and understood; a

---

47. I do not think it is coincidental that in the reproduced passage on the extreme strains of commitment facing the least advantaged under this principle, Rawls calls it the "principle of utility" or the "utility principle," dropping the "restricted" modifier: by doing so, he deemphasizes the very features of this principle that arguably reflect an ideal of reciprocity and so sharpens the contrast with the DP in a way helpful to his argument.

48. This said, the stability defense might be reconstructed so that it depended upon the §26 defense instead of the failed informal defense. For example, the relative strains of most and least advantaged might be explained by the fact that the DP better reflects the Kantian conception of persons—as shown by the OP defense of the DP—than the principle of restricted utility does. If we are all compelled by pure practical reason to adopt this conception, then the most advantaged will acquiesce in the economic disadvantages of the DP because it best reflects their nature as free and equal moral persons, while the least advantaged will reasonably bridle at the impositions of the restricted-utility principle because if fails to do so. Because the stability defense is by its nature a *secondary* defense, its plausibility hinges entirely on that of the primary defense. If the primary defense fails, so will the stability defense; if, on the other hand, the primary defense succeeds, the stability defense will play a strictly supporting role, as it cannot substitute for the primary defense.

society whose principles could meet this criterion would be "a society without ideology (understood in Marx's sense of false consciousness)."⁴⁹ Rawls suggests that any polity whose principles were nonreciprocal and/or unstable would have to depend to some extent upon ideology to buttress political authority and maintain order. He maintains that the restricted-utility principle fails on these counts; consequently, it must require ideological delusions for its support and therefore violate the full publicity criterion.⁵⁰ As we have seen, though, Rawls's reciprocity and stability defenses of the DP against this principle are unsuccessful. So if (contrary to Rawls's claims) it is a stable principle embodying an ideal of reciprocity, it will have no need of ideology and can serve as part of a public conception of justice. The failures of higher-order defenses have yet again induced failures in the lower-order defenses that depend upon them.⁵¹

IV. Conclusion

After completing his *Justice as Fairness* defenses of the DP, Rawls remarks that "while I view the balance of the reasons as favoring the difference principle, the outcome is certainly less clear and decisive" than in the argument for the basic liberties and their priority.⁵² In the preface to the revised edition of *Theory*, he goes even further, arguing that "the primary aim of justice as fairness is achieved once it is clear that the two principles would be adopted . . . or even [when] the mixed conception [i.e., the principle of restricted utility] . . .

49. JF 121; cf. KCMT 324–25. Also see my discussion of the publicity condition in chapter 1.
50. The delusions in question might include myths about natural endowments and the fruits that flow from them being earned or divinely sanctioned. I should also note that I am freely interpreting JF §35 here, as Rawls is unclear about the way the publicity defense is a defense of the DP against the principle of restricted utility. He does later suggest that the latter would not be "workably public" due to its reliance upon subjective rather than "objective features of peoples' circumstances," but my interpretation of the principle as maximizing average income rather than average utility largely deals with this concern (JF 126–27).
51. If the stability defense is a secondary defense (as I suggested in a previous footnote), then the publicity defense is best regarded as a *tertiary* defense. It hinges upon the primary defense and any supporting secondary defenses for its persuasiveness: principles that fail to gain support from these defenses will require ideological supports and will fall foul of the publicity rule as a consequence. If the reciprocity and stability defenses upon which it depends were to be reconstructed in line with the §26 defense of the OP, however, the publicity defense might be made to work.
52. JF 133; as Rawls notes at JF 94, the first fundamental comparison provides reasons for supporting the equal basic liberties, while the second fundamental comparison does the same for the DP.

is adopted rather than the principle of utility."⁵³ In other words, the chief objective of justice as fairness can be achieved even if the DP is rejected in favor of average-utility maximization subject to a decent social minimum. Needless to say, this late-life pronouncement is a significant shift from *Theory*'s original claim that "the force of justice as fairness would appear to arise from two things: the requirement that all inequalities be justified to the least advantaged, and the priority of liberty" (TJ 220).

What motivated Rawls to deemphasize the DP in this fashion over time? It has certainly been subjected to searching criticism over the years, but this fails to distinguish it from the many other components of his theory that have drawn sharp criticism. I think the reasons for its fading prominence are connected to Rawls's broader intellectual development. As I have argued in this chapter, Rawls's strongest defense of the DP is a Kantian reconstruction of the one given in §26 of *Theory;* its Kantianism comes out in numerous ways—in Condition 3's reliance on an idea of unavoidable ends (of duty, finitude, etc.), in Condition 2's Kantian-ascetic justification—but the most prominent is Condition 1's dependence on a thick veil, which deprives parties in the OP of any information that would allow them to make a heteronomous choice and thereby enables them to select principles from a position of negative freedom, one independent of the "alien causes" of natural, social, and fortuitous contingency (KCE 265; GMM 4:446). The trajectory of Rawls's defenses of the DP—like the trajectory of his political theory as a whole—has been away from Kantianism: away from the *Theory* §26 defense, away from the Kantian defense of *Theory* §29, away even from a significant reliance upon conditions (like Condition 1) that have a clear Kantian provenance. The arguments that have survived this transition—namely, the reciprocity, stability, and publicity defenses of *Justice as Fairness*—are relatively weak, being restatements and expansions of *Theory*'s less persuasive arguments for the DP. In this instance as in others, de-Kanting justice as fairness has undermined the case for its most distinctive principles.

---

53. TJ xiv (emphasis added); the preface was written in November 1990, while the JF comment was probably penned no later than 1989, at least a year earlier (JF xii).

PART 3

Kantian Foundations

7

Justifying the Kantian Conception of the Person

I. Introduction

As I have just shown in part 2, the only convincing arguments for the central principles of justice as fairness—the four priorities of right, political liberty, civil liberty, and fair equality of opportunity plus the difference principle—are tightly linked to and even require the radically Kantian conception of the person described in detail in chapter 2. Is this conception particularly compelling, however? The discussion so far has simply assumed that this conception has priority over alternative, maybe equally compelling conceptions (e.g., persons as sensuous beings, artistic creators, or children of God), but as we have seen, Rawls needs to justify this conception and its priority in order to complete the case for his principles of justice.

In this chapter, I will review Rawls's evolving efforts to justify his conception of persons. These efforts began in *Theory* with his celebrated justificatory method of reflective equilibrium.[1] As we shall see, though, this method contained certain ambiguities with respect to the conditions of moral objectivity, ambiguities that were resolved by Rawls in the early 1980s in a decidedly non-Kantian manner. After considering Rawls's reasons for adopting this resolution and offering two criticisms of it, I turn to his later justificatory technique in *Political Liberalism*, which offers a complete development of this resolution and at least implicitly responds to my two criticisms. I will return to and elaborate upon these two criticisms in chapter 8.

---

1. His development of reflective equilibrium in *Theory* was foreshadowed in a 1951 article, "Outline for a Decision Procedure in Ethics" (ODPE), which was a component of his Princeton University dissertation. (See CP x.)

II. *Theory*'s Justificatory Ambiguities

We can now return to a subject that I began to discuss at the end of chapter 1: Rawls's theory of moral justification. His justificatory strategy in *Theory* is ambiguous for reasons that I shall explain, but he eliminates this ambiguity in "Kantian Constructivism in Moral Theory" and by doing so exposes a veritable chasm between himself and Kant. As I noted above, Rawls's task is to justify his Kantian conception of the person, but why should this conception be normatively guiding, and in a way that trumps other conceptions? To answer this question, we must examine Rawls's coherentist justificatory technique, which he refers to as "reflective equilibrium."[2]

One way to justify principles of justice, Rawls says, is to show that they can be derived via a procedure of construction from a normatively guiding conception of the person, one that preferably incorporates "widely accepted but weak premises"; as we have seen, this is simply Kantian constructivism (TJ 16). A second way to justify principles, however, is to compare them to our "considered convictions of justice," that is, "those judgments in which our moral capacities are most likely to be displayed without distortion" caused by self-interest, fear, etc.; such convictions are calmly held, thoughtful, but pretheoretical commitments at various levels of abstraction, from ideals of the person (e.g., as free and equal, rational and reasonable) down to specific stances on public policy (e.g., that "religious intolerance and racial discrimination are unjust") (TJ 17–18, 42; IMT 288–89). When the conception of the person and the principles it yields via Kantian constructivism agree with these considered convictions—the "provisional fixed points" of our moral sense—we gain confidence in them; when they conflict, we lose confidence in the conception, the principles, and/or our own convictions (TJ 18).

Rawls's coherentist method of justification unites these two justificatory strategies. Once we have derived principles from an initially attractive conception of the person, we compare the principles and conception with our considered convictions. In cases of conflict, we have a pair of options: we can either change our convictions or modify our constructivism in order to resolve the conflict, where the latter might involve changing the conception of the person, the way it is interpreted in the procedure of construction, the way principles are derived in that procedure, etc. Taking the latter approach would generate

---

2. The discussion that follows draws freely from TJ §§4, 9, 87, and IMT 288–91.

a new conception of the person and/or new principles, which again are to be compared to our considered convictions. We are to repeat this procedure, adjusting our convictions and/or adapting our constructivism, until there is complete agreement among the conception of the person, the principles that mirror it, and our (modified) considered convictions; the reconciliation thus achieved is called "reflective equilibrium" (TJ 18). A conception of the person endorsed in reflective equilibrium is deemed justified: as Rawls says, "justification is a matter of the mutual support of many considerations, of everything fitting together into one coherent view" (TJ 19, 507).

This reflective equilibrium might be either narrow or wide. The narrow, local, or myopic kind of reflective equilibrium considers only those conceptions, principles, and convictions that bear a close resemblance to our current ones; consequently, the equilibrium that results is merely a neater, more internally consistent version of our old belief system. The wide or global kind of reflective equilibrium, on the contrary, ideally takes into account all "other plausible conceptions and . . . their supporting grounds"; this kind of equilibrium may involve a "radical shift" from our old belief system. As Rawls emphasizes, wide reflective equilibrium is what moral philosophy requires: only when we have considered all possible internally consistent belief systems (or, at minimum, a list of "representative theories from the history of moral philosophy") can we say with confidence that our own reflectively held beliefs are optimal.[3]

A question emerges at this point, one of the answers to which will lead us to the chasm mentioned earlier: under what circumstances will the wide reflective judgments (especially with respect to conceptions of the person) of different individuals coincide—a coincidence that Rawls calls "a necessary condition for objective moral truths" (IMT 290)? Rawls readily admits that even wide reflective equilibrium does not guarantee such a coincidence, because in it "many contrary moral conceptions may still be held" (IMT 290; cf. TJ 44). There are at least two sets of circumstances in which this sort of coincidence is expected to occur, both of which are described by Rawls and posited (or so I shall argue) in *Theory*. First, in the course of reflection, we may find "self-evident first principles" that are "so compelling that they lead us to revise all previous and subsequent judgments inconsistent with them" and create consistency in moral

3. TJ 43, 509; IMT 289. See Scanlon (2003) as well, who makes a parallel distinction between the "descriptive" and "deliberative" interpretations of reflective equilibrium (142–43, 147–48). Narrow and wide reflective equilibria are like local and global maxima: something can be a local maximum without being a global one—as anyone who thinks he has summited while hiking England's Scafell Pike will discover when the fog lifts (assuming that it does).

judgments across (fully reflective) persons (IMT 289). Rawls appears, at least, to take this approach in *Theory* whenever he refers to our "nature" as free and equal rational beings, as he often does in the text—and not only in the "Kantian Interpretation" section.[4] But how might such references to our "nature" count as reliance on first principles?

Given Rawls's consistent hostility to understanding moral truth "as fixed by a prior and independent order of objects and relations, whether *natural* or divine, an order apart and distinct from how we conceive of ourselves" and accessible via theoretical rather than practical reason, the most "natural" way to interpret Rawls's use of this term—and the one most compatible with his professed Kantianism—is to think of our freedom as a necessary presupposition or postulate of practical reason, as Kant does.[5] We can arrive at this postulate *directly*, as Kant does in the *Groundwork* (as a necessary presupposition of agency: something we must presuppose if we are to conceive of ourselves as agents, which is unavoidable), or *indirectly*, as he does in the second *Critique* (moral law, as a "fact of reason" that "forces itself upon us," first makes us conscious of our freedom, because "ought implies can" [i.e., morality presupposes freedom]).[6] Regardless of which path we take, however, we are forced by our own practical reason to conceive of ourselves as free beings. This necessary self-conception plays the role of a "self-evident first principle" in Kant's moral philosophy, and Rawls must have something like this in mind when he refers to our "nature"; otherwise, he would be relying illegitimately (from his perspective) on some notion of a natural moral order, accessible by theoretical reason and unmediated by our own conception of ourselves—which he says are among the sins of rational intuitionism.[7]

---

4. For example, TJ 222, 225, 475, 495, 501, 511. The p. 475 reference is interestingly ambiguous.

5. KCMT 306 (emphasis added); CPrR 5:3–5, 132. Rawls associates the idea of this "prior and independent order" with rational intuitionism, which he interprets Kant himself as opposing; see chapter 1 and KCMT 343–46.

6. GMM 4:447–48, 452, 459; CPrR 5:29–31. As Kant argues, "freedom and unconditional practical law reciprocally imply each other," a relationship sometimes referred to as the "reciprocity thesis" (CPrR 5:29 [cf. GMM 4:450]; Allison 1990, 201–13 [cf. Wood 1999, 171–72]). This relationship is purely analytic, though: without further argument, we have no idea whether either of these concepts applies to us as human beings. The two arguments from GMM and CPrR that I mention above attempt to show that they do.

7. I think Bernard Yack is absolutely right to complain that Rawls's assertions about our nature "act in his theory more as a placeholder for an absent justification than as that justification itself" (1993, 243n30). In the conclusion to this book, I will consider how a detranscendentalized Kantian foundational argument (based on GMM III) might replace these vague references to "our nature" in a reconstructed justice as fairness.

How exactly could this necessary self-conception lead to a coincidence of wide reflective judgments? The postulate in question holds for every finite rational being and thus for all human beings; every (fully reflective) person must therefore come to accept it as a first principle. Early in chapter 1, we saw that a presupposition of negative freedom of the will could be shown, by a series of steps, to imply positive freedom or autonomy, the highest form of which is moral; these qualities hold for each person and thus provide a basis for juridical and colegislative equality.[8] The postulate of freedom therefore implies a conception of ourselves as free, equal, and moral, which is precisely Rawls's Kantian conception of the person. If the postulate is necessary, then Rawls's Kantian conception of the person is necessary, and we have a reason to give priority to this conception over competitor ones. Moreover, if Rawls's Kantian constructivism is sound, we should *all* be led ineluctably from his Kantian conception of the person (which our own practical reason compels us to accept) to the three lexically ordered principles of justice that reflect it. If Kant's case for the postulate of freedom is compelling, therefore, the argument just adumbrated might be a powerful and persuasive way to make wide reflective judgments coincide on Rawls's justice as fairness.

Note, though, that this argument entails a degenerate notion of reflective equilibrium: any of our contrary considered convictions must be adjusted to reflect the Kantian conception of the person and the principles that follow from it; there is no "give and take" between the convictions and the constructivism. Kant would presumably view any contrary convictions as heteronomous moral commitments in simple need of revision.[9] Rawls clearly intended considered convictions to have some weight in his coherentist scheme of justification, however, so we may have reason to doubt that this argument best captures his preferred understanding of objectivity. Also notice that this argument's dismissive attitude towards contrary considered convictions remains even if they are conscientiously held by a cohesive social group (e.g., a nation); thus, the argument does not defer in the least to intensely held collective convictions and gives no independent weight to the value of *Gemeinschaft*, that is, ethical community. These features of the argument might explain why Rawls tacitly rejects it in "Kantian Constructivism in Moral Theory," where he says

---

8. I should note that the steps of this argument include elements from Kant's theoretical philosophy as found in the first *Critique*, as we saw in chapter 1; Rawls later parts ways with Kant on this matter (KCMT 352).

9. Cf. Pogge (1981), who has a different reading of the relationship between Kantianism and reflective equilibrium.

that his theory departs from Kant's view that the "conception of ourselves as fully autonomous is already given to us by the Fact of Reason [and therefore] implicit in individual moral consciousness, and the background social conditions for its realization are not emphasized or made part of the moral doctrine itself."[10] Five years later, in his seminal 1985 article "Justice as Fairness: Political Not Metaphysical," he explicitly rejects it, commenting that his argument for justice as fairness in *Theory* appears to depend "on philosophical claims I should like to avoid, for example, claims to universal truth, or claims about *the essential nature and identity of persons*. My aim is to explain why it does not."[11] Thus, by the early to mid-1980s, Rawls has decisively rejected the Kantian justification that I just outlined and must find another way to make wide reflective judgments coincide on justice as fairness.[12]

There is, however, a second set of circumstances under which this coincidence will (or at least can) occur: a preexisting consensus or near consensus on considered convictions of justice. Persons starting with identical or similar convictions are certainly more likely to arrive at *narrow* reflective judgments that coincide, and if original convictions exert a powerful influence on both the path and outcome of reflection—even with awareness of alternative conceptions—then *wide* reflective judgments are more likely to coincide as well.[13] Rawls assumes just such a consensus on considered convictions of justice in *Theory:* he says that "the argument for the principles of justice should proceed from some consensus," and he "take[s] for granted that these [considered convictions] are . . . approximately the same" (TJ 44, 508–9). Hence, he speaks of a "broadly shared agreement" on the "commonly shared presumptions" or "widely accepted but weak premises" that are at the roots of his constructivism, and

---

10. KCMT 340; cf. LP 86–88. Rawls appears to reject this approach even in *Theory* when he says that "I do not claim for the principles of justice proposed that they are necessary truths or derivable from such truths. A conception of justice cannot be deduced from self-evident premises or conditions on principles" (TJ 19). I believe that this is meant to be a direct criticism of rational intuitionism, however, which is discussed only eleven pages later (TJ 30–36). It is unclear whether Rawls meant to rule out Kant's approach at this stage; if he did, I am not sure how to interpret his frequent references to our "nature" as free and equal rational beings.

11. JFPM 388 (emphasis added); cf. JF 31. Intriguingly, he also says that he wants "to put aside the question whether the text of *A Theory of Justice* supports different readings from the one I sketch here" (JFPM 388). The Kantian justification that I outline above is just such an alternative reading.

12. Darwall (1976, 164–65; 1980, 331–32) was likely disappointed by this decision, as he himself had seen the promise of a "deeper justification" along Kantian lines of Rawls's political principles.

13. Rawls speculates that "perhaps the judgments from which we begin, or the course of reflection itself (or both), affect the resting point, if any, that we eventually achieve" (TJ 44).

he constantly uses "we" in describing considered convictions of justice, such as those opposing religious intolerance and racial discrimination, suggesting some underlying community of shared political belief (TJ 16–18).

This alternative elucidation of moral objectivity casts certain elements of Rawls's Kantian constructivism in a different, non-Kantian light. In chapter 1, for example, I presented Rawls's idea of the well-ordered society (WOS) as a product rather than a presupposition of his Kantian constructivism: a normatively guiding conception of the person entails certain principles via the OP, and when these principles are publicly ratified by citizens and applied to the basic structure, a WOS is achieved (TJ 4, 397–99, 475). By the time we reach "Kantian Constructivism in Moral Theory," though, the WOS has been assigned the status of one of "the three main model-conceptions of justice as fairness" and is connected there with citizens' membership in a "common polity" that preserves their "cultural and social life in perpetuity" (KCMT 323). This increasing prominence of WOS—a trend that continues in *Political Liberalism,* as we shall see— suggests that Rawls was beginning to realize the need for a preexisting national political culture with common values as a *foundation* for his constructivism.

As a way of securing the coincidence of reflective judgments on justice as fairness, this approach raises at least two questions, though. First, who is this "we" that "broadly shares" both the premises at the foundation of Rawls's constructivism and the more particular policy positions against which his principles of justice are tested? Second, why would this underlying community have considered convictions more favorable to justice as fairness than to plausible alternatives? Rawls never addresses these questions in *Theory,* but he begins to in "Kantian Constructivism," and the answers he gives mark a sharp break with Kant. On the former question, Rawls radically reduces his theory's range of application by saying that its most important function is to "settle a fundamental disagreement over the just form of basic institutions *within a democratic society under modern conditions*"; by restricting its applicability in this way, he hopes that there will be "a sufficient sharing of certain underlying notions and implicitly held principles so that the effort to reach an understanding has some foothold" (KCMT 305–6; emphasis added). As for the latter question, Rawls asserts that his Kantian conception of persons is "implicit in the public culture of a democratic society," "latent" or "embedded" in the "common sense" of democratic citizens, and that the task of philosophy is to excavate this shared understanding and present it in a clear and persuasive form to the demos, who will presumably recognize it and reflectively endorse it (KCMT 305–6).

These answers—that his theory is both relative to and implicit in a democratic political culture—are more fully developed in *Political Liberalism,* but we can already recognize certain advantages to this approach to moral objectivity. By limiting his theory's range of application to societies that are already democratic, Rawls can avoid charges of cultural imperialism. Justice as fairness, Rawls can say, is not an alien imposition on cultures lacking any democratic traditions, but rather is a compelling candidate conception of justice intended solely for those societies that can plausibly share its liberal-democratic assumptions—shared assumptions that can help secure a coincidence of wide reflective judgments, as required for moral objectivity. By arguing that his conception of persons is "latent" in a democratic political culture, he can similarly avoid charges of imperialism *within* that culture: Rawls believes that his Kantian conception of the person most fully reflects a liberal-democratic society's commitments to freedom and equality, so insofar as the adherents of *non*-Kantian doctrines participate in and endorse the values of that society, they must also (upon reflection) endorse the Kantian conception. The Kantian conception, in short, is not imposed upon non-Kantian liberal democrats but rather is shown to be an implication of their own belief systems.

Despite these apparent advantages, though, Rawls's approach to moral objectivity can be criticized for its handling of both questions. His reply to the first question in effect turns Kant on his head: Kant's Doctrine of Right was a ringing defense of universal republicanism in a world in which republics were virtually nonexistent; had it addressed only republican citizens, the French, Americans, and Swiss would have been the sole audiences. To say with Rawls that what justifies a conception of justice is that *"given* our history and the traditions embedded in our public life, it is the most reasonable doctrine for us" is to turn justification into a heteronomous enterprise, one that depends in a profoundly un-Kantian manner on historical contingency. The Rawls of *Theory* certainly recognized that his three lexically ordered principles of justice could not apply to every society regardless of its level of development, but this limit to their applicability was a temporary matter governed by his nonideal theory and its threshold conditions (namely, "strict compliance" and "favorable circumstances") (TJ §39). The Rawls of "Kantian Constructivism" extends this limit to his ideal theory as well and by doing so makes justice as fairness at best a parochial affair for those countries fortunate enough to have democratic political cultures (cf. Höffe 1984, 110; O'Neill 2003, 352–53, 360–63).

This domain restriction raises another question, however: why would justice as fairness and the Kantian conception of the person it relies upon be uncompelling outside the context of modern democratic societies? After all, the wide reflective equilibrium Rawls champions allows for the possibility of "radical shifts" in people's belief systems, presumably including shifts from nondemocratic to democratic ways of thinking. Rawls's domain restriction suggests a pessimism about the width of reflective equilibrium: if starting points strongly influence the conclusions we reflectively reach—an idea he entertains in *Theory* and later endorses, as we have seen—then the very possibility of wide reflective equilibrium is called into question (TJ 44). *Strong path dependence in reflection turns all reflective equilibria into narrow ones.* The communities of shared political belief that arise from such reflective processes remain "closed worlds" with respect to each other in the following sense: though they may come to understand (but not accept) each other's belief systems and though historical accidents may push them sufficiently within each other's orbits to make reconciliation a real possibility, the only principled ways to reconcile them—transcending these narrow worlds by appeal to a natural or divine moral order accessible by theoretical reason, to a practical postulate of freedom, or to some other kind of universal first principle—have been ruled out by Rawls. In avoiding what he took to be the Scylla of Kantian transcendentalism, he has apparently strayed into the Charybdis of ethical relativism.[14] In the conclusion to the book, I will suggest a way for Rawls to steer clear of both hazards: by adopting a detranscendentalized Kantian foundational defense of his conception of the person, one that holds across all times and cultures but is not dependent upon Kant's transcendental idealism.

As for Rawls's response to the second question—that his Kantian conception of persons is "implicit in the public culture of a democratic society" and can be philosophically excavated, persuasively presented, and reflectively ratified by the demos—I effectively assessed this claim in part 2 of the book. Most of part 2 was spent reconstructing Rawls's defenses of his principles of justice and showing how these reconceived defenses were tightly connected to the hierarchical Kantian conception of the person that was extended and

---

14. Ethical relativism is "the view that moral appraisals are essentially dependent upon the standards that define a particular moral code, the practices and norms accepted by a social group at a specific place and time. Given that there is in fact a plurality of social groups, with differing mores, the relativist argues that there exists no point of view from which these codes can themselves be appraised, no 'absolute' criteria by which they can be criticized" (Honderich 1995, 758). Also see my discussion of relativism in chapter 1.

elaborated in chapter 2. Over the course of these reconstructions, we slowly became aware of just how radical this conception really is, an awareness that was tough to achieve until we had seen the role that it and its various components played in the process of justification. Now that its radicalism has been made plain, however, it is extremely difficult to see how most democratic citizens could reflectively endorse either it or the principles of justice that flow from it—short of a "radical shift" in their belief systems of a kind that Rawls has effectively ruled out by his rejection of universal first principles. Though Rawls's Kantian conception of the person is certainly *one* way to embody the liberal-democratic values of freedom and equality, there are many other ways to do so that would surely be more attractive to non-Kantian liberal democrats.

In a sense, however, these criticisms are premature, for we have not yet seen Rawls's full development of this second approach to moral objectivity in *Political Liberalism*. The partial and tentative statements of this approach found in *Theory* and "Kantian Constructivism" are specially susceptible to my criticisms due in part to their sketchiness. As we shall see, *Political Liberalism* provides a much more complete and compelling presentation and offers (implicit) replies to both of my criticisms.

III. Political Liberalism: Motivation and Structure

From the essays marking Rawls's so-called political turn ("Justice as Fairness: Political Not Metaphysical" and "The Idea of an Overlapping Consensus") to his later book-length works (*Political Liberalism, The Law of Peoples*), political liberalism has developed its own conceptual apparatus, method of justification, and even terminology. Its complexity can be daunting, so we will make a gradual approach, beginning with a few rudimentary concepts and problems. By the end of this section, the reason for Rawls's rejection of the Kantian approach to moral objectivity that I sketched above will be evident.

The first Rawlsian term of art that needs to be defined is "comprehensive doctrine" (CD), which Rawls describes as a moral conception that is both general and comprehensive in scope, in the limit fully so:

> A moral conception is *general* if it applies to a wide range of subjects, and in the limit to all subjects universally. It is *comprehensive* when it includes conceptions of what is of value in human life, and ideals of

personal character, as well as ideals of friendship and of familial and associational relationships, and much else that is to inform our conduct, and in the limit to our life as a whole. A conception is *fully* comprehensive if it covers all recognized values and virtues within one rather precisely articulated system; whereas a conception is only *partially* comprehensive when it comprises a number of, but by no means all, nonpolitical values and virtues and is rather loosely articulated. Many religious and philosophical doctrines aspire to be both general and comprehensive. (PL 13 [emphasis added]; cf. IOC 424n4, 436n23)

Examples of philosophical and religious doctrines that would qualify as full CDs include Millian and Kantian liberalism and the Abrahamic faiths (Judaism, Christianity, and Islam), because they offer systematic judgments on a wide array of ethical and political issues in a variety of different contexts (IOC 427; PL 145, 170). To be more specific, Christianity explains what is of value in human life (God and his creation, as well as his intentions for it), which virtues are to be developed (e.g., piety, humility), and what precepts we are to live by (including the Ten Commandments in the Old Testament and the Golden Rule in the New). Late in life—and consistent with the argument of my book—Rawls viewed the liberalism of *Theory* as comprehensive: as he says in *The Law of Peoples*, "justice as fairness is presented there [i.e., in *Theory*] as a comprehensive liberal doctrine," and as I argued in chapter 1, *Theory* and several successor essays offer us a specifically Kantian liberalism, one with many ethical elements and aspirations towards moral comprehensiveness.[15]

Rawls regards a diversity of full and partial CDs to be a "permanent feature of the public culture of modern democracies," a truth that he refers to as the "fact of pluralism," and he thinks that several features of democratic society (e.g., freedom of speech and association) sustain and even promote such diversity.[16] He goes on to suggest two additional, closely related facts. First, he says

---

15. LP 179; see especially Rawls's discussions of the relationship between a well-ordered society and a kingdom of ends or "ethical commonwealth" and his belief that justice as fairness could be "extended to the choice of more or less an entire ethical system" at KCE 264 and TJ 15, 115, 221, 226, §§18–19, 51–52. See Hill (1989b) for a cautionary note about the possibility of such an extension. Finally, I should add that at times Rawls appears to suggest that *Theory* is already "politically liberal": for example, see JFPM 388–89, 396n14.

16. IOC 424–25. Rawls later distinguishes between this fact and the "fact of reasonable pluralism," i.e., a pluralism of *reasonable* CDs, which I will define and discuss shortly (PL 36–37). Such diversity has numerous causes, of course, including the Reformation and its aftermath, industrialization, mass immigration, etc.

that "a continuing shared understanding on one comprehensive religious, philosophical, or moral doctrine can be maintained only by the oppressive use of state power," which he calls the "fact of oppression"; hence, no society can be organized on the basis of one CD without the use of pervasive coercion and indoctrination, such as that found during the Inquisition (IOC 425; PL 37). Given the fact of pluralism, the fact of oppression closely follows: if diversity flows inexorably from liberal-democratic governance, then the only way to reduce diversity and secure consensus on a single CD is through undermining such governance. Second, if "we are concerned with securing the stability of a constitutional regime and wish to achieve free and willing agreement on at least the constitutional essentials, we must find another basis of agreement than that of a general and comprehensive doctrine," that is, the only way to achieve a *stable* and *legitimate* democratic regime is to find a "basis of agreement" sensitive to the fact of pluralism (IOC 421, 425; PL 38, 65, 137). We shall call this the "fact of legitimate stability."

If these three "facts" are indeed factual, *Theory*'s argument for the three lexically ordered principles of justice is highly problematic, as Rawls himself admits (JFPM 414n33; PL xv–xvii; LP 179). As I argued above, *Theory* grounds its case for the three principles on a Kantian CD, but the fact of pluralism suggests that a liberal-democratic society governed by such principles will host a wide variety of CDs, including but not limited to the Kantian one. If only a Kantian CD can underwrite these principles, though, then the only way to secure social consensus on it and the political principles that follow from it via Kantian constructivism is through coercion and indoctrination (by the fact of oppression).[17] Such methods are wholly at odds with the principles themselves, however, especially the equal-liberty principle and its lexical priority. Consequently, a Kantian CD cannot provide the basis for social unity and a well-ordered society, and any new attempt to ground the three principles must be sensitive to the fact of pluralism to achieve broad consent (by the fact of legitimate stability).

---

17. PL 37–38n39. Rawls, of course, thinks that *Theory*'s reliance upon a Kantian CD is narrower and more limited than I contend in part 2, consisting mainly in the Kantian presupposition about autonomy as a character ideal to be found in the argument for congruence (TJ 501, 503; also see S. Freeman 2003a). Indeed, Rawls believed that nearly all that was needed to "fix" *Theory* (i.e., to make it a political-liberal text) was a correction in its account of stability, which *Political Liberalism* provided; apart from these adjustments *Political Liberalism* assumed "the structure and content of *Theory* to remain substantially the same" (PL xv–xvii). As I argued in chapter 1, Rawls is absolutely right to view *Theory*'s congruence argument and the stability argument of which it is part as strongly Kantian in nature; as I have also argued throughout this book, however, the Kantianism of *Theory* runs—and must run—much deeper than this.

These three interrelated facts explain why Rawls must ultimately reject the first approach to moral objectivity that I sketched above. That approach gave no ground to contrary considered convictions of justice, even if conscientiously held by a cohesive group, such as, for example, devotees of various non-Kantian CDs. Therefore, it can offer us only a factitious moral objectivity based on coercion and indoctrination (by the fact of oppression). These facts also constitute an implicit reply to my first criticism above, namely, that Rawls's explicit abandonment of universal first principles amounts to a sort of ethical relativism. Rawls would undoubtedly respond that the ambition to realize such principles internationally would require a cultural imperialism backed by military force, because many societies—even ones that we would recognize as decent and humane—would be unable to endorse such principles reflectively due to their collectively and conscientiously held nonliberal, nondemocratic considered convictions of justice. (I will return to Rawls's extension of political liberalism to the international sphere in chapter 8.)[18]

We appear to have reached an impasse here: if a Kantian CD is required to underwrite the three principles, but no CD can provide a basis for social unity, then how are we to ground these principles in a stable and legitimate way? According to Rawls, the solution is political liberalism: we must reconceive justice as fairness as a "political conception of justice" (PCJ), which avoids any claims to universality and eschews any exclusive connection to a particular CD, such as the Kantian one (JFPM 388, 409). A PCJ will be (as Rawls puts it) "freestanding," that is, capable of being endorsed by numerous full and partial CDs (JFPM 411; PL 12). This plural affirmation will be feasible because the conceptions of person (as free and equal) and society (as a fair system of cooperation) that underlie justice as fairness and from which its distinctive political principles are derived (via what Rawls now calls "political constructivism") will not be drawn exclusively from a Kantian CD but instead from the "public culture of a democratic society," in which all the participating CDs are embedded (JFPM 396). This reconception of justice as fairness as a PCJ renders possible what he refers to as an "overlapping consensus" (OC) on its three principles by a host of CDs, which would constitute a widespread, durable, and willing endorsement as required by the fact of legitimate stability.

---

18. As he says in *The Law of Peoples*, "it is often thought that the task of philosophy is to uncover a form of argument that will always prove convincing against all other arguments. There is, however, no such argument" (LP 123). This holds just as strongly with so-called decent but illiberal peoples as with Rawls's subject here, expansionist peoples.

In order for such an argument to be compelling, however, a more detailed description of the proposed OC is needed, including information on its potential participants, the nature of their affirmation of the conceptions of person and society underlying justice as fairness, the manner in which the (joint) construction of principles takes place, and the scope of the proposed OC. As for participating CDs, Rawls suggests that an OC on justice as fairness could be joined by a Kantian or Millian liberalism, a "free-faith" religious doctrine such as Locke's, and certain types of partially comprehensive doctrines (PCDs) that give sufficient priority to political conceptions; excluded would be such CDs as the classical utilitarianism of Bentham or Sidgwick and certain kinds of religious fundamentalism.[19] He calls the former, included set *reasonable* CDs (RCDs) and the latter, excluded set *unreasonable* CDs (UCDs) (PL 58–66). Rawls himself defines RCDs as those CDs that "recognize the essentials of a liberal democratic regime and exhibit a reasoned ordering of the many values of life (whether religious or nonreligious) in a coherent and consistent manner," but this definition turns out to be peculiar to a particular domestic political context, because Rawls emphasizes that "whenever the scope of toleration is extended" in an international context so as to include certain nonliberal but "decent" peoples, "the criteria of reasonableness are relaxed" so that they may qualify as "reasonable" and therefore participate in a global society of well-ordered peoples.[20] Thus, the best definition of an RCD, one that is flexible enough to hold across different political contexts, may simply be *a CD capable of participating in an OC of some specification*. I will return to this issue in chapter 8, which is of substantial theoretical (not just terminological) interest.

RCDs are reasonable because they accept not only "the essentials of a liberal democratic regime" but also the conceptions of person and society that underwrite those essentials and lead to them via political constructivism. These conceptions, as Rawls repeatedly emphasizes, are not exclusively linked to a

---

19. JFPM 413; IOC 430–31, 438–39; PL 145–46, 170. Rawls later suggests that the classical utilitarianism of a Bentham or Sidgwick could also participate, which blatantly contradicts his earlier claims (PL 169–71; cf. IOC 433–34). I will criticize this suggestion and discuss utilitarianism in greater detail below. A *partially* comprehensive doctrine (PCD) "comprises a number of, but by no means all, nonpolitical values and virtues and is . . . loosely articulated" (PL 13).

20. LP 87; PL xviii; LP 561; cf. Wenar (1995, 35–38), on defining reasonable CDs and persons. Strictly speaking, Rawls reserves the term "reasonable" for those CDs/peoples who are liberal-democratic, preferring the term "decent" for those peoples who are nonliberal but who respect human rights and meet other criteria (LP 64–67, 71–78). However, a careful reading of the text (e.g., LP 70) indicates that "decent" is merely the *international analogue* of "reasonable."

specific RCD but rather are "implicit in the public culture of a democratic society," "latent" or "embedded" in the "common sense" of democratic citizens, including those adherents of RCDs (KCMT 305-6; PL xxi, 18-19). What form, however, does this acceptance, endorsement, or affirmation of these conceptions take? Rawls emphasizes that each RCD "accepts justice as fairness in its own way," but the various forms of acceptance do fall into two broad categories: first, the conceptions of person and society may be *derived from* the RCD, as is the case with Kantian or Millian forms of liberalism; second, the conceptions may simply be *compatible with* the RCD, as in the case of various PCDs that assign priority to these conceptions (i.e., allowing them to trump non-political concerns in most cases) without integrating them within a coherent system, which these PCDs by definition lack (JFPM 411; IOC 438-39, 441; PL 160). Whichever category the RCD falls into, Rawls insists that these conceptions be "affirmed on moral grounds," that is, *from within* RCDs and for *moral* reasons rather than strategic or self-interested reasons; otherwise, the OC degenerates into a mere modus vivendi, without the stability and legitimacy that Rawls demands of OCs (IOC 432). If the adherents of the non-Kantian RCDs can genuinely affirm these conceptions on moral grounds, my second criticism above—namely, that most democratic citizens could not endorse the radically Kantian conception of persons that is needed to underwrite justice as fairness—can be met: Kantians would *not* be the only citizens who could endorse a Kantian conception of the person and the principles that flow from it.

Just as RCDs are characterized by internal coherence and consistency and, more strongly, their moral endorsement of liberal conceptions of person and society, so reasonable citizens are characterized by their acceptance of an RCD and, relatedly, their recognition of the burdens of judgment. As I noted above, the fact of pluralism tells us that in a liberal-democratic society our fellow citizens will adopt a wide range of CDs—and if they are reasonable, these will be RCDs. We must see this diversity as itself reasonable, that is, the natural, expected result of fellow citizens exercising their "powers of reason and judgment in the ordinary course of political life" (PL 54-65 [§§2-3: "The Burdens of Judgment" and "Reasonable Comprehensive Doctrines"], here 56). Such exercise necessarily involves certain "hazards" generated by a variety of causes (e.g., conflicting empirical evidence, vagueness of the subject matter, etc.), hazards which explain the divergence of our judgments and the consequent diversity of RCDs. Reasonable citizens will both recognize and respect this capacity for, and divergent exercise of, reason and judgment by fellow citizens.

Justice as fairness, as a liberal PCJ, is to be "worked up from the fund of shared political ideas," especially the conceptions of person (as free and equal) and society (as a fair system of cooperation), that are held in common by RCDs (IOC 427). This joint construction of political principles by RCDs in an OC— moving from these conceptions of person and society through a procedure of construction to the three lexically ordered principles of justice—Rawls now terms "political constructivism," but it is equivalent in all of its essential features to the Kantian constructivism that we examined at great length in chapter 1.[21] The name change and restatement of method in *Political Liberalism* is simply meant to emphasize what was generally only implicit in "Kantian Constructivism in Moral Theory": that Rawls's constructivism is political rather than ethical and that its purely political nature (as well as its grounding in the shared ideas of democratic culture) makes it accessible to RCDs with widely varying, even incompatible conceptions of the good.[22] Thus, citizen adherents of such divergent RCDs are able to share not only a rich fund of political ideas but a systematic way of connecting them, of deriving some (e.g., principles of justice) from others (conceptions of person and society), without reference to the private or nonpolitical values that may be idiosyncratic to their own RCDs. Political constructivism is the joint manufacture of political principles among citizens within what Rawls calls the sphere of "public reason," that is, a realm of shared "principles, standards, and ideals" into which citizens of diverse private beliefs can emerge for purposes of common political discussion and decision making (IOC 441; PL 223-27; also see S. Freeman 2007a, 199-201, 215-56).

Finally, throughout this description I have suggested that the proposed OC is on a *single* liberal PCJ, namely, justice as fairness. At numerous points in his writings, however, Rawls suggests that a "more realistic and more likely" case of OC would be focused on "a *class* of liberal [PCJs, which] will be political rivals and no doubt favored by different interests and political strata" (JFPM 410; IOC 427; PL 164, 167-68; LP 180). I will discuss this possibility in much greater detail below, but I want to point out here that even if an OC on justice as fairness alone is impossible—as I will, in fact, argue in the next chapter—

---

21. PL 89-129, especially 90n1. Notice that I say "Kantian constructivism," not "Kant's constructivism": Rawls takes some care in *Political Liberalism* to distinguish the former from the latter (PL 99-101). See chapter 1 on this point.

22. These points are made, either directly or indirectly, in the earlier essay as well—see KCMT 305-6, 339-40, 355.

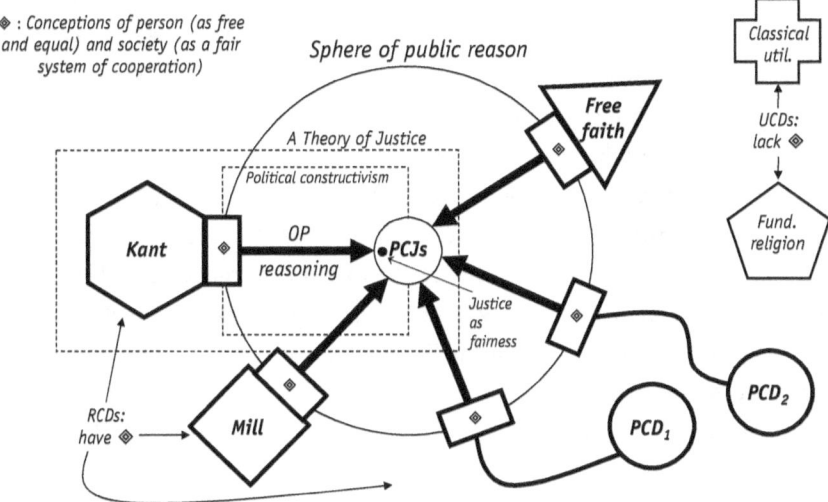

Fig. 11 Model overlapping consensus

an OC including justice as fairness among other liberal PCJs might still be possible; in it, justice as fairness would be endorsed by some RCDs but not by others. This possibility will raise a host of other questions, of course (such as, "Why not expand the OC further to include *illiberal* PCJs?"), which I will address in section III of the next chapter.

Figure 11 provides a graphical representation of the proposed OC that combines all of the elements we have just discussed. In it, CDs are represented by diverse geometric shapes (circles, hexagons, etc.). These CDs may be RCDs (such as Kantian or Millian liberalism) or UCDs (such as classical utilitarianism or some fundamentalist religious doctrines). What distinguishes RCDs from UCDs is the ability of the former to affirm (whether strongly or weakly, as with PCDs) the liberal conceptions of person and society; this difference is represented graphically by the RCDs' possession of "docking rings" (the boxes containing the ◆ symbol, which symbolizes the liberal conceptions of person and society) and the UCDs' lack of them. RCDs like Kantian and Millian liberalism have their docking rings attached directly to them (as the conceptions can be directly derived from them), while RCDs like the pictured PCDs are attached to their docking rings by a wire (as the conceptions are merely compatible with them). These docking rings allow the RCDs to dock with the sphere of public reason and therefore participate in the proposed OC. Once they are docked, the RCDs can jointly construct a liberal PCJ (or perhaps a family of them) by means of political constructivism: starting with their shared conceptions of person and society, they can utilize OP reasoning to generate principles of justice; the arrows represent this joint construction of a PCJ (or PCJs). I have drawn the focus of the OC broadly so that it could potentially contain several liberal PCJs, including justice as fairness (indicated as a dot inside the focus); this PCJ is more closely associated with the Kantian RCD for reasons that should be clear by now. Whether there are any PCJs in the focus other than justice as fairness will be discussed in the next chapter. Finally, to show the relationship between *Theory* (as interpreted by me as well as the late Rawls) and *Political Liberalism*, I display a dotted box around the Kantian RCD, conceptions of person and society, OP reasoning, and justice as fairness (understood narrowly here as simply the three lexically ordered principles).

IV. Conclusion

Over the course of this chapter, I have adumbrated the evolution of Rawls's justificatory strategy from *Theory* to *Political Liberalism* and *The Law of Peoples*. The basic method, which Rawls calls "reflective equilibrium," has stayed constant, but its interpretation and place within his larger Kantian (later political) constructivism has changed. *Theory*'s original presentation of it was ambiguous, as we saw, because it equivocated between two distinct methods of grounding moral objectivity: the first method was reliant upon universal first principles, the second upon a preexisting consensus on considered convictions of justice. In the early 1980s, he finally opted for the second method and by doing so opened up a chasm between his thought and that of Kant. Rawls ultimately believed that he was driven to do so by the facts of pluralism, oppression, and legitimate stability, and in *Political Liberalism* he spelled out in exquisite and compelling detail the full implications of this choice for the defense of justice as fairness. If it is really successful, this defense is a prodigy of parsimony: it shows that his radical and controversial principles of justice and the Kantian conception of persons upon which they are grounded can be reflectively endorsed not just by Kantians but by many reasonable non-Kantians as well. Is this in fact true, and if not, is there anything left of political liberalism worth salvaging? I turn to these questions in the remainder of part 3.

8

The Poverty of Political Liberalism

I. Introduction

In the preceding chapter, I in effect initiated a two-part critique of what Rawls eventually came to call "political liberalism," which offered a new justificatory basis for justice as fairness. The first part of this critique focuses on Rawls's proposed solution to the problem of securing a coincidence of wide reflective judgments across persons on a conception of justice, which Rawls sees as "a necessary condition for objective moral truths" (IMT 290; cf. JFPM 395, PL 112). After rejecting one means of securing such a coincidence—namely, "self-evident first principles," like Kant's practical postulates—Rawls opts for another: a preexisting consensus on (liberal) considered convictions of justice "implicit in the public culture of a democratic society" (IMT 289; KCMT 305). By limiting his justification in this way, however, Rawls demonstrates a profound pessimism about the potential width of reflective equilibrium: if starting points strongly influence the conclusions we reflectively reach, then dissimilar societies effectively become closed worlds with respect to one another, and justice as fairness (or any other liberal conception of justice, for that matter) can address only those fortunate enough to already have democratic public cultures and institutions. Political liberalism's rejection of universalism and muteness vis-à-vis nondemocratic societies has been critically discussed by several scholars, including Onora O'Neill and Sam Scheffler (O'Neill 1997, 422–28; Scheffler 1994, 20–22).

The second part of the critique says that even in the case of a "democratic society under modern conditions" it is unclear why justice as fairness would be more attractive than alternative conceptions of justice to adherents of non-Kantian comprehensive doctrines (KCMT 305–6). I have argued over the course of this book that the conception of the person required to support the three lexically ordered principles of justice (EL, FEO, and DP) is not only radical but distinctively Kantian—so much so, in fact, that it is hard to imagine how adherents of other comprehensive doctrines could *morally* endorse it, as Rawls insists (IOC 432). Such an affirmation would require a "radical shift" in their belief systems of a kind that Rawls has effectively ruled out by his rejection of self-evident first principles and his consequent pessimism regarding wide reflective equilibrium (TJ 43).

In this chapter, I will further develop this two-part critique, starting with the second part and then returning to the first. I reverse the order from the last chapter for the following reason: if political liberals were convinced by the second part, they might be tempted to "bite the bullet" and simply accept the fact that in a pluralistic democratic society, justice as fairness will be just one liberal conception of justice among many, with whatever political efficacy it might achieve being determined through constrained political competition. The first part shows, however, that political liberalism's poverty runs much deeper than an inability to support justice as fairness in overlapping consensus and that it is not an independently attractive form of justification.

Before continuing, I should say a bit more about the "target," so to speak, of this critique: political liberals, that is, adherents of the mature doctrine outlined at the end of the last chapter as a method of justification in political theory, whether in its narrow form (where the focus of the OC contains only justice as fairness) or its broad form (where the focus contains justice as fairness as well as other liberal PCJs). On this definition, the later Rawls was a political liberal, though there is a hint of ambiguity even here.[1] So are many

1. The ambiguity arises mostly in Rawls's very last writings. Earlier, around the time of the political turn, Rawls is reasonably clear that he views *Theory* as a political-liberal text, albeit one with certain flaws (notably with regard to its treatment of stability)—see, e.g., JFPM 388–89, 396n14. Given that *Theory* could be interpreted instead as advocating some kind of universalistic Kantian liberalism—a possibility that he does not completely exclude (JFPM 388)—Rawls can be seen here as offering an authoritative political-liberal interpretation of *Theory*, one intended to discount any universalistic elements. Political liberalism thus supplants any universalism that might have snuck into *Theory*. In one of his last published pieces, however, Rawls says that *Political Liberalism* simply answers a different question than *Theory*—viz. the question of how to achieve legitimate stability or stability for the right reasons—and thus that "the two books are asymmetrical" (IPRR 614–15). This at least raises the possibility that *Political Liberalism* does not supplant the universalistic elements of *Theory* at all but rather speaks to an entirely different question. The question is hardly unrelated, though: because *Political Liberalism* declares the well-ordered society of *Theory* to be "impossible," given the fact of (reasonable) pluralism, the former work relegates the latter to the genre of utopian literature, however much *Theory*'s WOS might have remained attractive to Rawls *qua* Kantian. My own sense is that the late Rawls is a thoroughgoing political liberal, but I cannot definitively rule out other possibilities.

scholars who work within a Rawlsian framework, ranging from orthodox Rawlsians like Samuel Freeman, arguably his leading interpreter, to those like John Tomasi who, though broadly political liberals, take strong exception to some elements of the theory (see S. Freeman 2007a; Tomasi 2001). Finally, we should include scholars like Charles Larmore and Donald Moon, who have developed closely related theories—though they might object to being called "Rawlsians" (see Larmore 1987; Moon 1993). These theorists and kindred ones will find the following critiques provocative, if not persuasive.

II. Narrow Critique: No Overlapping Consensus on Justice as Fairness Alone

If justice as fairness is to be the *only* PCJ in the focus of the proposed OC, then it must be the case that the political-constructivist module shown in figure 11—conceptions of persons as free and equal and of society as a fair system of cooperation, a constructive procedure mirroring these conceptions via OP reasoning, and the three lexically ordered principles of justice yielded by the procedure—is invariant across RCDs: each must affirm the identical conceptions, process, and principles.[2] This module, which is embedded in the structure of *Theory*, is liberated from its Kantian context in *Political Liberalism* and affirmed there by a host of Kantian and non-Kantian RCDs in OC. The conception of the person that each of these RCDs must endorse, though, is the same radical, controversial Kantian conception that I detailed in chapters 1 and 2 and showed in chapters 3-6 to be essential in the grounding of the three principles (EL, FEO, and DP) and their lexical priorities. Consequently, the very possibility of the proposed OC hinges on the answer to the following question, inter alia: *Is it really the case that adherents of most (or even many) of these RCDs could reflectively affirm this Kantian conception of the person on moral grounds, as Rawls requires?* Put somewhat differently, is such a conception really "latent" or "embedded" in the "common sense" of democratic citizens, including especially adherents of these RCDs (KCMT 306)?

2. PL 4-11. Rawls adamantly denies that the module itself—e.g., the three principles—has changed between *Theory* and *Political Liberalism:* "Some think the difference principle is abandoned entirely, others that I no more affirm justice as fairness than any other political conception of justice. And they do so despite the fact that early on I say that justice in fairness is held intact (modulo the account of stability) and affirmed as much as before in TJ" (1995 Santa Clara Conference comments, quoted in Daniels 2000, 135). I will call Rawls's account of his own work into question below.

We can only answer these questions by systematically reviewing not just the CDs that Rawls includes in his model OCs but also the other CDs that exist in democratic societies (e.g., those found in the United States) and then determining whether these CDs can affirm a Kantian conception of the person or justice as fairness more generally. As we shall see, what this review reveals is that there are innumerable competing conceptions of the person—even of the person as free and equal—among the CDs in a democratic culture and that virtually all of them are in some way *incompatible* with the Kantian one. This judgment continues to hold even if we consider just the reflective versions of these CDs and their associated conceptions (cf. Kaufman 2006, 27, 35–36). As we catalog these CDs and assess their ability to endorse the Kantian conception of persons, we shall gradually come to see the perceptiveness of Bernard Yack's comment that Rawls "simply writes his conception of moral personality into democratic public culture, rather than discovers it there" (Yack 1993, 232–34; cf. Hampton 1989, 805).

Before beginning this systematic review, I should note that it will only examine CDs that are (at least approximately) liberal. These are the tough cases, so to speak: liberal CDs are more likely to endorse a Kantian conception of persons as free and equal than illiberal ones, so if I can show that even they fail to do so, there will be no need to review the illiberal CDs, as they will surely fail as well. I will return to the case of illiberal CDs in the next section of this chapter, during what I shall term the "broad critique" of political liberalism.

A CD might fail to endorse a Kantian conception of the person or justice as fairness more generally for at least two kinds of reasons:[3]

1. Conceptual: If two distinct conceptions of the person (or of justice more broadly) flatly contradict one another, it is difficult to see as a conceptual matter how one could affirm them simultaneously, at least on moral grounds. Such an affirmation would constitute a sort of "justificatory schizophrenia," to use Norman Daniels's term.[4]

---

3. These two kinds of reasons are similar to John Tomasi's "rebutting" and "undercutting" defeaters, respectively, as well as to Kant's contradictions in conception and in will (Tomasi 2001, 22; GMM 4:424).

4. Daniels (2000, 135); cf. Wenar (1995, 53, "schizophrenic"). Will Kymlicka, for example, points out that the pursuit of full autonomy—which continues to be endorsed by political liberalism for mere *political* purposes—includes the development and exercise of the second moral power of rationality, which is the power to form, revise, and discard conceptions of the good and the plans of life that implement them. Thus, such a pursuit *by definition* intrudes upon the private realm and will be incompatible with CDs (such as conservative religious ones) that are

2. Empirical-psychological: Conceptual consistency may exist between two conceptions of the person or of justice more broadly, but one may nonetheless worry that affirmation of the political conception (and what follows from it) will ultimately erode one's loyalty to the private or nonpolitical conception on empirical-psychological grounds. These will include the tendency of political conceptions to insist upon the development of particular attitudes, skills, and virtues that might be in tension with those called for by nonpolitical conceptions and that might supplant the latter over time due to their priority in collective deliberation and action. John Tomasi refers to these unintended effects of endorsing the political conception as "spillovers" and to their long-term, cumulative consequences as "free erosion."[5]

With this rough taxonomy of reasons in hand, we can now begin systematically to examine CDs (both those included by Rawls in his model OCs and others of prominence in liberal-democratic societies) and to evaluate their compatibility with the Kantian conception of persons and justice as fairness more broadly. We shall first examine liberal CDs that fail to affirm these conceptions on conceptual grounds: they include the bourgeois, competitive-individualist CD, Rawls's "free-faith" religious CDs, and the teleological CDs (utilitarianism and perfectionism). Then we shall look at liberal CDs that fail to affirm on empirical-psychological grounds, including a romantic-liberal CD as well as reasonable PCDs. Following this fairly comprehensive review, I will argue that Rawls may have been aware of this problem (perhaps subconsciously) because he gradually made subtle changes to his theory after the "political turn" that appear designed to deal with it, such as watering down the content of justice as fairness, weakening the definition of liberalism, and widening the OC to include liberal PCJs other than justice as fairness. Finally, I will consider whether (some

---

fundamentally hostile to autonomy in private life. See Kymlicka (2002, 279n20) as well as below for further discussion.

5. Tomasi (2001, 14, 26). On the more general phenomenon, see Tomasi (2001, 12–16, 20–32); Macedo (1990, 62, 251–53, 263, 265–67, 278–79); Macedo (2000, 137, 278–79); and Kymlicka (2002, 236–43). Rawls begins to recognize this problem himself during a discussion of children's civic education, which is an education for merely *political* autonomy that may nonetheless have spillover effects; Rawls says that "the unavoidable consequences of reasonable requirements for children's education may have to be accepted, often with regret," but the consequences may include an inability by adherents of antiautonomy CDs to endorse the proautonomy political conceptions (PL 199–200; cf. KCMT 332, where Rawls seems to deny this implication). Again, see below for further discussion.

parts of) justice as fairness might still be affirmed by non-Kantian CDs—not in OC, of course, but perhaps in a constitutional or legislative consensus.

A. Conceptual-Failure CDs

1. *Bourgeois, Competitive-Individualist CD*

This CD has been described at some length by Gerald Doppelt and should be familiar to most citizens of liberal-democratic societies, especially the United States, where it is a dominant (if not *the* dominant) belief system (Doppelt 1989, 816, 842–48; cf. Yack 1993, 233, "justice rewards desert"). It holds that large economic and social inequalities can be justified "because they are perceived to be the proper rewards for unequal achievement, talent, rationality, and individual merit." The conception of the person it offers is both competitive and meritocratic: individuals "affirm their individuality and character through competitive economic and professional achievements of various sorts," which are rewarded appropriately in recognition of desert (Doppelt 1989, 843). This CD is comprehensive in that it views *all* fields of human endeavor (whether they are scholarly, artistic, athletic, etc.) as competitive settings where merit should be recognized and properly rewarded.[6] Its partisans see individual advantages and talents as the product of virtuous personal and familial struggle and sacrifice; unsurprisingly, it is a common belief system among first-generation American immigrants, as such beliefs frequently motivate migration itself.

This CD's personal ideal can be seen as an *alternative* conception of persons as free and equal: free to compete and formally equal before the law, just like participants in a game (e.g., a sporting event).[7] This conception has distributive-justice implications that diverge widely from justice as fairness, however: wage redistribution "might well be unfair from the standpoint of the bourgeois ideal because it drives an 'arbitrary' wedge between what individuals 'get' and what they 'earn' or 'deserve'" (Doppelt 1989, 844). Competitive individualists would be hard pressed to endorse FEO or DP, even in reflective equilibrium,

---

6. Walzer (1983, 18–20) would describe this as "tyranny," i.e., the intrusion of values, rules, etc. that are appropriate in one sphere into others where they are inappropriate. If bourgeois competitive-individualists were to restrict their claims to the economic sphere, this would convert their CD into a PCD.

7. Rawls himself commonly uses game metaphors—see, e.g., TJ 75, 460–61—though he draws different conclusions from them. See S. Freeman (2007a, 43–44, 212) for a very brief discussion of alternative, capitalistic conceptions of persons as free and equal, which he admits are "latent in a part of our culture."

because they begin with contrary considered convictions of justice (with respect to both conceptions of person and society and principles of justice) that are unlikely to be radically revised upon reflection. Such revision is unlikely because, as I indicated above, *they deny the arbitrariness of initial endowments,* seeing them as the deserved product of hard work and sacrifice by individuals and their families; also, this judgment is not vulnerable to mere factual contradiction, nor is it necessarily a product of self-interest or irrational bias (Doppelt 1989, 845–46). This CD's adherents would regard the abstraction from "social, natural, and fortuitous contingencies" involved with a thick veil of ignorance, which reflects a Kantian conception of the person, as the removal (if only in thought) of the most morally relevant features of persons (JF 55; cf. Nozick 1974, 213–16).

A competitive-individualist or kindred CD might be able to support what Rawls calls the "system of natural liberty," an alternative to justice as fairness with classical-liberal features.[8] It protects merely formal equality of opportunity ("careers open to talents": bans on discrimination on the basis of race and sex, on "closed shops" and exclusionary licensing arrangements, etc.) as well as encouraging economic efficiency and growth, with more focus on maximizing per capita income than guaranteeing an egalitarian distribution of it; it would, though, share with justice as fairness a commitment to the basic liberties and their priority, as they help create and sustain the competitive arenas in which different kinds of merit are pursued. Rawls worries that "it permits distributive shares to be improperly influenced by these factors [e.g., natural contingencies] so arbitrary from a moral point of view," but as we have seen, such a concern carries little weight with competitive individualists, as they see nothing arbitrary about such factors, even upon reflection.[9]

Again, even a casual familiarity with American political culture would indicate that this CD, with its distinctive conception of persons and policy commitments, is a major belief system, one that cuts across SES groupings—to the chagrin and also perplexity of economic egalitarians. Even the poor were hostile to estate taxes and remain skeptical of redistributive policies.[10] Their

---

8. TJ 57–58, 62–63. See Gauthier (1986) and J. Buchanan (1975) for Hobbesian defenses of classical liberalism.
9. TJ 63. Also see Rawls's criticisms of the idea of desert (TJ 88–89, 273–77), which are not very compelling: the fact that distributive principles reflecting desert would not be chosen in a *Rawlsian* OP begs some obvious questions.
10. On the "death tax" repeal of 2001 and its political context and constituencies, see Graetz and Shapiro (2005). Also see a November 23, 2006, article in *The Economist* with the title "Fanfare for the Common Man": "Douglas Schoen, another Democratic pollster, finds scant support

competitive-individualist sympathies may be dismissed by egalitarians as "false consciousness" that would be corrected in reflective equilibrium, but this is mere wishful thinking and reflects a failure to take seriously their considered convictions about merit and desert. While reflection and better information (about, say, class mobility in the United States) might temper their hostility to redistribution, there are simply no grounds for thinking that their equilibrium beliefs would settle anywhere near justice as fairness.

2. "Free-Faith" Religious CDs

Rawls defines free-faith religious CDs as those religious CDs (e.g., Locke's) that affirm a principle of religious toleration as a matter of doctrine: only faith that is freely given can have any worth in the eyes of God, so no compulsion is allowable in religion, and the state should not give inducements (rewards or punishments) to belief, treating citizens of all faiths in an impartial fashion.[11] Given the centrality of such CDs in liberal democracies, especially the United States, we might have expected Rawls to spend a great deal of time showing how they could endorse the Kantian conception of the person, the three lexically ordered principles, and the constructivist procedure that connects the former with the latter. Instead, Rawls is largely silent about such matters at the very moments in his texts when we might expect such discussions, and what he has to say about the potential for religious endorsement is at times less than encouraging: in *Political Liberalism,* he states at one point that "I shall suppose—*perhaps too optimistically*—that, except for certain kinds of fundamentalism, all the main historical religions admit of [an account of free faith] and thus may be seen as reasonable comprehensive doctrines."[12] Are there any reasons, however, to think that even free-faith religious CDs might be unreasonable, as Rawls understands that term?

The primary reason for thinking so has to do with the form of justification under political constructivism. Practitioners of the Abrahamic faiths, at least,

---

for economic redistribution. *Even amongst poorer Americans, large majorities prefer policies that boost economic growth to those that redistribute wealth*" (emphasis added).

11. PL 145; classic and very moving statements of this position include Locke (1990) and Madison (1999). Many of the major religions—e.g., Protestant Christianity, Catholicism (post-Vatican II), or Buddhism—would now qualify as free-faith religious CDs.

12. PL 170 (emphasis added). One point where a detailed discussion of endorsement might be expected but does not occur is IPRR §3; I will, however, return to two footnotes from this essay below (IPRR 590n46, 594n55).

do not see the principles of justice as self-constructed through practical reason but rather as given by God and discovered by means of theoretical reason and therefore heteronomous, even on Rawls's narrow account of autonomy in political liberalism. Even Thomists recommend the use of theoretical reason merely to discern God's will (e.g., as evidenced in natural law) and only as a supplement to revelation in scripture, never as something that would trump or override it; the priority of right, however, gives absolute precedence to practical reason and its principles over mere revelation, whereas Thomists would say that revelation and divine law are needed to temper and at times correct our fallible reason.[13]

We cannot avoid the conclusion of the previous paragraph by restricting ourselves to the political, as these faiths very explicitly deal with principles of right as God's edicts (e.g., the Ten Commandments in the Old Testament, the Golden Rule in the New, Shari'ah law as it developed out of the Qur'anic revelations, etc.), not as artifacts of our own practical reason. We also cannot avoid its conclusion—as Rawls might suggest we do—by focusing on doctrinal over constitutive autonomy. While constitutive autonomy says that "the order of moral and political values must be made, or itself constituted, by the principles and conceptions of practical reason," a doctrinal one (which is all that political liberalism requires) demands only that political values be ordered in a way consistent with political constructivism, and it is therefore more likely to be compatible with free-faith religious CDs (PL 98–99). Unfortunately for Rawls, this strategy of avoidance fails here, as political liberalism retains the idea of full autonomy, which is "realized by citizens when they act from principles of justice that specify the fair terms of cooperation they would *give to themselves when fairly represented as free and equal persons*," that is, citizens obey political principles that are "based on their practical reason" via political constructivism, as doctrinal autonomy demands (PL 77, 98). Adherents of these faiths cannot sincerely see principles of right as having such an origin rather than being God's edicts, however, so they will be reduced to a strategic or feigned

---

13. Wenar concurs in my analysis: "to be a Catholic is not only to think that God's word is authoritative on matters of basic justice, it is also to believe that there is no other source of authority on such matters. . . . Public reason can give citizens reasons for appealing in public to only part of what they believe, but it can't give citizens reasons to profess beliefs that contradict their comprehensive doctrines" (1995, 55–56; cf. Barry 1995, 905). Also see Thomas Aquinas's discussion of natural and divine laws, their relationship to eternal law, and our means of discerning them (1988, 46–52). Finally, on the heteronomy of religious rationalism, see Kant at GMM 4:443 and CPrR 5:40–41.

affirmation of the constructivist method and its associated ideal of full autonomy rather than the genuine moral affirmation that Rawls requires.

One might try to salvage the participation of free-faith doctrines in an OC by weakening its membership criteria. For example, one might relieve participating CDs of the need to endorse even the weaker, doctrinal form of autonomy, admitting instead any CD that can conscientiously endorse the principles of justice themselves.[14] As we shall later see, such a proposal would make the OC shallower and closer to a *constitutional* consensus, in which "these principles [of justice] are accepted simply as principles and not as grounded in certain ideas of society and person of a political conception, much less in a shared public conception" (PL 158). This proposal, however, would radically transform political liberalism, effectively changing it from a justificatory theory into a descriptive politico-sociological one. No longer would it contain a conception of citizens jointly constructing principles of justice from shared ideals of person and society with a shared method of construction (the OP and reflective equilibrium more broadly); public reason would be hived off into the separate, private spheres of comprehensive belief. Even the weaker, doctrinal notion of autonomy would be thrown overboard, relegated to any politically constructivist CDs that may participate in the OC. This said, there is an undeniable logic to this proposal: if the aim of political liberalism is stability for the "right reasons," but those reasons turn out to be objectionably demanding and exclusionary, then weakening them is an obvious way to expand the support base for the political principles at the focus of the OC—or as I noted earlier, whenever "the criteria of reasonableness are relaxed . . . the scope of toleration is extended" and more CDs can consequently participate in the OC (LP 561). As I will suggest during my broad critique of political liberalism, though, this flexibility is not a sign of political liberalism's robustness but rather of its moral poverty.

Is there any other way to square this circle, at least within the Abrahamic faiths?[15] There are at least two possibilities, the second perhaps more promising than the first. First, there is the compatibilist path taken by Kant's moral religion. In his *Religion*, Kant says that "each [person] indeed obeys the law . . . which he has prescribed for himself, yet must regard it *at the same time* as the

---

14. Wenar (1995, 52–60) advises this approach as part of an internal critique and reconstruction of political liberalism.

15. I pass over Buddhism and other non-Abrahamic faiths here. On Buddhist morality, see Noss (2003, 170–71, 179–84).

will of the world ruler [i.e., God] as revealed to him through reason."[16] That is, we can see political principles as constructions of practical reason and also as edicts of God if we see all rational beings—finite (e.g., man) and infinite (e.g., God)—as colegislators of the principles of right. True, humans will be bound by these principles in a way that God is not (specifically, man will experience them as imperatives, that is, constraints on his potentially untoward Will$_B$), but they can nevertheless be seen as joint legislators, allowing both autonomy and God's legislative role to be preserved.

Were the Abrahamic faiths to adopt such a position by importing ideas of autonomy into their religious doctrines, they would become consistent not just with doctrinal autonomy but also with the constitutive sort, and their hostility to political constructivism would surely evaporate. It would be only a slight exaggeration, though, to say that most of the present practitioners of these faiths would regard Kant's notion of colegislation as blasphemous hubris: they would judge it as an outrageous presumption (reminiscent of Lucifer's own) to think of man and God as coequals in *any* sphere, especially in the creation of foundational principles of right; man's proper stance towards God is one of submission and humble obedience, as we are subjects, not citizens, of the moral world. Only a Unitarian or a specimen of the most rarefied Protestant species could even entertain the idea of Kantian colegislation—a point to which I will return shortly.

The second, more promising possibility is Locke's religious liberalism. Locke begins his defense of liberal constitutionalism with a conception of the person as free and equal, as shown by both reason and revelation, then proceeds to derive political principles from this conception via practical reason.[17] His defense might be reconceived as a constructivist project and hence as autonomous, at least in the more limited doctrinal sense; it would not, of course, be autonomous in the constitutive sense, because Locke considers our freedom and equality to be gifts of God rather than products of our own practical reason.[18] Hence,

---

16. Rel 6:122 (emphasis added). To someone who questions the consistency of this doctrine with scripture, Kant can reply with an equally controversial claim: "since . . . the moral improvement of human beings . . . constitutes the true end of all religion of reason, it will also contain the supreme principle of all scriptural exegesis" (Rel 6:112).

17. Locke (1988, 269–78, 303–18 [*Second Treatise,* chaps. 2 and 6]). A good example of this juxtaposition of reason and revelation occurs while Locke is discussing the (nascent) freedom and equality of children: he begins by speaking of freedom and equality "by Nature," then moves seamlessly to a discussion of Adam and Eve's children (304–5).

18. Rawls believed that "average utilitarianism might be presented as a kind of constructivism," and he may have held such views about other CDs as well (KCMT 323n1; TJ §27). Like

a Lockean religious liberalism might be able to participate in an OC on justice as fairness: just like a Kantian or Millian liberalism, it could endorse a conception of persons as free and equal and, using shared political-constructivist techniques, work this conception up into common liberal principles of justice. The fact that this CD sees freedom and equality as having a different source than in Kantian and Millian doctrines is of no concern, as it lies outside the sphere of public reason in the private or nonpolitical belief systems of the participating RCDs; one of political liberalism's key strengths is in allowing CDs to integrate liberal conceptions of person and society in idiosyncratic ways, thereby making wide participation in an OC on a liberal PCJ a possibility, at least in liberal-democratic societies.

However, the same question that arose with the Thomists arises here as well: could Locke give the kind of priority to the products of practical reason over revelation that Rawls demands? Locke generally believes that natural law (which we can think of as being arrived at via political constructivism) and divine law are consistent, so that the issue of priority does not arise.[19] When the two appear to be in conflict, however, Locke almost invariably (re)interprets Scripture so that it is consistent with natural law; this interpretive strategy is particularly evident in his defense of private property against scriptural evidence of original communism in God's grant to Adam.[20] So Locke's exegesis effectively gives priority to practical reason over revelation, just as required by political constructivism.

Locke, Thomas Jefferson maintained in his 1774 *Summary View of the Rights of British America* that "the God who gave us life gave us liberty at the same time."

19. For example, in his discussion of paternal power, he says that whether "we consult Reason or Revelation, we shall find [the mother] hath an equal Title" to rule over the children with their father (Locke 1988, 303).

20. Ibid., 156–71, 285–302 (*First Treatise*, chap. 4; *Second Treatise*, chap. 5). I say "almost invariably," because at times Locke seems to waver on this issue. Consider the example of divorce. Locke wonders why marriages should be treated differently from other "voluntary Compacts, there being no necessity in the nature of the thing, nor to the ends of it [for Locke, primarily the bearing, education, and financial support of children], that it should always be for life; I mean, to such as are under no Restraint of any *positive Law*, which ordains all such Contracts to be perpetual" (ibid., 321). Locke seems to suggest here that "natural Right" militates in favor of a right of divorce so long as duties to children are discharged and "positive Law" allows. But positive law for Locke includes what "God has ordered by divine declaration," i.e., scriptural revelation, and the New Testament clearly bans divorce except in cases of marital infidelity (Locke 1997, 94, 119–20 [*Essays on the Law of Nature* III and VI]). As Jesus says, "anyone who divorces his wife and marries another woman commits adultery against her" (Mark 10:11). Thus, one can interpret Locke as saying that those who *are* "under . . . Restraint of . . . positive Law" (here, Christians) may not divorce. In this case, divine law would constrain natural law, and revelation would trump practical reason and its products.

If the preceding analysis is correct, religious liberals of a Kantian or Lockean persuasion could—in principle at least—be part of an OC focused on justice as fairness because their beliefs are consistent with constitutive and doctrinal autonomy, respectively. So an *enlightened* religious liberalism might be autonomous in the required way. What bearing does this have, though, on the possibility of an OC on justice as fairness in the United States, for example? Both of the religious doctrines we just surveyed are highly unorthodox (and were considered so by contemporaries) in their promotion of autonomy and practical reason and their subordination of scriptural revelation. Neither bears much relation to dominant religious practices and doctrines, be they in eighteenth-century Europe or twenty-first-century America, nor is it easy to imagine them developing in this direction in the near future. Rawls's confidence that all of the main historical religions, "except for certain kinds of fundamentalism," could take part in this OC is either heroic or perhaps prospective: he might be saying that these religions, *were they properly enlightened as a result of reflection over time,* could so participate, an interpretation supported by his claim that "these adjustments or revisions we may suppose to take place slowly over time as the political conception shapes comprehensive views to cohere with it" (PL 160, 170). Such an evolution in doctrine may be prompted, in fact, by the nature of reasonable citizens, who want to make a good-faith effort to conform their doctrines to public principles of justice already endorsed by their fellow citizens.

However, such prospective evolution assumes both too much flexibility in the CDs under question and too little flexibility in those publicly endorsed PCJs. CDs in liberal democracies are often rather resilient to changes in the political climate, even perversely so: for example, the rise of fundamentalist Christianity in the United States at the same time as—and perhaps in response to—the greater protection of liberal rights by the judiciary in the second half of the twentieth century suggests that the evolution of doctrine might run in the other direction; the fact that mainstream denominations that liberalized their doctrines lost much of their membership just reinforces this point. Relatedly, justice as fairness is not the only liberal PCJ available. If there is some tension between a religious doctrine and justice as fairness—as is the case in the United States with all but the most left-wing denominations (e.g., Quakers, Unitarians)—why would adherents of that doctrine not instead affirm some alternative form of liberalism, one that did not insist upon such radical changes in their doctrine? As I mentioned above and will further discuss below, the focus of an OC may contain a variety of liberal PCJs; if so, the supposed evolution in doctrine is even less likely to occur. Granted, these claims are empirically contestable, but at least with respect to religious CDs I believe they are largely (though not wholly) borne out by the historical record.[21]

Let us suppose for the sake of argument, however, that Rawls is right and that all of the main historical religions are at least consistent with doctrinal autonomy and so could in principle participate in an OC on justice as fairness. I keep saying "in principle" because the acceptance of political-constructivist methodology is a necessary but not a sufficient condition for participation in such an OC; an additional condition is the ability to endorse, inter alia, a Kantian conception of the person. With the obvious exception of Kantian ethico-theology, do we have reason to believe that *any* religious doctrine—including even Locke's heterodox religious liberalism—would see a Kantian conception of persons or justice as fairness more broadly as an implication of its tenets? Certainly there are affinities. A free-faith doctrine gives a picture of the person as autonomous in religious matters, at least, and could lead via political constructivism to lexical priority for liberty of religious conscience.[22] The main historical religions all have a firm commitment to reciprocity, as evidenced by their support for charity and (in some cases) for state welfare provision.[23] Others no doubt exist as well—for example, the Gospel's Parable of the Talents as a possible support for FEO and its priority (Matthew 25:14–30).

Still, there remains a substantial gap between religious autonomy and personal autonomy more generally, between charity and the DP, and between injunctions to cultivate one's talents and the lexical priority of FEO. Some conservative Protestants (like the bourgeois competitive-individualists) may be able to endorse justice as fairness's commitment to religious autonomy, priority

---

21. They are not wholly borne out because religious doctrines in the West have gradually become more supportive of religious liberty of conscience (see PL xxv, 145; IPRR 588–91, 603n). There is no indication, however, that they are moving any closer to an affirmation of justice as fairness and its presuppositions. For example, as Catholic doctrine has become more liberal post-Vatican II, it has not affirmed anything as strong as justice as fairness, as even Rawls confesses: he identifies "Habermas's discourse conception of legitimacy . . . as well as Catholic views of the common good and solidarity when they are expressed in terms of political values" as *alternatives* to justice as fairness (IPRR 582–83). Cf. S. Freeman (2007a, 169), who sees "liberal Thomism" as compatible with justice as fairness.

22. Rawls suggests a "strains of commitment" argument to defend the lexical priority of religious liberty (TJ 475).

23. This commitment comes in various forms, such as Islam's almsgiving injunction (one of its "Five Pillars") and Catholicism's social doctrine (especially in its "liberation theology" mode). As Rawls himself notes, such concern for the poor might be grounded in the "Good Samaritan" story or similar scriptural parables (IPRR 594n55; Luke 10:29–37).

for the basic liberties, and formal equality of opportunity, but balk at its wider Kantian conception of the person and the highly egalitarian liberalism that flows from it. One might say of these citizens that they are being unreasonable, as they are failing to recognize the burdens of judgment: their fellow citizens might be incapable of endorsing more conservative principles of justice, and they should therefore moderate their claims and accede to a more egalitarian political society than they would prefer. As I noted earlier, however, citizen reasonableness requires more than just recognizing the burdens of judgment and acting appropriately: reasonable citizens must also be able to conscientiously affirm a PCJ *from within their own RCDs;* as Rawls puts it, "each recognizes its concepts, principles, and virtues as the shared content at which their several views coincide" (IOC 432). Otherwise, their "affirmation" of the PCJ may only be a public-spirited capitulation, one that sows the seeds of long-term discontent, alienation, and withdrawal.[24]

Other religious doctrines, on the other hand, might be *roughly* consistent with a Kantian conception of the person, but that is very different from saying that they imply it. The most that we could say for these doctrines is that they may qualify as reasonable PCDs: they might be able to participate in an OC on justice as fairness, but only because their conception of the person and their principles of justice are "loosely articulated" enough to be consistent with justice as fairness (including both its conceptions and principles) and because, in cases of conflict, they may assign a certain priority to political conceptions and principles, perhaps on the grounds that we should "render . . . unto Caesar the things which are Caesar's; and unto God the things that are God's."[25] Such an interpretation may lead to additional problems, however, which I will return to below in my discussion of reasonable PCDs.[26]

---

24. See Rawls's discussion of the second, milder species of "strains of commitment" at JF 128.

25. Matthew 22:21. Brian Barry expresses skepticism about whether even this much is true: he emphasizes the limited implications of "free faith" not just for nonreligious liberties but even for liberty of religious conscience, points out the historical friendliness of the major faiths towards monarchy rather than democracy, and also notes their frequent toleration of brutal socioeconomic inequalities (Barry 1995, 910–11).

26. I have had little to say so far about non-Christian religious doctrines. Interestingly, Rawls suggests that Islam may qualify as an RCD—so long as it is properly interpreted—and discusses the work of a contemporary Islamic scholar to make his point. His case, however, suffers from the same weaknesses I have already discussed: it is uncertain that even a reinterpreted Islam could accept doctrinal autonomy (as it sees Shari'ah as a binding "divine law"), and even its purported commitment to "equality of men and women and complete freedom of choice in matters of faith and religion" is still some way from a Kantian conception of persons and justice as fairness more broadly. See IPRR 590n46 for an extended discussion.

3. Two Teleological CDs: Utilitarianism and Perfectionism

Insofar as they address themselves to political matters, utilitarianism and perfectionism are straightforwardly incompatible with justice as fairness, not because they are (necessarily) hostile to constructivism and its presuppositions but because their conceptions of the person contradict that associated with justice as fairness and lead to opposed political principles (e.g., ones hostile to the priority of liberty).[27] The classical utilitarianism of Bentham and Sidgwick is hedonistic: it seeks to maximize a sum of pleasures net pains across persons and therefore has a conception of persons as sensuous beings, equal only in having a capacity to experience pleasure and pain.[28] This maximizing, hedonistic conception of the good is unlikely to generate principles of right consistent with justice as fairness, and for this reason Rawls suggests that it may have to be excluded from the proposed OC: as he says in his "Idea of an Overlapping Consensus," "there appears to be no assurance that restricting or suppressing the basic liberties of some may not be the best way to maximize the total (or average) social welfare," and given the centrality of these liberties and their priority to justice as fairness, one is hard pressed to see how utilitarianism can participate in the OC.[29] Surprisingly, Rawls later changes his position: in *Political Liberalism*, he states that the "utilitarianism of Bentham and Sidgwick" *could* participate in such an OC, where it would endorse justice as fairness as a "workable approximation to what the principle of utility, all things tallied up, would require."[30] Rawls offers two sets of reasons why such an affirmation might be possible: one, involving our "limited knowledge of social institutions" and "the bounds on complexity of legal and institutional rules," I will return

---

27. As I noted earlier, Rawls suggests that "average utilitarianism might be presented as a kind of constructivism," so teleological theories are not necessarily hostile to constructivism (KCMT 323n1; TJ §27). Following Rawls, I define a teleological theory here as one in which "the good is defined independently from the right, and then the right is defined as that which maximizes the good" (TJ 21–22).

28. Bentham sees pleasure and pain as mankind's "two sovereign masters" and endorses a "greatest felicity principle" of the kind described above (Mill 1962, 33–34n1). Sidgwick's doctrine of "universalistic hedonism" further develops that "taught by Bentham and his successors" (Sidgwick 1981, 11). One of the best-known contemporary exponents of classical utilitarianism is J. J. C. Smart, to whom I will return below (e.g., see Smart and Williams 1973).

29. IOC 433. In *Theory*, of course, justice as fairness is presented as a systematic alternative to utilitarianism, so it is prima facie unremarkable that utilitarianism is unlikely to endorse it in OC.

30. PL 170. This shift has perplexed many interpreters: see, e.g., Scheffler (1994, 9–11) and Wenar (1995, 39n11, 50). I should note that Rawls is a bit slippery in his claim, saying that utilitarianism would endorse "a political conception of justice liberal in content," which may or may not be justice as fairness proper.

to later when looking at the potential for *constitutional* consensus; the second, which recommends restricting utilitarianism's range of application for the sake of *indirect* utility-maximization, I will address shortly.[31]

Perfectionism comes in different varieties, but all have conceptions of the person and associated political principles inconsistent with justice as fairness. I will focus here on just two classes of perfectionism, what we might call *plural* and *cultural* perfectionism, respectively. The first or plural variety is exemplified by the writings of Wilhelm von Humboldt and J. S. Mill, the first of whom declared (in a passage which serves as the epigraph of Mill's *On Liberty*), "The true end of Man, or that which is prescribed by the eternal and immutable dictates of reason, and not suggested by vague and transient desires, is the highest and most harmonious development of his powers to a complete and consistent whole. Freedom is the first and indispensable condition which the possibility of such a development presupposes; but there is besides another essential—intimately connected with freedom, it is true—a variety of situations."[32] This objective of maximal development of our multifaceted intellectual, physical, and spiritual capacities does, as Humboldt indicates, have generally liberal implications—freedom, as well as the diversity that flows from it, can strongly contribute to such development, "since by it there are as many possible independent centres of improvement" as there are persons—but not exclusively so: as Mill himself admits, "the spirit of improvement is not always a spirit of liberty, for it may aim at forcing improvements on an unwilling people."[33] The problem with teleological theories, perfectionist or otherwise, is that they are intrinsically hostile to any principle that constrains the maximization of the good, and though the good of personal perfection is normally served by the protection of basic liberties, it is sometimes served (as Mill indicates) by their abrogation.[34] Thus, even a plural perfectionism would probably

---

31. PL 170; IOC 433–34. This range restriction might involve ignoring certain types of desires (e.g., so-called external preferences, like envy), limiting utilitarianism's writ to nonpolitical matters, etc. Rawls mentions the first kind of restriction at IOC 433; I will examine the second kind shortly. Rawls, following John Gray, identifies John Stuart Mill as an advocate of indirect utilitarianism, but as we shall see, even Sidgwick was open to indirectness (IOC 434n20).

32. Humboldt (1993, 10). Contemporary liberal plural-perfectionists would include Joseph Raz and William Galston, although it is unclear to what extent their theories are maximizing—see Galston (1991, chap. 8) and Raz (1986, chaps. 13 and 14).

33. Mill (1962, 200). Obviously, a development "index" would need to be created, as there can only be one maximand.

34. I offer two examples. First, content regulations on speech that encourages consumerism (e.g., bans or restrictions on certain types of commercial advertising) might be justifiable on plural-perfectionist grounds if such speech had a pronounced tendency to distract people from

be unable to endorse the *lexical* priority of the basic liberties and so could not participate in the proposed OC on justice as fairness.

The second, cultural variety of perfectionism is more obviously inconsistent with justice as fairness and liberalism more broadly, as Rawls himself notes. In it, the principle of perfection acts as "the sole principle of a teleological theory directing society to arrange institutions and to define the duties and obligations of individuals so as to maximize the achievement of human excellence in art, science, and culture."[35] Nietzsche offers the most extreme version of cultural perfectionism, in which the priority assigned to cultural excellence is so high that even slavery can be justified in its support:

> In order that there may be a broad, deep, and fruitful soil for the development of art, the enormous majority must, in the service of a minority, be slavishly subjected to life's struggle to a greater degree than their own wants necessitate. . . . [S]lavery is of the essence of culture. . . . The misery of toiling men must still increase in order to make the production of the world of art possible to a small number of Olympian men. Here is to be found the source of that secret wrath nourished by Communists and Socialists of all times, and also by their feebler descendants, the white race of the "Liberals," not only against the arts, but also against classical antiquity.[36]

Even less extreme versions, *so long as they retain a narrow conception of human excellence,* are unlikely to be consistent with justice as fairness: the many excluded forms of excellence are very likely to have their supporting conditions (e.g., basic liberties, egalitarian distribution of income) sacrificed to promote culture and its conditions (e.g., surplus income for an artistic elite). In what

---

self-improving activities. Second, bans or restrictions on certain kinds of unhealthy foods might be justifiable as a means to improving citizens' physical capacities. (Variances might be granted to epicures who make a conscious and informed choice to trade off physical health for the sake of a more refined palate, which is itself a kind of physical/intellectual capacity—we might call this the *foie gras* exception.)

35. TJ 285–86 and §50, which also covers the case in which the principle of perfection is held as "one standard among several in an intuitionist theory" (TJ 286). I effectively cover this other case in my discussion of PCDs.

36. Nietzsche (2006, 166, "The Greek State"). Rawls "feebly" remarks that "if for example it is maintained that in themselves the achievements of the Greeks in philosophy, science, and art justified the ancient practice of slavery (assuming that this practice was necessary for these achievements), surely the conception is highly perfectionist. The requirements of perfection override the strong claims of liberty" (TJ 286).

follows, therefore, I will only discuss the pluralist species of perfectionism, which is more likely to be liberal (though probably not *Rawlsian* liberal, as we have seen).

Could these two theories—classical utilitarianism and plural perfectionism—be restricted to the private or nonpublic realm, however? That is, could we be Kantians in our public lives but utilitarians or perfectionists in our private lives? Given the maximizing quality of these theories, surely not: by their very nature, they are intended to apply to all realms of life because all realms are arenas for utility or development maximization. Why would politics alone be excluded from the felicific or perfectionist calculus? The only compelling reasons, from the perspective of these theories' adherents, would be internal reasons. Classical utilitarians, for example, might believe that by restricting their theory's range of application to the nonpolitical realm they would (a bit paradoxically) maximize utility; this kind of strategy is sometimes called *indirect* utilitarianism and has been advocated by utilitarians from Sidgwick to J. J. C. Smart. Sidgwick explains it as follows:

> The doctrine that Universal Happiness is the ultimate *standard* must not be understood to imply that Universal Benevolence is the only right or always best *motive* of action. For, as we have before observed [p. 405], it is not necessary that the end which gives the criterion of rightness should always be the end at which we consciously aim: and if experience shows that the general happiness will be more satisfactorily attained if men frequently act from other motives than pure universal philanthropy, it is obvious that these other motives are reasonably to be preferred on Utilitarian principles.[37]

To put this in terms relevant to our discussion: acting from a nonutilitarian *motive* in a political context might be utility maximizing, even if classical utilitarianism is the appropriate *standard* in all contexts. Let us suppose, for the sake of argument, that this is in fact true, perhaps because nonutilitarian motives seem more elevated and can therefore be acted upon with greater

---

37. Sidgwick (1981, 413); cf. Smart (1973, 48–51). Sidgwick sees this not as an innovation on, but rather an explication of, Bentham (432). Moreover, in a passage particularly relevant to our context, Sidgwick explains that "the pursuit of . . . Freedom . . . for [its] own sake . . . is indirectly and secondarily, though not primarily and absolutely, rational; on account not only of the happiness that will result from [its] attainment, but also of that which springs from [its] disinterested pursuit" (405–6).

pleasure. Such a strategy, however, cannot be used by utilitarians with regard to themselves, as this would be a recipe for schizophrenia: how could I, as a utilitarian, act from a nonutilitarian motive in a political context when I know that a utilitarian standard applies in that context as in every other? Doing this would require self-deception, or at the very least an unreflective approach to political action, in which proximate motives were systematically mistaken for ultimate ones.

Such a strategy *could* be used by utilitarians, however, *with regard to nonutilitarians*. To wit, suppose (heroically) that a society organized on Rawlsian principles would maximize utility. Further suppose, as just asserted, that affirming such principles on Kantian rather than utilitarian grounds is better for utilitarian reasons, that is, affirming a Kantian conception of the person and the three lexically ordered principles that follow from it via political constructivism produces greater utility than affirming such principles for utilitarian reasons. Were all of this true, then utilitarians might have reason to defend and publicly endorse the Kantian conception in the hope that others would do so as well, even though the conception is absolutely alien to their doctrine. In this case, classical utilitarianism would become both indirect and *esoteric*, two qualities that are commonly paired in utilitarian tracts.[38] Utilitarians would profess one thing in public but believe something entirely different in private—and all for impeccably utilitarian reasons. As Sidgwick puts it, "a Utilitarian may reasonably desire, on Utilitarian principles, that some of his conclusions should be rejected by mankind generally" (Sidgwick 1981, 489–90).

Given these (not particularly plausible) suppositions, could an indirect, esoteric classical utilitarian be part of an OC on justice as fairness? Clearly not, for two interrelated reasons. First, the utilitarian's affirmation of the Kantian conception of the person and of what follows from it would not be sincere and moral but rather instrumental and strategic and therefore unacceptable on Rawlsian grounds. Second, the endorsement would violate the publicity condition, which is a formal constraint on principles of right, because the actual reasons for the public affirmation stay hidden (KCMT 324–25; TJ 115, 398). The classical utilitarian's treatment of Rawlsian justice as a "socially useful illusion" is unacceptable, as political principles must be "publicly accepted and followed *as* the fundamental charter of society," not merely as a handy tool for utility enhancement (TJ 25, 158; cf. Scheffler 1994, 10–11). Consequently, classical

---

38. For example, see Smart (1973, 49–50), which defends esotericism in the midst of a defense of indirectness.

utilitarians could not participate in an OC on justice as fairness, even making the most generous assumptions conceivable—Rawls should have maintained his earlier position.

Could a Millian plural-perfectionist sincerely endorse a Kantian conception of the person and justice as fairness more generally, without such a reliance upon esotericism? I earlier argued that this would be untenable because perfectionism, as a teleological theory, is inherently hostile to any principle that constrains maximal development, and though personal perfection is usually served by the protection of basic liberties, it may sometimes be served by their abrogation, which would violate their lexical priority. Suppose, however, that only *autonomously chosen* perfection has any value to such a perfectionist. That is, personal perfection is only considered valuable if it is self-directed, which requires the capacities that we earlier called self-realization (to produce a plan of self-development in pursuit of an ideal of personal perfection) and personal autonomy (to produce a plan of life in pursuit of a conception of the good, of which personal perfection is but a component). As I noted in chapter 2, though Mill tends to conflate these two facets of autonomy, he clearly endorses them, urging us to develop our own "plan of life" instead of letting the world choose one for us, an activity that will require us to "employ all [our] faculties" in the process of "perfecting and beautifying" ourselves (Mill 1962, 187–88). Millian plural-perfectionists need not regard all powers as equally important, and insofar as they give a special priority to the metapowers just described and to the political principles that protect their exercise and development (namely, EL and FEO), they have gone a long way toward affirming a Kantian conception of the person and justice as fairness more broadly on sincere moral grounds.[39]

There remains some distance, however, between this Millian conception of persons and a Kantian one. First, given the way Mill grounds his conception and the principles that follow from it, it is again doubtful that *lexical* priority can be sustained. As he avows in On Liberty, "I forego any advantage which could be derived to my argument from the idea of abstract right, as a thing

---

39. Interestingly, Rawls notes that justice as fairness, like perfectionism but unlike utilitarianism, is an ideal-regarding rather than a want-regarding theory, as it defines "an ideal of the person" and attempts to "encourage certain traits of character, especially a sense of justice," that are central to the ideal. Rawls emphasizes that justice as fairness, unlike perfectionism, defines this ideal "without invoking a prior standard of human excellence," but the more this standard resembles Rawls's own ideal of the person, the closer the associated perfectionism is to justice as fairness (TJ 287).

independent of utility. I regard utility as the ultimate appeal on all ethical questions."[40] Giving lexical priority to these metapowers and to political principles that guard their development and exercise would be utility maximizing only under the most unusual of circumstances, as profitable trade-offs would surely arise on occasion, and we have just seen that indirect-utilitarian strategies fail as well. Second, and perhaps more importantly, plural perfectionists such as Mill and Raz are very hostile to Kantian *moral* autonomy, the highest form of autonomy in the Kantian conception of the person and the one that grounds the priorities of right and political liberty.[41] Unless some approach can be found to reconcile plural-perfectionists to Kantian moral autonomy, they, like the classical utilitarians, would seem unable to endorse a Kantian conception of the person or participate in an OC on justice as fairness.

B. Empirical-Psychological-Failure CDs

1. Romantic Liberalism

The romantic tradition of liberalism stands in sharp contrast to the dispassionate system building of Kantian liberalism that has been our focus throughout most of this book: it has been called a liberalism of "individuality, spontaneity, and self-expression," and its major exemplars in the American tradition—Henry David Thoreau and Walt Whitman—offer us "Promethean" or "heroic" individualist variations on its rich themes.[42] Thoreau, for instance, defended

---

40. Mill (1962, 136). The quotation ends with Mill's claim that "it must be utility in the largest sense, *grounded on the permanent interests of man as a progressive being*" (emphasis added). To the extent that some "prior standard of human excellence" underwrites Mill's notion of utility, too—a standard that he might consider self-evident, part of a natural or divine moral order accessible through theoretical reason, or perhaps aesthetic—he would be immune to this first line of criticism. However, sustaining such an alternative reading would require a radical reinterpretation of Mill's theory, one that does not have a clear basis in his writings. For Rawls's analysis of Mill's "psychologized" perfectionism, see LHPP 269–70, 299, 307–9, and 311–13. Incidentally, similar comments could be made on Raz's theory, which is perfectionist and ultimately grounded on notions of "well-being" and "the good life" (1986, 19, 370, 425).

41. In his essay *Utilitarianism,* Mill notoriously dismisses Kantian moral autonomy (as found in the FUL formulation of The CI) as either empty or crypto-consequentialist (1962, 254, 308). Raz's theory similarly does without any idea of moral autonomy and specifically criticizes Kant's variety, distinguishing it from the personal autonomy that plays a central role in Raz's theory and appearing to question whether it qualifies as autonomy at all: "in Kant's [variety of moral autonomy] authorship reduced itself to a vanishing point as it allowed only one set of principles which people can rationally legislate and they are the same for all" (1986, 370n2). I criticize this claim in Taylor (2005).

42. Rosenblum (1987, 6, 103); Larmore (1996, 129). George Kateb is a contemporary expositor and advocate of this strand of liberalism—see Kateb (1984). Nancy Rosenblum (1987, chap. 5) provides a superb overview of heroic individualism as found in the writings of Thoreau and Whitman.

provocative public acts of self-assertion, authenticity, and integrity (engaging in several himself) and the idea of personal rather than collective consent to governmental authority, which he believed should be minimal.[43] Another distinctive feature of Thoreau's heroic individualism is its "methodology": as Nancy Rosenblum notes, "personal inspiration takes priority over reason" in it, and motivation is supplied by an "inner voice" that "does not necessarily speak consistently or in terms of rules" (Rosenblum 1987, 107; also see 109 ["hyperbole [not] social analysis"] and 114 ["unreflective"]). Thoreau's liberalism, in short, is one of unmediated and at times unreflective self-expression and an accompanying demand for recognition and respect from both state and society; it is a reaction as well against sociopolitical conformism and complicity in the collective crimes of the polity.

Romantic liberalism, especially its heroic-individualist variant, would be unlikely to yield political constructivism or a Kantian conception of the person as free and equal: in contrast to the Kantian CD (and, as Rawls argues, the Millian one), there is no "derivation" of these conceptions from a romantic liberalism, as its philosophy is too fluid and variable across individual adherents to generate any consistent, systematic method or personal ideal (IOC 441; PL 160). This being said, there does not seem to be any *conceptual* incompatibility between romantic liberalism and justice as fairness. In fact, there are quite a few points of contact between the two: romantic liberalism's stress on self-authorship and authenticity in both personal and political matters fits well with the three forms of autonomy that constitute the Kantian conception of the person, as does its individualistic demand for personal freedom and equal respect within the framework of limited, democratic government. One could therefore imagine a romantic liberal affirming the conceptions and methods of justice as fairness for his or her own idiosyncratic reasons and participating in an OC on it.

The techniques and presuppositions of justice as fairness may, however, have long-term, indirect effects on the beliefs of its romantic supporters, progressively eroding their commitment to the priority of "personal inspiration" over reason. Political constructivism's stress on practical reasoning and on the intellectual and moral capacities required to exercise it could even reverse this priority: as John Tomasi suggests, "insofar as people begin to consider their interests from a more detached, impersonal perspective they may begin to see

---

43. See especially his essay "Civil Disobedience," where these sentiments are succinctly defended (1962, 85–104).

their interests differently" from the embedded or first-personal perspective of romantic liberalism (Tomasi 2001, 23). So even Kantian constructivism for merely political purposes might ultimately erode antirationalist elements in our nonpolitical comprehensive doctrines. As noted earlier, this effect is likely to be especially prominent across generations: the civic education needed to prepare the young for political autonomy on a Kantian model will inevitably inculcate attitudes, skills, and virtues in some tension with those taught in romantic-liberal homes.[44] Consequently, romantic liberals may reject justice as fairness out of a not unreasonable fear that acceptance of it might lead in the long run to the erosion of their own romantic commitments, which offer a valued and comprehensive (if not particularly systematic) approach to living.

2. Reasonable PCDs

Rawls says that a moral conception is only *partially* comprehensive when "it comprises a number of, but by no means all, nonpolitical values and virtues and is rather loosely articulated"; he also characterizes PCDs as "pluralist" and "not systematically unified" (PL 13, 155). The "looseness" of such conceptions makes it easier for them to affirm justice as fairness and assign it priority over any conflicting nonpolitical values and virtues, in which case they are *reasonable* PCDs. In such PCDs, "the political conception can be seen as part of a comprehensive doctrine but it is not a consequence of that doctrine's nonpolitical values"; that is, reasonable PCDs are only able to "cohere loosely" with justice as fairness because "there is lots of slippage" in them (PL 155, 159, 160; cf. Tomasi 2001, 19, "B-people"). For this reason, figure 11 shows reasonable PCDs being connected to the Kantian conceptions of person and society by slender wires. The political and nonpolitical conceptions are simply not as tightly integrated in such PCDs as they are in unified, systematic doctrines like the Kantian one.

It is difficult to say anything general about reasonable PCDs given their diverse natures. Some of them, for example, may be "loosely articulated" throughout, whereas others may have a few constituent parts that are internally well

---

44. For example, reconsider the model of agency discussed in chap. 2, which provides some guidance regarding the process needed to build an autonomous agent on a Kantian model. The emphasis on self-criticism and detachment as a prelude to discipline and control of oneself stands in some tension with romanticism's inclination toward uncritical celebration of one's idiosyncratic traits, whether these are seen as peculiar to the individual (the heroic-individualist strain of romanticism) or to the individual's nation, race, ethnicity, etc. (the communitarian strain of romanticism). See Rosenblum (1987, chaps. 5 and 7).

developed and systematic (e.g., professional ethics) while the whole remains barely coherent. Yet others, such as the religious CDs discussed above, may be moderately comprehensive—telling their adherents what they should value in life, which virtues they should develop, and which precepts they should abide by—but still fail to imply any specific PCJ, merely being consistent with several, including justice as fairness. The "free-faith" religious CDs have this quality, as their commitment to religious freedom and reciprocity make them well disposed to justice as fairness but not exclusively so; that is, the relationship between the former and the latter is not "derivative," even after setting aside doctrinal-autonomy issues. The one thing that these varied reasonable PCDs do have in common is a weak connection to justice as fairness: they are consistent with it and may even be generally sympathetic to its values, but they do not entail it and, at least in principle, remain compatible with other PCJs as well.

Rawls contends that the "looseness" of PCDs and their prevalence among citizens will make the evolution of an OC on justice as fairness considerably more likely, so he loads a great deal of justificatory weight upon them—they effectively become the guarantors of the system's stability (PL 159–60, 208 ["much depended on the fact" that most CDs are "only partially comprehensive"]). I want to suggest, however, that they cannot play the vitally important role that Rawls assigns them, regardless of whether their "looseness" is principled or unprincipled. Suppose, for example, that their looseness is *unprincipled*: adherents of such PCDs may simply be complacent and unreflective about their belief systems, unconcerned by the possibility that profound internal conflicts within and between the various components of their "loosely articulated" doctrine may exist—including conflicts between political and nonpolitical values.[45] Justice as fairness, though, is committed to the development of the two moral powers of rationality and reasonableness in all citizens and must therefore take some interest in their intelligent exercise—a theory that went to great lengths to encourage capacities whose exercise was a matter of indifference to it would be a peculiar theory indeed. Yet Rawls's case for the stability of an OC on justice as fairness seems to rely here on citizen failure to (fully) exercise these capacities: he appears oddly untroubled about such citizens' lack of reflection and says of those who "cannot fully explain [their] agreement" in an OC that

45. See PL 160, where Rawls speaks of such adherents "affirming" political principles "without seeing any particular connection, one way or the other, between those principles and their other views." First, is this "affirmation" or just acquiescence? Second, do they not "see" any "particular connection" (or conflict, for that matter) only because they are not looking very hard?

they "may not expect, or think they need, greater political understanding than that" (PL 156). Is this *Rawls's* stance as well, and if so, is it consistent with his concern for the development and exercise of the two moral powers? Perhaps Rawls would say that citizens cannot be obligated in any enforceable way to reflect fully on their commitments, but could we not still identify this as some kind of politico-ethical failure (like incivility in deliberation) on Rawls's own grounds? If unreflectiveness does qualify as a political vice, a refusal to make use of our political autonomy, then making an OC's stability depend upon it would have a distinctly nonideal, even paradoxical quality to it: an OC on principles dedicated, inter alia, to protecting our capacity for reflection can only survive if most of its participants do not think too hard about it. Relatedly and perhaps more importantly, how stable would an OC composed largely of PCD adherents actually be? Rawls is concerned that consensus on political principles not be a mere modus vivendi, which could shift with changes in the underlying distribution of power, be it socioeconomic or otherwise (PL 146–48). If such shifts were to occur in an OC composed largely of PCDs, however, would their adherents be able or willing to offer much resistance? Their faithfulness to justice as fairness is weak by definition, and they may be able to "endorse" closely related PCJs nearly as easily. The lesson to draw from this is that while reasonable PCDs may not cause instability themselves, they will also do little to buttress an OC's stability, making it vulnerable to "shocks" to the underlying power distribution.

Now suppose that their looseness is *principled,* as Rawls himself sometimes suggests. For example, he claims with regard to a reasonable PCD's "large family of nonpolitical values" that "each subpart . . . has its own account based on ideas drawn from within it, leaving all values to be balanced against one another"; as described, the PCD is intuitionist, so "while the complexity of the moral facts requires a number of distinct principles, there is no single standard that accounts for them or assigns them their weights" (PL 155; TJ §7, esp. 30). In this case, the looseness is principled: adherents of these PCDs may think that any such attempt to assign weights or priority—in short, to create an internal architecture for our belief systems—is futile and that looseness is simply an irremediable consequence of moral complexity. If allegiance to intuitionism explains the looseness, however, a different problem emerges, one that we encountered above: the possibility of "free erosion" (Tomasi 2001, 26–32). Justice as fairness offers a systematic approach to weighing different values within the political conception of justice, namely, a hierarchy based upon the three-tiered Kantian conception of the person. Given that this conception of persons has certain implications for virtue as well as right (as we saw in chapter 1), it is unlikely that adherents of intuitionist PCDs will be able to contain its effects permanently within the political sphere.[46] They are likely to spill over into other areas, partially or wholly supplanting the intuitionistic balancing of values even in nonpolitical settings; as Rawls admits, "the political conception shapes comprehensive views," and this influence will be particularly strong when such views lack rival schemes for weighting or prioritizing values (PL 160n25). Adherents of intuitionist PCDs may therefore have reason to reject justice as fairness on erosion grounds, somewhat like the romantic liberals: in both cases, a rationalistic, hierarchical political conception, given priority in cases of conflict and supported by a system of civic education, will over time and across generations remake loose or impressionistic CDs in its own image— and as we have seen, those non-Kantian CDs coherent enough to resist will fail to affirm on conceptual grounds instead.

C. An Inconvenient Truth

As I noted at the beginning of this section, Rawls believes that the political-constructivist module displayed in figure 11 is invariant across RCDs, that is, he believes that his three lexically ordered principles of justice can be supported not just by a Kantian CD (*Theory*'s assertion) but by a whole series of non-Kantian CDs as well. In other words, we can liberalize the justificatory framework—admitting a wide variety of CDs into an OC—without watering down the content of the principles being justified. As John Tomasi describes it: "Political liberals think they can move to a broader, more inclusive foundation but make few corresponding adjustments in the design of their existing house. The nature of the liberal virtues and of even the content of justice itself are said

---

46. In §§18, 19, 51, and 52 of *Theory*, Rawls offers a preliminary discussion of those principles that would apply to individuals rather than institutions of the basic structure, including obligations of fairness and fidelity, natural duties of mutual aid and respect, and supererogatory behavior such as benevolence, heroic self-sacrifice, etc. He does not, however, systematically develop a Rawlsian doctrine of virtue (or even a wider, nonpolitical doctrine of right) in *Theory*, though he does say that justice as fairness could be "extended to the choice of more or less an entire ethical system" (TJ 15). Were such an extension carried out, the virtues supported would undoubtedly be closely related to the Kantian ones: natural and moral self-perfection, beneficence, respect, etc. These virtues would take priority over others (e.g., solidaristic ones, such as patriotism, hostility to outsiders, etc.), thereby imposing an architecture on the universe of virtues that may be inconsistent with intuitionism. See Taylor (2005) for a more complete discussion.

to be left largely untouched by the shift from a comprehensive to a political form of justification" (Tomasi 2001, 126). Were this trick possible, the law of parsimony alone would require it: *ceteris paribus,* the weaker the assumptions, the more compelling the justification.

Perhaps unsurprisingly, we have discovered that a more parsimonious justification is not possible: *there can be no overlapping consensus on a Kantian conception of persons or justice as fairness more broadly,* or at least none built with the participation of the liberal CDs that have been surveyed in this section.[47] Only a Kantian CD can morally endorse a Kantian conception of the person and what follows from it via political constructivism, namely, the three lexically ordered principles of justice.[48] Some of the candidate OC participants that we examined were friendlier to justice as fairness and its presuppositions than others, of course, but only the Millian plural-perfectionist CD came close to endorsing it, thanks in large part to its commitments to personal autonomy and self-realization.[49] Even in this case, however, the gap remained sizable, due to its residual utilitarian sympathies and, even more awkwardly, its hostility to moral autonomy. If this section's argument is correct, Rawls's hopes for an OC on justice as fairness alone are illusory.

D. Was Rawls Aware of This Truth?

Interestingly, Rawls appeared to be aware of this problem on a number of different levels. First, late in his life he started to water down the content of justice as fairness, or at the very least to open it up to such revisions—a claim that he sharply denied, as I indicated at the beginning of this section.[50] For example, he expresses some second thoughts about the lexical priority of FEO in *Justice as Fairness: A Restatement,* as the following footnote (apparently

---

47. I cannot, of course, rule out the possibility that some non-Kantian CD exists that could participate. No survey of this kind can be exhaustive—the number of *potential* CDs is infinite, of course—so I have simply reviewed what I take to be the most important or widespread candidate CDs. (Cf. TJ 106–9, where Rawls is forced to limit the set of contemplated alternatives to justice as fairness to "a short list of traditional conceptions of justice . . . together with a few other possibilities suggested by the two principles of justice" themselves.)

48. Wenar (1995, 59) arrives at the same conclusion by distinct but nonetheless complementary reasoning. Only the relationship between the Kantian CD and justice as fairness is called "deductive" by Rawls (PL 169).

49. Thus, Rawls's claim that justice as fairness can be "derived from" Kantian *and Millian* liberalisms as well as the implication that only Kantian liberalism has a closer connection to justice as fairness are not baseless (IOC 441).

50. See the Rawls quotation at Daniels (2000, 135), which was reproduced in note 2 above.

written sometime in the early 1990s) indicates: "Some think that the lexical priority of fair equality of opportunity over the difference principle is too strong, and that either a weaker priority or a weaker form of the opportunity principle would be better, and indeed more in accord with fundamental ideas of justice as fairness itself. At present I do not know what is best here and simply register my uncertainty. How to specify and weight the opportunity principle is a matter of great difficulty and some such alternative may well be better."[51] Even more surprisingly, Rawls's preface to the revised edition of *Theory* (written in 1990) states that "the primary aim of justice as fairness is achieved" even when the "mixed conception" (i.e., justice as fairness, but with the principle of average utility substituted for the DP) is chosen over the principle of average utility as the sole principle of justice; in other words, the "primary aim" of Rawls's theory of justice can be realized without the DP (TJ xiv). This position is a far cry from the one succinctly expressed in §39 of *Theory*: "the force of justice as fairness would appear to arise from two things: the requirement that all inequalities be justified to the least advantaged, and the priority of liberty" (TJ 220). Here the DP is treated as the priority of liberty's coequal—if not as more important, given the textual sequencing.

Again, what Rawls seems to be doing here at minimum is opening up the interpretation of the principles and priorities and thereby admitting the possibility of alternative, weaker versions of justice as fairness. What might motivate him to do something like this? In part 2 of this book, I suggested that powerful scholarly criticisms of these features of justice as fairness might have reduced his confidence in their correctness. I want to propose an additional explanation here that is more speculative than the first but fully compatible with it: *weaker versions of these principles and priorities would make an OC on justice as fairness more likely*. Utilitarianism, for example, would be significantly happier with a watered-down priority for FEO—why rule out the trade of opportunities for income if it might be utility enhancing?—and with a mixed conception, even if it were constrained by a decent social minimum or other limitations on income dispersion. If one is having a hard time making the case that "weaker assumptions will yield identical results," then fudging a bit on the "identical" may become an attractive strategy.[52]

---

51. JF 163n44; approximate date confirmed by e-mail correspondence with Erin Kelly, editor of JF (April 14, 2003).
52. This fudging sometimes takes related forms, as when Rawls brings classical utilitarians into his model OC and says they may have reason to endorse a PCJ "liberal in content" (PL 170).

A second, closely related change over time is his loosening of the definition of liberalism itself. In *Theory*, liberalism appears to be almost synonymous with justice as fairness (with a few exceptions: e.g., "liberal equality," which embraces FEO but not DP) (TJ 57, 63–65). By *Political Liberalism* Rawls is stating that justice as fairness is simply one "egalitarian form" of liberalism; liberalism is defined by a "specification of certain basic rights, liberties, and opportunities," giving "special priority" to them, and assuring to all citizens "adequate all-purpose means to make effective use of their liberties and opportunities" (PL 6; cf. IOC 440). Rawls says here that liberal PCJs need not protect the fair value of political liberties, FEO, or the DP; moreover, his use of the word "special" (rather than "lexical") may suggest a weakening in the priority relation. Lastly, in "The Law of Peoples," he repeats this definition but substitutes "high priority" for "special priority," further indicating that lexical priority has been weakened (LP 536; cf. LP 14, which retains the PL wording). This increasingly ecumenical reading of liberalism serves a vital purpose, as I will now show: to "decenter" justice as fairness and place greater emphasis on a more realistic alternative OC on a *class* of liberal PCJs, of which justice as fairness will be only one member, affirmed by the Kantian CD but rejected by all others, as I argued above.

Even at the earliest stages of his "political turn," Rawls is considering the possibility of a broader OC in which justice as fairness is merely the "kernel"; as he later states, "it is also likely that more than one political conception may be worked up from the fund of shared [democratic] political ideas; indeed, this is desirable, as these rival conceptions will then compete for citizens' allegiance and be gradually modified and deepened by the contest between them" (JFPM 410; IOC 427). In *Political Liberalism*, Rawls presents the "more realistic and more likely" case of an OC that is focused on "a *class* of liberal conceptions [which] will be political rivals and no doubt favored by different interests and political strata."[53] The width of this OC is driven not just by the competing social and economic interests but also (and even more importantly) by different

---

Throughout PL, Rawls has a tendency to talk about the OC being on a "political conception" or a "liberal political conception," which would include justice as fairness *but might include other PCJs as well*. I will elaborate on this point below. Incidentally, Rawls himself suggests the possibility of weakening the principles to achieve stability at PL 66 (cf. Hill 2000, 256–57).

53. PL 164 (emphasis added). Contra Daniels (2000, 133, 135–36, 150), there is no firm proof that Rawls thinks such an OC puts us in the nonideal world, as would be the case with a mere constitutional consensus (CC). See especially his comments about those PCJs that would be "typical of the focal *class* of an overlapping consensus, *should such a consensus ever be reached*" (emphasis added): he evidently sees even the wide OC as an ideal that is approached out of CC (PL 167). Rawls does note that CCs are characterized by competition among diverse "liberal

understandings of the "fundamental ideas of society and person found in the public culture of a constitutional regime," *with respect to not just what those ideas are but also how they should be interpreted* (PL 167–68). To give some examples, a republican or communitarian might place more emphasis on the "public good" than on a conception of persons as free and equal, while a liberal utilitarian might interpret "free and equal persons" in a different way than a Kantian liberal, stressing our equality in the ability to feel pleasure and pain.[54] At best, it seems, Rawls can hope for "justice as fairness to specify the center of the focal class," but not for this focal class to collapse to a single element; the fact of reasonable pluralism that Rawls highlights with regard to CDs has apparently been extended here to liberal PCJs, with justice as fairness as just one competitor conception among others, its centrality decided through ideological competition and the strength of its supporting social and economic interests.[55] This expanded OC may include, in addition to justice as fairness, Rawls's classical-liberal "system of natural liberty" (perhaps affirmed by competitive individualists and Lockean religious liberals), weaker versions of justice as fairness (possibly endorsed by Millian plural-perfectionists, liberal utilitarians, and adherents of reasonable PCDs), and, if the scope of political toleration is extended even further, *nonliberal* PCJs, as we shall see in section III.

Towards the end of his life, Rawls decisively confirmed this interpretation. As he admits in "The Idea of Public Reason Revisited," "The content of public reason is given by a family of political conceptions of justice, not by a single one. There are many liberalisms and related views, and therefore many forms of public reason specified by a family of reasonable political conceptions. Of these, justice as fairness, whatever its merits, is but one" (IPRR 581). As Samuel Freeman points out, this implies that "a well-ordered society of justice as fairness is not feasible, at least not as originally conceived," because in a WOS "everyone accepts the same conception of justice," and he is right to suggest that this

---

principles," but such competition can characterize *both* OCs and CCs, with the latter being narrower and shallower than the former (PL 158). Rawls is also absolutely clear that he is talking about OCs, not CCs, in the key passages of PL 167–68. Finally, although Rawls does state that in the presence of such competition among liberal PCJs *"full* overlapping consensus cannot, it seems, be achieved," the mere fact that an OC fails to be "full" does not necessarily put us in the nonideal world—and if it does, then we are *permanently* in the nonideal world, because as I have shown, a full OC on justice as fairness is as "utopian" as Rawls fears it might be (PL 158, 168).

54. On the compatibility of classical republicanism with justice as fairness, see PL 205.
55. PL 168. Cf. Waldron (1999, 153–56), who says that given the "circumstances of politics," ideological disagreement among liberal-democratic citizens is permanent. See LP 180 too, where Rawls states that RCDs "support reasonable political conceptions—although not necessarily the most reasonable."

must have been a "difficult concession" for Rawls to make (S. Freeman 2007a, 255–56). Having said this, Rawls continues to believe that "justice as fairness has a certain special place in the family of political conceptions," although he admits that "this opinion of mine is not basic to the ideas of political liberalism and public reason" (IPRR 582n27). One is hard pressed to see the basis for the claimed "special central place" for justice as fairness, however, especially in light of my preceding narrow critique: only a Kantian CD can support justice as fairness; thus, unless the *Groundwork* is unusually popular in a particular liberal-democratic society, there is no reason to think justice as fairness will be more "central" than any other liberal PCJ (IPRR 583). Perhaps he is only revealing here his personal penchant for Kant or (more strongly) that in a democracy with many competing liberal PCJs in a wide OC, *he* would endorse justice as fairness and the Kantian CD that underwrites it.

E. A Constitutional Consensus on Justice as Fairness?

Even if an OC on justice as fairness alone is a utopian prospect, constitutional consensus (CC) on (parts of) justice as fairness might still be a possibility. CC is both narrower and shallower than OC. It is narrower because it is a consensus only on "certain liberal principles of political justice," applied only to "political procedures of democratic government," such as the protection of "basic political rights and liberties," and it is shallower because it is a consensus merely on the principles themselves, "not as grounded in certain ideas of society and person of a political conception, much less in a shared public conception."[56] Although no OC is possible on Rawls's three lexically ordered principles of justice, a CC could be achieved on the constitutional analogues of (some of) these principles. One example might be the constitutional analogue of the priority of liberty, civil libertarianism, which resists violations of basic liberties for the sake of socioeconomic equality, conceptions of the good, greater security, etc., and could be institutionalized through a combination of written bills of rights and judicial review or even effected through unwritten norms that constrain legislative behavior (as in Great Britain).

A Kantian CD could obviously endorse civil libertarianism in CC because it affirms the priority of liberty, from which civil libertarianism would follow in the constitutional stage. Some non-Kantian CDs might also be able to endorse

---

56. PL 158–59. The various types of consensus parallel the stages in Rawls's so-called four-stage sequence (TJ §31).

civil libertarianism in CC, however, even though they reject the priority of liberty as a principle of justice. For instance, liberal utilitarians, who by Rawls's definition of liberalism support "special" or "high" priority for the basic liberties but not lexical priority (as we saw above), might endorse civil libertarianism in CC: if they believed that basic liberties would otherwise be severely eroded through legislative encroachment, they might be able to affirm it as a kind of "second-best" corrective. The following example will explain in more detail how such a prima facie counterintuitive affirmation might be possible. Suppose that minor content regulations on the speech of atheists, racists, and other assorted miscreants would produce higher social welfare than no content regulations: maybe the pleasure of their unfettered expression is outweighed by the intense pain caused to some fainthearted listeners. Now further suppose that in the absence of a court-enforced content neutrality, balancing decisions regarding free-speech issues (i.e., decisions about trade-offs between free speech and other values) would be made in the legislature, as seems likely. Under these conditions, dominant political and religious groups might use their considerable influence to secure adoption of content regulations favoring their particular viewpoints, and the extent of content regulations might grow far beyond the level that would be socially optimal due to the political dynamics of "communicative rent seeking," so to speak. Consequently, social welfare at the legislative-equilibrium extent of content regulations (generated through unconstrained communicative rent seeking) could be even lower than it was at the admittedly second-best level of no content regulations. Thus, under the right set of political conditions, a second-best, court-enforced institution of content neutrality might generate greater social welfare than the only politically feasible alternative of legislative "overshoot," and liberal utilitarians might therefore endorse civil libertarianism as a second-best solution.[57]

Figure 12 gives a graphical depiction of this example. The extent of content regulations is measured on the horizontal axis, while social welfare is measured on the vertical one. The level of social welfare with minor content regulations is A, with no content regulations is B, and with substantial content regulations is C, where $A > B > C$. If the first-best solution of minor content regulations is

---

57. Such worries motivated numerous features of the U.S. Constitution. As Seth Kreimer notes, "its combination of judicial supremacy and difficulty of amendment makes the American Constitution a pre-commitment device, designed to guard against the particular popular excesses that are likely to sweep through our system. Our First Amendment doctrine rejects 'content regulation' and 'prior restraints' because of our documented tendency to populist intolerance" (Kreimer 1999, 642).

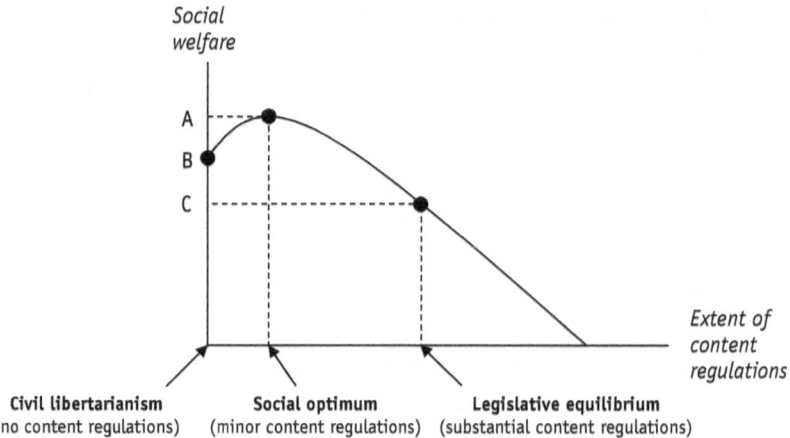

Fig. 12 Utilitarian civil libertarianism

unavailable due to the likelihood of communicative rent-seeking in the legislature, then the second-best solution of civil libertarianism may be preferred, even by liberal utilitarians. One might call this the "cold-turkey" defense of civil libertarianism: just as a very low level of tobacco or television consumption may be infeasible for an addict, so a very low level of content regulation may be impossible for a democratic government, leading it to give up such regulation entirely through constitutional means.[58]

Adherents of other liberal CDs might endorse civil libertarianism for the same or similar reasons. Lockean religious liberals, for example, might be open in principle to content regulation of nonreligious speech but worry about the capacity of legislatures and even courts to distinguish between religious and nonreligious speech; if so, they might endorse a generally civil-libertarian approach to speech in order to prevent any "chilling effects" on religious speech, whose security is of overriding importance to them. Constitutional or legislative analogues of other components of justice as fairness might also be endorsed in constitutional or legislative consensus, though we would have to analyze each

---

58. Earlier I noted Rawls's claim that classical utilitarianism might be able to endorse justice as fairness due to our "limited knowledge of social institutions" and "the bounds on complexity of legal and institutional rules" (PL 170). Such constraints are at work here: our limited ability to understand and design sophisticated institutional structures prevents us from attaining the social optimum, and we are instead forced to adopt a second-best solution of judicial review and civil libertarianism. Rawls consequently has the right idea but applies it at the wrong stage of the four-stage sequence: classical utilitarianism cannot endorse the priority of liberty, but it *can* endorse its constitutional analogue, civil libertarianism, on the very grounds that Rawls identifies.

on a case-by-case basis for feasibility.[59] Each such consensus may be broader and deeper than Rawls had foreseen, because the constitutional provisions and laws agreed to might address the basic structure of society and might be endorsed in a principled and moral way by the various participating liberal CDs. However, the consensus arrived at would not be an *overlapping* one, as the agreement would not be over conceptions of person and society or over principles of justice assembled from them, nor could it be expected to evolve into one given the fact of reasonable pluralism.[60] Hence, this kind of consensus will lack the depth and stability that Rawls had hoped for, and its survival will be more politically and historically fortuitous.

III. Broad Critique: Moral Philosophy or "Philosophical Anthropology"?

As the last section demonstrated, there can be no OC on a Kantian conception of persons or justice as fairness more broadly, or at least none built with the participation of the liberal CDs that we surveyed there. Only a Kantian CD can morally endorse a Kantian conception of persons and what follows from it via political constructivism—namely, three lexically ordered principles of justice. This conclusion, insofar as it is defensible, effectively presents political liberals with a dilemma: they can either

1. retain Rawls's three principles of justice but abandon political liberalism and its fixation on legitimate stability in favor of the only kind of liberalism able to ground them, namely, a comprehensive Kantian liberalism, or
2. remain political liberals but give up an exclusive commitment to Rawls's three principles, accepting that their efficacy will be determined not through philosophical argumentation but rather through bounded political competition in a wide OC that is inclusive enough (with respect to liberal PCJs and affiliated RCDs) to guarantee legitimate stability.[61]

---

59. Rawls defines a division of labor between the constitutional and legislative stages, with the former dealing with basic liberties and other essentials and the latter dealing with socioeconomic matters (TJ 174–75; PL 336–37). Though formal equality of opportunity is a constitutional matter, FEO and DP are legislative.

60. PL 4, 36–37, 164–68. As noted above, this "fact" holds with respect to not only CDs but also PCJs.

61. Can one simultaneously be a political *and* comprehensive liberal? This would require "hollowing out" one or the other. To see this, imagine that U.S. politics were dominated by a

Political liberals might not hesitate, however, to choose the second horn: if Rawls's arguments against the possibility of a well-ordered society—that is, one with a stable and legitimate political order and culture—being grounded upon any kind of shared comprehensive moral doctrine are sound, then they may reluctantly abandon an exclusive commitment to Rawls's three principles of justice for the sake of the greater political goods of stability and legitimacy (PL 65, 137). As we saw in the last section, there is strong evidence that Rawls himself implicitly recognized this dilemma and chose the second horn (e.g., by weakening the content of justice as fairness and conceding the necessity of a wider OC on a family of liberal PCJs). To complete my critique, then, I must demonstrate why political liberals would be ill-advised to choose the second horn over the first. In this section, I will therefore argue that political liberalism does not offer us an independently attractive mode of justification and that we should not sacrifice Rawls's political principles for the sake of the particular forms of stability and legitimacy it promises. I will turn to the alleged infeasibility of the first horn of the dilemma in the conclusion to the book.

A. Extending the Scope of Toleration, Domestically and Internationally

Recall from chapter 7 that Rawls defines RCDs as those CDs that can "recognize the essentials of a liberal democratic regime and exhibit a reasoned ordering of the many values of life (whether religious or nonreligious) in a coherent and consistent manner" (LP 87; PL xviii, 58–60; cf. Wenar 1995, 35–38, on defining reasonable CDs and persons). This description of reasonableness turns out to be peculiar to a particular domestic political context, though. Once we move to an international context, as Rawls does in "The Law of Peoples," nonliberal but still "decent" peoples are said to qualify as reasonable and thus as fit to participate

---

Rawls-Kant Party, owing to its rhetorical, strategic, and tactical brilliance. (To make this even more unrealistic, give it a charismatic leader too.) Few if any outside this minority party could endorse its RCD and the PCJ (justice as fairness) following from it, but a consistent majority of voters backed it anyway due to its leader's charm, its slick ads, etc. Should it implement justice as fairness? If it did, it would hollow out its *political* liberalism: only a minority of voters can endorse its sectarian conception of persons, which is part of the now balkanized sphere of public reason (due to the OC's width and consequent disagreement on the meaning of "free and equal," etc.), so stability for the right reasons is absent. If it did not, it would hollow out its *comprehensive* liberalism: to hold political power legitimately yet not implement one's political program is in effect to privatize it and thereby neuter it, making it a fit object for political discussion and action only at party confabs.

in a global society of well-ordered peoples.⁶² Is there some understanding of reasonableness, then, that holds across these domestic and international contexts? Rawls suggests there is when he states that "whenever the scope of toleration is extended . . . the criteria of reasonableness are relaxed."⁶³ Put differently, in order to increase the number of CDs or peoples who can participate in a principled agreement on a political conception of right (i.e., extend the scope of toleration), one must be less exacting in the standards for association (i.e., relax the criteria of reasonableness). The best definition of reasonableness, then—one that is flexible enough to hold across different political contexts—is simply *the capacity to participate in an OC of some specification*. According to this description, reasonableness is always relative to an OC of a particular scope, and the wider it is, the weaker its associated criteria of reasonableness.⁶⁴

We can see this definition of reasonableness at work in three exemplary OCs, domestic and international, that Rawls uses in his works. First, an OC might consist of all CDs capable of affirming at least one conception of person and society yielding a liberal PCJ by way of political constructivism. As we saw in section II, this wide OC may include Kantians, liberal utilitarians, Millian plural-perfectionists, Lockean religious liberals, and others. This OC could be reached in the following manner: we begin with a degenerate OC focused solely on justice as fairness and affirmed by a Kantian CD alone; we then consider expanding this OC (i.e., extending the scope of toleration) by widening the OC's focus to include all liberal PCJs, members of which can be endorsed by a wide variety of CDs, including those listed above; this expansion is achieved by relaxing the criteria of reasonableness, that is, participating CDs need no longer affirm the Kantian conceptions of person and society but rather any conceptions that lead, by way of constructivism, to liberal PCJs (LP 561n56; LP 180; PL 164–68). Once the focus of the OC has been expanded in the way described, many CDs

---

62. Strictly speaking, Rawls reserves the term "reasonable" for those CDs/peoples who are liberal-democratic, preferring the term "decent" for those peoples who are nonliberal but who respect human rights and meet other criteria (LP 64–67, 71–78). However, a careful reading of his texts indicates that "decent" is merely the international analogue of "reasonable," and he therefore uses the term "reasonable" to refer to decent peoples in both the essay (e.g., LP 530) *and* the book (e.g., LP 70, where he uses the term "reasonably" three times in relation to decent peoples and their OP representatives). Any difference here between the essay and book is wholly semantic.

63. LP 561. Rawls is fairly explicit about the way reasonableness works across political contexts at LP 529n2–30.

64. Cf. S. Freeman (2007a, 227), who in a not very analytic moment says that "any attempt to provide a definition of 'reasonable' would be incapable of capturing all that is involved in the many uses of this rich concept."

become reasonable that were unreasonable before, when the focus was limited solely to justice as fairness.

The second OC, strongly suggested by Rawls though not explicitly spelled out by him, is an international version of the first. Imagine an international society (regional or global) that has as its members liberal peoples of varying degrees of egalitarianism: some are liberal egalitarian, others are classical liberal, etc.[65] Because they share countless values, their form of association may be much deeper than the international norm—more like the European Union than the United Nations. They may unite in (internal) defense of not just human rights but also liberal rights, and they may agree in advance to their partners' intervention in their internal affairs to preserve these rights, as a kind of mutual insurance.[66] This OC on an international doctrine of right for a liberal federation might arise in the following way: we start with a set of degenerate OCs, in which each of these liberal societies considers (most of) the other liberal societies to be unreasonable in their practices of liberalism and so unfit for federation, and therefore remains unaffiliated; we can then consider a wider international OC consisting of all liberal societies, where the focus is not on any particular form of liberalism but rather on shared liberal values (e.g., the high priority of personal liberty, democracy, etc.) and their protection by means of federative institutions; this extension is achieved by relaxing the criteria of reasonableness, that is, each liberal society ceases to hold fellow federation members to its own peculiar standard of liberalism but rather to an ecumenical liberal standard agreed to by all, egalitarians and classical liberals alike. Liberal practices earlier thought unreasonable become reasonable in an expanded and more tolerant international-liberal OC.

The third and final OC is Rawls's own international society of well-ordered peoples, who unite on an international doctrine of right that forbids aggressive war and calls for the defense of human rights (LP 63). This OC's

---

65. This example is suggested by Rawls's claim that "if we start with a well-ordered liberal society that realizes an egalitarian conception of justice such as justice as fairness, the members of that society will nevertheless accept into the society of peoples other liberal societies whose institutions are considerably less egalitarian" (LP 561). Also of relevance is Rawls's suggestion that "we can go on to third and final stages once we think of groups of societies joining together into regional associations or federations of some kind, such as the European Community or a commonwealth of the republics of the former Soviet Union" (LP 550n35; cf. LP 70; also see Follesdal 2006).

66. For a very explicit and extreme form of such mutual insurance, see article IV, section 4 of the U.S. Constitution: "The United States shall guarantee to every State in this Union a Republican Form of Government." The European Union practices a milder form via internal sanctions, such as those imposed on Austria in 2000 when the Christian Democrats invited the xenophobic populist Jörg Haider's Freedom Party into the governing coalition.

participants include not only all liberal societies but also what Rawls calls "decent-hierarchical" peoples, that is, nonliberal societies that are nonaggressive and respectful of human rights and that have a "decent consultation hierarchy," allowing their populations some measure of influence on state policy through informal corporate representation.[67] This OC on an international doctrine of right might emerge in the following way: we begin with an international liberal federation of the kind defined in the previous example; its members then decide to enlarge the scope of toleration by watering down the content of their international doctrine of right (e.g., limiting it to *human*-rights protection), which would allow decent-hierarchical peoples to join as well; this inclusion of all well-ordered peoples once again relaxes the criteria of reasonableness, that is, liberal societies come to see some nonliberal societies as reasonable in their willingness to abide by human rights, refrain from aggressive war, etc., even though they earlier saw them as unreasonable by a different, more demanding set of (liberal) standards.

Might the "criteria of reasonableness" be relaxed more, the "scope of toleration" further extended, whether in the international or domestic cases? Rawls believes not—he says there are "limits of toleration" that cannot be crossed—but there are in fact no reasons internal to political liberalism for not considering such relaxations/extensions (LP 561–52). I will start with international cases. Consider a society of well-ordered peoples like the one just described (consisting of both liberal and "decent-hierarchical" peoples) but with the scope of toleration modestly extended to include "benevolent absolutisms," which Rawls defines as nonaggressive societies that guarantee human rights but do "not give [their] members a meaningful role in making political decisions" and so do not have decent consultation hierarchies and are not well ordered (LP 4, 63, 92). He points out that these societies retain the "right of self-defense" but excludes them from his society of peoples, yet his reasons for doing so are unstated. If a benevolent absolutism is nonaggressive and human-rights respecting, though, why could it not participate in a wider international OC made up of societies sharing similar features? They could collaborate on their shared ends of peace and human-rights protection, perhaps even creating joint institutions for such purposes. For the scope of toleration to be extended in this way, the criteria of

---

67. LP 64–67, 71–78; LP 561–62. See Doyle (2006, 116–18) for a list of countries that may qualify as decent-hierarchical societies. He singles out Kuwait, Bahrain, and Oman as the best candidates, though I suggest below that the last two might be better classified as malevolent absolutisms given their mediocre human rights records and limited political participation, corporate or otherwise.

reasonableness would have to be relaxed—any pacific, rights-respecting society would be deemed "reasonable"—but given that Rawls entertains *tighter* international institutions (e.g., EU), it is unclear why *looser* ones could not also be considered.[68] Perhaps he thinks that any society lacking a decent consultation hierarchy would also fail to have a "common good idea of justice" and that its own citizens would therefore "see their duties and obligations as mere commands imposed by force," making the society's government illegitimate, unstable, and an unreliable partner in international cooperation (LP 66). There are bases of legitimacy, however, other than corporate representation, including economic prosperity, ethnic nationalism, and a shared religious identity.[69] This kind of legitimacy is not *liberal* legitimacy, of course, but neither is that of the decent-hierarchical peoples that Rawls unhesitatingly admits into his society of well-ordered peoples.[70] Thus, Rawls has given us no reason to resist the idea of extending the scope of toleration to include benevolent absolutisms.[71]

Now consider an international society of peoples like the one just described (consisting of liberal, decent-hierarchical, and benevolent-absolutist societies) but with the scope of toleration extended once more to include what I will call "malevolent absolutisms," that is, societies that deny both political influence and human-rights protection to their citizens but that renounce aggressive war as a policy instrument. Rawls himself considers the fanciful example of a developed version of "Aztec" society, which is nonaggressive but "holds its own lower class as slaves, keeping the younger members available for human sacrifices in its temples."[72] Malevolent absolutisms could in principle take part

---

68. Rawls does speak of "certain institutions, such as the United Nations, capable of speaking for all the societies of the world," presumably including benevolent absolutisms and even "outlaw states" like North Korea (LP 70, 90).

69. Examples abound, including China and Singapore (economic prosperity), the Balkans (ethnic nationalism), and Saudi Arabia (shared religious identity). Some of these countries are not benevolent absolutisms, because many if not most of them fail to respect human rights, but their internal legitimacy—which is impressive in many cases, as with Singapore—is not primarily grounded on corporate political representation.

70. On liberal legitimacy, see PL 135-37.

71. Coming up with real-world examples of benevolent absolutisms is difficult, as most societies that deny citizens any political role also violate human rights. Tonga provides an admittedly imperfect example: it is an authoritarian monarchy with limited political consultation but a robust press and an independent judiciary; Freedom House 2008 gives it a score of only 5 for political freedom but a 3 on civil liberties (on a scale of 1-7, where 7 is least free). See http://www.freedomhouse.org/template.cfm?page=22&year=2008&country=7505.

72. LP 93-94n. There are numerous real-world examples of malevolent absolutisms—though their lack of aggression towards their neighbors may be more a result of small size than good will. Bhutan in Asia and many of the Persian Gulf states (e.g., Qatar, Oman, and Bahrain) are fully autocratic but have little to no history of militarized disputes, according to Polity 4 and Correlates of War scoring, respectively. Swaziland may provide the "best" example: it is a fully

in both international cooperation and organization for the shared but limited purpose of preserving peace, at least if the criteria of reasonableness were appropriately relaxed. Rawls implies that "their participation in [a transnational] system of social cooperation is simply impossible," but he does not elaborate (LP 94n). While it might be true *domestically* that "human rights are recognized as necessary conditions of any system of social cooperation" (as only when these rights are recognized is such association likely to be mutually beneficial), it is not clear why they are such *internationally:* not only might a cruelly exploitative ruling class have good reasons to cooperate internationally to prevent cross-border military conflict, but they might even do so for principled moral reasons (e.g., in the belief that such conflict fails to respect national autonomy), suggesting that even such a wide OC might be more than a mere modus vivendi, which offers the wrong kind of stability.[73] We may finally have run up against the real "limits of toleration" here, however: military aggression is surely an alternative to, not a kind of, cooperation and so marks off the boundaries of toleration; we cannot extend the scope of toleration or relax the criteria of reasonableness any further internationally.[74]

Moving back now to a national setting, consider an expanded version of the wide OC that we discussed in section II: a domestic society composed of adherents of not just liberal CDs but also illiberal yet decent ones together in wide OC, modeled on a well-ordered society of peoples. Such a society would have wider scope for toleration and more relaxed criteria of reasonableness than the liberal society of section II. Some of its citizens would have their full panoply of liberal democratic rights defended (political freedom, civil liberties, etc.), while others would have only their *human* rights and *corporate* political representation protected. Affiliates of illiberal groups might live in enclaves (e.g., Hutterites and Native American tribes) or intermixed with the larger, liberal population

---

autocratic absolute monarchy (Polity 4) with utterly brutal social conditions but no recent history of militarized disputes (Correlates of War); Freedom House 2008 gives it an abysmal score of 7 on political freedom and only a 5 on civil liberties. See http://www.freedomhouse.org/template.cfm?page=363&year=2008&country=7496.

73. LP 44-45, 68. As an empirical matter, such cooperation—principled or not—may be unlikely, except in those cases where the malevolent absolutism is small and/or weak; see note 72. S. Freeman (2007a, 277-78) briefly discusses such an expansion of the scope of toleration to include malevolent absolutisms.

74. Is even this true, however? Suppose that *aggressive* malevolent absolutisms were willing to recognize certain rules of war—might this not constitute a very limited kind of international social cooperation? Again, they might endorse such rules for principled moral reasons (e.g., aristocratic notions of military honor or "fair play"). See the discussion of "combat contractualism" in Chiu (2007).

(e.g., some Orthodox Jews or fundamentalist Christians). Myriad details would need to be settled (e.g., secession from illiberal groups), but there are at least historical models to guide us, most notably the Ottoman Empire and its "millet" system of autonomous Orthodox and Jewish communities.[75] The political principles of such a society would be endorsed by agents of both liberal and illiberal groups in a "second-level" OP, providing the grounds for a wide OC.[76] As in the international case, of course, we could entertain even wider domestic OCs that include benevolent-absolutist CDs, etc.; I will return to this possibility shortly.

Again, what these examples (both Rawls's and mine) demonstrate is that *reasonableness is relative to the width of OC and thus the scope of toleration*. As I have claimed, the "limits of toleration" are extremely capacious: OCs of greatly varying widths can survive in both domestic and international political contexts, at least in principle, and each one is associated with a certain scope of toleration and particular criteria of reasonableness (LP 561–62; cf. IOC 439). Therefore, although one can offer a definition of reasonableness that holds across political contexts—namely, the capacity to participate in an OC of some description—it is completely parasitic upon the OC with which it is associated. The most significant consequence of this is that *reasonableness cannot give us an independent criterion by which to judge the appropriate width of OC or scope of toleration*—which, as we shall see, means that it hardly qualifies as a moral standard at all, leaving political liberals with few if any resources to pass judgment in some extremely important categories of cases.[77]

B. What Is the Appropriate Scope of Toleration?

How much and what kind of moral guidance does political liberalism offer in judging the proper width and content of an OC in any given domestic or international setting? In order to fix ideas, let us consider this question in the context of three model examples:

---

75. For a discussion of the Ottoman case, see Kymlicka (2002, 230–31) and Walzer (1997, 17–18). See Kukathas (2003) for a defense of one form of such a society.

76. LP 68–70; see especially the discussion there of churches and universities in domestic society.

77. Rawls suggests that "political constructivism does not criticize, then, religious, philosophical, or metaphysical accounts of the truth of moral judgments and of their validity. Reasonableness is its standard of correctness, and given its political aims, it need not go beyond that" (PL 127). If reasonableness does not provide such a standard even in key political contexts, however, then we must question its usefulness and that of the theory of which it is part. The weakness of reasonableness as a standard will prove emblematic of the poverty of political liberalism.

1. *Hutterites:* Suppose that an illiberal but decent group like the Hutterites—who segregate themselves in colonies where all assets are owned collectively, there is little privacy and no personal property, men control all decision making while women remain subservient and fecund, and individuals are expected to submit completely to the doctrines and edicts of the colony church—wants its members excluded from liberal protections of both civil and political freedoms (opting for a mere defense of human rights and corporate political representation instead) and from childhood education for political autonomy that would make the effective exercise of such rights possible. Should a liberal society impose these rights and the supporting education upon the Hutterites, or should the scope of toleration and width of OC be extended instead so that the criteria of reasonableness include rather than exclude the Hutterites and their doctrines?[78]

2. *Confederacy:* Suppose that a slave society like the antebellum South wants to protect its "peculiar institution" against threats of "expropriation" by those with whom it happens to be in political union; assume too that this society is nonaggressive and liberal with regard to its white citizens but malevolent-absolutist toward its black subjects. Should those with whom this society is in liberal political union impose liberal rights upon it without regard for race—by force if necessary—or should the scope of toleration and the width of OC be extended (whether through a looser form of confederation *or* by separation/secession and the conversion of the relationship into an international one) and its content appropriately watered down, limited to the maintenance of peace, mutual defense, free trade, etc.?[79]

---

78. See Kymlicka for a discussion of seminal Hutterite and Amish court cases, the former dealing with reasonable rights of exit, the latter with childhood education (2002, 237–38). Rawls briefly addresses this category of cases in *Political Liberalism*, where he says that the "unavoidable consequences of *reasonable* requirements for children's education may have to be accepted, often with regret" (PL 199–200). However, Rawls never really considers the option of expanding the scope of toleration here, on the model of his later global society of well-ordered peoples, nor does he give sufficient attention to the frequency of such groups in modern liberal nations (especially the United States, Canada, and other immigrant societies) and the likelihood that their participation in *liberal-democratic* OCs would be instrumental/strategic at best rather than principled/moral.

79. One way to have achieved a looser form of confederation is that proposed by John C. Calhoun in his 1850 treatise *A Disquisition on Government:* the concept of "concurrent majorities," in which a society is considered to be "made up of different and conflicting interests" or subcommunities and the government "takes the sense of each through its majority or appropriate organ" (Calhoun 1953, 23). Compare this approach with the Ottoman model of "toleration" discussed by Walzer (1997, 17–18).

3. *Taliban:* Suppose that a nonaggressive but malevolent absolutism wishes to be admitted into a duly expanded society of peoples and thereby secured against invasion, embargoes, etc. Afghanistan under the Taliban—had they not been *indirectly* aggressive by harboring international terrorists—would have provided a splendid real-world example: the Taliban effected a complete exclusion of women from employment and education, the destruction of non-Islamic religious sites, the implementation of cruel forms of criminal punishment, even against apostates, etc. Should a society of well-ordered peoples try to impose human rights on such a people—by force if needed—or again should the scope of toleration and the width of the international OC be expanded to bring this people within a framework of (very limited) international cooperation on peace, trade, etc.?[80]

What I will now contend is that political liberalism provides little moral guidance in answering these vitally important questions. Specifically, with regard to the three model examples we just surveyed, could political liberalism offer any *moral* reasons to *oppose* the proposed expansions in the scope of toleration domestically or internationally?

One approach to doing so is to suggest that there are universal values (such as human or even liberal rights) that can be justified by reference to a natural or divine moral order accessible by theoretical reason, to a practical postulate of freedom, or to some other brand of universal first principle. On grounds such as these, the proposed impositions of rights could be justified and the expansions in the scope of toleration could not. Rawls rules out such reasoning, however, at least after his political turn: as I noted in chapters 1 and 7, he rejects rational intuitionism and Kantian transcendentalism as foundational doctrines and tries to find a form of justification based not on universal first principles but rather on the shared values of liberal-democratic political

---

80. Apostasy is punishable by death throughout much of the Muslim world, including Saudi Arabia and Iran. Rawls, in the case of his nonaggressive but malevolent-absolutist "Aztec" society, asks, "is there ever a time when forceful intervention might be called for? If the offenses against human rights are egregious and the society does not respond to the imposition of sanctions, such intervention in the defense of human rights would be acceptable and would be called for" (PL 94n6). Again, however, he does not consider the possibility of expanding the scope of toleration to include such societies, mistakenly arguing that "without honoring human rights, their participation in a system of social cooperation is simply impossible"; see my discussion of this (unsubstantiated) claim above.

culture.[81] Whether this approach to justification can have any purchase when these values are *not* shared, as appears to be the case in my three model examples, is a question I will return to momentarily. For the time being, though, compare Rawls's approach to that of Amartya Sen, whose defense of universal human rights is grounded proximately on the importance of freedom as it is understood within a capabilities framework but ultimately on a global Habermasian argument that "the status of . . . ethical claims must depend ultimately on their survivability in unobstructed discussion"; this discussion is explicitly "nonparochial," that is, not tied to any specific national political culture—a major point of departure from Rawls's political liberalism, as Sen himself points out.[82]

At least two other approaches, both of dubious moral status, are available for opposing the proposed expansions. First, the expansions may simply be *infeasible* due to indelible power arrangements, cultural traditions, economic constraints, etc. "Ought," after all, implies "can" (CPrR 5:125). For example, attempts to bring a nonaggressive Taliban within even a very minimal framework of international cooperation on peace and trade might founder on irreconcilable religious beliefs, incompatible commercial assumptions (e.g., as regards banking), inconsistent product standards and contract law, etc. Strictly speaking, however, these are not moral reasons at all but rather the constraints—cultural, managerial, technological, economic—within which moral reasoning

---

81. KCMT 306, 340, 343–46, 352; JFPM 388; LP 86–88. Rawls's claim that "human rights are recognized as necessary conditions of any system of social cooperation" implicitly relies on such universalism (LP 68). What, after all, is so important about human relations being cooperative as opposed to constituting "command by force, a slave system"? Presumably, the reason is that "the well-being and freedom of every individual are of fundamental importance," and they would be systematically violated in a command or slave system (A. Buchanan 2006, 163–65). The only way that we can vindicate such an argument, however, is by the very methods that Rawls has ruled out. The only attempt that I know of to defend human rights universally *without* the use of such techniques is Pettit (2006), which does so on the grounds that human rights are necessary conditions for treating peoples as "group agents" and therefore subjects of justice in the international arena. It depends, however, on a highly controversial, illiberal, and collectivist "ontology of peoples"; moreover, it is not even clear that human (versus liberal) rights are sufficient to secure group agency, as the required identification with the group by unequal, partly free citizens may just be the result of false consciousness.

82. Sen (2004, 330–38, 348–55); cf. Nussbaum (2000), Shue (1996). One might picture this discussion occurring in a global OP, but given that discussion is not tied to national cultures, the agents in this OP would represent *individuals* rather than nations, contra Rawls. National identity is the mother of all social contingencies, after all, having an unrivaled effect on life prospects, so for an OP and the principles it generates to have full authority, it must abstract from (by placing behind the VI) all "social, natural, and fortuitous contingencies," especially national identity (JF 55). Thus, cosmopolitanism necessarily follows from a properly Kantianized Rawls, at least at the level of ideal theory.

and action take place, so their force is only as strong as their indelibility: were they easily overcome, we might have good moral reason to modify or perhaps circumvent them. Additionally, political philosophers are not well qualified in terms of knowledge, training, or disposition to make these kinds of difficult empirical assessments; rather, they must rely upon the expert opinions of social scientists and others to assess feasibility—another point to which I will recur below.

Second, these expansions might be criticized for infringing the *self-understanding* of the participants, who at least in the domestic cases may share traditions of political culture and their associated goals, principles, etc. For example, the Hutterites and antebellum Southerners can be seen as participants in an ongoing social practice, the liberal political order of the United States, which has certain objectives (e.g., goods it is meant to distribute) that are pursued in accord with certain rules (e.g., equal consideration before the law). Whether these participants recognize it or not, they are invested in and implicated by this social practice, and if we can demonstrate that the "reforms" they have proposed undermine rather than support the immanent goals and principles of the practice, then they can be rightly rejected and contrary reforms—here, the enforcement of human or liberal rights—can be entertained.

How might such a demonstration be made?[83] One possibility that has been discussed in this context is by means of the "constructive interpretation" of social practices, which involves a three-stage process. In the first stage, a social practice is tentatively sketched in a noncontentious manner (or what is hoped to be one). In the second stage, it is morally redescribed in such a way as to bring out its distinctive purposes, principles, etc. (e.g., via constructivism). In the third and last stage, the existing social practice is subjected to reformist critique to identify ways in which it must be changed to make it conform to its morally redescribed and purified form as discovered in the second stage. To translate this into the terms of the current examples: one might argue that the Hutterites and antebellum Southerners already implicitly accept liberal conceptions of person and society, as evidenced by their participation in as well as practical acceptance of liberal social practices; by means of constructivism, we can trace out the political implications of these liberal conceptions of person and society, implications that together constitute an ideal social

---

83. In this paragraph, I follow R. Dworkin (1986, 65–66) and James (2005, 282, 298–308), especially the latter's excellent explication of the former. Rawls describes his own constructivist technique in similar terms at LP 533.

practice; if current practices deviate from this ideal—as they presumably do, at least with respect to the two groups in question—then proposed reforms that move us away from the ideal (e.g., certain kinds of political decentralization) should be rejected and those that move us towards it (e.g., universal application of human or liberal rights) should be adopted. In summary, tracing out the theoretical implications of these groups' practical commitments undermines their case for greater toleration and supports the case for enforcing rights within them, with or without their consent.

There are numerous problems with this approach, two of which I will mention here. First, any given "constructive interpretation" of an existing social practice is bound to be controversial and lead to *alternative interpretations*. The Hutterites, for example, might very well dispute their status as participants, given their isolationism. Antebellum Southerners, on the other hand, might admit their status as participants but dispute the way the goals and principles of the U.S.'s liberal political order have been characterized: they would certainly emphasize our history of federalism and the innumerable compromises reached to preserve the South's "peculiar institution" (e.g., the Three-Fifths Compromise of article 1, section 2, paragraph 3 of the U.S. Constitution) as signs of national acceptance and even complicity; moreover, they would argue that the Constitution is a foundational compact of states, not of persons, and that as such its provisions take priority over the sonorous phrases of the liberal Declaration, a revolutionary rather than governing document. Neither of these alternative interpretations can be rejected out of hand as bizarre or indefensible, nor does it seem likely that additional interpretive labor would definitively resolve the issues in dispute—or even substantially narrow the parameters of the debate.[84] Therefore, the notion that "constructive interpretation" can be unproblematically used to oppose expansions in the scope of toleration is itself highly problematic, as it frequently fails to provide a compelling answer to the central question: what is the appropriate width and content of the OC?

---

84. The Hutterites do engage in trade with the surrounding world, which might be deemed a form of "participation," but they would surely maintain that this economic interaction no more commits them to the United States's liberal political order than China's trade with the United States commits them—like the Old Order Amish, they consider themselves to be a people apart. The antebellum-Southern position may *seem* bizarre and indefensible, but I would suggest that this is only because of the intervening political history: any doubts about federal supremacy and the liberal implications of the Constitution (which strike me, at least, as entirely reasonable *at that time*) have been resolved by military force and subsequent court orders backed by same, not shared interpretive labor—except of an ex post facto kind. To be clear, I believe that this resolution was morally required, but we should not kid ourselves about what was involved: coercion, not persuasion. (Cf. IPRR 609–10, where Rawls discusses the Lincoln-Douglas debates and slavery.)

A second problem is that even if we assume that these exegetical difficulties can (in some situations, at least) be sufficiently overcome to give localized moral force to such interpretations, it remains the case that this approach gives no purchase in those contexts, especially international ones, where there is no shared tradition upon which to draw for purposes of immanent criticism. This would appear to be the case for a nonaggressive Taliban and perhaps for the Hutterites, who are so insular as almost to constitute a separate society. We have returned here to a concern about political liberalism that I first raised in chapter 7: the communities of shared political beliefs and practices are frequently "closed worlds" with respect to one another, with no common social text to interpret, and in these cases political liberalism cannot offer us a principled basis for criticism or intervention.[85] We are then left with two unappetizing options: either to enlarge the scope of toleration and admit these societies into a watery sort of moral community (which may, as in the case of a nonaggressive Taliban, mean sharing nothing but a desire for peace and trade), perhaps in the hope that they will develop in a liberal direction over time and therefore become amenable to deeper forms of moral community; or to deal with them in realpolitik style, with nothing but counsels of prudence and rules of skill—be they diplomatic or military—to guide interaction.[86]

C. What Is the Appropriate Role for Political Philosophers?

What both of these approaches to resisting enlargement of the scope of toleration—I will call them the *feasibility* and *self-understanding* approaches—have in common is that they require political philosophers to play a very different role than they have hitherto played, drawing upon a radically different skill set. In both approaches, philosophers must use the skills of legal scholars, intellectual historians, anthropologists, sociologists, economists, political scientists, and others to determine whether a proposed expansion of the scope

---

85. See Doppelt (1989, 846) on closed worlds (e.g., "these ordinary judgments parse into *clusters* which presuppose the very conflicting ideals of personhood between which we are trying to adjudicate").

86. It seems that such "hope" for liberal evolution if not revolution must remain just that: as Rawls cautions, "it is not reasonable for a liberal people to adopt as part of its own foreign policy the granting of subsidies to other peoples as incentives to become more liberal," as it would fail to respect their "self-determination" (LP 85). Again, as I said in chapter 7, we must apparently wait for historical accidents to push societies sufficiently within our orbit to make a real political reconciliation possible. Finally, on the distinction between the categorical imperatives of morality and the hypothetical imperatives of prudence and skill, see GMM 4:414–16.

of toleration is both feasible and consistent with the best interpretation of an existing social practice. Why, though, should these tasks not be left to the specialists in the enumerated disciplines instead? What, if anything, can philosophers *qua* philosophers add to this discussion?

Once an existing social practice has been identified and described by others, philosophers can perform the useful albeit limited task of morally redescribing the practice (a procedure that is itself firmly constrained by the prior interpretive work of other scholars) and thereby pointing out and possibly resolving internal contradictions within it. For example, an OC on a class of liberal PCJs may be discovered in a particular society, but that society might deny even formal equality of opportunity to homosexuals, such as rights to enlist in the military and get married. Philosophers would have a comparative advantage (given their analytical abilities, knowledge of logic, etc.) in showing how such a policy might be in tension with a liberal principle of equality before the law and the conceptions of person and society that underwrite it via constructivism. This role should be a familiar one: it is simply that of discovering a *narrow* reflective equilibrium, "describing a person's sense of justice more or less as it is although allowing for the smoothing out of certain irregularities"; the point of such a process is not to bring about a "radical shift" in the interpreted social practice but to make it more internally consistent or true to itself, since in a social universe of "closed worlds" there is no other kind of moral truth—or at least none that political liberalism can recognize (TJ 43).

Under either the feasibility or self-understanding approaches, political philosophy's role is effectively reduced to that of a handmaiden of the social sciences or simply a maid, tidying up all messy belief systems or social practices: for any particular RCD or OC on a class of PCJs, its job is to identify which of our considered convictions of justice must be adjusted or pruned in narrow reflective equilibrium to achieve internal consistency.[87] The questions of which RCD is the best or what the most appropriate width and content of a specific OC is—questions that require wide reflective judgments—are set aside as unanswerable by political liberalism, whether explicitly (the first question) or implicitly (the second, as we have just seen) (PL xix–xx). This agnosticism is yet another aspect of political liberalism's poverty—or modesty, as Rawls would describe it.

---

87. Cf. Kaufman (2006, 35–36), who believes that *wide* reflective equilibrium is indeed at stake here.

I exaggerate only slightly by saying that such a role change for philosophers would mean the death of political philosophy as we have known it. No longer would it be about the discovery and realization of universal moral ideals through politics; rather, it would be about discerning the meaning and limits of existing political practices and delivering up more internally consistent versions of them. This role change would constitute a collapse of moral horizons and a deeply parochial and balkanized political-philosophical practice. Some political liberals are admirably frank about this implication of their doctrine. Norman Daniels, for example, stresses the radically narrower scope for political-philosophical inquiry after Rawls's political turn: the idea that we can convert those who have illiberal or un-Kantian "starting beliefs" to liberalism or justice as fairness is dismissed as a mere "philosopher's dream" that we have a "reluctance to be wakened from"; philosophy's task is at most to "*refine* . . . democratic ideas" in those cultures where they are already embraced, and even this is less a philosophical task than a "historical process" that is a "far cry . . . from the role ascribed to the individual seeking *wide* equilibrium, as opposed to groups seeking to make their political surroundings accommodate to them" (Daniels 2000, 141–42, 146–48; emphasis added). Similarly, Aaron James argues that once we properly read political liberalism, we will see that "Rawls is largely unconcerned with pure moral ideals" and that "even his concern with the ideal theory requirements of social justice is not, and never has been, fundamentally divorced from *philosophical anthropology*."[88] Whether we should be so sanguine about the prospect of such a diminutive, unambitious, and provincial political-philosophical practice is another matter entirely.

IV. Conclusion

I have endeavored to demonstrate in this chapter that political liberalism is impoverished in at least two senses. First and more narrowly, it cannot ground an OC on justice as fairness—at best, it suggests the possibility of an OC on a

---

88. James (2005, 285); cf. Daniels (2000, 146, 148). To be fair here, James's objective is not "overall assessment" of Rawls's theory of justice (285, 307), and he admits that "it is fair to wonder why reasoning about fundamental justice should be sensitive to existing practices at all, an issue on which Rawls is largely silent" (316)—apart from his rather Tory desire to build a "realistic utopia" that "reconciles us to our political and social condition" (LP 11).

class of liberal PCJs, with justice as fairness as just one competitor conception among others, its centrality determined through political competition and the strength of supporting social and economic interests. Second and more broadly, it offers little moral guidance, whether in a domestic or an international context, regarding the appropriate width and content of OC, and its agnosticism leads to a dramatically diminished role for political philosophy, which is effectively turned into a handmaiden of the social sciences.

Rawls frequently expressed his great admiration for Abraham Lincoln as a statesman and held him as a personal hero, but what would Lincoln have thought of the impoverished, parochial liberalism of the later Rawls?[89] We can draw inferences from his speeches. Lincoln's liberalism, limited though it was in other ways, was always universalistic. He would have been perplexed by the idea that he was merely offering one interpretation, inter alia, of the text of American political history, with application solely to his American audience; instead, he saw himself and his nation as defending the universal human values of freedom and equality. The universalism of one of his most famous speeches, the Gettysburg Address, is unremitting: "dedicated to the proposition that *all men* [not 'all Americans'] are created equal"; "testing whether . . . *any* nation so conceived and dedicated . . . can long endure"; "the *world* will little note"; and "government of the people, by the people, for the people, shall not perish *from the earth* [not merely 'from America']." All of these excerpts emphasize the global moral implications of a local military struggle and suggest that the blessings of liberal-democratic government are the birthright not merely of a fortunate subset of men and women but of all human beings. Only a comprehensive, universalistic liberalism could possibly lead one to such a conclusion.[90]

Being true to Lincoln's legacy (and that of the American Founders) requires us to reject political liberalism in favor of the sort of universalistic liberalism that can be found in, or can at least be reconstructed from, Rawls's writings during his earlier Kantian period, as I have argued over the course of this book. To use Bill Galston's terminology, we must eschew Reformation liberalism

---

89. LP 97. The provincialism of Rawls's political liberalism is a bit like that of Unitarianism: the Unitarian trinity has been described as "the Fatherhood of God, the Brotherhood of Man, and the Neighborhood of Boston." Adherents of the RCDs in Rawls's model OC—Kantians, Millians, classical utilitarians, liberal Christians—sound more like a roll call of those denizens of Cambridge, Massachusetts, than a representative sample of the American population or that of any other liberal-democratic society.

90. On Lincoln's liberal universalism and its Transcendentalist origins, see Wills (1992, chap. 3, esp. 99, 102 [Lincoln: the Declaration of Independence is for "all people of all colors everywhere"], and 105).

and return to a liberalism of the Enlightenment, preferably the Prussian one (Galston 1995). What, however, of Daniels's implication that the hope for a Kantian comprehensive liberalism that can be persuasive to liberals and non-liberals alike and can therefore serve as a global "fighting faith" is a vain "philosopher's dream," because there are no first principles that could possibly gain the assent of most or even many people? I will address this claim in the conclusion by offering there a detranscendentalized Kantian foundational argument for a *practical postulate of freedom*—one modeled on the argument of GMM III—that has some hope of succeeding as the required kind of first principle from which a Kantian conception of persons and, through Kantian constructivism, justice as fairness more generally can be derived.[91] I will also suggest that even if we ultimately admit the force of Rawls's fact of (reasonable) pluralism, which provided the major impetus for his political turn, we should still choose to devote the lion's share of our philosophical labor to the construction, refinement, and propagation of universalistic, comprehensive liberalisms.

---

91. I began in chapter 1 to outline how this ascent would work once a practical postulate of freedom was established. Cf. Estlund (1998, 254), who says a "single point of contact with the moral truth" is required for political liberalism to operate effectively.

Conclusion
Justice as Fairness as a Universalistic Kantian Liberalism

I. Introduction

In the second section of chapter 7, I discussed two sets of circumstances in which wide reflective judgments (especially regarding conceptions of the person) of different individuals could potentially coincide—a coincidence that Rawls calls "a necessary condition for objective moral truths" (IMT 290). The second of these was critiqued in the last chapter: a preexisting consensus or near consensus on considered convictions of justice reflecting the shared beliefs of an underlying political community. To attain this sort of consensus for justice as fairness and those conceptions of person and society that support it, Rawls restricted his theory's range of application to modern societies with liberal-democratic traditions and found his Kantian conception of the person to be "implicit in the public culture" of those societies (KCMT 305). As I argued in chapter 8, though, this political liberalism cannot ground an OC on justice as fairness, because only a Kantian CD can endorse a Kantian conception of the person and those political principles that follow from it, and even if it could ground such an OC, it possesses few if any theoretical resources for determining the proper scope of OC—whether in a domestic or an international context—and offers us an impoverished conception of political philosophy's practical role.

The first of these two sets of circumstances, on the other hand, was one in which we find "self-evident first principles" that are "so compelling that they lead us to revise all previous and subsequent judgments inconsistent with them" and create consistency in moral judgments across (fully reflective) persons (IMT 289). Rawls appears to suggest such an approach himself when he refers to our "nature" as free and equal rational beings, as he often does in

Theory (TJ 222, 225, 475, 501, 511). I suggested in chapter 7 that the best way to interpret Rawls's language there—and the one that is most compatible with his professed Kantianism—is to think of our freedom as a necessary presupposition or postulate of (pure) practical reason, as Kant does (CPrR 5:3–5, 132). Suppose that this postulate holds for each finite rational being and thus for all human beings; every fully reflective person must therefore come to accept it as a first principle. Earlier, in chapter 1, I verified that a presupposition of negative freedom of the will could be shown, by a series of steps, to imply positive freedom or autonomy, the highest form of which is moral; these qualities hold for each person and thus provide a basis for juridical and colegislative equality. The postulate of freedom therefore implies a conception of ourselves as free, equal, and moral, which is precisely Rawls's Kantian conception of the person. If such a postulate is necessary, then Rawls's Kantian conception of the person is necessary, and we have a reason to give priority to this conception over competitor ones (e.g., conceptions of the person as a sensuous being, artistic creator, or child of God). Furthermore, if Rawls's constructivism is sound, we should each be led ineluctably from his Kantian conception of the person, which our own practical reason compels us to accept, to the three lexically ordered principles of justice that reflect it. Thus, if this presupposition of negative freedom of the will is sufficiently compelling, it might serve in the needed role of self-evident first principle, providing Rawls's justice as fairness with a universalistic Kantian grounding.

What reason do we have, however, to believe that this postulate of freedom applies to us, that is, that our $Will_B$ (free choice or *Willkür*) is indeed undetermined by "alien" and external forces, such as nature, culture, God, etc. (GMM 4:446)? Kant offers two different ways to arrive at this postulate. One, found in *Groundwork* III, is direct: Kant claims there that the postulate of freedom is a necessary presupposition of agency, something we must presuppose if we are to conceive of ourselves as agents, which is unavoidable (GMM 4:447–48, 452, 459). The second one, found in the Analytic of the second *Critique,* is indirect: moral law, as a "fact of reason" that "forces itself upon us," first makes us conscious of our own freedom, because "ought implies can" (i.e., morality assumes freedom) (CPrR 5:29–31). Both of these approaches, however, rely upon the controversial metaphysical claims of Kant's transcendental idealism, including the distinction between noumenal (intelligible) and phenomenal (empirical) character and the latter's grounding in the former. The idea that such strongly contested claims could ever be "self-evident" to non-Kantian liberals and nonliberals alike might reasonably be judged fanciful—just a "philosopher's dream," as Norman Daniels would put it (Daniels 2000, 142).

Consequently, over the course of this concluding chapter I will examine and reconstruct Kant's claims in *Groundwork* III in favor of warranted faith in the negative freedom of our wills, that is, the freedom of Will$_B$ (*Willkür*) from determination by "alien" causes. What I will contend is that Kant's argument can be given a *narrower* construction than the one he suggests, allowing us to dispense with transcendental idealism and adopt a more modest, detranscendentalized account of our negative freedom. This narrower account offers the hope that the postulate of freedom can become a generally accepted first principle and that justice as fairness—which can be shown to be a consequence of this principle by way of Rawls's Kantian conceptions of person and society and his constructivist methods—can thus be reconceived as a universalistic Kantian liberalism. I will conclude this chapter and the book by arguing that the lion's share of philosophical labor by analytic liberals should be devoted to perfecting, extending, as well as popularizing universalistic comprehensive liberalisms of *all* stripes—Lockean, Kantian, Millian—as part of a shared liberal philosophical project: to undermine ideological support for the illiberal political institutions and values that are still widespread in the world today. If we expand our political horizons beyond the generally well-functioning (in comparative and historical terms) "democratic societies under modern conditions," we shall see that the universalistic comprehensive liberalisms that behave as competitors in such contexts will usefully complement one another in a global environment that continues to harbor innumerable theocratic, secular authoritarian, and even totalitarian regimes.

II. Grounding Kantian Liberalism

A. The Necessity of the Practical Presupposition of Freedom

Do human beings have free wills? Kant believes that we must *presuppose* the freedom of our wills *on practical grounds*. That is, something about human agency itself forces us to believe that our power of choice (*Willkür*) is undetermined by alien forces. Before reconstructing Kant's argument for this claim, we should note what he is *not* claiming. First, he is not claiming that we can *know* that we are free, such as through logical proof or empirical observation.

We cannot derive freedom from anything, and we cannot observe our own free agency—and if we could, it would no longer be free, but rather subsumed under natural law like all other observable phenomena.[1] Second and relatedly, the claim is not one of theoretical or speculative reason. Mathematics and science have nothing to say about freedom (so understood), as it is neither susceptible of proof nor falsifiable, as we shall soon see. Finally, and perhaps most surprisingly, Kant's claim is not inconsistent with freedom being an illusion. On practical grounds we must presuppose it, but it may be false—though mathematics and science are incapable of demonstrating its falsity.

Kant's argument for this limited, practical claim in *Groundwork* III is distressingly brief and imprecise, but we can reconstruct it in two steps:

> *STEP 1:* While I am choosing, I *can* consider myself free, that is, as undetermined by natural law.

I cannot observe [i] *myself* [ii] *while I am choosing*, that is, I cannot step outside myself while I am in the process of deciding and simultaneously observe myself in that process. I can, on the other hand, observe [i'] *others* while they are choosing or [i] *myself* [ii'] *before or after I choose*, that is, I can make predictions about my future choices, and I can observe myself retrospectively or after the fact (perhaps through audio-visual aids, recollections of other people, my own memory, etc.). In other words, there is a "blind spot" in my observational field, an epistemic limit that cannot be overcome. In order to subsume something under principles of natural causality, however, it must be observable, at least in principle. Consequently, I can use natural and social sciences to explain and/or predict in circumstances [i'] or [i] + [ii'] but not in circumstance [i] + [ii]. I *can* therefore see myself as free (undetermined by natural law) while I am choosing. Notice the very limited nature of this claim: it is both first-person and immediate, and it does not require belief in freedom even under the specified circumstance but rather subverts contrary claims of natural compulsion when one is in that circumstance.

> *STEP 2:* While I am choosing, I *must* consider myself free, that is, as undetermined by natural law (GMM 4:447–48).

---

1. Though see CPrR 5:29–31, where Kant seems to "derive" it from The CI itself: if freedom is a necessary condition of moral action and we are bound by morality, then we must be free—or at least must think ourselves to be so.

If I reflect on what I am doing while I am choosing, I will see that I necessarily presuppose a free will under such circumstances. Take the example of choosing a political-party identity. Perhaps I believe with Alford, Funk, and Hibbing that genes play a significant role in the determination of party identity (see Alford, Funk, and Hibbing 2005). However, when I myself must choose such an identity, the process I go through to do so—collecting information, analyzing policy positions and past performance, weighing the benefits and costs of each option, and so forth—simply takes as given that each of these options can (in principle) be chosen, that is, that my choice is not predetermined. More generally, the very process of choosing comes with certain implicit assumptions: while I am choosing, I necessarily assume that my choice set is not limited to one option, that my choosing is not a charade. I might come to see it otherwise after the fact ("I was always going to make that choice") or even give a prediction about my decision in advance ("given who I am, one choice seems inevitable"), but as a purely practical matter I cannot in any coherent way think that I am choosing and not choosing simultaneously. To be clear, Kant's claim is that I *must* consider myself free *only in the midst of choice;* at any other time I may—like a good determinist—think that free choice in general, and mine in particular, is entirely an illusion. Man *qua* agent, however, must assume his own free agency while he is exercising it.

With this phenomenology of choice as background, we can now more easily understand Kant's otherwise obscure claim that "every being that cannot act otherwise than *under the idea of freedom* is just because of that really free in a practical respect, that is, all laws that are inseparably bound up with freedom hold for him just *as if* his will had been validly pronounced free also in itself and in theoretical philosophy" (GMM 4:448). If I must think of myself as free when I choose, then while I am choosing I must see myself as constrained by laws "that are inseparably bound up with freedom," which as we have seen are Imperatives and, more specifically, universal moral law (The CI). The "as if" in this passage is key: theoretical philosophy cannot pronounce us free, but practical philosophy can, and it binds us just as efficiently to universal moral law. The derivation of The CI that we began in chapter 1 is now complete.

Before moving on, I want to point out that the general strategy Kant employs here—what we might irreverently call the "Kantian two-step"—will be utilized again in the second *Critique* to make the case for the practical postulates of God and immortality. Step 1 is to free up space, so to speak, in the proper domain of theoretical/speculative reason by showing that such reason cannot pronounce on some subject (such as the existence or nonexistence of freedom, God, and immortality) (CPrR 5:142: "I cannot prove these by my speculative reason, although I can also not refute them"). Step 2 is to occupy this space with a postulate, belief in which is "a need of pure [practical] reason." This is in fact the meaning of the priority of practical over theoretical reason: theoretical reason must tolerate supernatural claims if and only if (1) these claims are essential to the operation of pure practical reason and (2) they are not contradicted by equally valid claims of theoretical reason.[2]

B. The Antinomy of Freedom

Strictly speaking, the derivation completed above is valid on its own terms: it proves as a practical matter that we are bound by the moral law and that we can (consistent with theoretical reason) believe in the freedom of our own will due to a "blind spot" in our observational fields that keeps us from subsuming all aspects of our agency under natural law. This being said, there still seems to be a contradiction here between the broader implications of the claims of practical and theoretical reason:

a. We are *free* agents, subject to *moral* law. {implied by (pure) practical reason}
b. We are *unfree* agents, subject to *natural* law. {implied by theoretical reason}

We skirted this contradiction above by painstakingly qualifying the respective claims of practical and theoretical reason, but the reconciliation thereby achieved is not wholly satisfying: surely we must be either free or unfree—how can we be both, as the derivation above seems to suggest?

---

2. Freedom, God, and immortality are all practical postulates, but the first has special status, as it is a precondition of the moral law itself, whereas the others are only preconditions of the moral law's object, i.e., the highest or complete good—see CPrR 5:3-5. It is also important to note that the two enumerated criteria must work in tandem; otherwise, a boundless proliferation of metaphysical concepts may result. For example, the second criterion alone might appear to permit belief in invisible guardian angels who imperceptibly steer us clear of danger (as their existence cannot be scientifically disproven), but the first criterion would rule out such belief as delusional because presumably it is not a precondition of the moral law or its object, i.e., it is not a need of *pure* practical reason. See CPrR 5:144n.

To answer this question, we must first examine the Third Antinomy of the first *Critique,* commonly called the "Antinomy of Freedom."[3] The antinomy presents a rationalist thesis and an empiricist antithesis, which parallel claims (a) and (b) above:

Thesis

Causality in accordance with laws of nature is not the only one from which all the appearances of the world can be derived. It is also necessary to assume another causality through freedom in order to explain them. . . .

Antithesis

There is no freedom, but everything in the world happens solely in accordance with laws of nature.

The proof of each proceeds by *reductio ad impossibile:* the thesis is proven by pointing out that the antithesis leads to an infinite regress of causes, which itself contradicts the natural law "that nothing happens without a cause sufficiently determined a priori," while the antithesis is proven by pointing out that the thesis posits an uncaused cause and therefore a "transcendental freedom [that] is contrary to causal law" and, indeed, "the guidance of *all* rules." Although this antinomy is most obviously related to cosmological arguments for God's existence, it has a bearing as well on our concern, the question of practical freedom: as Kant argues, "it is this *transcendental* idea of *freedom* [as pure spontaneity] on which the practical concept of freedom is grounded" (CPuR A533/B561). If the idea of transcendental freedom present in the thesis is overturned, in other words, then practical freedom would be as well. Unsurprisingly, then, a resolution of the Antinomy of Freedom is required for a reconciliation of claims (a) and (b) above.

C. Resolution of the Antinomy Through Transcendental Idealism

In order to resolve this antinomy, Kant makes his (in)famous distinction between things-in-themselves (*noumena*) and things as they appear to us

---

3. CPuR A444–51/B472–79. An "antinomy" is conventionally defined as "a contradiction between conclusions that seem equally logical, reasonable, or necessary" (OED2).

(*phenomena*). We are all familiar with the idea that appearances can be deceptive (e.g., optical illusions), but Kant's distinction is more fundamental than this: all we *can* know are things as they appear; what lies behind and generates or grounds these appearances, on the other hand, cannot be known. Phenomena, because they can be known through observation, can be subsumed under natural law; noumena, on the other hand, cannot be so subsumed, so a noumenon "will not be determined in its causality by appearances even though its effects [i.e., phenomena] appear and so can be determined [caused] through other appearances. Thus the intelligible cause [i.e., noumenon], with its causality, is outside the series [of phenomenal cause and effect]; its effects, on the contrary, are encountered in the series of empirical conditions. *The effect can therefore be regarded as free in regard to its intelligible cause and yet simultaneously, in regard to appearances, as their result according to the necessity of nature*" (CPuR A537/B565; emphasis added). In other words, anything that we observe in the phenomenal world can be considered both free and unfree: free with respect to its noumenal cause (which cannot be observed and need not be subsumed under natural law) but unfree in its connection to other phenomena (in which it must stand, like everything else in nature, in a cause/effect relationship governed by natural law). The application of this "transcendental idealism" to a human being is then straightforward: "one can consider the causality of this being in *two aspects,* as intelligible in its action as a thing in itself, and as sensible in the effects of that action as an appearance in the world of sense." In other words, we have an intelligible/noumenal character that generates or provides the ground for our empirical/phenomenal character, where the former character is governed by moral laws and the latter by natural laws. Consequently, we can be simultaneously free and unfree, so that there is no contradiction between claims (a) and (b) (CPuR A538–39/B566–67; cf. GMM 4:450–55).

To relate this back more directly to the derivation of the moral law: when we take up the perspective of *agents,* we will necessarily "think of ourselves as free [and] transfer ourselves into the [noumenal] world of understanding as members of it and cognize autonomy of the will along with its consequence, morality"; on the other hand, when we take up the perspective of *observers* of ourselves or of others, we will "regard ourselves as belonging to the world of sense and yet *at the same time* to the [noumenal] world of understanding" (GMM 4:453). Kant seems to believe that this "two-world" or "two-perspective" metaphysics is implicit in the derivation of the moral law.

Kant is adamant throughout the last pages of the *Groundwork* that we not read too much into the idea of a noumenal realm: it is just a "negative thought" or a "*standpoint* that reason sees itself constrained to take outside appearances *in order to think of itself as practical*" (GMM 4:458). Practical reason "oversteps all its bounds" if it tries to learn more about this realm, because we "have not the least cognizance of it nor can we ever attain this by all the efforts of our faculty of reason," as it is beyond sensibility and hence beyond knowledge: as Kant indicates, "where determination by laws of nature ceases, there all *explanation* ceases as well, and nothing is left but *defense*, that is, to repel the objections of those who pretend to have seen deeper into the essence of things and therefore boldly declare that freedom is impossible" (GMM 4:458–59, 462). Kant clearly believes that transcendental idealism is a "minimal" or "modest" metaphysics, doing no more than is absolutely necessary to protect practical freedom from the depredations of both empiricism and unbounded rationalism: "Here, then, is the highest limit of all moral inquiry; and it is already of great importance to determine it just so that reason may not, on the one hand, to the detriment of morals search about in the world of sense for the supreme motive and a comprehensible but empirical interest, and that it may not, on the other hand, impotently flap its wings without moving from the spot in space, which is empty for it, of transcendental concepts called the intelligible world, and so lose itself among phantoms" (GMM 4:462). With transcendental idealism, Kant attempts to chart a course between the Scylla of empiricism (Plato's "many-headed beast" of desire) and the Charybdis of hubristic metaphysics (a vortex of ever-proliferating but empty transcendental concepts—angels on pinheads and the like) (Homer 1996, 273–74 [12.81–121]; Plato 1991, 271 [588c]).

D. Detranscendentalizing Kantian Liberalism

As I noted earlier, the derivation of the moral law in *Groundwork* III is, strictly speaking, valid on its own terms even if unsupplemented by transcendental idealism, as it demonstrates that freedom is a necessary presupposition of agency for creatures such as ourselves, a presupposition that is fully consistent with theoretical reason (due to the "blind spot" in our observational fields) and implies the subordination of our wills to moral law. Such a derivation may seem incomplete, though, leading us to hunger for a deeper explanation of how we can be simultaneously free and unfree. Kant warns us that "where determination by laws of nature ceases, there all *explanation* ceases as well," but he nevertheless proceeds to provide an explanation for our dual nature with his transcendental idealism (GMM 4:459). He appears to offer us a choice here between a sound but narrow derivation and a fuller derivation that relies upon his controversial metaphysics.

I believe we should resist the hunger for deeper explanation here for precisely the reasons that Kant provides: once we start to theorize about the supernatural realm, there is no way to test the validity of our claims, as we have departed the known world of logic and science. Although Kant's metaphysics may seem relatively modest, it itself involves a proliferation of concepts as well as questions; for example, what is the noumenal realm like? how do noumena "cause" phenomena? how is dual causation of a phenomenon (by both noumena and other phenomena) possible? Kant tries to cut off such speculation, but these metaphysical flights of fancy are inevitable as we seek deeper and deeper explanations for things that, as Kant admits, can be given no explanation. We may be better off—so long as we find the narrower derivation to be sound—simply accepting the mystery of our free and unfree selves and getting on with the difficult business of living morally. Surely this is one implication of Kant's belief in the priority of practical over theoretical reason.

Put a bit differently, Ockham's razor would appear to slice away transcendental idealism, at least in this setting. As long as (1) the practical postulate of freedom is a need of pure practical reason, (2) its possibility is not definitively ruled out by theoretical reason, and (3) the derivation is sound from this postulate to the moral law *or* to justice as fairness by way of Rawls's Kantian conception of persons and his constructivism, additional controversial metaphysical assumptions would serve no purpose and would consequently need to be avoided on grounds of parsimony. A further, more compelling reason to avoid such assumptions is provided by Rawls: transcendental idealism is too controversial a doctrine to supply the basis for an OC, which explains in part why he believes that a Kantian comprehensive liberalism cannot serve as the public charter of liberal-democratic societies without (paradoxically) the "sanctions of state power" (PL 37–38n; cf. PL 99–100, LP 87; also see S. Freeman 2007a, 161).

Assuming we can strip away transcendental idealism from Kantian liberalism, would the doctrine that remains be sufficiently compelling to all fully reflective persons? The answer to this question depends, of course, on the obviousness of its grounding postulate: the presupposition of negative freedom of the will. The extreme modesty of the postulate militates in its favor here. To expand on what was noted earlier, this postulate is a practical claim of warranted faith rather than a theoretical or speculative claim of knowledge. That is, the postulate is something that has to be assumed in the exercise of agency, which is unavoidable for finite rational beings; consequently, it has practical rather than theoretical necessity, though it is consistent with speculation and may even be of use to it for its own purposes.[4] As Kant points out, this postulate and those of God and immortality are "not theoretical dogmas but presuppositions having a necessarily practical reference and thus, although they do not indeed extend speculative cognition, they give objective reality to the ideas of speculative reason in general . . . and justify its holding concepts even the possibility of which it could not otherwise presume to affirm" (CPrR 5:132). Moreover, this presupposition of practical reason does not claim the status of knowledge but rather that of warranted faith.[5] It does not force itself upon us like the conclusion of a mathematical proof but rather asks us for a voluntary assent grounded in our reflective recognition of "a need of pure [practical] reason," namely, the requisites of our own agency, including moral agency; it therefore qualifies as a special form of faith, what Kant calls "pure practical rational belief" (*reiner praktischer Vernunftglaube*).[6]

Even in this weak form, shorn of metaphysical accompaniment, the practical postulate of freedom will meet resistance from certain quarters. For instance, committed determinists, such as La Mettrie and his modern descendants, would balk at any such postulate due to its inconsistency with a thoroughgoing materialism; La Mettrie would simply deny that speculative reason cannot pronounce on the existence of freedom, God, and immortality—he holds that it rejects all three.[7] However, insofar as one holds that speculative reason cannot pronounce on metaphysical claims and should remain agnostic towards them (except as guided by pure practical reason), a postulate of freedom of the kind described should be compelling: as we have seen, it must be presupposed in

---

4. For example, the postulate of God, one condition of the possibility of the highest good, is practically necessary as well; it is consistent with speculative reason (as such reason cannot disprove the postulate) and even serves certain of its purposes (e.g., it provides a possible explanation for evidence of "purposiveness in nature" [CPrR 5:142]).

5. Kant speaks of the practical postulates as having a "warrant" or "authorization" (*Befugnis*) from our pure practical reason—see CPrR 5:5n.

6. CPrR 5:5, 146. The detranscendentalized Kant is therefore not a realist—see the chapter 1 discussion of realism.

7. La Mettrie (1987), to which Kant seems to allude at WIE 8:42, where he says man is "now more than a machine."

the exercise of human agency, which is itself unavoidable, and when stripped of metaphysical baggage it is likely to be consistent with (if not implied by) a wide variety of belief systems. The practical postulate of freedom therefore stands some hope of becoming a generally accepted first principle, and insofar as this postulate implies justice as fairness by way of a Kantian conception of persons and Kantian constructivism, Rawls's three lexically ordered principles of justice may similarly gain the assent of all reflective persons and thereby constitute a genuinely universalistic Kantian liberalism. This possibility would call into question the validity of Rawls's so-called fact of pluralism as well as the other facts following from it: if the postulate and what it implies were actually endorsable by all fully reflective persons, then non-Kantian CDs might be systematically abandoned upon reflection, at least insofar as they (or elements of them) were inconsistent with a Kantian comprehensive liberalism; this process would generate a consistency in moral judgments across persons—a condition of moral objectivity—and would allow a Kantian liberalism such as justice as fairness to serve as the public charter of all liberal-democratic societies, without the use of illegitimate state coercion.[8] *Theory*'s initial universalistic promise would thus be redeemed.

III. On the Proper Use of Pluralism in Liberal Theorizing

The idea just surveyed—that non-Kantian CDs would be systematically abandoned in the face of a practically necessary postulate with its myriad implications for politics and ethics—will strike most as hopelessly optimistic. Even if we restrict attention to liberal CDs alone, there is so far little indication that the many sorts of comprehensive liberalism—Lockean, Kantian, classical utilitarian, Millian—are converging toward one of their number or some hybrid, even after many generations of thoughtful reflection by scholars on these theories' assumptions and implications. The likelihood that one more addition to this conversation, in the form of a reinterpretation of the foundations of Kantian liberalism, is going to alter this situation significantly is simply nil. There are many reasons for this, of course, not the least of which is the complexity of the argument that leads from the postulate of freedom to justice as

---

8. IOC 421–25. PCDs would be even more likely, of course, to make this transition without difficulty, as they are so loosely articulated as to be consistent with a variety of CDs, including the Kantian one.

fairness, which creates many possible points for disagreement. From the postulate to positive freedom or autonomy; from autonomy to the utmost form of autonomy, moral autonomy; from moral autonomy to a Kantian conception of persons as free, equal, and moral; from this conception to the three lexically ordered principles of justice by means of OP reasoning and wide reflective equilibrium—any one of these stages of the argument (which themselves have numerous substages) could become a stumbling block for conscientious moral agents. My book has been an attempt to refine and clarify these argumentative stages, but I am not under the illusion that many adherents of competitor liberalisms will find the argument as a whole to be compelling, and I recognize that there may be errors at particular stages, including ones that invalidate the whole. The facts of pluralism, oppression, and legitimate stability might be more durable than I suggested at the end of the last section.[9]

Given this likelihood, one might be tempted to conclude that, in one respect at least, the later, post-Kantian Rawls was right: given the stubborn diversity of CDs, political philosophers should dedicate themselves principally to the conservative tasks of refinement and reconciliation in liberal-democratic political cultures. As we saw in chapter 8, they might best reconceive their vocation as the identification of wide OCs and/or constitutional and legislative consensuses and the philosophical "smoothing out" of their rough ways (e.g., showing that equal opportunity for homosexuals is demanded by these cultures' own principles and traditions, rightly understood) (Luke 3:5). This kind of fine-tuning is certainly not unimportant—the injustices that remain in these societies are made all the more galling by their ostensible commitment to liberal principles—but it should also be said that, comparatively and historically speaking at least, these societies are already very close to the liberal-democratic ideal, that is, the distance between them and the ideal is almost trivial compared to that between the overwhelming majority of societies in the world

---

9. Should a Kantian comprehensive liberalism be embarrassed by this prospect? Maybe not. If we seize the first horn of the dilemma presented in the last chapter, thus abandoning the idea of legitimate stability, we are not necessarily driven towards anything as dramatic as "oppression," at least on the common understanding of that term. After all, Kantian liberals might peacefully obtain political power and implement their PCJ in a manner fully consistent with their own principles (e.g., respectful of liberal rights and publicity, offering justification to all who request it), with non-Kantians *acquiescing* in this outcome. This wouldn't be "stability for the right reasons," of course, but it could be a liberal form of stability nonetheless, one resulting from democratic procedures and without the use of illiberal means (such as censorship, indoctrination, etc.). This would be an alternative, Kantian understanding of legitimate stability. Why should a more demanding standard be applied, at least if the indicated circumstances obtained?

today as well as in history (including ones that are now liberal-democratic) and the same ideal. Perhaps, though, this is the most that we can hope for, at least if we eschew philosophical hubris.

I believe that this would be the wrong conclusion to draw, however, one that results from overly narrow political horizons. Seen from the domestic context of liberal-democratic societies, the interminable conflict among liberal PCJs (e.g., that between liberal-egalitarian and classical-liberal variants) appears to be a problem that cannot be solved but only finessed via the exercise of political-liberal meliorism. Seen from the wider context of an international society filled with theocratic, secular authoritarian, and totalitarian regimes, however, the diversity of liberal RCDs appears to be less of a problem than an opportunity. These illiberal regimes and their supporting ideologies, in addition to being burdens for their oppressed populations, are a continuing affront to liberalisms of all stripes, suggesting that the various liberal CDs could set aside their domestic political squabbles (at least as a temporary matter) and make common cause against international illiberalism. Granted, all existing societies (including supposedly liberal-democratic ones) fail to meet liberal ideals, however they might be characterized, but the *extent* of the failure varies quite dramatically across societies. Focusing our philosophical labor on those societies with relatively modest failures might be forgiven as a regrettable example of intellectual provincialism were the stakes not so high for the victims of these illiberal regimes and for the success of liberalism more generally, both as a philosophical position and as a governing doctrine.

The idea that liberal CDs, which jockey for philosophical and political position in liberal-democratic societies, might cooperate with and even complement one another in the larger world may be counterintuitive, but once we recognize that different comprehensive liberalisms will be appealing to different persons and groups, the practical uses of this diversity of liberal theorizing will become clear. For example, the comprehensive religious liberalisms of Kant or Locke might be attractive to some Christians as well as adherents of other Abrahamic faiths; a Millian plural-perfectionist approach may persuade artists, romantics, and polytheists; and a classical-utilitarian variety of liberalism like that constructed by Bentham and Sidgwick may hold a special allure for engineers, economists, and other natural and social scientists.[10] Working together,

---

10. I list polytheists as potential adherents of Millian plural-perfectionism partly in jest, but partly because Mill wrote so admiringly of "pagan self-assertion," especially in contrast with a Christian ideal of "abstinence from evil, rather than energetic pursuit of good." As Mill

these assorted comprehensive liberalisms might be able to do what none could do on its own: persuade a broad swath of people in illiberal societies of the virtues of liberal principles and governance. If such a conversion could be carried out, the likelihood of a liberal political transformation—whether of a reformist or revolutionary kind—would surely improve, perhaps dramatically.[11]

If this is indeed the proper use of pluralism in liberal theorizing, then how should analytic liberals reallocate their philosophical labor? Without ignoring the need for a little political-liberal meliorism in existing democratic societies, analytic liberals should dedicate themselves chiefly to perfecting, extending, and popularizing the canonical comprehensive liberalisms and to devising entirely new ones. Examples of scholars who have done the former kind of work include Joseph Raz and William Galston (plural perfectionism), Rawls (Kantianism, as I have argued), and Peter Singer (utilitarianism).[12] Singer's output is especially noteworthy on this count: he has worked to refine utilitarianism in professional journals, expanded it to address (inter alia) animal rights and euthanasia, and promoted it by means of innumerable popular books, several of which have been translated into a wide variety of languages.[13] These kinds of efforts to defend and promote liberal CDs—not just through scholarly works but also by way of popular lectures and books, especially when they are translated into the languages of illiberal societies—are precisely what is needed to wage an effective international war of ideas against illiberal doctrines and regimes.

One way in which analytic liberals could usefully extend these theories is by developing their nonideal components, that is, those components dealing with the requirements of justice under nonideal conditions, including ongoing injustices, reactionary political cultures, severe economic underdevelopment, etc. (TJ 215–16; LP 106). These are commonly the very conditions under which

---

memorably puts it, "it may be better to be a John Knox than an Alcibiades, but it is better to be a Pericles than either." See Mill (1962, 177, 191–92); cf. Milton (1999, 24).

11. Lest this prospect be thought naïve, many of the anticommunist revolutionaries and reformers of former Soviet Bloc countries speak of the powerful influence that smuggled copies of contemporary classical-liberal texts (by such scholars as Milton Friedman and Friedrich Hayek) had on their thinking. See, e.g., Klaus (2005).

12. See Raz (1986), Galston (1991), and Singer (1999). Singer is in many ways the true heir to Bentham: his utilitarianism is rigorous and unflinching, sometimes leading to discomforting—even illiberal—conclusions.

13. The professional articles include ones on act-utilitarianism and vegetarianism (Singer 1972, 1980); early popular works include his renowned *Animal Liberation* (Singer 1975), which has been translated into seventeen languages, including Chinese. For a complete list, see his Web site: http://www.princeton.edu/~psinger/.

illiberal societies struggle, so further progress in this area of liberal theorizing is crucial for the extension of liberal ideas and institutions globally. Many of the great thinkers of the liberal tradition, including Kant, Tocqueville, and Mill, speculated on the necessary conditions for successful transitions to liberal democracy, but most contemporary liberals have shown scant interest in nonideal theory, perhaps due to their focus on existing liberal-democratic societies.[14] Even Rawls gave little attention to it, though *The Law of Peoples* does propose ways in which well-ordered societies (including liberal and decent regimes) can help what he calls "burdened peoples" overcome cultural, political, and economic disadvantages.[15] Further development of liberal nonideal theory will be challenging, of course, because (like political liberalism) it must draw extensively upon the intellectual resources of the humanities and social sciences, but such interdisciplinary labor is key to the construction of sophisticated liberal nonideal theories and to the success of liberalism more broadly.

This book has been an attempt to recover not simply the Kantian foundations of Rawls's justice as fairness but also the cosmopolitan Enlightenment spirit that has animated the best and most ambitious work in the liberal tradition. As I argued in chapter 8, what William Galston has called the "Reformation liberalism" of scholars like Charles Larmore and the "political" Rawls is largely impotent before the greatest contemporary challenges to liberal theory and practice, such as the spread of fundamentalist political Islam in the Middle East, increasing global inequality in longevity and wealth, ongoing oppression and poverty in sub-Saharan Africa, and the economic and military rise of a politically authoritarian China (Galston 1995; Larmore 1987). What is needed to meet these challenges is the spread of liberal values and forms of government, yet Reformation liberalism is too unsure of its own relevance in illiberal societies to spearhead such efforts effectively; its accommodationist instincts and excessive tolerance of diversity leave it nearly powerless to critique illiberal values and practices outside its comfort zone of existing liberal-democratic societies. Cultural relativism in this context will create a vacuum into which

14. See Mill (1991) and Tocqueville (2003); I write about Kant and democratic transitions in Taylor (2006). Two major exceptions to my claim about the lack of contemporary-liberal interest in nonideal theory are G. A. Cohen (2000) and Murphy (2003).

15. LP §15. Rawls does, of course, give substantial attention to civil disobedience and conscientious objection as responses to existing injustices—see TJ §§55–59. I conjectured at the end of chapter 3 about whether Rawls's nonideal theory could tolerate temporary restrictions on political liberties if such restrictions were required to safeguard economic growth (as a precondition of the eventual full and effective exercise of *all* basic liberties), but this discussion was purely speculative.

the myriad religious and secular authoritarianisms will expand, as they (unlike Reformation liberalism) have no qualms about imposing themselves in alien or even hostile environments.

As different as the Enlightenment liberalisms of Locke, Kant, Mill, and the earlier Rawls are, they all offer universalistic, cosmopolitan theories, intended to apply (eventually, at least) to all societies on earth, up to and including international society. Only they possess the intellectual resources to defend and advance liberal principles in every corner of the globe and to help realize historical liberalism's grandest ambition: "a republicanism of all states, together and separately," as Kant described it.[16] Though I believe that some version of Kantian liberalism, such as Rawls's reconstructed justice as fairness, offers the most compelling interpretation of the liberal ideals of freedom and equality, all of these forms of comprehensive liberalism inspire by their willingness to provide justification to every person, not as a member of a particular nation, race, or faith, but as a human being, as a citizen of the world. It is this quality above all that makes them deserving of our best philosophical labor and highest hopes.

---

16. MM 6:354. Lest I be misunderstood: in spite of my "militaristic" rhetoric of conflict, conquest, and appeasement, cosmopolitanism does not necessarily imply a commitment to military (as opposed to ideological) intervention. On this important and often neglected point, see Tan (2006, 77, 91–92) and Macleod (2006, 137, 146).

References

Alexander, Larry. 1985. "Fair Equality of Opportunity: John Rawls' (Best) Forgotten Principle." *Philosophy Research Archives* 11:197–207.
Alford, John, Carolyn Funk, and John Hibbing. 2005. "Are Political Orientations Genetically Transmitted?" *American Political Science Review* 99 (2): 153–67.
Allison, Henry. 1990. *Kant's Theory of Freedom*. Cambridge: Cambridge University Press.
Anderson, Elizabeth. 1999. "What Is the Point of Equality?" *Ethics* 109 (2): 287–337.
Aquinas, Thomas. 1988. *St. Thomas Aquinas on Politics and Ethics*. Trans. and ed. Paul E. Sigmund. New York: W. W. Norton.
Aristotle. 1958. *The Politics*. Trans. Ernest Barker. Oxford: Oxford University Press.
Arneson, Richard. 1999. "Against Rawlsian Equality of Opportunity." *Philosophical Studies* 93 (1): 77–112.
———. 2000. "Rawls Versus Utilitarianism in Light of *Political Liberalism*." In Davion and Wolf 2000.
Arrow, Kenneth. 1973. "Some Ordinalist-Utilitarian Notes on Rawls' Theory of Justice." *Journal of Philosophy* 70 (9): 245–63.
Barry, Brian. 1973a. "John Rawls and the Priority of Liberty." *Philosophy and Public Affairs* 2 (3): 274–90.
———. 1973b. *The Liberal Theory of Justice: A Critical Examination of the Principal Doctrines in "A Theory of Justice" by John Rawls*. Oxford: Clarendon Press.
———. 1989. *Theories of Justice*. Berkeley and Los Angeles: University of California Press.
———. 1995. "John Rawls and the Search for Stability." *Ethics* 105 (4): 874–915.
Berk, Laura. 2003. *Child Development*. 6th ed. Boston: Allyn and Bacon.
Blasi, Vincent. 1977. "The Checking Value in First Amendment Theory." *American Bar Association Foundation Research Journal* 2 (3): 521–649.
Blaug, Ricardo. 1986. "John Rawls and the Protection of Liberty." *Social Theory and Practice* 12 (2): 241–58.
Bork, Robert. 1971. "Neutral Principles and Some First Amendment Problems." 47 *Indiana Law Journal* 1.
Bratman, Michael. 2003. "Autonomy and Hierarchy." *Social Philosophy and Policy* 20 (2): 156–76.
Buchanan, Allen. 2006. "Taking the Human out of Human Rights." In Martin and Reidy 2006.
Buchanan, James. 1975. *The Limits of Liberty: Between Anarchy and Leviathan*. Chicago: University of Chicago Press.
Budde, Kerstin. 2007. "Rawls on Kant: Is Rawls a Kantian or Kant a Rawlsian?" *European Journal of Political Theory* 6 (3):339–58.
Calhoun, John C. 1953. *A Disquisition on Government and Selections from the Discourse*. Ed. C. Gordon Post. Indianapolis: Bobbs-Merrill.
Chiu, Yvonne. 2007. "Combat Contractualism: A Secular Theory of Just War." Ph.D. diss., University of California, Berkeley.
Christman, John. 1988. "Constructing the Inner Citadel: Recent Work on the Concept of Autonomy." *Ethics* 99 (1):109–24.
———, ed. 1989. *The Inner Citadel: Essays on Individual Autonomy*. New York: Oxford University Press.

———. 2009. "Autonomy in Moral and Political Philosophy." In *The Stanford Encyclopedia of Philosophy*. http://plato.stanford.edu/entries/autonomy-moral/.
Cicero. 1994. *The Republic*. Trans. Clinton W. Keyes. Cambridge, Mass.: Harvard University Press.
Cohen, G. A. 2000. *If You're an Egalitarian, How Come You're So Rich?* Cambridge, Mass.: Harvard University Press.
Cohen, Joshua. 1989. "Democratic Equality." *Ethics* 99 (4): 727–51.
———. 2003. "For a Democratic Society." In S. Freeman 2003b.
Constant, Benjamin. 1988. "The Liberty of the Ancients Compared with That of the Moderns." In *The Political Writings of Benjamin Constant*, ed. Biancamaria Fontana. Cambridge: Cambridge University Press.
Daniels, Norman. 1989a. "Equal Liberty and Unequal Worth of Liberty." In Daniels 1989b.
———, ed. 1989b. *Reading Rawls: Critical Studies on Rawls' "A Theory of Justice."* Stanford: Stanford University Press.
———. 2000. "Reflective Equilibrium and Justice as Political." In Davion and Wolf 2000.
Darwall, Stephen. 1976. "A Defense of the Kantian Interpretation." *Ethics* 86 (2): 164–70.
———. 1980. "Is There a Kantian Foundation for Rawlsian Justice?" In *John Rawls' Theory of Social Justice: An Introduction*, ed. H. Gene Blocker and Elizabeth H. Smith. Athens: Ohio University Press.
Davidson, Arnold. 1985. "Is Rawls a Kantian?" *Pacific Philosophical Quarterly* 66 (1–2):48–77.
Davies, J. K. 1993. *Democracy and Classical Greece*. Cambridge, Mass.: Harvard University Press.
Davion, Victoria, and Clark Wolf, eds. 2000. *The Idea of a Political Liberalism*. Lanham, Md.: Rowman and Littlefield.
DeMarco, Joseph, and Samuel Richardson. 1977. "A Note on the Priority of Liberty." *Ethics* 87 (3): 272–75.
Denis, Lara. 2006. "Kant's Conception of Virtue." In *The Cambridge Companion to Kant and Modern Philosophy*, ed. Paul Guyer. Cambridge: Cambridge University Press.
Doppelt, Gerald. 1989. "Is Rawls's Kantian Liberalism Coherent and Defensible?" *Ethics* 99 (4): 815–51.
Doyle, Michael. 2006. "One World, Many Peoples: International Justice in John Rawls's *The Law of Peoples*." *Perspectives on Politics* 4 (1): 109–20.
Dupor, Bill, and Wen-Fang Liu. 2003. "Jealousy and Equilibrium Overconsumption." *American Economic Review* 93 (1): 423–28.
Dworkin, Gerald. 1988. *The Theory and Practice of Autonomy*. Cambridge: Cambridge University Press.
Dworkin, Ronald. 1986. *Law's Empire*. Cambridge, Mass.: Harvard University Press.
———. 2000. *Sovereign Virtue*. Cambridge, Mass.: Harvard University Press.
Elster, Jon. 1985. *Making Sense of Marx*. Cambridge: Cambridge University Press.
———. 1986. "Self-Realization in Work and Politics: The Marxist Conception of the Good Life." *Social Philosophy and Policy* 3 (2): 97–126.
Estlund, David. 1998. "The Insularity of the Reasonable: Why Political Liberalism Must Admit the Truth." *Ethics* 108 (2): 252–75.
Fehige, Christoph. 2000. "Justice Beyond Desires?" In Davion and Wolf 2000.
Feinberg, Joel. 1989. "Autonomy." In Christman 1989.
Flanagan, Owen. 1991. *The Science of the Mind*. Cambridge, Mass.: MIT Press.
Follesdal, Andreas. 2006. "Justice, Stability, and Toleration in a Federation of Well-Ordered Peoples." In Martin and Reidy 2006.

Frank, Robert H., and Philip J. Cook. 1996. *The Winner-Take-All Society: Why the Few at the Top Get So Much More than the Rest of Us*. New York: Penguin.

Frankfurt, Harry. 1988. "Freedom of the Will and the Concept of the Person." In *The Importance of What We Care About: Philosophical Essays*. Cambridge: Cambridge University Press.

Freeman, A. Myrick. 1993. *The Measurement of Environmental and Resource Values: Theory and Methods*. Washington, D.C.: Resources for the Future.

Freeman, Samuel. 2003a. "Congruence and the Good of Justice." In S. Freeman 2003b.

———, ed. 2003b. *The Cambridge Companion to Rawls*. Cambridge: Cambridge University Press.

———. 2007a. *Justice and the Social Contract: Essays on Rawlsian Political Philosophy*. Oxford: Oxford University Press.

———. 2007b. *Rawls*. London: Routledge.

Frost, Robert. 1969. *The Poetry of Robert Frost: The Collected Poems, Complete and Unabridged*. Ed. Edward Connery Lathem. New York: Henry Holt.

Galston, William. 1991. *Liberal Purposes: Goods, Virtues, and Diversity in the Liberal State*. Cambridge: Cambridge University Press.

———. 1995. "Two Concepts of Liberalism." *Ethics* 105 (3): 516–34.

Gauthier, David. 1989. *Morals by Agreement*. Oxford: Oxford University Press.

———. 1997. "Political Contractarianism." *Journal of Political Philosophy* 5 (2):132–48.

Gilligan, Carol. 1982. *In a Different Voice: Psychological Theory and Women's Development*. Cambridge, Mass.: Harvard University Press.

Goldman, Alan H. 1976. "Rawls's Original Position and the Difference Principle." *Journal of Philosophy* 73 (21): 845–49.

Gowans, Chris. 2008. "Moral Relativism." In *The Stanford Encyclopedia of Philosophy*. http://plato.stanford.edu/entries/moral-relativism/.

Graetz, Michael, and Ian Shapiro. 2005. *Death by a Thousand Cuts: The Fight over Taxing Inherited Wealth*. Princeton: Princeton University Press.

Gray, John. 1996. *Mill on Liberty: A Defense*. 2nd ed. London: Routledge.

Gutmann, Amy, ed. 1998. *Freedom of Association*. Princeton: Princeton University Press.

Guyer, Paul. 2000. *Kant on Freedom, Law, and Happiness*. Cambridge: Cambridge University Press.

Habermas, Jürgen. 1995. "Reconciliation Through the Public Use of Reason: Remarks on John Rawls's Political Liberalism." *Journal of Philosophy* 92 (3): 109–31.

———. 1996. *Between Facts and Norms: Contributions to a Discourse Theory of Law and Democracy*. Cambridge, Mass.: MIT Press.

Habibi, Don. 1999. "The Moral Dimensions of J. S. Mill's Colonialism." *Journal of Social Philosophy* 30 (1): 125–46.

Haksar, Vinit. 1979. *Equality, Liberty, and Perfectionism*. Oxford: Clarendon Press.

Hampton, Jean. 1989. "Should Political Philosophy Be Done Without Metaphysics?" *Ethics* 99 (4): 791–814.

Hart, H. L. A. 1989. "Rawls on Liberty and Its Priority." In Daniels 1989b.

Haworth, Lawrence. 1991. "Dworkin on Autonomy." *Ethics* 102 (1): 129–39.

Herman, Barbara. 1993. *The Practice of Moral Judgment*. Cambridge, Mass.: Harvard University Press.

Hill, Thomas. 1989a. "The Kantian Conception of Autonomy." In Christman 1989.

———. 1989b. "Kantian Constructivism in Ethics." *Ethics* 99 (4): 752–70.

———. 2000. *Respect, Pluralism, and Justice: Kantian Perspectives*. Oxford: Oxford University Press.

Höffe, Otfried. 1984. "Is Rawls' Theory of Justice Really Kantian?" *Ratio* 26 (2): 103–24.

Homer. 1996. *The Odyssey.* Trans. Robert Fagles. New York: Viking.

Honderich, Ted. 1995. *The Oxford Companion to Philosophy.* Oxford: Oxford University Press.

Hopkins, Ed, and Tatiana Kornienko. 2004. "Running to Keep in the Same Place: Consumer Choice as a Game of Status." *American Economic Review* 94 (4): 1085–1107.

Humboldt, Wilhelm von. 1993. *The Limits of State Action.* Ed. J. W. Burrow. Indianapolis: Liberty Fund.

Hume, David. 1969. *A Treatise of Human Nature.* London: Penguin Books.

James, Aaron. 2005. "Constructing Justice for Existing Practice: Rawls and the Status Quo." *Philosophy and Public Affairs* 33 (3): 281–316.

Johnson, Oliver. 1974. "The Kantian Interpretation." *Ethics* 85 (1): 58–66.

Johnston, David. 1994. *The Idea of a Liberal Theory: A Critique and Reconstruction.* Princeton: Princeton University Press.

Kahneman, Daniel, Alan B. Krueger, David Schkade, Norbert Schwarz, and Arthur A. Stone. 2006. "Would You Be Happier If You Were Richer? A Focusing Illusion." *Science* 312 (5782): 1908–10.

Kalven, Harry. 1964. "The New York Times Case: A Note on 'The Central Meaning of the First Amendment.'" *Supreme Court Review* 191.

Kant, Immanuel. 1900. *Gesammelte Schriften.* Ed. Royal Prussian Academy of Sciences. Berlin: Georg Reimer.

———. 1996. *Practical Philosophy.* Ed. and trans. Mary Gregor. Cambridge: Cambridge University Press.

———. 1998a. *Critique of Pure Reason.* Ed. and trans. Paul Guyer and Allen Wood. Cambridge: Cambridge University Press.

———. 1998b. *Religion Within the Boundaries of Mere Reason and Other Writings.* Ed. and trans. Allen Wood and George di Giovanni. Cambridge: Cambridge University Press.

———. 2000. *Critique of the Power of Judgment.* Ed. Paul Guyer. Trans. Paul Guyer and Eric Matthews. Cambridge: Cambridge University Press.

Kateb, George. 1984. "Democratic Individuality and the Claims of Politics." *Political Theory* 12 (3): 331–60.

Kaufman, Alexander. 1999. *Welfare in the Kantian State.* Oxford: Oxford University Press.

———. 2006. "Rawls's Practical Conception of Justice: Opinion, Tradition, and Objectivity in Political Liberalism." *Journal of Moral Philosophy* 3 (1): 22–43.

Keat, Russell, and David Miller. 1974. "Understanding Justice." *Political Theory* 2 (1): 3–31.

Keynes, John Maynard. 1920. *The Economic Consequences of the Peace.* New York: Harcourt, Brace and Howe.

Klaus, Vaclav. 2005. *On the Road to Democracy: The Czech Republic from Communism to Free Society.* Dallas: National Center for Policy Analysis.

Kohlberg, Lawrence. 1963. "The Development of Children's Orientation Toward a Moral Order: Sequence in the Development of Moral Thought." *Vita Humana* 6:11–33.

———. 1969. "Stage and Sequence: The Cognitive Developmental Approach to Socialization." In *Handbook of Socialization Theory and Research,* ed. David Goslin. Chicago: Rand McNally.

Korsgaard, Christine. 1996a. *Creating the Kingdom of Ends.* Cambridge: Cambridge University Press.

———, with G. A. Cohen, Raymond Geuss, Thomas Nagel, and Bernard Williams. 1996b. *The Sources of Normativity.* Ed. Onora O'Neill. Cambridge: Cambridge University Press.

———. 2003. "Realism and Constructivism in Twentieth-Century Moral Philosophy." In "Philosophy in America at the Turn of the Century," APA Centennial Supplement, *Journal of Philosophical Research* 28:99–122.
Krasnoff, Larry. 1999. "How Kantian Is Constructivism?" *Kant-Studien* 90:385–409.
Kreimer, Seth. 1999. "Invidious Comparisons: Some Cautionary Remarks on the Process of Constitutional Borrowing." *University of Pennsylvania Journal of Constitutional Law* 1:640–50.
Kukathas, Chandran. 2003. *The Liberal Archipelago: A Theory of Diversity and Freedom.* Oxford: Oxford University Press.
Kymlicka, Will. 2002. *Contemporary Political Philosophy: An Introduction.* 2nd ed. Oxford: Oxford University Press.
Laden, Anthony Simon. 1991. "Games, Fairness, and Rawls's *A Theory of Justice.*" *Philosophy and Public Affairs* 20:189–222.
———. 2001. *Reasonably Radical: Deliberative Liberalism and the Politics of Identity.* Ithaca: Cornell University Press.
Laden, Anthony Simon, and David Owen, eds. 2007. *Multiculturalism and Political Theory.* Cambridge: Cambridge University Press.
La Mettrie, Julien Offray de. 1987. *Man a Machine.* La Salle, Ill.: Open Court.
Larmore, Charles. 1987. *Patterns of Moral Complexity.* Cambridge: Cambridge University Press.
———. 1996. *The Morals of Modernity.* Cambridge: Cambridge University Press.
Layard, Richard. 2005. *Happiness: Lessons from a New Science.* New York: Penguin.
Lessnoff, Michael. 1971. "John Rawls' Theory of Justice." *Political Studies* 19 (1): 63–80.
Levine, Andrew. 1974. "Rawls' Kantianism." *Social Theory and Practice* 3 (1): 47–63.
Locke, John. 1988. *Two Treatises of Government.* Ed. Peter Laslett. Cambridge: Cambridge University Press.
———. 1990. *A Letter Concerning Toleration.* Amherst, N.Y.: Prometheus Books.
———. 1997. *Political Essays.* Ed. Mark Goldie. Cambridge: Cambridge University Press.
Macedo, Stephen. 1990. *Liberal Virtues: Citizenship, Virtue, and Community in Liberal Constitutionalism.* Oxford: Oxford University Press.
———. 2000. *Diversity and Distrust: Civic Education in a Multicultural Democracy.* Cambridge, Mass.: Harvard University Press.
MacIntyre, Alasdair. 1984. *After Virtue.* Notre Dame: University of Notre Dame Press.
MacKinnon, Catharine. 1987. *Feminism Unmodified: Discourses on Life and Law.* Cambridge, Mass.: Harvard University Press.
Macleod, Alistair M. 2006. "Rawls's Narrow Doctrine of Human Rights." In Martin and Reidy 2006.
Madison, James. 1999. "Memorial and Remonstrance Against Religious Assessments." In *James Madison: Writings,* ed. Jack Rakove. New York: Library of America.
Martin, Rex, and David A. Reidy, eds. 2006. *Rawls's Law of Peoples: A Realistic Utopia?* Oxford: Blackwell.
Mehta, Uday Singh. 1999. *Liberalism and Empire: A Study in Nineteenth-Century British Liberal Thought.* Chicago: University of Chicago Press.
Mele, Alfred. 2001. *Autonomous Agents: From Self-Control to Autonomy.* Oxford: Oxford University Press.
Mill, John Stuart. 1962. *Utilitarianism, On Liberty, Essay on Bentham: Together with Selected Writings of Jeremy Bentham and John Austin.* Ed. Mary Warnock. Cleveland: Meridian Books.
———. 1991. *Considerations on Representative Government.* Amherst: Prometheus Books.

———. 1998. *On Liberty and Other Essays*. Ed. John Gray. Oxford: Oxford University Press.
Milton, John. 1999. *Areopagitica and Other Political Writings of John Milton*. Ed. John Avis. Indianapolis: Liberty Fund.
Mischel, Walter. 1996. "From Good Intentions to Willpower." In *The Psychology of Action*, ed. Peter Gollwitzer and John Bargh. New York: Guilford.
Mischel, Walter, and Nancy Baker. 1975. "Cognitive Appraisals and Transformations in Delay Behavior." *Journal of Personality and Social Psychology* 31 (2): 254–61.
Moon, J. Donald. 1993. *Constructing Community: Moral Pluralism and Tragic Conflicts*. Princeton: Princeton University Press.
Murphy, Liam. 2003. *Moral Demands in Nonideal Theory*. Oxford: Oxford University Press.
Nietzsche, Friedrich. 2006. *On the Genealogy of Morality*. Ed. Keith Ansell-Pearson. Cambridge: Cambridge University Press.
Noss, David S. 2003. *A History of the World's Religions*. Upper Saddle River, N.J.: Prentice Hall.
Nozick, Robert. 1974. *Anarchy, State, and Utopia*. New York: Basic Books.
Nussbaum, Martha. 1997. "Kant and Stoic Cosmopolitanism." *Journal of Political Philosophy* 5 (1): 1–25.
———. 2000. *Women and Human Development*. New York: Cambridge University Press.
Okin, Susan. 1989. *Justice, Gender, and the Family*. New York: Basic Books.
O'Neill, Onora. 1989. *Constructions of Reason: Explorations of Kant's Practical Philosophy*. Cambridge: Cambridge University Press.
———. 1997. "Political Liberalism and Public Reason: A Critical Notice of John Rawls, *Political Liberalism*." *Philosophical Review* 106 (3): 411–28.
———. 2003. "Constructivism in Rawls and Kant." In S. Freeman 2003b.
Palmer, Monte. 1997. *Comparative Politics: Political Economy, Political Culture, and Political Interdependence*. Itasca, Ill.: F. E. Peacock.
Parfit, Derek. 1997. "Equality and Priority." *Ratio* 10 (3): 202–21.
Paton, H. J. 1947. *The Categorical Imperative: A Study in Kant's Moral Philosophy*. Philadelphia: University of Pennsylvania Press.
Pettit, Philip. 2006. "Rawls's Peoples." In Martin and Reidy 2006.
Piaget, Jean. 1928. *Judgment and Reasoning in the Child*. Trans. Marjorie Warden. New York: Harcourt, Brace.
———. 1950. *The Psychology of Intelligence*. Trans. Malcolm Piercy and Daniel Berlyne. London: Routledge.
Plato. 1991. *The Republic*. Trans. Allan Bloom. New York: Basic Books.
Pogge, Thomas W. 1981. "The Kantian Interpretation of Justice as Fairness." *Zeitschrift für philosophische Forschung* 35:47–65.
———. 1989. *Realizing Rawls*. Ithaca: Cornell University Press.
Rawls, John. 1971. *A Theory of Justice*. Cambridge, Mass.: Harvard University Press.
———. 1993. *Political Liberalism*. New York: Columbia University Press.
———. 1999a. *Collected Papers*. Ed. Samuel Freeman. Cambridge, Mass.: Harvard University Press.
———. 1999b. *The Law of Peoples*. Cambridge, Mass.: Harvard University Press.
———. 1999c. *A Theory of Justice*. Rev. ed. Cambridge, Mass.: Harvard University Press.
———. 2000. *Lectures on the History of Moral Philosophy*. Ed. Barbara Herman. Cambridge, Mass.: Harvard University Press.
———. 2001. *Justice as Fairness: A Restatement*. Ed. Erin Kelly. Cambridge, Mass.: Harvard University Press.

———. 2007. *Lectures on the History of Political Philosophy*. Ed. Samuel Freeman. Cambridge, Mass.: Harvard University Press.
Rawls, John, and Philippe van Parijs. 2003. "John Rawls and Philippe van Parijs: Three Letters on *The Law of Peoples* and the European Union." In "Autour de Rawls," special issue, *Revue de philosophie économique* 7:7–20.
Raz, Joseph. 1986. *The Morality of Freedom*. New York: Oxford University Press.
Reath, Andrew. 1989. "Hedonism, Heteronomy, and Kant's Principle of Happiness," *Pacific Philosophical Quarterly* 70 (1):42–72.
Reath, Andrew, Barbara Herman, and Christine Korsgaard, eds. 1997. *Reclaiming the History of Ethics: Essays for John Rawls*. Cambridge: Cambridge University Press.
Reidy, David A. 2002. "Hate Crimes, Oppression, and Legal Theory." *Public Affairs Quarterly* 16 (3):259–85.
Roemer, John. 1994. *Egalitarian Perspectives: Essays in Philosophical Economics*. Cambridge: Cambridge University Press.
Rosen, Allen D. 1993. *Kant's Theory of Justice*. Ithaca: Cornell University Press.
Rosenblum, Nancy. 1987. *Another Liberalism: Romanticism and the Reconstruction of Liberal Thought*. Cambridge, Mass.: Harvard University Press.
Rousseau, Jean-Jacques. 1997. *The Social Contract and Other Later Political Writings*. Ed. Victor Gourevitch. Cambridge: Cambridge University Press.
Sandel, Michael. 1982. *Liberalism and the Limits of Justice*. Cambridge: Cambridge University Press.
Scanlon, Thomas. 1972. "A Theory of Freedom of Expression." *Philosophy and Public Affairs* 1 (2): 204–26.
———. 2003. "Rawls on Justification." In S. Freeman 2003b.
Schapiro, Tamar. 1999. "What Is a Child?" *Ethics* 109 (4):715–38.
Scheffler, Samuel. 1994. "The Appeal of Political Liberalism." *Ethics* 105 (1): 4–22.
———. 2003. "What Is Egalitarianism?" *Philosophy and Public Affairs* 31 (1): 5–39.
Schneewind, J. B. 1996. "Kant and Stoic Ethics." In *Aristotle, Kant, and the Stoics: Rethinking Happiness and Duty*, ed. Stephen Engstrom and Jennifer Whiting. Cambridge: Cambridge University Press.
Sen, Amartya. 1985. "The Moral Standing of the Market." In *Ethics and Economics*, ed. Ellen Frankel Paul, Jeffrey Paul, and Fred D. Miller Jr. Oxford: Blackwell.
———. 1992. *Inequality Reexamined*. Cambridge, Mass.: Harvard University Press.
———. 2004. "Elements of a Theory of Human Rights." *Philosophy and Public Affairs* 32 (4): 315–56.
Shue, Henry. 1975. "Liberty and Self-Respect." *Ethics* 85 (3): 195–203.
———. 1996. *Basic Rights: Subsistence, Affluence, and U.S. Foreign Policy*. Princeton: Princeton University Press.
Sidgwick, Henry. 1981. *The Methods of Ethics*. Indianapolis: Hackett.
Singer, Peter. 1972. "Is Act-Utilitarianism Self-Defeating?" *Philosophical Review* 81 (1):94–104.
———. 1975. *Animal Liberation: A New Ethics for Our Treatment of Animals*. New York: Random House.
———. 1980. "Utilitarianism and Vegetarianism." *Philosophy and Public Affairs* 9 (4):325–37.
———. 1999. *Practical Ethics*. Cambridge: Cambridge University Press.
Smart, J. J. C., and Bernard Williams. 1973. *Utilitarianism: For and Against*. Cambridge: Cambridge University Press.
Steamer, Robert, and Richard Maiman. 1992. *American Constitutional Law: Introduction and Case Studies*. New York: McGraw-Hill.
Stephens, Otis, and John Scheb. 1988. *American Constitutional Law: Essays and Cases*. New York: Harcourt Brace Jovanovich.

Tan, Kok-Chor. 2006. "The Problem of Decent Peoples." In Martin and Reidy 2006.
Taylor, Robert S. 2003. "Rawls's Defense of the Priority of Liberty: A Kantian Reconstruction." *Philosophy and Public Affairs* 31 (3): 246–71.
———. 2004. "Self-Realization and the Priority of Fair Equality of Opportunity." *Journal of Moral Philosophy* 1 (3): 333–47.
———. 2005. "Kantian Personal Autonomy." *Political Theory* 33 (5): 602–28.
———. 2006. "Democratic Transitions and the Progress of Absolutism in Kant's Political Thought." *Journal of Politics* 68 (3): 556–70.
———. 2009. "Rawlsian Affirmative Action." *Ethics* 119 (3): 476–506.
———. 2010. "Kant's Political Religion: The Transparency of Perpetual Peace and the Highest Good." *Review of Politics* 72 (1): 1–24.
The Economist. 2008. *Pocket World in Figures.* London: Profile Books.
Thoreau, Henry David. 1962. *Walden and Other Writings.* Toronto: Bantam Books.
Tocqueville, Alexis de. 2003. *Democracy in America and Two Essays on America.* Trans. Gerald Bevan. New York: Penguin Classics.
Tomasi, John. 2001. *Liberalism Beyond Justice: Citizens, Society, and the Boundaries of Political Theory.* Princeton: Princeton University Press.
Van Parijs, Philippe. 1995. *Real Freedom for All.* Oxford: Oxford University Press.
———. 2003. "Difference Principles." In S. Freeman 2003b.
Varian, Hal. 1992. *Microeconomic Analysis.* New York: Norton.
Waldron, Jeremy. 1993. "John Rawls and the Social Minimum." In *Liberal Rights: Collected Papers, 1981–1991.* Cambridge: Cambridge University Press.
———. 1999. *The Dignity of Legislation.* Cambridge: Cambridge University Press.
———. 2005. "Moral Autonomy and Personal Autonomy." In *Autonomy and the Challenges to Liberalism,* ed. John Christman and Joel Anderson. Cambridge: Cambridge University Press.
Walzer, Michael. 1983. *Spheres of Justice: A Defense of Pluralism and Equality.* New York: Basic Books.
———. 1997. *On Toleration.* New Haven: Yale University Press.
Wenar, Leif. 1995. "Political Liberalism: An Internal Critique." *Ethics* 106 (1): 32–62.
Williams, Bernard. 1962. "The Idea of Equality." In *Philosophy, Politics, and Society,* ed. Peter Laslett and W. G. Runciman. Oxford: Basil Blackwell.
Wills, Garry. 1992. *Lincoln at Gettysburg: The Words That Remade America.* New York: Simon and Schuster.
Wood, Allen. 1999. *Kant's Ethical Thought.* Cambridge: Cambridge University Press.
Yack, Bernard. 1993. "The Problem with Kantian Liberalism." In *Kant and Political Philosophy: The Contemporary Legacy,* ed. Ronald Beiner and William James Booth. New Haven: Yale University Press.
Yovel, Yirmiahu. 1980. *Kant and the Philosophy of History.* Princeton: Princeton University Press.

Index

absolutism, 149
absolutisms, benevolent and malevolent, 287–89, 291–92
abstraction, 34, 90–92, 94, 104–5
action
  in agency model, 104–5
  duty and, 119–20
  knowledge and, 8–9
agency model
  introduction to, 104–6
  Kantian moral autonomy in, 110–11
  personal autonomy in, 108–10
  romantic liberalism and, 272 n. 44
  self-realization in, 106–8
  stages in, 104–6
akrasia, 187
Alexander, Larry, 174, 175 n. 5, 177 n. 7
Allison, Henry, 17 n. 29
alternative principles of justice, 29–32, 204
Antinomy of Freedom, 307–8
apartheid, 182–83
appearances, 308–9
aristocracy, 148–49
Aristotelian principle, 175, 177–79, 180–81, 185, 187
Arneson, Richard, 174, 186
Arrow, Kenneth, 154
association, freedom of, 142–44, 164, 166
authenticity, contingency problem and, 81–83
authenticity conditions, 68
autonomous law, 15 n. 27, 18, 110–11
autonomous will
  the categorical imperative and, 18
  Kantian moral autonomy and, 64–65
  negative property of, 94, 96
  personally, 213
autonomy. *See also* moral autonomy
  conceptions of, 61
  constitutive autonomy, 257
  in Enlightenment liberalism, xvii
  external autonomy, 60
  formula of autonomy, 28, 51, 134
  full autonomy, 24, 118–21, 132, 257–58
  rational autonomy, 35
  rationality as form of, 164–65
  three-stage sequence for deriving, 96–100

auxiliary political liberties
  defined, 121–22, 152
  identifying, 123 n. 13
  regulation of, 138
  role and priority of, 139–42

Barber, Benjamin, 150
Barry, Brian, 9 n. 14, 13 n. 20, 154, 263 n. 25
basic liberties. *See also* lexical priority of basic liberties; priority of basic liberties
  constitutional consensus and, 280–83
  difference principle and, 204–6
  fair equality of opportunity and, 185
  principles of justice and, 44–45
  priority of civil liberty and, 153
basic needs threshold, 197–98, 199, 202–8, 214
basic structure of society, 48–50
beneficence, 38–39, 76–77, 78–80, 214
benevolent absolutisms, 287–88
Bentham, Jeremy, 264
Berk, Laura, 103 n. 57
Berlin, Isaiah, xvii, 125
black holes, indispensability and, 181–84
Blasi, Vincent, 172 n. 20
Blaug, Ricardo, 154
Bork, Robert, 144
Brandenburg v. Ohio (1969), 171
Brandt, R. B., 9 n. 14
Buchanan, James, 7 n. 11
Budde, Kersin, xviii
Burke, Edmund, 147–48, 173

Calhoun, John C., 291 n. 79
Camus, Albert, 63
categorical commands of morality, 89–90, 188. *See also* moral law
the categorical imperative. *See also* specific formulations of The CI
  construction of, 16, 18–20
  defined, 6
  free will and, 306
  priority of right and, 120
  universal-law formulation of, 89, 96
  universal subjective end of happiness and, 42
categorical imperatives, 17–20, 42, 46–47

categories, 15
causality, 15, 308–9
Christianity, 241
Christman, John, 68–69, 98
Cicero, 112 n. 68
civic friendship, 50
civil liberties. *See also* lexical priority of civil liberties; priority of civil liberty
  American application of, 170–72
  constitutional consensus and, 280–83
  defined, 152
  priority of political liberty and, 124–27, 135–37, 142–44
  as supports for rationality, 165–68
classical utilitarianism, 268–69
Cohen, G. A., 49 n. 84
Cohen, Josh, 150, 198, 203 n. 19
commands of morality. *See* moral law
common assets, 222
communities, hierarchy of, 111–14
competency conditions, 68–69
competitive-individualist comprehensive doctrine, 254–56
comprehensive doctrines. *See also* reasonable comprehensive doctrines; unreasonable comprehensive doctrines
  competitive-individualist comprehensive doctrine, 254–56
  defined, 3 n. 3
  free-faith religious comprehensive doctrines, 256–63
  Kantian comprehensive doctrines, 275–81
  in Kantian conception of the person, 240–48
  partially comprehensive doctrines, 272–75
  perfectionism and, 264–70
  pluralism and, 313–16
  political liberalism and, 249–53
  principles of justice and, 275–76
  romantic liberalism and, 270–72
  utilitarianism and, 264–70
comprehensive liberalism, 313–16. *See also* Kantian comprehensive liberalism
conception of justice, 30, 40, 154, 185–86, 238. *See also* political conception of justice
conception of the good
  difference principle and, 198, 209
  fair equality of opportunity and, 186
  free revisability of, 27
  perfectionism and, 264
  priority of political liberty and, 128–30, 136
  utilitarianism and, 264

conception of the person. *See also* Kantian conception of the person
  the categorical imperative and, 18–19
  comprehensive doctrines and, 251–52, 254–55
  conclusions on, 54–55
  difference principle and, 220, 222–23
  justificatory ambiguities in, 232–33
  Kantian constructivism and, 11–14
  Kantian liberalism and, 302–3
  perfectionism and, 264
  principles of justice and, 30–32
  priority of right and, 43
  Thin Theory of the Good and, 35
  utilitarianism and, 264
  veil of ignorance and, 32–34
confederacy, 291, 294–95
congruence, 42 n. 67, 52
consensus. *See* constitutional consensus
considered convictions of justice, 232–33, 235
Constant, Benjamin, 125, 135
constitutional consensus, 258, 280–83, 302
constitutionalism, liberal, 123
constitutional process, 133
constitutive autonomy, 257
constructivism. *See also* Kantian constructivism
  categories of, 13 n. 20
  defined, 5–6
  political constructivism, 246, 256–60, 271–72
  variants and competitors, 7–11
consumption, 177–79, 181
content regulation, 281–82. *See also* freedom, of speech
contingency, knowledge of, 91–92, 94
contingency problem, 80–83
core political liberties. *See also* lexical priority of core political liberties
  auxiliary political liberties and, 139–42
  defined, 121, 152
  extent of, 125
  fair value of, 122 n. 11
  sacrificing, 153 n. 3
counsels of prudence, 17, 42, 60–61, 89–90. *See also* hypothetical counsels of prudence
cultural perfectionism, 265–66

Daniels, Norman, 154, 252, 298, 300, 304
Darwall, Stephen, xix n. 10, 4
decent peoples, 244, 284–85, 287
decision rules, 194–99, 201
deductive method, 60

deliberative rationality, 25, 67, 68, 92, 98, 210
DeMarco, Joseph, 154
deontological moral theories, 42 n. 67, 116–17
detachment, 65–66
detranscendentalization, of Kantian liberalism, 310–12
difference principle
  conclusions on, 226–27
  defense(s) of, 194–99, 220–23
  fair equality of opportunity and, 173–76, 183–84, 276–77
  informal defense of, 215–20
  introduction to, 192–93
  Kantian conception of the person and, 231
  Kantian constructivism and, 12
  Kantian defense of, 220–23
  objections to condition 1, 199–202
  objections to condition 2, 207–14
  objections to condition 3, 202–7
  principles of justice and, 43–46
  priority of civil liberty and, 165
  reciprocity defense of, 223–26
discontinuity problem, 81, 83–84
distancing, 104, 105, 110
distributive principles, 199, 201
divorce, 260 n. 20
docking rings, 247–48
doctrine of right, international, 286–87
Doppelt, Gerald, 254
duties
  of noncoercion, 76
  to others, 77
  priority of political liberty and, 119–20
  of right, 76, 77 n. 25, 96
  to self, 77, 96
  social, 176–78, 180–81, 189–90
  of virtue, 38–39, 76–80, 214
Dworkin, Gerald, 68, 74 n. 20, 82–83, 97

economic growth, 129, 146–49
egoism, 40–41
elections, economic growth and, 147–49
Elster, Jon, 187
empirical practical reason, 42–43, 64, 96
Enlightenment liberalism, xvii–xviii
equal basic liberties, 204–6
equal citizenship, 156–57
equality. See also fair equality of opportunity
  auxiliary political liberties and, 139
  in conception of persons, 27–28
  freedom and, 29 n. 46
  political, 156–57
  principles of justice and, 47–48
  priority of political liberty and, 132
equal liberty, 43–46, 121, 259–60
equal liberty of conscience argument, 155, 158–62
equal participation, principle of, 28 n. 46
Establishment Clause of the First Amendment, 170–71
ethics
  ethical relativism, 239
  objectivity in, 10
existentialist autonomy, 63, 65–66
external autonomy, 60

fact of legitimate stability, 242, 243, 248, 314
fact of oppression, 242–43
fact of pluralism, 241–42, 245, 300, 313
fair equality of opportunity, 43–46, 138, 165, 262–63. See also lexical priority of fair equality of opportunity; priority of fair equality of opportunity
fair value of political liberties
  advancing conceptions of the good and, 128–30
  conclusions on, 150
  economic growth and, 146–47
  freedom of association and, 142
  in priority of political liberty, 121–22, 127–28, 139
feasibility approach to toleration, 293–94, 296–97
finite rational agency
  Kantian conception of the person and, 60–61, 88–89, 234–35
  Kantian constructivism and, 14–19
  in Rawlsian and Kantian doctrines, 53–54
  Thin Theory of the Good and, 37–39
First Amendment, 170–71
formal equality of opportunity, 45, 122, 173, 181–82, 255, 263
formula of autonomy, 28, 51, 134
formula of humanity, 19 n. 32, 26–27, 51, 188
formula of the kingdom of ends, 19, 132–33
formula of the law of nature, 38–39
formula of universal law, 18, 38, 51, 119–20, 134
four-stage sequence, 92–96, 133, 137, 204
four-step CI-procedure, 38–39
Frankfurt, Harry, 68, 81, 82
free choice, 26–27, 304–6. See also *Willkür*
free choice of occupation, 182, 189

freedom. *See also* negative freedom; positive freedom
  antinomy of, 307-8
  of association, 142-44, 164, 166
  detranscendentalization of Kantian liberalism and, 310-11
  Kantian conception of the person and, 235
  of movement, 182
  of occupation, 182, 189
  of the person, 26-27, 124, 166
  postulate of, 303-4
  practical postulate of, 60, 239, 300, 311-14
  practical presupposition of, 304-7
  principles of justice and, 47-48
  of speech, 141, 143-44, 161-62, 166, 281-82
  of thought, 166
  universal principle of right and, 38 n. 58
free erosion, 253, 274-75
free-faith religious comprehensive doctrines, 256-63, 273
Freeman, Samuel, xix n. 10, 3-4, 92, 251, 279-80, 285 n. 64
free movement, 182
free will, 26-27, 304-6. See also *Willkür*
friendship, civic, 50
full autonomy, 24, 118-21, 132, 257-58. *See also* moral autonomy
full publicity condition, 31-32, 225-26
fundamental interests, 36, 158-63

Galston, William, xvii, 70 n. 13, 265 n. 32, 299-300, 316
Gauthier, David, 7
generality, 29-31, 73, 93
good. *See* conception of the good
good of the sense of justice, 52
goods of stability, 128-30, 167
good will, 117, 119-20, 212-13
Gray, John, 70 n. 13
guilt, moral, 51 n. 88

Habermas, Jürgen, 64 n. 5, 122, 130, 135, 137, 150
Habibi, Don, 149
Haksar, Vinit, 70 n. 13
happiness
  beneficence and, 78
  counsels of prudence and, 17
  deontological theories and, 117
  Kantian conception of the person and, 25-26
  Kant on, 18 n. 31
  plan of life and, 210-11
  psychology of justice and, 52-53
  Sidgwick on, 267
Harman, Gilbert, 10
Hart, H. L. A., 154, 159 n. 11
hereditary prerogative, 20 n. 34, 47-48, 148, 173-74. *See also* natural aristocracy
Herman, Barbara, xvii
Herzog, Don, xvii
heteronomous law, 15 n. 27
hierarchy argument, 155, 162-70
hierarchy of communities, 111-14
higher-order preferences, 68, 92, 95, 97-98
Höffe, Otfried, xviii, 51 n. 87
Holmes, Oliver Wendell, 171
Honig, Bonnie, 150
humanity, formula of, 19 n. 32, 26-27, 51, 188
human rights, 286-95
Humboldt, Wilhelm von, 70, 265
Hutterites, 291, 294-96
hypothetical counsels of prudence, 89-90
hypothetical imperatives, 16-17, 25-26, 60-61
hypothetical political liberty, 132-34
hypothetical rules of skill, 89-90, 188

ideal theory, 41, 238, 298
identity
  in agency model, 104-5
  contingency problem and, 81-84
imperatives, 15-19
imperfect duties of virtue, 76-80, 96-97, 214
incitement, 170-71
income. *See* median income, maximizing; social minimum income; social primary goods
indirect utilitarianism, 265, 267
indispensability, 181-84
inference fallacy, 124, 129, 154, 157, 159, 163
infinite rational beings, 53
institutions of justice, 23 (table), 41, 48-51
instrumentalism, 88, 125, 128, 215, 221-23
insufficient reason, principle of, 200-201
integrity of the person, 124-25, 159, 161-63
internal autonomy. *See also* moral autonomy; personal autonomy; self-realization
  versus external autonomy, 60 n. 2
  interpreting, 72-75
  three conceptions of, 61, 62-72
  in three-stage sequence, 90-100
international doctrine of right, 286-87
international societies, 286-90

intuitionism, 9–10, 274–75. *See also* rational intuitionism

James, Aaron, 298
Jefferson, Thomas, 260 n. 18
Johnson, Oliver, xviii, 3
Johnston, David, 69
justice. *See also* principles of justice; sense of justice
   conception of justice, 30, 40, 154, 185–86, 238
   considered convictions of justice, 232–33, 235
   institutions of justice, 41, 48–51
   political conception of justice, 243, 246–48, 251, 261–63, 278–79
   principles, institutions, and psychology of justice, 23 (table)
   psychology of justice, 41, 51–53
just legislation, 127–28

Kalven, Harry, 144
Kantian comprehensive doctrines, 275–81, 283–84
Kantian comprehensive liberalism, 300, 311, 313
Kantian conception of the person
   comprehensive doctrines and, 252–53, 275, 276, 283–84
   conclusions on, 111–14, 248
   difference principle and, 199–200, 202, 207–10, 222–23
   four-stage sequence and, 92–96
   internal autonomy and, 62–72
   internal autonomy hierarchy and, 72–75, 90–100
   introduction to, 59–62, 231
   iterative model of agency and, 104–10
   justificatory ambiguities in, 232–40
   Kantian personal autonomy and, 75–84
   Kantian self-realization and, 84–88
   liberalism and, 271, 302–3
   Millian conception and, 269–70
   overview of, 22–28
   perfectionism and, 269
   political liberalism and, 240–48
   provenance and degree of, 88–90
   theory of moral development and, 100–104
   utilitarianism and, 268
Kantian constructivism
   conception of the person and, 22–28, 235–37
   conclusions on, 53–55
   definition and derivation of, 11–22
   difference principle and, 193, 207, 219–20
   institutions of justice and, 48–51
   political liberalism and, 246
   principles of justice and, 42–48
   procedure of construction in, 28–41
   psychology of justice and, 51–53
Kantianism of Rawls
   constructivism and, 5–11
   introduction to, 3–5
   Kantian constructivism and, 11–22
Kantian liberalism
   grounding, 304–13
   introduction to, 302–4
   pluralism and, 313–14
Kantian moral autonomy, 64–66, 74–75, 96–97, 110–11
Kantian personal autonomy, 74–88, 97–98
Kantian prudential reasoning, 25–26, 89
Kantian self-realization, 74–75, 84–88, 99–100
Keat, Russell, 154
Keynes, John Maynard, 147
kingdom of ends
   formula of, 19, 132–33
   imagining, 34
   publicity and, 32
   well-ordered society and, 21, 24, 50
knowledge
   action and, 8–9
   of contingency, 91–92, 94
Kohlberg, Lawrence, 101, 103 n. 57
Korsgaard, Christine, xvii, 6, 7 n. 10, 8–9
Krasnoff, Larry, xviii, 20 n. 35
Kreimer, Seth, 281 n. 57
Kymlicka, Will, 252 n. 4

La Mettrie, Julien Offray de, 312
Larmore, Charles, xvii, 251, 317
law of nature, formula of, 38–39. *See also* natural law(s)
laws. *See also* moral law
   duty and, 119–20
   formula of the kingdom of ends and, 19–20
   free-faith religious comprehensive doctrines and, 258–59
   heteronomous law, 15 n. 27
   natural, 308, 310–11
   objective, 15
   priority of political liberty and, 127–28
legitimate stability, fact of, 242, 243, 248, 314
leisure. *See* social minimum income
Letter Concerning Toleration (Locke), xvii n. 3
Levine, Andrew, xviii, 3

lexical ordering, 151, 181
lexical priority
  black holes and, 144-45
  defined, 123
  justification of, 124
  lexical ordering and, 151
lexical priority of basic liberties, 154-55, 157-58, 162-63, 165-67
lexical priority of civil liberties, 126-27, 155
lexical priority of core political liberties, 127, 150
lexical priority of equal liberty of conscience, 159-60
lexical priority of fair equality of opportunity
  application of, 185
  conclusions on defense of, 189-91
  defined, 44-45
  difference principle and, 276-77
  indispensability and, 181, 183
  introduction to, 174-76
  versus priority of right, 186
  self-realization and, 85
lexical priority of political liberty
  conceptions of the good and, 128-30
  conclusions on, 150-51
  defined, 123
  guaranteeing just legislation, 127-28
  justification of, 124-27
lexical priority of right, 121
liberal constitutionalism, 259
liberalism. *See also* political liberalism
  change in definition of, 278
  comprehensive liberalism, 313-16
  Enlightenment liberalism, xvii-xviii
  Kantian comprehensive liberalism, xxiii n. 14, 300, 311, 313
  Reformation liberalism, xvii-xviii, 317-18
  religious liberalism, 259-62
  romantic liberalism, 270-75
liberal theory, types of, xvii-xviii
liberal utilitarianism, 281-82
liberty of conscience, 124-25, 164, 166. *See also* equal liberty of conscience argument
Lincoln, Abraham, 299
Locke, John, xvii n. 3, 260
luck egalitarianism, 193

Macedo, Stephen, xvii
Madison, James, xvii
malevolent absolutisms, 288-89, 291-92
marriage, 260 n. 20
maximax rule, 194-99
maximin rule, 194-99, 201
maximization, 207

maxims
  of action, 37-39
  formula of universal law and, 119-20
  will and, 14-18, 27-28
means of production, 205 n. 23
median income, maximizing, 196, 208
mediating devices, 12-13
Mele, Alfred, 60 n. 2, 97 n. 53
metaskills, 99, 188
Mill, John Stuart
  absolutism and, 149
  perfectionism and, 265
  political liberty and, 125
  on self-realization, 70-71, 88
  on utility, 269-70
Miller, David, 154
model of agency. *See* agency model
Moon, Donald, xvii, 251
Moore, G. E., 9 n. 14
moral agency, 84, 312
moral autonomy. *See also* Kantian moral autonomy; reasonableness
  the categorical imperative and, 18
  as conception of internal autonomy, 62-66
  conception of the person and, 59-60
  core political liberties and, 139
  exercising, 16
  full autonomy and, 24
  in hierarchy of communities, 112
  Kantian moral autonomy and, 74-75
  personal perfection and, 270
  positive freedom and, 27
  principles of justice and, 120-21
  priority of political liberty and, 133-36
  rationality and, 164-65
moral conceptions, 240-41, 272
moral development, theory of, 100-104
moral guilt, 51 n. 88
moral imperatives, 16, 24, 89, 188
morality, categorical commands of, 89-90, 188
moral law. *See also* morality, categorical commands of
  colegislation in, 27-28
  derivation of, 309, 310-11
  freedom and, 303, 307
  Kantian conception of the person and, 60-61
  moral autonomy and, 62-64, 74
  overview of, 17-18
  psychology of justice and, 51
moral objectivity, 10, 231, 237-38, 240, 243, 248
moral perfection, 78

moral personality, 22–24, 26–27, 36–37, 132
moral philosophy, 19, 49, 233, 283–84
moral powers. *See also* rationality; reasonableness
  civil liberties and, 135–37
  difference principle and, 198
  indispensability and, 183
  Kantian conception of the person and, 22–26, 59
  priority of political liberty and, 131–32
  priority of right and, 118–20
  romantic liberalism and, 273–74
moral principles, 5, 10, 28, 32, 62
moral relativism, 10–11
moral shame, 51 n. 88
moral theory
  constructivist, 5–6
  of Kant, 7–20, 37–39
  of Rawls and Kant, 53–55
moral truth, 233–34, 249, 302
movement, freedom of, 182
Moynihan, Pat, 206
mutual disinterest, 35, 40–41
myopia, 109, 187

natural aristocracy, 174, 176, 190. *See also* hereditary prerogative
natural inequalities, 190, 193
natural law(s), 260, 305, 307–11. *See also* formula of the law of nature
natural liberty, system of, 48, 255, 279
natural perfection, 77–80, 189
natural powers, 188–89
natural primary goods, 85–86
natural talents, 97–98, 221–22
nature, 18 n. 31, 26 n. 44, 234, 302–3. *See also* formula of the law of nature
negative freedom, 14–16, 20–21, 26–27, 235, 303–4, 311–13
Nietzsche, Friedrich, 186–87, 266
nonideal theory, 41, 146, 149, 238, 317
nonpolitical liberties, 124–27, 135. *See also* civil liberties
noumena, 308–10, 311
Nozick, Robert, 7 n. 11

objective moral law, 63, 65
objective moral principle, 19–20
objective moral truth, 233, 249, 302
objective principles, 14–18
objective probability estimates, 200, 202
obscenity, 143
occupation, free choice of, 182, 189
Okin, Susan, 49

O'Neill, Onora, xvii, 5, 6 n. 8, 69, 249
oppression, fact of, 242–43
ordering, 29–30, 204, 206. *See also* lexical ordering
original position
  conclusions on, 53–54
  defense of difference principle and, 194–99
  deliberative rationality and, 92
  formal constraints on alternative principles and, 29–32
  four-stage sequence and, 92–96
  in Kantian constructivism, 11–13, 20–21, 23 (table)
  objections to condition 1, 199–202
  objections to condition 2, 207–14
  objections to condition 3, 202–7
  overview of, 28–29
  Thin Theory of the Good and, 34–41
  veil of ignorance and, 32–34
overlapping consensus
  broadened, 278–79
  comprehensive doctrines and, 258, 273–74
  constitutional consensus and, 280
  political liberalism and, 243–48, 251–52
  reasonableness and, 285–90
  utilitarianism and, 264

Parfit, Derek, 206–7, 218
partially comprehensive doctrines, 244–45, 272–75
perfect duties of virtue, 38, 76, 80
perfection. *See also* moral perfection; natural perfection; self-perfection
  of others, 77 n. 26
  personal, 269
perfectionism, 70 n. 13, 85, 145, 186, 191, 264–70
person, freedom of the, 26–27, 124, 166
personal autonomy. *See also* Kantian personal autonomy; rationality
  in agency model, 108–10
  conception of the person and, 59–60, 66–69
  in hierarchy of communities, 112–13
  Kantian personal autonomy, 74–84
  personal perfection and, 269
  plan of life and, 212–13
personal perfection, 269
phenomena, 308–9, 311
philosophers, political, 296–98, 314
Piaget, Jean, 101, 103 n. 57, 104 n. 58
Pitkin, Hanna, 147–48
plan of life
  civil liberties and, 166
  difference principle and, 209–14

execution and revision of, 24–25
Kantian personal autonomy and, 74, 98
Kantian self-realization and, 86–87
as moral enterprise, 36 n. 55
political liberties and, 152 n. 1
self-realization and, 72, 187
plan of self-development, 72, 74–75, 187–89
pluralism
  fact of, 241–42, 245, 300
  in liberal theorizing, 313–18
plural perfectionism, 265–67, 269–70
political conception of justice, 243, 246–48, 251, 261–63, 278–79
political constructivism, 246, 256–60, 271–72
political elites, 148–49
political liberalism
  comprehensive doctrines and, 254–63, 270–75
  conclusions on, 298–300
  constitutional consensus and, 280–83
  introduction to, 249–51
  Kantian conception of the person and, 240–48, 275–80
  narrow critique of, 251–54
  perfectionism and, 264–70
  political philosophers and, 296–98
  principles of justice and, 283–84
  toleration and, 284–96
  utilitarianism and, 264–70
political liberty. *See* lexical priority of political liberty; priority of political liberty
political philosophers, 296–98, 314
pornography, 143
positive freedom, 14–21, 27–28, 63
practical love of others, 78–79, 98
practical postulate of freedom, 60, 239, 300, 311–14
practical reason. *See also* empirical practical reason; pure practical reason; *Wille*
  constructivism and, 5, 8–9
  free-faith religious comprehensive doctrines and, 257, 259, 260, 261
  Kantian conception of the person and, 54–55
  political constructivism and, 271
  priority of fair equality of opportunity and, 188
  self-conception and, 234–35
  transcendental idealism and, 310–12
  virtue and, 52
primary goods. *See* natural primary goods; social primary goods
principle of equal participation, 28 n. 46

principle of insufficient reason, 200–201
principle of restricted utility, 202–8, 221–26
principle of utility, 225 n. 47, 227. *See also* principle of restricted utility
principles of justice. *See also* alternative principles of justice; difference principle; equal liberty; fair equality of opportunity
  comprehensive doctrines and, 242–43, 275–76
  conclusions on, 54
  constitutional consensus and, 280
  four-stage sequence and, 92–96
  full autonomy and, 120–21
  institutions of justice and, 49–50
  justifying, 232–33
  Kantian conception of the person and, 23 (table)
  overview of, 41, 42–48
  political liberalism and, 283–84
  priority of political liberty and, 137–38, 153
prioritarianism, 206–7
priority of auxiliary political liberties, 139–42
priority of basic liberties. *See also* lexical priority of basic liberties
  equal liberty of conscience argument and, 158–62
  hierarchy argument and, 162–70
  priority of civil liberty and, 153
  self-respect argument and, 156–58
priority of civil liberty. *See also* lexical priority of civil liberties
  conclusions on, 170–72
  equal liberty of conscience argument and, 158–62
  hierarchy argument and, 162–70
  introduction to, 152–55
  Kantian conception of the person and, 231
  self-respect argument and, 156–58
priority of fair equality of opportunity. *See also* lexical priority of fair equality of opportunity
  conclusions on, 189–91
  defense of, 175–84
  defined, 45
  introduction to, 173–75
  Kantian conception of the person and, 231
  priority of right and, 186–89
  self-realization and, 59
priority of liberty
  conclusions on, 170–72
  constitutional consensus and, 281
  defined, 44–45

priority of liberty (continued)
    difference principle and, 277
    equal liberty of conscience argument and, 158-62
    hierarchy argument and, 162-70
    introduction to, 153-55
    three arguments for, 155-64
    thresholds for, 185-86
priority of political liberty. See also lexical priority of political liberty
    conclusions on, 150-51
    defending intrinsic value of political liberty, 130-39
    defined, 121-24
    implications for, 139-49
    introduction to, 115-16
    Kantian conception of the person and, 231
    protection of nonpolitical or civil liberties, 124-27
priority of right
    conclusions on, 150-51
    defined, 116-18
    free-faith religious comprehensive doctrines and, 257
    introduction to, 115-16
    justification for, 118-21
    Kantian conception of the person and, 231
    lexical priority of right, 121
    principles of justice and, 42-43
    priority of fair equality of opportunity and, 186-89
probability estimates, 194, 195, 200-202, 208
production, means of, 205 n. 23
property ownership, 205 n. 23
prudential reasoning, 25-26, 61, 89
psychology of justice, 23 (table), 41, 51-53
publicity, 30-32, 73, 225-26
publicity defense of the difference principle, 223-26
public reason, 246-48, 257 n. 13
pure practical reason
    duty of self-perfection and, 79
    freedom and, 303
    good will and, 117
    Kantian personal autonomy and, 75, 96
    moral autonomy and, 42-43, 64
    theoretical reason and, 307

rational autonomy, 35
rational intuitionism, 8, 234, 236 n. 10, 292-93
rationality. See also personal autonomy
    civil liberties and, 136
    conception of the person and, 59
    deliberative, 92
    hierarchy argument and, 164-68
    highest-order interest in, 163-64, 169
    Kantian conception of the person and, 31
    Kantian personal autonomy and, 97-98
    overview of, 24-27
    romantic liberalism and, 273-74
    three regulative interests and, 35-36
rational nature, 26 n. 44, 188 n. 15
Raz, Joseph, 66, 67-68, 69-70, 265 n. 32, 316
realism, 7-9
reasonable comprehensive doctrines, 244-48, 251, 260, 272-75, 284-89, 297
reasonableness. See also moral autonomy
    of citizens, 263
    civil liberties and, 136
    conception of the person and, 31, 59
    defined, 22-24, 285
    priority of political liberty and, 132
    priority of right and, 118-20
    romantic liberalism and, 273-74
    three regulative interests and, 35-36
    toleration and, 285-90
    will and, 27-28
reasonable partially comprehensive doctrines, 272-75
"reasonably favorable conditions," 145-47
reciprocity defense of the difference principle, 223-26
reciprocity thesis, 234 n. 6
redistributive taxation, 46, 128, 147, 174. See also wage redistribution
reflective equilibrium, 231, 232-35, 239, 248-50, 297
Reformation liberalism, xvii-xviii, 317-18
relativism, 10-11
religion, 97 n. 54, 158-60, 170-71, 241. See also free-faith religious comprehensive doctrines
religious interest, 159-60
religious liberalism, 259-62
representation, economic growth and, 147-49
Rescher, Nicholas, 9 n. 14
respect, 51, 76, 78
responsibility, 27
restricted utility, principle of, 202-8, 221-26
Richmond, Samuel, 154
risk aversion, 97, 187, 194-95, 200
romantic liberalism, 270-75
Rosenbulm, Nancy, 271
Rousseau, Jean-Jacques, 63-64, 65-66, 101
rules of skill, 16-17, 25-26, 42, 60, 85. See also hypothetical rules of skill

Index   335

Sandel, Michael, 66
Sartre, Jean-Paul, 63
Scanlon, Thomas, 172 n. 21
Scheffler, Sam, 249
Schenck v. United States (1919), 171
Schneewind, J. B., 84
self-control, 97-98, 105, 111. *See also* self-discipline
self-criticism, 105, 110
self-development, 72, 74-75, 187-89
self-discipline, 67, 104, 105. *See also* self-control
self-perfection, 38-39, 71, 75, 214
self-realization. *See also* Kantian self-realization
  in agency model, 106-8
  Aristotelian principle and, 177-79
  conception of the person and, 59-60, 69-72
  in hierarchy of communities, 113
  indispensability and, 181-83
  interest in, 176-77
  Kantian self-realization, 74-75, 84-88
  personal perfection and, 269
  priority of fair equality of opportunity and, 186-87, 190-91
  rules of skill and, 89
self-reflection, 104
self-respect argument, 156-58
self-understanding approach to toleration, 294, 296-97
Sen, Amartya, 218, 293
sense of justice
  good of the sense of justice, 52
  happiness and, 21
  moral autonomy and, 62, 118-21
  moral powers and, 135-36
  perfectionism and, 179, 269 n. 39
  principles of justice and, 22 n. 39, 24, 50
  in well-ordered society, 101
shame, 51
Shue, Henry, 154
Sidgwick, Henry, 264, 267, 268
Singer, Peter, 316
skill(s)
  rules of skill, 16-17, 25-26, 42, 60, 85
  self-realization and, 187-89
  social union and, 180-81
slavery, 266
Smart, J. J. C., 267
social duties, 176-78, 180-81, 189-90
social inequalities, 183, 190, 254
social minimum income, 45-46, 181, 192-93, 196-98, 202-6

social practices, constructive interpretation of, 294-95, 297
social primary goods
  division of, 218-20
  lexical ordering of, 181
  natural primary goods and, 86
  principles of justice and, 44
  in Thin Theory of the Good, 35, 36-37, 39-40
social stability, 129-30
social union, 130, 175, 180-81
society, basic structure of, 48-50
speculative reason, 15, 305, 306-7, 312
speech, freedom of, 141, 143-44, 161-62, 166, 281-82
stability, goods of, 128-30
stability defense of the difference principle, 223-26
stage theories, 101-3
status competition, 211-12
strains-of-commitment argument, 160-62
subjective probability estimates, 200-201, 202, 208
substantive equality of opportunity, 45, 173, 182-83
surplus income, 209-14
system of natural liberty, 48, 255, 279

Taliban, 292, 293-94, 296
taxation, redistributive, 46, 128, 147, 174. *See also* wage redistribution
teleological theories, 42 n. 67, 116, 264-70
theoretical reason
  constructivism and, 5
  free-faith religious comprehensive doctrines and, 257
  Kantian liberalism and, 310-12
  practical reason and, 307
  in realism, 8-9
  self-conception and, 234
theory of moral development, 100-104
Thin Theory of the Good, 33, 34-41, 198-99, 202, 207
Thoreau, Henry David, 270-71
thought
  in agency model, 104-5
  freedom of, 166
three regulative interests, 35-36, 40, 49, 208-9
three-stage sequence for deriving autonomy, 96-100
threshold, of basic needs, 197-98, 199, 202-8, 214

threshold condition for applying the priority of liberty, 168–70
toleration
  appropriate scope of, 290–96
  extending scope of, 284–90
  political philosophers and, 296–98
Tomasi, John, 251, 253, 271–72, 275–76
transcendental idealism, 303–4, 308–12
transcendentalism, 239, 292–93

uncertainty, 200, 204
universality, 30–31
universal law, formula of, 18, 51, 119–20, 134
universal principle of right, 19–20, 38 n. 58, 47, 134
universal principle of virtue, 19, 47
universal subjective end of happiness, 25, 42
universal values, 292–93
unreasonable comprehensive doctrines, 244, 247
utilitarian civil libertarianism, 281–82
utilitarianism, 7, 264–70, 277, 281, 316
utility function, 196
utility principle, 225 n. 47, 227. *See also* principle of restricted utility

veil of ignorance
  the categorical imperative and, 20–21
  competitive-individualist comprehensive doctrine and, 255
  difference principle and, 198, 200–202, 207
  four-stage sequence and, 92–96
  in original position, 32–34
virtue
  imperfect duties of, 38–39, 76–80, 96–97, 214
  perfect duties of, 38, 76, 80
  psychology of justice and, 52
  universal principle of, 19, 47
virtuosity, 177–79, 180, 184–85, 187
von Humboldt, Wilhelm, 70

wage redistribution, 254–55. *See also* redistributive taxation
Waldron, Jeremy, xvii, 59
Walzer, Michael, 150
Warren, Earl, 170
well-ordered society
  full autonomy and, 24
  institutions of justice and, 50
  international, 286–87
  Kantian constructivism and, 237
  possibility of, 279–80, 284
  priority of political liberty and, 130–31
  psychology of justice and, 51
Wenar, Leif, 257 n. 13
Whitman, Walt, 270
will. *See also Wille; Willkür*
  autonomous will, 18, 64–65, 94, 96, 213
  free will, 26–27, 304–6
  good will, 117, 119–20, 212–13
Wille, 14–16, 27, 89. *See also* practical reason
Willkür, 14–16, 26, 27, 303–6. *See also* free choice
Wolin, Sheldon, 150
Wong, David, 10
Wood, Allen, xvii, 17 n. 30, 26 n. 44, 79

Yack, Bernard, 36 n. 55, 234 n. 7, 252

www.ingramcontent.com/pod-product-compliance
Lightning Source LLC
Chambersburg PA
CBHW021352290426
44108CB00010B/213